Property-Owning Democracy

Property-Owning Democracy

Rawls and Beyond

Edited by
Martin O'Neill and Thad Williamson

A John Wiley & Sons, Ltd., Publication

This edition first published 2012
© 2012 Blackwell Publishing Ltd.

Blackwell Publishing was acquired by John Wiley & Sons in February 2007. Blackwell's publishing program has been merged with Wiley's global Scientific, Technical,
and Medical business to form Wiley-Blackwell.

Registered Office
John Wiley & Sons Ltd, The Atrium, Southern Gate, Chichester, West Sussex, PO19 8SQ, UK

Editorial Offices
350 Main Street, Malden, MA 02148-5020, USA
9600 Garsington Road, Oxford, OX4 2DQ, UK
The Atrium, Southern Gate, Chichester, West Sussex, PO19 8SQ, UK

For details of our global editorial offices, for customer services, and for information
about how to apply for permission to reuse the copyright material in this book please see
our website at www.wiley.com/wiley-blackwell.

The right of Martin O'Neill and Thad Williamson to be identified as the authors of the editorial material in this work has been asserted in accordance with the UK Copyright, Designs and Patents Act 1988.

All rights reserved. No part of this publication may be reproduced, stored in a retrieval system, or transmitted, in any form or by any means, electronic, mechanical, photocopying,
recording or otherwise, except as permitted by the UK Copyright, Designs and Patents Act 1988, without the prior permission of the publisher.

Wiley also publishes its books in a variety of electronic formats. Some content that appears
in print may not be available in electronic books.

Designations used by companies to distinguish their products are often claimed as trademarks.
All brand names and product names used in this book are trade names, service marks,
trademarks or registered trademarks of their respective owners. The publisher is not associated with any product or vendor mentioned in this book. This publication is designed to provide accurate and authoritative information in regard to the subject matter covered. It is sold
on the understanding that the publisher is not engaged in rendering professional services.
If professional advice or other expert assistance is required, the services of a competent professional should be sought.

Library of Congress Cataloging-in-Publication Data

Property-owning democracy : Rawls and beyond / edited by Martin O'Neill and Thad Williamson.
    p. cm.
  Includes bibliographical references and index.
  A collection of original essays that represent the first extended treatment of political philosopher John Rawls' idea of a property-owning democracy.
  ISBN 978-1-4443-3410-4 (hardcover : alk. paper)
 1. Social justice–Philosophy. 2. Rawls, John, 1921-2002–Political and social views. I. O'Neill, Martin, 1975- II. Williamson, Thad.
  HM671.P78 2012
  320.01'1–dc23
                                                                    2011038089

A catalogue record for this book is available from the British Library.

This book is published in the following electronic formats: ePDFs ISBN 9781444355161;
Wiley Online Library ISBN 9781444355192; ePub ISBN 9781444355178;
Mobi ISBN 9781444355185

Set in 10/12.5pt Galliard by Thomson Digital, India
Printed in Malaysia by Ho Printing (M) Sdn Bhd

1 2012

Contents

Notes on Contributors   vii
Acknowledgments   xi
Foreword   xiii
   Joshua Cohen and Joel Rogers

Introduction   1
   Martin O'Neill and Thad Williamson

Part One: Property-Owning Democracy: Theoretical Foundations   15

1 Justice or Legitimacy, Barricades or Public Reason? The Politics of Property-Owning Democracy   17
   Simone Chambers

2 Property-Owning Democracy: A Short History   33
   Ben Jackson

3 Public Justification and the Right to Private Property: Welfare Rights as Compensation for Exclusion   53
   Corey Brettschneider

4 Free (and Fair) Markets without Capitalism: Political Values, Principles of Justice, and Property-Owning Democracy   75
   Martin O'Neill

5 Property-Owning Democracy, Liberal Republicanism, and the Idea of an Egalitarian Ethos   101
   Alan Thomas

6 Property-Owning Democracy and Republican Citizenship   129
   Stuart White

Part Two: Interrogating Property-Owning Democracy: Work, Gender, Political Economy — 147

7 Work, Ownership, and Productive Enfranchisement — 149
  Nien-hê Hsieh

8 Care, Gender, and Property-Owning Democracy — 163
  Ingrid Robeyns

9 Nurturing the Sense of Justice: The Rawlsian Argument for Democratic Corporatism — 180
  Waheed Hussain

10 Property-Owning Democracy or Economic Democracy? — 201
  David Schweickart

Part Three: Toward a Practical Politics of Property-Owning Democracy: Program and Politics — 223

11 Realizing Property-Owning Democracy: A 20-Year Strategy to Create an Egalitarian Distribution of Assets in the United States — 225
  Thad Williamson

12 The Empirical and Policy Linkage between Primary Goods, Human Capital, and Financial Capital: What Every Political Theorist Needs to Know — 249
  Sonia Sodha

13 The Pluralist Commonwealth and Property-Owning Democracy — 266
  Gar Alperovitz

14 Is Property-Owning Democracy a Politically Viable Aspiration? — 287
  Thad Williamson

Index — 307

Notes on Contributors

Gar Alperovitz is Lionel R. Bauman Professor of Political Economy at the University of Maryland, a former Fellow of King's College Cambridge, and a Founding Principal of the Democracy Collaborative. His books include *America Beyond Capitalism*, *Atomic Diplomacy*, *The Decision to Use the Atomic Bomb*, *Rebuilding America* (with Jeff Faux), *Unjust Deserts* (with Lew Daly), and *Making a Place for Community* (with David Imbroscio and Thad Williamson).

Corey Brettschneider is Associate Professor of Political Science (and, by courtesy, of Philosophy and Public Policy) at Brown University. He is author of *Democratic Rights: The Substance of Self-Government* as well as the forthcoming *Democratic Persuasion: Promoting Public Values in Private Life*, as well as numerous articles in journals including *Political Theory* and the *American Political Science Review*.

Simone Chambers is Professor of Political Science, University of Toronto. She is the author of *Reasonable Democracy: Jürgen Habermas and the Politics of Discourse*, and co-editor of *Deliberation, Democracy and the Media* (with Anne N. Costain) and *Alternative Conceptions of Civil Society* (with Will Kymlicka). She is currently working on a book titled *Public Reason and Deliberation*.

Joshua Cohen is Marta Sutton Weeks Professor of Ethics in Society, and professor of political science, philosophy, and law at Stanford University. He is co-director of Stanford's Program on Liberation Technologies, and co-editor of the *Boston Review*. His books include *On Democracy* (with Joel Rogers), *Associations and Democracy* (with Joel Rogers), *The Arc of the Moral Universe and Other Essays*, *Rousseau: A Free Community of Equals*, and *Philosophy, Politics, Democracy*. Cohen is also on the faculty of Apple University.

Nien-hê Hsieh is Associate Professor of Legal Studies and Business Ethics at the Wharton School, University of Pennsylvania. His work has been published by *Economics and Philosophy*, *Journal of Political Philosophy*, *Philosophy & Public Affairs*, *Utilitas*, and numerous other academic journals.

Waheed Hussain is Assistant Professor of Legal Studies and Business Ethics at the Wharton School, University of Pennsylvania. His work has appeared in a variety of academic journals, including *Journal of Business Ethics*, *Journal of Moral Philosophy*, *Journal of Social Philosophy*, *Journal of Value Inquiry*, and *Social Theory and Practice*. He is currently working on a book titled *Freedom and Democracy in Economic Life*.

Ben Jackson is University Lecturer in Modern History at Oxford University and a Fellow of University College. He is the author of *Equality and the British Left: A Study in Progressive Political Thought, 1900–1964*, and is currently working on the intellectual history of neoliberalism. He is a Commissioning Editor of *Renewal: A Journal of Social Democracy*.

Martin O'Neill is Lecturer in Political Philosophy in the Department of Politics at the University of York. His work has been published in the *Journal of Moral Philosophy*, *Journal of Social Philosophy*, *Philosophy & Public Affairs*, and various other journals. He is currently working on the political philosophy of corporations, banks, and financial institutions, and is co-editing (with Shepley Orr) a collection on *Taxation and Political Philosophy*. He has also written about philosophical issues in current politics and public policy for nonacademic publications, including the *Big Issue*, the *Guardian*, and the *New Statesman*.

Ingrid Robeyns is Professor of Practical Philosophy at Erasmus University, Rotterdam. Her work has appeared in *Feminist Economics*, *Journal of Human Development*, *Journal of Social Philosophy*, *Political Studies*, *Social Theory and Practice*, and many other publications. She is co-editor (with Harry Brighouse) of *Measuring Justice: Primary Goods and Capabilities* and (with Bina Agarwal and Jane Humphries) *Amartya Sen's Work and Ideas: A Gender Perspective*.

Joel Rogers is Professor of Law, Politics, and Sociology at the University of Wisconsin, and director of the Center on Wisconsin Strategy. His many books include *On Democracy* (with Joshua Cohen), *Associations and Democracy* (with Joshua Cohen), *What Workers Want* (with Richard Freeman), and *American Society: How It Really Works* (with Erik Olin Wright).

David Schweickart is Professor of Philosophy at Loyola University of Chicago. His books include *Against Capitalism*, *Market Socialism: The Debate Among Socialists* (with James Lawler, Bertrell Ollmann, and Hillel Ticktin), and *After Capitalism*. His work has been translated into Spanish, Catalan, French, and Chinese.

Sonia Sodha was until recently a Senior Research Fellow at Demos, the London-based independent think tank. She has co-authored numerous policy reports on poverty and social exclusion, education, asset-based welfare policy, and civic service in the UK. She now works in the office of Ed Miliband MP, the Leader of the British Labour Party, and remains an Associate of Demos.

Alan Thomas is Professor of Ethics at Tilburg University and Director of the Tilburg Hub for Ethics and Social Philosophy (THESP). He is author of *Value and Context: The Nature of Moral and Political Knowledge* and *Thomas Nagel*, and editor of *Bernard Williams*, as well as many publications for academic journals, including *Mind*, *Utilitas*, and the *European Journal of Philosophy*.

Stuart White is Fellow and Tutor in Politics and University Lecturer at Jesus College, University of Oxford. He is the editor of *New Labour: The Progressive Future?* and *The Citizen's Stake: Exploring the Future of Universal Asset Policies* (with Will Paxton), and is the author of *The Civic Minimum: On the Rights and Obligations of Economic Citizenship* and *Equality*. He is an Associate Editor of *Philosophy & Public Affairs*.

Thad Williamson is Associate Professor of Leadership Studies and Philosophy, Politics, Economics and Law at the University of Richmond. He is author of *Making a Place for Community: Local Democracy in a Global Era* (with Gar Alperovitz and David Imbroscio) and *Sprawl, Justice and Citizenship: The Civic Costs of the American Way of Life*, and co-editor (with Douglas Hicks) of the forthcoming *Leadership and Global Justice*. In addition to his academic writing, he is a frequent contributor to newspapers and progressive popular publications in the United States, including *The Nation*, *Tikkun*, and *Dollars & Sense: The Magazine of Economic Justice*.

Acknowledgments

This book has its origin in a panel organized by Thad Williamson in collaboration with Nien-hê Hsieh, Waheed Hussain, and Martin O'Neill on the topic of "property-owning democracy" for the 2007 annual meeting of the American Political Science Association (APSA), held in Chicago. Each collaborator presented original papers on the subject, and we received insightful responses from panel respondents Corey Brettschneider and David Schweickart. The papers from that initial conference were eventually published as a symposium in a 2009 issue of the *Journal of Social Philosophy* (edited by Carol Gould).

The collaborators for the APSA panel simultaneously decided to go forward with a more ambitious book project on the topic of property-owning democracy, judging that the topic deserved a more thorough treatment from a variety of disciplinary, philosophical, and political perspectives. O'Neill and Williamson took primary responsibility as editors, but we would like to acknowledge and thank Hsieh and Hussain for being integrally involved as we collectively shaped the book's table of contents and recruited authors. To our delight, we found a great deal of interest in the project, and were able to assemble an outstanding set of authors who were willing to join with us in engaging seriously with the idea of property-owning democracy. Our thanks go to all of the authors for their contributions, their wise input, their enthusiasm, and their patience throughout this process. It has been an enormous pleasure working with such a wonderful group of political philosophers.

Many of the individual authors' chapters have been presented at a variety of academic conferences and university departments in the United States, United Kingdom, and Europe. We would like in particular to acknowledge feedback received on presentations concerning property-owning democracy and related ideas at a Jepson School of Leadership Studies research symposium at the University of Richmond (April 2008), the annual meetings of the Society for the Advancement of Socio-Economics in Philadelphia (June 2010), and the annual meeting of the American Political Science Association in Washington, DC (September 2010).

We would also like to acknowledge helpful comments and encouragement provided by a variety of people not directly involved in the book project, including Chris Brooke, Thom Brooks, Francis Cheneval, Matthew Clayton, Richard Dagger, Stephen Elkin,

Archon Fung, Carol Gould, Joe Guinan, Shepley Orr, Philippe Van Parijs, and anonymous reviewers for the *Journal of Social Philosophy*, *Living Reviews in Democracy*, and Wiley-Blackwell. O'Neill is grateful to James Hodgson for efficient research assistance, and especially also to Pablo Gilabert and Miriam Ronzoni, who prompted him think further about property-owning democracy and liberal socialism through helpful questioning at the Joint Sessions of the ECPR (European Consortium for Political Research) in Helsinki in 2007. Joshua Cohen provided helpful advice at an early stage of the book project, and we thank him and Joel Rogers for their generous preface to this volume.

O'Neill thanks Mary Leng for limitless love and support, and thanks his sons Tommy and Joe (both of whom arrived during the gestation of this book) for joyful distraction. Williamson thanks Adria Scharf and daughter Sahara for their inspiration, companionship, and patience.

Our thanks as well go to the editorial team at Wiley-Blackwell who have patiently worked with us through the process of putting this book together: Nick Bellorini, who commissioned the volume, Tiffany Mok, who inherited the book, and Nicole Benevenia and Caroline Richards, who oversaw the production process.

We owe a considerable debt to Michael Sandel of Harvard University. We (the editors) first met as teaching fellows for Sandel's course on "Justice" at Harvard in Fall 2000. In addition to being a *tour de force* introduction to questions of justice for undergraduates, the weekly meetings of the teaching staff conducted by Sandel served as an excellent seminar on theories of justice, with Sandel actively encouraging challenges to his own views and fostering a lively debate among the teaching fellows. Despite – or because of – our differences in nationality, discipline, philosophical starting points, and choice of English football clubs (Arsenal and Manchester City, in case you were wondering), we struck up a lively ongoing discussion of politics and justice (and football) that has both generated and sustained this project. In a tangible sense, this book is the offspring of Michael Sandel's now-famous course and the intellectual space that it provided.

Our greatest intellectual debt is to John Rawls, whose work provides the impetus for this book (as for so much recent political philosophy). Each of us first encountered Rawls's work as undergraduates at a time in which he was seen as rather mainstream, if not staid – unlike many of our students today, who (quite rightly!) view his ideas as radical. But like many others before us, our respect for Rawls's work, and his accomplishment in working out a conception of a just society that gives expression to our commitments to freedom and equality, has only grown over time. To be sure, each of us also has been shaped by rival trains of thought drawn from both inside and outside of philosophy. But we remain convinced that Rawls's approach to social justice, and the ideals that it embodies, remains a compelling starting point for both the critical analysis of contemporary society and for disciplined inquiry into how our societies might be made substantially more just. While we do indeed think it necessary to move far "beyond" Rawls's own work in considering the justification, structure, and political plausibility of a "property-owning democracy," we see this inquiry as in continuity with Rawls's commitment to the hope of creating a just society of free and equal citizens.

Martin O'Neill and Thad Williamson
Oxton, UK and Richmond, Virginia
November 2011

Foreword

Joshua Cohen and Joel Rogers

In *A Theory of Justice* (1971), John Rawls proposed a conception of justice he called "justice as fairness." A synthesis of liberal and egalitarian political values, justice-as-fairness comprises two principles of justice – principles that require our institutions to ensure equal basic liberties, provide genuinely equal opportunities, and limit socioeconomic inequalities to those that maximally benefit the least advantaged (Rawls, 1999). Recognizing the distance of such institutions from current realities, Rawls nevertheless says that justice-as-fairness presents a *realistic* utopia – a utopia because it meets the demands of our fundamental political values, realistic because it is politically feasible, taking people as they are and institutions as they might be (Rawls, 2001, p. 4).

This concern for realism, for institutional feasibility, was central to Rawls's idea of the aims of political philosophy. Political philosophy, an exercise of practical reason, aims, inter alia, to play a role in the political world by "provid[ing] guidance where guidance is needed" (Rawls, 1999, p. 18) – in particular, by guiding our judgment on large, open questions about the demands of justice. A very large open question is how, if at all, we can balance the demands of liberty and equality in the institutions of a modern political society. Given this aim, a case for institutional feasibility cannot be relegated to a "from-theory-to-practice" appendix, treated as a supplemental application of principles fully justified prior to such argument. Instead, that case is an ingredient of "reflective equilibrium" – of the justification of a conception of justice (Rawls, 1999, pp. xix, 171, 577–578).

Rawls's own account of just institutions has several features, including democracy, both constitutional and deliberative. But one especially striking part was the idea of a *property-owning democracy*, drawn from ideas of Nobel Prize-winning economist James Meade (1964). A property-owning democracy is defined by its broad dispersion of private productive assets. Already present in *A Theory of Justice*, this idea plays a large role in Rawls's later *Justice as Fairness: A Restatement* (Rawls, 2001, pp. 135–140). There he expresses skepticism that justice-as-fairness can be realized in a capitalist welfare state, which he assumes to rely principally on a tax-transfer redistribution of market incomes to achieve fair distribution. Capitalist welfare states do not, as Rawls describes them, worry about the dispersion of income-generating assets – human and nonhuman capital. But asset inequalities threaten a concentration of economic and political power damaging to democracy and equal opportunity. Achieving a reconciliation of liberty and equality in a private ownership economy requires, then, a broad distribution of those assets.

But Rawls did not say much about property-owning democracy: that is the purpose of this volume, the basis of the "Rawls and Beyond" in its subtitle. The essays collected here provide a serious, critical exploration of the appeal and potential of property-owning democracy. Beginning with Martin O'Neill and Thad Williamson's illuminating and instructive introduction, the volume is historically grounded, philosophically informed, and inspiringly alive with good practical and moral sense.

One of the lessons of the book is that property-owning democracy is a complex theme with many variations and a rich history. Rather than briefly sketching (thus simplifying) that complexity, we propose to locate the argument on a wider political-philosophical canvass.

First, the book focuses on a problem of *just institutions*. This focus – embraced by Rawls in his emphasis on the "basic structure of society" – belongs to the central traditions of political theory: from Plato's *kallipolis*, ruled by philosopher-kings, to Locke's case for the rule of law and separated powers, to Marx's communism, with common property and free cooperation without subjection to a state. But post-Rawlsian political philosophy has been less concerned with institutions, concentrating instead on alternative principles of justice (as in the vast literature on responsibility-sensitive variants of egalitarianism), or on the complexities of justifying principles of justice under conditions of pluralism, or on the importance of outcomes or "realizations" rather than institutions (Sen, 2009, pp. 5–6). These philosophical challenges raise important questions about the precise role of institutions in an account of justice. But even if a concern with just institutions is less fundamental than political theorists have traditionally supposed, even if they are only a tool for producing independently defined just outcomes, they are an important tool and command close attention. As Amartya Sen, a sharp critic of an exclusively institutional focus, says, "Any theory of justice has to give an important place to the role of institutions..." (Sen, 2009, p. 82).

Second, the book focuses on *domestic* justice and institutions. For the past 15 years, much political philosophy has focused on global justice, especially global distributive justice – important subjects in view of the extraordinary importance of globalization, global politics, global inequality, and global poverty. Still, justice in a domestic society is a subject of great importance, and a focus on domestic institutions has much to be said for it. To be sure, it *might* be said that we simply cannot work out what a just domestic society is except as part of a larger argument about global justice; perhaps, for example, a global difference principle makes concern for the least advantaged in wealthier societies less pressing. But most reasonable ideas about global justice permit us to reflect, as a distinct practical matter, on principles and institutions for domestic justice. The discussion here accepts that invitation. Without minimizing the importance of global justice, the authors are betting that they can make progress understanding just domestic institutions while abstracting from the global setting.

Finally, the book focuses on economic justice and *class* – a central focus of modern politics and of the Rawlsian concern to respond to radical democratic and socialist criticisms of liberalism. To be sure, a focus on these issues abstracts from other important concerns – race, gender and family, ethnicity, nationality, culture, and language – that raise large issues of justice and have provided a focus of much work in political philosophy since the mid-1980s. Here again, the editors and contributors do not slight these other issues, but lay a bet – like Rawls's in *A Theory of Justice* – that they can make headway in analyzing certain institutions of economic justice while abstracting from the more complete picture of a just society that fuller engagement with those issues might permit.

Readers will decide for themselves if this bet – like the bets on a domestic and institutional focus – is likely to pay off. We like the odds and happily join them in their wager.

References

Meade, J. (1964) *Efficiency, Equality, and the Ownership of Property*, George Allen and Unwin, London.
Rawls, J. (1999) *A Theory of Justice*, rev. edn, Harvard University Press, Cambridge, MA.
Rawls, J. (2001) *Justice as Fairness: A Restatement* (ed. E. Kelly), Harvard University Press, Cambridge, MA.
Sen, A. (2009) *The Idea of Justice*, Harvard University Press, Cambridge, MA.

...there is a question about how the limits of the practicable are discerned and what the conditions of our social world in fact are; the problem here is that the limits of the possible are not given by the actual, for we can to a greater or lesser extent change political and social institutions, and much else.

Rawls, *Justice as Fairness*, p. 5

Introduction

Martin O'Neill and Thad Williamson

Justice as Fairness and Property-Owning Democracy

Forty years have passed since the publication of John Rawls's *A Theory of Justice* (1971), an event that has literally set the agenda for contemporary political philosophers and political theorists on both sides of the Atlantic throughout the intervening years. In the decades of debate that have followed, Rawls's basic framework for thinking about justice has acquired many strong adherents, as well as attracting the widest range of criticism – from relatively friendly early critics such as H.L.A. Hart to, more recently, the fundamental critique of the entire project of "ideal" political theory articulated by Amartya Sen (himself once a reviewer of *A Theory of Justice* for Harvard University Press). Rawls's aim was to articulate principles of justice for a society committed to the idea of free and equal persons engaged in a system of social cooperation for mutual advantage. The pursuit of this aim placed Rawls simultaneously in a multitude of debates: the debate between liberal egalitarianism and utilitarianism; the debate between liberal egalitarianism and libertarianism; the debate between liberalism and Marxism; the debate between liberalism and communitarianism (and, later, civic republicanism); the debate between "political" liberalism and "comprehensive" or perfectionist liberalism; and most recently, the debate between "ideal theory" and approaches to politics anchored in "nonideal" assumptions about both the circumstances of highly imperfect modern societies and the nature of the political condition itself.

Much attention in these varied debates has been devoted to interpreting and developing Rawls's liberal egalitarian position, with Rawls himself an active participant in those debates, right up until the publication of his *Justice as Fairness: A Restatement* in 2001 (Rawls, 2001). Over the years, Rawls made numerous revisions – *some technical, some more far-reaching – to his theory, but never gave up the project of specifying an internally consistent conception of social* justice appropriate for modern democratic societies, in which commitment to religious beliefs or

Property-Owning Democracy: Rawls and Beyond, First Edition. Edited by Martin O'Neill and Thad Williamson.
© 2012 Blackwell Publishing Ltd. Published 2012 by Blackwell Publishing Ltd.

other "comprehensive" life ideals are viewed as an impossible basis for achieving political unity.

In his recent work, *The Idea of Justice*, Amartya Sen, Rawls's colleague and frequent interlocutor, suggests that Rawls's contributions to thinking about justice have more or less run their course. Instead of attempting to specify principles of justice that would be adopted under ideal conditions, and then crafting institutional arrangements designed to realize those principles, Sen suggests that we need to focus on developing a clear metric that will allow us – actual persons in actual societies with actual histories – to judge whether marginal changes of policy and resource distribution do or do not lead to more just outcomes. Sen argues that knowing that point A is the ideal gives no clear guidance to the person at point D regarding whether it is better to move toward point B or point C, given that point A is unattainable (Sen, 2009).

Speaking for ourselves (and not necessarily for all the contributors to this book), we believe that, while it *is* critically important to move the terrain of debate from purely ideal theory to discussion of institutional arrangements, nevertheless Sen's epitaph for Rawls's project is quite premature, for (at least) two reasons. First, the proposed move from institutional analysis to comparative policy analysis threatens to obscure what is perhaps Rawls's greatest contribution to social thought: the commitment to viewing questions of justice as holistic *institutional* questions, and not simply as questions of either individual ethics or piecemeal political reform. Contrary to the views of a figure like F.A. Hayek (1984), who argued that conceptions of "social justice" were flawed because no individual agent within market society intends to produce the particular distribution of goods that actually obtains, Rawls secured a great breakthrough by insisting that the proper locus of attention in evaluating justice is critical examination of a society's institutional arrangements – including the market itself. Put another way, Rawls's theory draws moral attention not just to the consequences of capitalism, but to its foundational institutions. Rawls does not accept that existing forms of capitalism are the best that we can do, and that advocates for justice must simply push for incremental changes within the existing institutional framework. While we agree with Sen that being able to judge which sort of *policies* promote justice is important, we see no need – and much to be lost – in allowing a focus on policies alone to obscure or distract from fundamental institutional questions.

Second, for all the debates about Rawls's theory of justice, attention to the mechanics of Rawls's "point A" – the preferred institutional arrangements of a just society under modern conditions – remains underdeveloped, particularly with respect to its political economy. For all the ink spilled and academic careers devoted to the finer points of Rawls's theory, the core question of how Rawls's theory of justice can be realized institutionally under contemporary conditions has received only intermittent attention. A primary aim of this volume is to take a big step toward correcting that imbalance through critical and constructive discussion of Rawls's idea of a "property-owning democracy."

What is "property-owning democracy"? In *Justice as Fairness* (2001), Rawls contrasts it to four other institutional alternatives: laissez-faire capitalism, command economy socialism, welfare state capitalism, and liberal democratic socialism. It is not surprising that Rawls quickly rejects the first two alternatives as inconsistent with his principles of justice. A command economy violates personal liberty by allowing the state to dictate where a person works, and also in all likelihood will violate or severely compromise political liberty as well (by concentrating political and economic power in the same hands). A laissez-faire market economy with private control of capital will tend to produce nearly unlimited inequality of outcomes as well as systemic inequality of opportunity, and will also severely compromise political liberty by allowing the rich and powerful disproportionate influence in politics and government.

The most surprising contrast Rawls makes, however, is between property-owning democracy and welfare state capitalism. This contrast is surprising because Rawls often has been understood – to this very day – as providing the definitive philosophical argument for the systemic redistribution of resources ("primary goods"), by means of the institutions of the traditional welfare state, operating within a market system. The idea of "limiting inequalities to those that benefit the least well off" has often been conceptualized as using the tax and transfer system to provide all with a minimum income. Indeed, Rawls can be seen as doing this himself in *A Theory of Justice* (1971, p. 276), and in *Political Liberalism* (1993, pp. 228–229) where he argues that a minimum income should be a constitutional right. Yet, while Rawls does want to maximize the position of the least well off, and does think minimum incomes should be provided as a matter of right, he does not believe that a traditional welfare state can realize the principles of justice, for three kinds of reasons.

First, because capital is concentrated in private hands under welfare state capitalism, it will be difficult if not impossible to provide to all "the fair value of the political liberties"; that is to say, capitalist interests and the rich will have vastly more influence over the political process than other citizens, a condition which violates the requirement of equal political liberties. Second, Rawls suggests at points that welfare state capitalism produces a politics that tends to undermine the possibility of tax transfers sufficiently large to correct for the inequalities generated by market processes. The relatively well off will resist proposals to tax their incomes at a rate sufficiently high to maximize the position of the least well off, and will often (if not always) have the political capacity to do so. As Rawls puts it, while such a regime "has some concern for equality of opportunity, the policies necessary to achieve that are not followed" (Rawls 2001, p. 138). Third, welfare state capitalism undercuts the possibility of equal relationships between citizens based on a principle of reciprocity in a deeper sense, by creating a divide between those primarily "dependent" on the government for income and resources and those who obtain resources through market processes and, in particular through, paid employment.

Consequently, Rawls judges that welfare state capitalism – even if it provides a decent social minimum – is inconsistent with the two principles of justice. A society that assures the fair value of political liberty, provides substantive equality of opportunity, and limits inequalities to those benefiting the least well off must have a different political–economic architecture. Rawls argues that there are two plausible possibilities: either a form of liberal democratic socialism that is organized so as to secure the liberty principle as well as strong economic equality; or else a "property-owning democracy," a term Rawls borrows from the British economist James Meade.

Rawls says very little about the specifics of democratic socialism. Even in his late publications, he does not engage with various recent efforts by left political economists and philosophers such as John Roemer (1994) and David Schweickart (1993) to specify the institutional form of a workable form of market socialism – other than to indicate that he does not see any reason why a democratic socialism cannot work and also be fully supportive of the liberty principle. (This judgment, of course, is controversial: many conservative and libertarian critics – i.e., Friedman (1962) – have argued that a society based on democratic control of the economy with a strong steering and planning function for government inevitably will violate liberty.)

Rawls says rather more about "property-owning democracy," and in *A Theory of Justice* goes so far as to specify several of the key institutional features of such an economy. Government is to be engaged (through several "branches" of activity) in macroeconomic planning, regulation of economic institutions, establishing market rules, and implementing resource transfers; it is also to be engaged in providing both essential and nonessential public goods. The primary aim of this public activity is *not* to maximize economic growth (or to maximize utility) but rather to ensure that capital is widely distributed and that no group is allowed to dominate economic life; but Rawls also assumes that the economy needs to be successful in terms of conventional measures (i.e., by providing full employment, and lifting the living standards of the least well off over time). A stiff inheritance tax is envisioned as the principal mechanism by which large accumulations of capital are to be diluted over time (Rawls, 1971).

This account is suggestive, and Rawls certainly made a good faith effort to engage with the work of contemporaneous economists (especially in *A Theory of Justice*). Rawls takes seriously economic rationality, and is not interested in describing an unworkable utopia: he is fully serious in the intention that property-owning democracy can be realized in modern societies. Yet Rawls never followed through on this institutional prospectus by providing a more detailed specification of the architecture of a fully functioning property-owning democracy, or any explanation of how modern capitalist economies might be converted into property-owning democracies, given the stiff resistance serious proposals for wealth redistribution inevitably face in existing capitalist democracies. Rawls, quite plausibly, may have felt that going into institutional details, or discussions of contemporary politics, would have involved stepping outside the appropriate role of political philosophy. But the results of this relative silence are that property-owning democracy is still not well understood as a central idea in Rawls's entire theory of justice, and that the idea itself has only rarely been subject to critical examination.

This volume aims to end that silence. But the motivation for this book has other sources beyond simply explication and critical assessment of a crucial but underexamined aspect of Rawls's project. First, one need not subscribe to the Rawlsian paradigm of justice, or the entire approach to political philosophy that Rawls exemplifies, to maintain a practical interest in the idea of property-owning democracy. Prominent scholars from broadly republican political perspectives such as Richard Dagger (2006) and Stephen Elkin (2006) have also in recent work taken up the idea of a property-owning democracy – that is, a political economy based on wide dispersal of capital with the political capacity to block the very rich and corporate elites from dominating the economy and relevant public policies. Likewise, discussion of property-owning democracy dovetails with – and to some extent, overlaps with – debates over the past 20 years aimed at specifying a workable and normatively attractive model of democratic socialism. Further, among academic scholars of social policy there has been increasing attention over the past decade to the extraordinary concentration of *wealth* in advanced capitalist societies, particularly the United States and the United Kingdom, as a crucial factor shaping both individuals' life prospects and their political agency, independent of the impact of annual income (Conley, 2009). Those with accumulated assets can easily pay for college or professional training, make down-payments on homes, invest in risky but potentially lucrative enterprises, take trips, donate money to candidates, and cope with a period of unemployment or underemployment. (See Erikson and Goldthorpe, 2002; Barry, 2005, pp. 186–199.) Those who do not enjoy these endowments of wealth typically must borrow money to do these things (if they can do them at all) and live in constant threat of downward economic mobility.

Academic interest in the question of whether it is possible to have a market society that meaningfully disperses wealth thus extends far beyond the subset of political philosophers and theorists working in the Rawlsian paradigm of social justice. But the idea of property-owning democracy potentially has much broader political significance as well. Simply put, left-of-center parties in both the United States and the United Kingdom, as well as in Europe as a whole, have lacked a clear programmatic direction for nearly a generation. Labor parties often have been reduced to trying to defend the welfare state against pressures generated by globalization, as well as from internal political attack from the right. In the United States, where social democratic politics is even weaker and where there is no true labor party, the electoral success of a "progressive" president (Barack Obama) has thus far reinforced rather than challenged the primacy of corporate, especially financial, interests over public policy (Kuttner, 2010; Suskind, 2011). One might judge that an historic opportunity to use public power in a large-scale way to reshape the basic contours of the economy has been bypassed in favor of a very expensive attempt to restore the status quo ante.

An intriguing question, then, is whether the vision of a society based on the wide dispersal of both tangible and intangible capital might, if sufficiently fleshed out, constitute both an alternative to the welfare state and an attractive alternative to the predominant neoliberal paradigm. The answer to that question cannot be provided in the absence of a serious effort to convert the broad concept of "property-owning democracy" offered by Rawls and others into a concrete political program, and a serious effort to construct a political coalition that favored and advocated for such a program. As supporters of the Labour Party in Britain come to terms both with the eviction of their party from office in 2010, and with a balanced understanding of the significant limitations of their party's achievements while in office, and as liberals and progressives in the United States come to terms with the limitations of Barack Obama's presidency and the fact that the substance of his policy agenda has rarely matched the boldness of his rhetoric, the need to develop a coherent alternative agenda for the next generation of progressive politics has become an urgent *political* task as well as an intriguing philosophical challenge.

It is appropriate here to expand upon these initial comments about the political relevance of property-owning democracy. Increasingly, scholars, activists, and politicians have come to recognize the structural basis of the current economic crisis and the steady decay of traditional social democratic strategies for containing capital and forging a version of welfare state capitalism that secures the traditional goals of full employment, rising living standards for workers, and a strong safety net. Rawls himself came to recognize the degree to which the American political economy had drifted away from the ideals of justice as fairness (i.e., Rawls, 2001, p. 101, n23), but in the most recent period two structural developments in particular have further emphasized our distance from the idea of a well-ordered, just polity in the Rawlsian vein. Importantly, both developments were in a sense anticipated by Rawls in his critique of welfare state capitalism.

First, the concentration of capital and the emergence of *finance* as a driving sector of capitalism has generated not only instability and crisis; it also has led to extraordinary political power for private financial interests, with banking interests taking a leading role in shaping not only policies immediately affecting that sector but economic (and thereby social) policy in general. These interests typically have a strong controlling role over economic policy, no matter which political party controls the White House and Congress. Second, the 2010 Supreme Court decision (*Citizens United v. Federal Election Commission*) reaffirming the view that corporations are to be treated as persons for the purposes of free speech, and the consequent invalidation of (already modest) regulations on the ability of large corporate interests to flood the media with political advertising in the run-up to elections, opened the door to a further expansion of corporate political voice in the United States. The United States is now further than ever from realizing what Rawls termed the "fair value of the political liberties" – that is, the core value of political equality.

In a similar vein, politics on the other side of the Atlantic looks to be moving further away from, rather than closer toward, the Rawlsian ideal of a stable, well-ordered, and just polity. Despite widespread public perceptions that financial interests were to blame for the financial crisis that began in 2007, there has been little reassertion of the power of democratic institutions over corporate and financial power in the years since. In countries such as the UK, inequality is at levels not seen since before World War II, while social mobility has stalled, and public contempt for the political process continues to grow. The failures of private capital have not ushered in a more mixed and stable economy, but have instead led to the further encroachment of the market as democratic states see their room for operation undercut by the fiscal crisis created by the costs of the financial collapse. During the onward march of social democracy, with rising living standards and flattening inequalities during the postwar years, one might have thought that a broadly Rawlsian society was a plausible destination of historical trends. But the overwhelming trend in OECD (Organization for Economic Cooperation and Development) countries over the past two decades has been toward steadily growing inequality, with incomes of the top decile growing much faster than incomes of the bottom decile (OECD, 2011, Table 1). Throughout the advanced capitalist countries, it is now abundantly clear that the realization of a just and well-ordered society will require a much more systemic transformation of the structure of the economy.

Altering these structural features of politics in the USA, UK, and other nations will require forging a different political-economic order. To this extent, Rawlsian justice as fairness shares with socialist perspectives not only a critique of capitalism but a determination to find a different way to organize a modern economy. Just what that different way is (and whether we could achieve it) remains an underexplored question. Socialist writers within the traditional Marxist paradigm have argued (and continue to argue) that either workers or the public at large must take a controlling interest in the bulk of productive capital in society to prevent large-scale private concentrations of capital from coming to have a dominant role in economic and political life (Lebowitz, 2010). Similarly, heterodox conceptions of market socialism such as David Schweickart's conception of "Economic Democracy" also require doing away with large-scale private control of capital (Schweickart, 2002).

"Property-owning democracy," as Rawls and others have envisaged it, aims – at least at first glance – at a different approach. Rawls's account of property-owning democracy openly embraces markets for many purposes, and does not condemn private control of capital as such. Rather, property-owning democracy is to aim at the *wide* distribution of capital, so that many people have access to productive assets and giant concentrations of accumulated wealth are melted away through taxation or incentivized bequests (gifts given to avoid stiff inheritance taxes). Some recent commentators have extended the idea further to propose versions of property-owning democracy based not just on "wide" but on *universal* distribution of capital, with all households having access to one or more forms of wealth in substantial quantity (see Williamson, 2009, and in Chapter 11 of this volume).

It remains an open question whether a fully realized property-owning democracy can *in practice* be meaningfully distinguished from democratic forms of market socialism (see the chapters by O'Neill and Schweickart in this volume). But property-owning democracy does seem to appeal to a political and cultural ideal distinct from the aims of traditional socialism, one that is more celebratory of entrepreneurialism and welcoming of individuals and households using their own assets to make whatever they wish of themselves. Socialist critics of property-owning democracy (such as Schweickart in this volume) will be skeptical of the hope that cultural ideals of that sort can easily be decoupled from capitalism as a *system*, and that market systems that allow for substantial private control of investment can be reined in sufficiently to realize any substantive distributive goals. Equally skeptical will be neoliberals who contend that capitalism cannot be moderated or reformed in substantial measure without killing off the golden goose of continually increasing productivity and technological innovation. Any modern conception of property-owning democracy necessarily must revive the idea of a mixed economy based on multiple forms – a "mix" – of ownership. Interestingly, contemporary post-Soviet visions of democratic socialism such as Schweickart's "Economic Democracy," and to an even larger extent Gar Alperovitz's "Pluralist Commonwealth" and Erik Olin Wright's "Social Empowerment" economy, point in just this direction – and also point to the idea that it is possible to nurture alternative, more democratic forms of ownership even within a context of economic crisis and the prolonged decay of social democratic politics (Schweickart, 1993; Alperovitz, 2004; Wright, 2010).

This volume thus also speaks to this wider set of reasons for engaging with the idea of property-owning democracy. The essays assembled here fall into three rough categories: those concerned with relating the idea of a property-owning democracy to a philosophical conception of justice; those concerned with broader institutional implications of property-owning democracy; and those concerned with converting the basic idea into a practical political agenda. What unites these essays is that each seeks to take the idea of "property-owning democracy" seriously, whether the assessment offered is one of critical appreciation, qualified support, or outright rejection. Careful readers will note numerous tensions, and on occasion out-and-out disagreements, between the arguments provided by the authors. Such tensions and disagreements are healthy and inevitable – they are the necessary price of taking a complex idea seriously. This book certainly does not (and does not hope to) offer a programmatic approach to how we should think about the philosophical, institutional, and political aspects of a property-owning democracy. Rather, it addresses those questions from a variety of perspectives, and hopes to shed light on these issues from a variety of directions. The aim of this book is to open up a number of fertile but neglected avenues for further debate. Taken together, these essays help to clarify both the idea of property-owning democracy and the major questions – philosophical, institutional, practical – about the idea that must be addressed if it is to move from philosophical sketch to a meaningful political program. It is the hope of the editors of and contributors to this volume that these issues will then be further taken up by others, and the ideas presented in this book will be subjected to ongoing development and critical engagement.

The remainder of this Introduction aims to provide a brief tour of the chapters and arguments comprising the volume.

Part One: Property-Owning Democracy: Theoretical Foundations

The opening chapter by Simone Chambers lays the groundwork for the volume by deftly summarizing much of the debate about how to understand Rawls's economic agenda. Chambers points to the following paradox: while Rawls's tone of writing is often understated and preoccupied with procedural and technical issues, the conclusions he reaches are unmistakably radical with respect to the political status quo in advanced capitalist societies. Rawls – perhaps at odds with his own claims to be simply working out the implications of widely shared ideas about liberty and equality – provides neither an apologia for existing institutional arrangements nor much reassurance that these arrangements can easily be reformed so as to realize his principles of justice. His theory of justice thus stands in critical tension with current institutional arrangements and the belief systems (however widespread) that justify them.

But what of Rawls's alternative? In Chapter 2, historian Ben Jackson shows in highly illuminating detail that the idea of "property-owning democracy" appropriated by Rawls has a curiously complicated history. Ironically, the term actually owes its origin to the efforts of a Scottish conservative political thinker and Unionist politician, Noel Skelton (1880–1935), who articulated a constructive social alternative in opposition to the British Labour Party's trade union socialism in the 1920s. Later the idea was taken up by the left-leaning economist James Meade (winner of the 1976 Nobel Memorial Prize in Economics), whose writings on property-owning democracy (POD) most immediately influenced Rawls. Historically, then, there has been both a left egalitarian democratic POD tradition and a right conservative POD tradition, with the former often blurring into defenses of both socialism and the welfare state, in that it seeks to foster greater collective capital ownership and collective social provision, *as well* as a wider distribution of private property. Jackson's enlightening historical excavation highlights the possible worry that a POD agenda focused only on private property ownership is, in the present day, likely to advance the right-conservative strand of this thinking rather than the radical egalitarian strand, and suggests that the contemporary pursuit of a left egalitarian property-owning democracy needs to proceed with a due appreciation of the way in which the institutions of a property-owning democracy can be integrated with some elements of the traditional welfare state.

In Chapter 3, Corey Brettschneider explores the idea of property-owning democracy in light of his own insightful analysis of one of the fundamental questions of political philosophy: when and under what circumstances can private ownership of property be legitimated? Engaging with Locke as well as contemporary libertarian writers, Brettschneider develops the position that private property ownership can be made both legitimate and just when it is coupled with provision of a positive basic right to a livelihood and other material resources to *all* citizens, including those who do not own property. This argument can be used to undergird a right to welfare; it also can be used to undergird a positive right to control of at least some material assets, in the spirit of property-owning democracy.

In Chapter 4 Martin O'Neill examines more closely Rawls's specific criticisms of welfare state capitalism, as well as interrogating Rawls's positive case for a property-owning democracy with regard to the central political values of liberty, equality, and reciprocity. O'Neill calls into question the force of Rawls's argument in *Justice as Fairness* that assuring the fair value of the political liberties strictly requires adoption of a property-owning democracy. In certain well-developed social democracies, mechanisms may be available to constrain political inequalities short of large-scale redistribution of wealth. O'Neill goes on to argue, however, that with regard to the value of equality – and, more particularly, with regard to the difference principle – there is an extremely strong case to be made on behalf of property-owning democracy and against welfare state capitalism. Thus while Rawls's own writings may be seen as overstating the strength of the liberty-based case for property-owning democracy, Rawls nevertheless may have *understated* the strength of the equality-based case against welfare state capitalism, and in favor of the institutions of a property-owning democracy.

Chapters 5 and 6 by Alan Thomas and Stuart White relate – and to a considerable extent defend – Rawls's commitment to property-owning democracy to (and against) two alternative lines of criticism. In Chapter 5, Thomas defends Rawls against G.A. Cohen's well-known criticism that there is a moral inconsistency in Rawls's theory of justice: that is, Rawls's view that citizens can simultaneously be egoists in economic life (claiming as much as they can in the market) and motivated primarily by principles of justice in political life (modifying market outcomes so as to ensure equality of opportunity and to maximize the position of the least well off). Thomas argues that the entire point of a just political economy is to achieve social justice via institutional arrangements without having to rely on individual good will or beneficence. He further argues that a Rawlsian property-owning democracy can indeed achieve a liberal egalitarian conception of justice, and can circumvent Cohen's internal criticisms of Rawls's approach, provided that the institutions of a property-owning democracy are hard-wired into society's constitutional arrangements. Here, Thomas suggests, Rawls can legitimately be faulted for leaving too much of basic economic arrangements to be decided by the vagaries of democratic politics, while nevertheless making the case for a constitutionalized property-owning democracy as the core element of a just society.

In Chapter 6, White argues that Rawls's basic framework and the recent revival of republican thinking in a variety of quarters can largely be reconciled once it is recognized that, as a matter of sociological fact, robust political participation is essential to the preservation and further development of any socially just society. White uses Tocqueville's account of democratic culture in nineteenth-century America to illustrate how democratic concern with the common good can deform into a destructive hyper-individualism, and to describe possible remedies to this process. White then goes on to argue that Rawlsians should opt for a "republican" rather than "liberal" conception of citizenship that places more demands on ordinary people in daily life to be politically aware and engaged. The requirement that citizens be more than just voters, that they should also be active, co-equal citizens on roughly equal footing with one another, strengthens the argument for property-owning democracy.

Part Two: Interrogating Property-Owning Democracy: Work, Gender, Political Economy

Part Two of the book considers both institutional implications of property-owning democracy and critical comparisons of property-owning democracy with other institutional alternatives. In Chapter 7, Nien-hê Hsieh builds on the discussions in Part One by showing how Rawls's critique of the welfare state relates to the issue of *work* and workplace democracy. A full-blown, attractive liberal egalitarian conception of justice must have an explicit conception of just work at its core. While Rawls's writings exhibit concerns with the character of work, including a concern that work not replicate social relations based on domination, and that persons have an opportunity to do meaningful work, these concerns do not play a central role in the explicit argument for property-owning democracy. This chapter assesses how well property-owning democracy might address these concerns and thereby contribute to the "productive enfranchisement" of citizens – the ability to participate in economically productive activity on terms consistent with their self-respect. By reducing the degree to which workers' choice of jobs is governed by economic necessity, property-owning democracy affords workers opportunity to pursue meaningful work as well as protection from "arbitrary interference" – that is, managerial authoritarianism – at work. Widespread ownership of productive assets also helps to ensure that labor market arrangements do not create deep inequalities of power and status in the workplace. This chapter argues that the implications of distributing productive assets broadly for the content, governance, and status of work form a significant rationale for favoring property-owning democracy over other types of redistributive strategies.

In Chapter 8, Ingrid Robeyns examines the relationship between property-owning democracy and questions of gender justice and care. How might a property-owning democracy impact social policies that structure how care for children (and other dependents) is provided, and consequently how gender norms are constructed? Robeyns compares several different conceptions of care regimes, and argues on behalf of a "mixed care regime" that combines generous support for leaves to provide care with professional (extra-familiar) provision of care. Implementing a full-blown mixed care regime in ways that meet all the relevant concerns (i.e., adequate care for children;

support for parent–child relationships, especially when children are very young; and ensuring that parenthood does not excessively damage career prospects of parents, especially mothers) will typically be an expensive undertaking requiring many transfers. From the standpoint of gender justice, an important question is whether the institutions of property-owning democracy might shift resources away from the kinds of universal care support a gender-just society must provide. If property-owning democracy is adopted in such a way that *reduces* the kinds of transfers required for a just gender regime, it could have a negative impact; likewise, Robeyns argues that the provision of universal basic incomes could have a negative impact on women if it induces them to drop out of the labor market. On the other hand, property-owning democracy could benefit women by tending to equalize wealth (since most women are below the net median worth level) and especially by promoting workplace democracy (and hence more just workplace arrangements and practices). In short, property-owning democracy as such poses both possible benefits and possible risks for gender justice, and careful attention must be given to issues of gender justice in elaborating the details of any specific institutional realization of a property-owning democracy.

The following two chapters each in different ways pose critiques of property-owning democracy, as well as suggesting alternatives to it. In Chapter 9, Waheed Hussain argues that Rawls's theory is most consistent with a form of property-owning democracy that incorporates elements of social corporatism. The burgeoning literature on the "varieties of capitalism" has renewed interest in corporatist institutions, such as the codetermination system in Germany, society-wide collective bargaining in Sweden and Norway, and other features of labor markets in European social democracies. Hussain focuses in particular on what he calls a "democratic corporatist" property-owning democracy, an arrangement that would enable workers and owners to participate collectively in rule-making processes that structure competition in an industry (not unlike collective bargaining in some American professional sports leagues). He argues that this arrangement is more consistent with Rawls's ideal of "stability," which says that liberal democratic institutions must be anchored in a liberal democratic spirit among citizens. Rawls thinks that citizens in a just society come to care about liberal democratic ideals when they see how these ideals have contributed to their own lives and the lives of the people and communities they care about. By involving workers and owners more directly in economic governance, democratic corporatism puts more people in a position to see and feel how they have benefited from liberal democratic institutions, and thereby strengthens the liberal democratic sense of justice among citizens. Although noncorporatist arrangements can take measures to improve political participation in other spheres – measures such as those described by Tocqueville and endorsed by Stuart White – Hussain argues that participation in the economic realm is essential because people in modern societies care so intensely about their careers and their economic aspirations.

In Chapter 10, David Schweickart critically compares property-owning democracy to his own model of "Economic Democracy" – a form of democratic market socialism with a strong role for worker control of productive assets. Schweickart argues, on Rawls's own terrain, that democratic socialism provides a far more secure basis for securing the principles of justice than does property-owning democracy. To make the case, Schweickart first outlines seven major criticisms of capitalism; then distinguishes property-owning democracy from existing forms of capitalism; and finally, asks how well property-owning democracy fares vis-à-vis "Economic Democracy" (ED) in addressing the problems generated by capitalism. In Schweickart's view, while property-owning democracy may actually generate more egalitarian distributive results than economic democracy, ED would fare better on the other dimensions, especially those having to do with society's ability to direct investment in a rational direction. This advantage of ED rests mostly on the presumption that in property-owning democracy, the financial sector would remain in private hands. Schweickart then goes on to consider the possibility of "Property-Owning Democracy Plus," which would add public control over finance to other property-owning democracy policies. "POD+," Schweickart contends, could indeed address fairly well most of the central problems with capitalism – precisely by adopting explicitly socialist mechanisms for determining how investment takes place. If this is the case, the choice between ED and "POD +" is best made on grounds of political plausibility; Schweickart thus closes the chapter by arguing the case for why, despite initial appearances, economic democracy may actually be a more realistic political possibility than "property-owning democracy plus."

Part Three: Toward a Practical Politics of Property-Owning Democracy: Program and Politics

The final section of the book takes up the question of how property-owning democracy might begin to be realized in practice. In Chapter 11, Thad Williamson provides a fairly detailed sketch of how (in the context of the contemporary United States), policies might implement a full-blown property-owning democracy over the course of the next generation. One consequence of the lopsided distribution of current wealth is that it is *possible* to provide all households with a substantial pool of wealth simply by redistributing a substantial proportion of the existing wealth held by the most wealthy (i.e., the top 1%). Williamson proposes taking advantage of that fact by using ongoing taxation of the wealthy (targeted at both inherited wealth and very high incomes) to fund a series of funds providing *all* citizens with access to three kinds of capital: housing (real property); cash (savings); and productive capital (stock ownership). The long-term goal is to provide all households with access to real assets of at least $100,000: that is, to achieve a society in which all citizens truly do control or have access to substantial property holdings. Williamson describes how this goal might be achieved in an evolutionary fashion over a 20–30-year time period.

In Chapter 12, Sonia Sodha moves from consideration of long-term visions of implementing property-owning democracy to smaller-bore policies, achievable in the near term, aimed at promoting widespread distribution of assets. Drawing on examples from the United Kingdom, Sodha both surveys existing policies and describes a number of forward-looking proposals for providing citizens with ownership stakes on a universal basis. This chapter also provides an informative overview of the idea of "asset-based" social policy as it has emerged in the United States and in the UK since the 1990s. Where Williamson's chapter provides an aerial view of the systemic transformation that would be needed for the full enactment of a property-owning democracy, Sodha takes a more incremental approach, showing how the extension or radicalization of recent approaches to social policy could be used to move a society toward the goals associated with a property-owning democracy.

In Chapter 13, attention turns back from the question of asset-enhancing social policy to the question of how to nurture democratic forms of capital. Gar Alperovitz begins by providing a sober assessment of the limited capacity of social democratic politics in the United States (and often elsewhere) to achieve its stated goals, such as establishing equal opportunity or providing a meaningful safety net. In this political context, ironically, there may actually be greater public interest in more radical strategies aimed at democratizing capital – simply because nothing else works, and traditional liberal policies are so obviously inadequate. Alperovitz goes on to survey and document a wide variety of examples of democratic capital ownership already in practice, in a variety of different sectors and geographic locations, including worker-owned firms, networks of cooperatives, community-owned enterprise, and local and state public enterprise. Taken together, these examples suggest the outlines of an alternative political–economic system, termed by Alperovitz a "pluralist commonwealth," that could realize many of the same goals as property-owning democracy, but with a richer attention to questions of how to stabilize geographic communities over time. The moral basis for this program, Alperovitz suggests, should rest on an understanding of modern forms of wealth as inherently a social product – the "inheritance" of decades of developing knowledge – not the result of the individual contributions of wealthy entrepreneurs.

In Chapter 14, Thad Williamson closes the volume by discussing in greater detail the potential *politics* of property-owning democracy, in the context of the United States. What political actors and groups are likely to be attracted to the idea, and who would be opposed? What reasons do we have for thinking that property-owning democracy might fare better politically than traditional conceptions of the welfare state or social democratic modes of redistribution? Williamson argues that advocates for property-owning democracy must take the offensive in offering strong moral arguments against the near-monopolization of wealth by the very wealthy (the top 1%) and especially the super-wealthy (the top 0.1%). If effective arguments can be made that the very rich ought not dominate the economy as a whole, then many other aspects of property-owning democracy, including (as Rawls hinted) its consistency with cultural ideas about the value of individual entrepreneurship, would likely be attractive to large swathes of the American public. Political resistance to serious calls for redistribution of wealth would likely be intense. But any serious effort in the direction of property-owning democracy will require intense ideological struggle over the purposes of a modern economy – a struggle that progressives and egalitarians, in the USA, UK, and elsewhere, have arguably put off for far too long.

References

Alperovitz, G. (2004) *America Beyond Capitalism*, John Wiley & Sons, Inc, Hoboken, NJ.
Barry, B. (2005) *Why Social Justice Matters*, Polity Press, Cambridge.
Conley, D. (2009) *Being Black, Living in the Red: Race, Wealth and Social Policy in America*, 2nd edn, University of California Press, Berkeley.

Dagger, R. (2006) Neo-republicanism and the civic economy. *Politics, Philosophy and Economics*, 5, 151–173.

Elkin, S. (2006) *Reconstructing the Commercial Republic: Constitutional Theory After Madison*, University of Chicago Press, Chicago.

Erikson, R. and Goldthorpe, J.H. (2002) Intergenerational inequalities: A sociological perspective. *Journal of Economic Perspectives*, 16, 31–44.

Friedman, M. (1962) *Capitalism and Freedom*, University of Chicago Press, Chicago.

Hayek, F.A. (1984) "Social" or distributive justice, in *The Essence of Hayek* (eds C. Nishiyama and Kurt Leubke), Hoover Institution Press, Stanford, CA.

Kuttner, R. (2010) *A Presidency in Peril: The Inside Story of Obama's Promise, Wall Street's Power, and the Struggle to Control Our Economic Future*, Chelsea Green, White River Junction, VT.

Lebowitz, M. (2010) *The Socialist Alternative: Real Human Development*, Monthly Review Press, New York.

OECD (Organization for Economic Cooperation and Development) (2011) *Growing Income Inequality in OECD Countries: What Drives It and How Can Policy Tackle It?* OECD Forum on Tackling Inequality, Paris, May 2, 2011. Available at www.oecd.org/dataoecd/32/20/47723414.pdf (accessed August 11, 2011).

Rawls, J. (1971) *A Theory of Justice*, Harvard University Press, Cambridge, MA.

Rawls, J. (1993) *Political Liberalism*, Columbia University Press, New York.

Rawls, J. (2001) *Justice as Fairness: A Restatement* (ed. E. Kelly), Harvard University Press, Cambridge, MA.

Roemer, J. (1994) *A Future for Socialism*, Harvard University Press, Cambridge, MA.

Schweickart, D. (1993) *Against Capitalism*, Rowman & Littlefield, Lanham, MD.

Schweickart, D. (2002) *After Capitalism*, Rowman & Littlefield, Lanham, MD.

Sen, A. (2009) *The Idea of Justice*, Harvard University Press, Cambridge, MA.

Suskind, R. (2011) *Confidence Men: Wall Street, Washington, and the Education of a President*, HarperCollins, New York.

Williamson, T. (2009) Who Owns What? An Egalitarian Interpretation of John Rawls's Idea of a Property-Owning Democracy. *Journal of Social Philosophy*, 40, 434–453.

Wright, E.O. (2010) *Envisioning Real Utopias*, Verso, New York.

Part One
Property-Owning Democracy: Theoretical Foundations

Part One

1

Justice or Legitimacy, Barricades or Public Reason?
The Politics of Property-Owning Democracy

Simone Chambers

Thinking about the sorts of politics that Rawls's work might lead to or inspire presents us with something analogous to a *trompe l'oeil*. Not the *trompe l'oeil* of open windows painted on brick walls, but the optical puzzle of a picture that looks first like a vase, then like two profiles, and then a vase again, and indeed the painting is both a vase and the profile of two faces but – and here is the puzzling part for the viewer – they cannot be seen as both simultaneously. Looking at Rawls's work from a philosophical perspective, he moved from philosophical questions of justice to political questions of stability and legitimacy. Thus his work became more political over the years and spoke more directly to the politics of constitutional democracies. But looking at his work from the point of view of politics, Rawls's work become less political over the course of years because it became less about justice.

What do I mean by "less political" in this context? *A Theory of Justice* is a radical book that claimed (among other things) that strongly egalitarian social institutions are the proper and only conclusion to draw from thinking through our liberal commitments. Thus *A Theory of Justice* contained a deep indictment of contemporary schemes of distribution. In particular, welfare state capitalism was essentially unjust and should be replaced with property-owning democracy. But replacing welfare state capitalism with property-owning democracy would – certainly in the political world within which Rawls lived, the late twentieth-century United States – require something close to a revolution.

Rawls a revolutionary? Could one ever imagine the careful, gentle, and eminently sensible figure of John Rawls manning a barricade? The very strangeness of this image is part of the shifting ideas of politics that come in and out of focus as we read Rawls from two different perspectives. Rawls's egalitarian vision would take nothing short of a revolution to bring about and yet Rawls was anything but a revolutionary.

In this chapter I trace out the shifting terms of the politics of egalitarianism. In particular I look at the reasons why Rawls refused to embrace the type of politics that would be necessary to bring about the type of justice he appeared to be advocating.

Property-Owning Democracy: Rawls and Beyond, First Edition. Edited by Martin O'Neill and Thad Williamson.
© 2012 Blackwell Publishing Ltd. Published 2012 by Blackwell Publishing Ltd.

Rawls's views on equality are radical, indeed utopian, and as such quite far ahead of prevailing public culture. Outlining the political implications of the difference principle in any detail would involve stepping out of the existing liberal order into a radical critical theory.[1] This is to say it would involve taking a critical stand toward existing distributive schemes. The difference principle does not point to a more progressive tax system but rather to a rethinking of the basic structure of our property relations. This is radical. This sort of radicalism not only did not interest Rawls; it appears to undermine his main justificatory strategy, namely the argument that "justice as fairness" was simply a rendering of certain core ideas central to our existing liberal order.

Furthermore, in moving from his Archimedean stage to his political stage, Rawls moved from outlining a theory of justice to outlining how such a theory of justice could become widely accepted and stabilized under conditions of pluralism. The central idea in this move is to seek out principles of justice that have both a strong philosophic justification as well as a strong citizen endorsement, despite the fact that citizens might have very different religious and moral world-views. This is what Rawls calls political liberalism. It is political rather than metaphysical. We need not find agreement on questions of truth and or a full moral view in order to agree on principles to govern the basic structure of our political community. Legitimacy becomes tied to what can be publically justified under conditions of reasonable pluralism, and Rawls had to concede that many of the egalitarian principles he championed in *A Theory of Justice* could not be publically justified even though he still was convinced that they were just (Freeman, 2007).

Controversial principles concerning social justice moved into the background and more widely accepted views concerning rights and freedoms moved into the foreground. In particular, the difference principle, which is the jewel in the crown of Rawls's egalitarianism and the foundational principle for the endorsement of property-owning democracy, was essentially just but could not be shown to be legitimate (Freeman, 2007). In what follows I trace out the move from justice to legitimacy and ask, "Is there a way back from legitimacy to justice?" In order to see why the difference principle causes problems from the point of view of legitimacy we need to begin at the beginning: with basic ideas of equality.

What Is Equality?

Rawls's discussion of equality is complex and multileveled, and, despite becoming less prominent in his later work, remained an enduring theme throughout his career. Very broadly, we can discern three interlocking spheres of equality at work in Rawls's writings: fundamental equality, political equality, and social and economic equality. Fundamental equality involves some initial claim about the moral status of individuals, namely, that all persons are of equal worth (Barry, 2001). It is this sort of claim that is expressed in the Declaration of Independence, for example, with the words "We hold these truths to be self-evident, that all men are created equal." There are three things to note about fundamental equality: it is notoriously difficult to "prove," it is not self-evident what follows from such a claim, and it is the closest thing liberal democracy has to an axiom. All of Rawls's work begins from the premise that we are free and equal in a fundamental and essentially pre-political sense. There is no attempt – nor does Rawls think there is any need – to "prove" this as a universal truth. Nor does he claim it as a fact. It is simply the way we must begin if we are to think about what follows from our broadest liberal commitments.

Although it is not self-evident what follows from fundamental equality, political equality, sometimes called equality of democratic citizenship, is the most common next step (Arneson, 1993). Here we move from making a general claim about moral status to a claim about how institutions should treat individuals. Political equality then encompasses such things as equal basic liberties – for example, freedom of expression, religion, and association; equal right to vote and run for office; equality before the law and due process.

Finally, we come to social and economic equality or, more precisely, social and economic inequality. Few claim that in this sphere there *is* equality (as in the moral realm) or that there *ought* to be or *could* be full equality (as in the political realm). The debate is usually about how much inequality we ought to allow. For strong egalitarians like Rawls, the benchmark is equality, but the question is not how to achieve equality, but rather, how far ought we to let distribution fall away from the benchmark. While there is a great deal still to be said about fundamental equality (and we should never tire of reminding ourselves of its importance), and we have yet to get political equality quite right, there appears to be a broad consensus on these ideas within Western liberal democracies. Social and economic equality is the hard case and so the more interesting case.

In justice as fairness, Rawls's favored conception of justice, political and social equality are embodied in his two principles of justice. The first principle runs as follows: "each person has the same indefeasible claim to a fully adequate scheme of equal basic liberties, which scheme is compatible with the same scheme of liberties for all" (Rawls, 2001, p. 42). The status and centrality of this principle to Rawls's political philosophy never changed and it appears to have deep roots in American political culture.[2] The first half of Rawls's second principle also remained central to his conception of justice and also appears to have significant popular support: social and economic inequalities "are to be attached to offices and positions open to all under conditions of fair equality of opportunity" (2001, p. 42).[3] It is the second half of the second principle, the difference principle, that has seen the most change and which appears to have the least support in public culture: social and economic inequalities "are to be to the greatest benefit of the least advantaged members of society" (Rawls, 2001, p. 43).[4] This principle is the heart and soul of Rawls's egalitarianism. But he pushed this egalitarianism into the background as his work become more political. Why this should be so is worth considering.

From the Fact of Inequality to the Fact of Pluralism

In *A Theory of Justice*, Rawls argues that questions of justice are really questions about the basic structure of society: that is, they are questions about how things like constitutions, markets, and private property determine and shape life chances. These institutions, however they are set up, necessarily "favor certain starting places over others." This is a fact of social life, and for Rawls "[i]t is these inequalities, presumably inevitable in the basic structure of any society, to which the principles of social justice must in the first instance apply" (Rawls, 1971, p. 7). Social inequality is inevitable but it is also man-made. Inequality is the result of structures that are subject to our choices and control. There are an infinite number of ways to regulate a market. Thus, although inequality is inevitable, no particular pattern or configuration of inequality is necessary. We must decide which pattern or configuration is justifiable. This is the central problematic of *A Theory of Justice*. It leads Rawls to develop principles of justice that regulate the basic structure and hence determine life chances. These principles of justice are highly egalitarian and he never repudiates or significantly alters his commitment to them. But things do change.

One way to read that change is as a shift from a concern about the problems raised by the fact of inequality to a concern for the problems raised by the fact of pluralism. These two facts play vastly different roles in his theory. The fact of inequality asks for justification against a benchmark of equality; the fact of pluralism asks for accommodation against a benchmark of autonomy. The first fact must be viewed with suspicion, the second with approval. The fact of inequality demands that we think about and come up with principles of justice; the fact of pluralism demands that we think about and come up with ways of justifying and defending principles of justice in a world characterized by deep disagreement. Thus, one can understand the move from *A Theory of Justice* to *Political Liberalism* as a move from the question "What principles of justice follow from our general liberal commitments?" to the question "Why should we think citizens would accept these principles as legitimate?"[5]

The problem of inequality in *A Theory of Justice* is posed as a philosophical problem to be worked out in the original position, while the problem of pluralism in *Political Liberalism* is posed as a political problem to be worked out among citizens. The difference here is not that Rawls moves from ideal theory to the nonideal world of messy politics. In both *A Theory of Justice* and *Political Liberalism* ideal theory is the medium; Rawls is working within the assumption of a well-ordered society. A well-ordered society is "a society effectively regulated by a public conception of justice" (Rawls, 2001, p. 5). The Rawlsian strategy is to think about moral and political problems in a context where everything pretty much works as it should and where everyone pretty much acts as she should. Once we get a handle on how things might work in a well-ordered society, we can begin to introduce the problems, uncertainties, and contingencies of the real world.

So *Political Liberalism* is not political in a pragmatic sense. It is political because it describes the citizen point of view and argues that citizens can endorse a political conception of justice without at the same time having to endorse a shared moral, religious, or deep philosophical perspective.

Although citizens are, of course, present in *A Theory of Justice*, the most important character is the chooser in the original position. She is asked to view the problem of inequality from an impartial perspective. This perspective requires that she know nothing about her particular place in society. Citizens, in contrast, know everything about themselves and in particular they are very aware of the way their fundamental moral and religious ideas diverge. Citizens, while not under the radical impartiality of the veil of ignorance, are asked to adopt a stance of neutrality while arguing with each other.

Public reason eclipses the original position as the perspective from which citizens view questions of justice. Public reason in its earliest articulation (Rawls, 1993) was the reasoning and deliberation that would be necessary to work out the constitutional and legislative elaboration of the principles of justice chosen in the original position. In a well-ordered society, everyone would share a basic but very general conception of justice (for example, justice as fairness) and would argue from that conception. There would still be lots of room for difference of opinion but it would be about the application and elaboration of principles of justice and not about the principles themselves. But as Rawls became more interested in citizens and legislators working out the constitutional essentials necessary to any conception of justice, he became less insistent that justice as fairness was the only conception of justice that could fit the bill. Justice as fairness became one among many possible conceptions of justice that could serve the function of shared starting point for deliberation. Rawls began to use the phrase "justice as fairness or something like it" when appealing to a conception of justice. Not only did justice as fairness become just one possible conception of justice among a number of possible sets of liberal principles but questions of economic distribution and property rights fell completely outside of public reason (Rawls, 1993, p. 229; Freeman, 2007). Rawls came to accept that there was no shared starting principle from which we could argue about distribution and therefore distribution should not be addressed as a constitutional essential. This in turn has thrown social justice back into the political arena in a very interesting way. But we get ahead of ourselves. We need to take a closer look at the difference principle to see why it falls outside of public reason and back into a political sphere of contestation.

The Difference Principle

At the heart of Rawls's egalitarianism is the intuition that institutions should be arranged in such a way as to improve the life chances of the worst off in society. Rawls is not alone in making concern for those at the bottom of the social and economic ladder the *sine qua non* of egalitarianism (Nagel, 1991; Arneson, 1993). This intuition is expressed in the difference principle and leads to the conclusion that if there is some scheme of unequal distribution that makes individuals at the bottom better off than they would be under an equal distribution, then the unequal scheme is preferable to the equal distribution. A great deal of ink has been spilt on the justification and defense of this principle and its connection to equality (e.g., Richardson and Weithman, 1999). At first sight it does not appear to be a principle of equality at all as it seems to give unequal moral weight to the least advantaged of society. Before I spill even more ink on this subject, I want to jump ahead and offer a hint at what is at stake; that is, I want to look briefly at what it might mean to implement this principle. Some people have implied that it wouldn't mean much. On the left, this principle has sometimes been read as a disingenuous defense of capitalism and huge inequalities (DiQuattro, 1983). But if

Rawls himself is anything to go by, the difference principle is a far cry from the conservative adage that a rising tide lifts all boats.

It is not just that Rawls's egalitarianism appears to be tacking quite hard against neoliberalism and a retrenchment of the welfare state. Rawls himself sees the institutional implication of the difference principle in much more radical terms. He has clearly and without equivocation stated that it is not just laissez-faire capitalism that is incompatible with his view of equality; welfare state capitalism also fails to pass muster. Rawls endorses what, following James Meade (1964), he calls property-owning democracy, while admitting that some form of democratic socialism might also be compatible with the difference principle. Few people have taken Rawls up on this topic, and, as noted by Krouse and McPherson (1988), many commentators have simply assumed that Rawls is advocating an egalitarian brand of welfare state capitalism. On this mistaken reading, the redistribution mandated by the difference principle would predominantly involve a redistribution of income to those identified as the least well off in society. At the end of each "period," whatever that might be, we would look at how everyone was doing and reshuffle the outcome deck. This is not what Rawls had in mind.

Rawls is interested in "securing background justice over time" (Rawls, 2001, p. 135). To do this, the difference principle must be applied directly to the basic structure. A capitalist welfare system tolerates not just an uneven distribution of wealth but a world in which there are some without property altogether. By contrast, "background institutions of property-owning democracy work to disperse the ownership of wealth and capital. And thus to prevent a small part of society from controlling the economy" (Rawls, 2001, p. 39). Welfare capitalism redresses the inequalities produced by the basic structure; property-owning democracy offers a redesigned basic structure to ensure minimum or only justifiable inequalities in outcomes. While some income transfers will always be necessary within property-owning democracy, Rawls is interested in a system that has no need of large-scale income *re*distribution.

What would a property-owning democracy really entail? Rawls says very little on the subject. Very generally, it would mean establishing and maintaining "widespread ownership of productive property and limits to the concentration of property over time" (Krouse and McPherson, 1988, p. 99). This in turn would probably mean "some sort of once and for all redistribution of property holding, accompanied by institutional reforms . . . to keep the redistributed property from becoming reconcentrated" (Krouse and McPherson, 1988, p. 103). However one looks at it, property-owning democracy, with its insistence that property, understood both as human and real capital, be "put in the hands of citizens generally" (Rawls, 2001, p. 140), is a radical departure from property arrangements in contemporary America, or in other contemporary liberal democratic societies. The more Rawls said about it, the more he seemed to be inching toward the barricades. Perhaps he adopted the strategy of "the less said, the better." But Rawls did say enough about property-owning democracy to conclude that any plausible interpretation of such a system would require something quite different than the existing property arrangements in contemporary America. But here is the puzzle. Rawls claims to be articulating beliefs that, although latent, are nevertheless constituent of our political culture. This in turn implies that existing property relations and the distribution of wealth are out of line with political culture. But are they? Can Rawls find the deep cultural resources he needs to defend egalitarianism?[6] He sometimes appears to go back and forth between two strategies. One is to insist that the difference principle is the consistent answer to the question of what follows from our deep commitments to fundamental equality (Rawls, 2001, p. 49). The other strategy is to admit that the difference principle is controversial and so not insist on its inclusion in a conception of justice (Rawls, 1993, p. 157). I take up the first strategy in the following section, before moving on to address the alternative strategy in the final section.

Ideals Latent in Public Political Culture

Why should we care more about the worst off than other groups in society? There is an original position answer to this question, of course. Briefly, it states that if you did not know where you would end up in society, you would be most concerned about what would happen if you ended up at the bottom. From this vantage point you would choose a distributive scheme that maximized the possibilities for the minimum stake (Cohen, 1989). From the point of view of the original position, then, we care about ourselves first and the least well off only to the extent that we might be one of them. This, however, is not the most important or persuasive argument in defense of the difference principle and Rawls himself admits that without appeal to substantive ideals in our political culture, the difference principle might appear "eccentric or bizarre" (Rawls, 1971, p. 75).

There are two arguments in particular that deserve our attention: the distinction between persons and the concept of moral arbitrariness. The "distinction between persons" argument brings us back to ideas of fundamental equality. In Rawls's early career he was partly motivated by the fact that moral philosophy had been dominated by utilitarianism. Utilitarianism also begins from a strong idea of fundamental equality: no one shall count for more than one. For utilitarians, justice is realized when "major institutions are arranged so as to achieve the greatest net balance of satisfaction summed over all the individuals belonging to any given society" (Rawls, 1971, p. 22). The problem is that for utilitarians, "it does not matter, except indirectly, how this sum of satisfactions is distributed among individuals" (Rawls, 1971, p. 26). This would allow – in principle, anyway – the losses of some to be compensated for by the greater gains of others. Such trade-offs are incompatible with an alternative view of fundamental equality in which each individual is considered to have equal *immeasurable* worth, or dignity, rather than each individual being considered as numerically equal. The equal dignity of each individual prohibits a scheme in which some people's losses are justified because they are a means to other people's gains.[7]

So we cannot just make the pie bigger – especially if making the pie bigger involves sacrificing someone's life chances for the greater good. We can only make the pie bigger if we can be assured that no one will be made worse off by it. Thomas Nagel points out that in contrast to utilitarianism, this Kantian concern for everybody "must contain a separate and equal concern for each person's good" (Nagel, 1991, p. 66). From such a concern, "a ranking of urgency naturally emerges" (Nagel, 1991, p. 68). It is not that the worst off have more moral worth; it is that in looking at everybody as having equal moral worth we ought to be most concerned with those who fall farthest from an ideal of well-being, whatever that might be.[8] Thus, there is a certain intuitive affinity between an idea of equal dignity and a special concern for those at the bottom. However, it is not clear that this alone could produce the difference principle.

The second fundamental idea that underpins the difference principle is the intuition that people should not be disadvantaged or penalized by factors outside their control or factors that are otherwise arbitrary from a moral point of view. No one thinks that shoe size should significantly determine one's life chances or social position. Race and gender are equally arbitrary from a moral point of view and so should not determine one's life chances or social position. To these widely accepted examples of arbitrariness, Rawls adds talents and abilities. He claims that it is one of the fixed points of our considered judgments "that no one deserves his place in the distribution of native endowments, any more than one deserves one's initial starting place in society" (Rawls, 1971, p. 104). A person does not deserve the talents she was born with any more than she can be said to deserve or have earned the size of her feet. Rawls goes further still and maintains that "even the willingness to make an effort" is dependent upon – or, at any rate, inextricable from – morally arbitrary factors like social circumstances and family (Rawls, 1971, p. 74).

According to Rawls we may – and indeed should – benefit from our talents, not because we deserve such benefit in any strong moral sense, but only because rewarding certain talents and abilities is good for everyone: "Those who have been favored by nature, whoever they are, may gain from their good fortune only on terms that improve the situation of those who have lost out" (Rawls, 1971, p. 101). The two important ideas here are, first, that a person should not be penalized or lose out in life because of circumstances beyond her control. Natural abilities constitute such a circumstance. Second, society is a joint venture from which we are all supposed to benefit. Each and every individual's cooperation in this joint venture, including those with fewer talents than others, is premised on the deck not being stacked against them from the very beginning. Joshua Cohen (2002, p. D1) puts this nicely when he says: "Rawls's large point is that we ought to reject the idea that our economic system is a race or talent contest, designed to reward the well-born, the swift, and the gifted. Instead, our economic life should be one part of a fair system of social cooperation, designed to ensure a reasonable life for all." But what if the idea that our economic system is a race or a talent contest has a deep hold on us, or at least on many of us?

How Egalitarian Are We?

Here is the puzzle thus far: Rawls begins with ideas implicit in our political culture but ends with an egalitarian vision far removed from anything the political culture within which he lived seemed prepared to contemplate. In what follows I rely mostly on studies and data about how Americans feel about equality, and this arguably is different than European political culture. Perhaps the difference principle, and by extension property-owning democracy, has more purchase within European understandings of liberal democracy than in America. Be that as it may, the underlying point is still the same. Rawls's egalitarianism relies on controversial claims about the basis of just distribution. The claims articulate ideas that are so latent as to be invisible to the naked eye, by which I mean measurable in any social scientific sense, and indeed appear to conflict with other aspects of our political culture that are less latent. This is especially clear with regard to the moral arbitrariness argument. Rawls is right to point out that modern liberal democratic culture grew out of a rejection of the moral significance of natural facts:

> The natural distribution [of talent] is neither just nor unjust; nor is it unjust that persons are born into society at some particular position. These are simply natural facts. What is just and unjust is the way that institutions deal with these facts. Aristocratic and caste societies are unjust because they make these contingencies the ascriptive basis for belonging to more or less enclosed and privileged social classes. The basic structure of these societies incorporates the arbitrariness found in nature. But there is no necessity for men to resign themselves to these contingencies. The social system is not an unchangeable order beyond human control but a pattern of human action. In justice as fairness men agree to share one another's fate. In designing institutions they undertake to avail themselves of the accidents of nature and social circumstance only when doing so is for the common benefit. (Rawls, 1971, p. 102)

This strikes me as a very powerful idea and one that is, in many ways, deeply embedded in contemporary American public culture. But it competes with an equally strong and apparently contradictory principle of desert and personal responsibility (Scheffler, 1992). Even though we might admit that no one deserves the particular talent they are born with, it is still strongly felt that people deserve the rewards and benefits that they can get by exercising that talent, even if that means large inequalities. Some of the earliest empirical work addressing public opinion on income equality comes from Robert Lane's 1962 interviews of 10 working-class and five white-collar American males. He concludes that his respondents view inequality as just: "Most of my subjects accepted the view that America opens up opportunity to all people, if not in equal proportions, then at least enough so that a person must assume responsibility for his own status." He summarizes their opinions this way: "the upper classes deserve to be upper," and "the lower classes deserve no better than they can get" (Lane, 1962, pp. 61, 69, 71). Ideas of desert are often strongly connected to ideas of personal responsibility. McCloskey and Zaller, note, for example, that public opinion research generally indicates that "although most Americans think that government should intervene positively to promote social and economic equality, they also believe that the primary responsibility for personal advancement ought to remain with the individual" (McCloskey and Zaller, 1984, p. 91). In her qualitative study of 28 working adults in New Haven, Jennifer Hochschild also concludes that her respondents "all want to believe that upward mobility is possible for those with drive, talent, and ambition. But they are dubious" (Hochschild, 1981, p. 143). Even scholars like Benjamin Page and Larry Jacobs, who argue that public opinion data show that Americans are very open to government policy redressing economic inequality, admit that the deep political culture is conservative. Americans "embrace the 'American Dream' – the idea that individuals should enjoy the opportunity to go as far as their work and skill will take them. Responsibility for an individual's economic position and life conditions rests chiefly with him- or herself" (Page and Jacobs, 2009, pp. 2–3; see also Bartels, 2008, pp. 127–161).

So talent and desert appear firmly embedded in public culture even for those who are uncertain whether the American economic system can really deliver the goods.

Although some elements of Rawls's egalitarianism are present, they conflict with a view of equality that Kymlicka has described this way:

> in a society where no one is disadvantaged by their social circumstances, the people's fate is in their own hands. Success (or failure) will be the result of our own choices and efforts. Hence whatever success we achieve is "earned," rather than merely endowed on us. In a society that has equality of opportunity, unequal income is fair, because success is "merited," it goes to those who "deserve" it. (Kymlicka, 2002, p. 58)

Rawls too, of course, thinks that people should be rewarded for hard work and talent; indeed, they have a legitimate expectation of such a reward. Under the difference principle unequal income is fair. However, the ultimate justification for the reward is not desert; rather, it is that a system that offers such a reward can be shown to be good for everyone and especially the least well off in society. Is this an important difference? I think it is. There is evidence to suggest that citizens in the USA today are willing to tolerate much higher levels of inequality as result of a natural lottery than one could possibly imagine in a Rawlsian well-ordered society.[9] As Hochschild's study shows, even those at the bottom who do not necessarily think that the system is very fair have a conception of social justice based on desert not constrained by a higher principle of egalitarianism (Hochschild, 1981, p. 111). The willingness to tolerate high levels of inequality can be tied back to notions of desert and a view of economic justice that sees it more as a fair race then as a cooperative joint venture.[10]

Public culture goes as far as the first part of the second principle but not much farther. In *A Theory of Justice* Rawls insists that there is a glaring inconsistency here: "once we are troubled by the influence of either social contingencies or natural chance on the determination of distributive shares, we are bound, on reflection, to be bothered by the influence of the other. From a moral standpoint the two seem equally arbitrary" (Rawls, 1971, pp. 74–75). If we think race and gender should not count then we must also think that natural talent should not count from a moral point of view. Indeed, Rawls often talks about the difference principle as an integral part of a vision of fundamental equality that has reciprocity at its center: "It is nevertheless important to try to identify the idea of equality most appropriate to citizens viewed as free and equal, and as normally and fully cooperating members of society over a complete life. I believe that idea involves reciprocity at the deepest level and thus democratic equality properly understood requires something like the difference principle" (Rawls, 2001, p. 49). Here Rawls is connecting the three levels of equality I mentioned at the outset: that we are all free and equal in a fundamental sense leads to the recognition of political equality, which in turn should lead to the difference principle and the economic institutions that could instantiate this principle. But the fit is not perfect and Rawls finally came to admit that reasonable people could and did come to very different conclusions.

As Rawls moved beyond *A Theory of Justice*, the difference principle began to take on an oddly double life. On the one hand, Rawls never wavered from the opinion that the difference principle (or something very much like it) is part of the most reasonable conception of justice (Rawls, 2001, p. 49). It retains a central place in the last and fullest articulation of justice as fairness. Thus until the end he held to the conviction that welfare state capitalism is in some fundamental way unjust. On the other hand, in articulating a political conception of justice he realizes that principles of distribution cannot become constitutional essentials because, among other reasons, there is too much controversy surrounding them (Rawls, 1993, pp. 229–230). They simply do not flow smoothly and obviously from ideas latent in our public culture. Therefore a liberal conception of justice need only include "measures to insure that all citizens have sufficient material means to make effective use of... basic rights" (Rawls, 1993, p. 157). An adequate social minimum (Rawls, 1993, p. 230) replaces the difference principle. It is a very long way indeed from an adequate social minimum to property-owning democracy.

The difference principle lives on as Rawls's favored interpretation of economic justice and indeed throughout *Political Liberalism* he uses it as the exemplar of economic justice even while no longer insisting that it is the only possible candidate for a fair principle. But in addition to demoting its status within the theory, there is a subtler fading away of the topic. Social justice is no longer front and center. His growing concern to find a view of justice compatible with pluralism, came to overshadow his deep commitment to egalitarianism. He thought that egalitarianism flowed from ideas latent in public culture but had to concede that an overlapping consensus on strongly egalitarian principles (difference principle or otherwise) did not seem a realistic possibility. So he kept the difference principle but did not insist on it (or anything like it). To insist on the difference principle would be to take a strongly political and critical stance at a time when Rawls was more interested in arguing why we already possess the grounds for an overlapping consensus on justice. Thus we have the odd picture that as Rawls's theory became more political in one sense, that is, more about the citizen's point of view, it had to become less political in another sense, that is, seen to advocate a normative agenda on social justice.

Outside of the Bounds of Public Reason

But now I want to try and see another story in this picture. I want the vase to recede and the faces to come to the surface. Public reason proceeds from shared principles to constitutional essentials. Its foundations are political not metaphysical in the sense that the shared principles are the object of an overlapping consensus of comprehensive views. Thus Rawls has no problem imagining convergent agreement on the first principle of justice: "each person has the same indefeasible claim to a fully adequate scheme of equal basic liberties, which scheme is compatible with the same scheme of liberties for all" (Rawls, 2001, p. 42). We do not need to inquire let alone fight out the best metaphysical justification of this principle. We can each endorse it for our own comprehensive reasons, from an embrace of Kant to religiously based universalism. If we start the arguments from the shared political principle then we bypass the irresolvable metaphysical questions and head straight for political principles that are widely acceptable. This is the idea behind public reason.

There has been much interesting debate about the feasibility of public reason as a restraint on public justification. This is not the place to pursue that line of thought, however. Instead I am interested in what happens outside the bounds of public reason. Not all political conversations are governed by public reason. Rawls is a little bit cagey about where to draw the line. At first he insists that public reason should primarily concern and govern the deliberation and public justification of public officials (Rawls, 1993, p. 220). They are under especially stringent requirements to appeal to reasons that can be shown to be acceptable to all because their deliberation justifies coercive laws. But in a later discussion he adds that citizens too, when deliberating about important constitutional matters, should think "as if they were legislators" and seek reasons drawn from shared ideas of justice (Rawls, 2005, p. 444).

As was noted in the previous section, with regard to constitutional essentials, citizens and legislators may base arguments on general ideas of a social minimum but not on the difference principle. Or at least Rawls implies that the difference principle is not an appropriate principle to instantiate in a constitution because (a) there is too much uncertainty and disagreement about what would constitute its instantiation, and (b) the principle itself does not appear to enjoy the support of an overlapping consensus even though it follows from our other commitments (Rawls, 1993, p. 229). So the difference principle fades into the background – but it does not go away, and from this new perspective I am describing can be said to become truly political. There are two things to keep in mind here. First, the difference principle still describes the most just system of economic distribution. Second, there is a large and active world of politics outside the "political" world governed by public reason. Indeed, Rawls's idea of the political strangely inverts what we might normally think of as the domain of politics.

Rawls (1993, p. 231) tells us that the institution that most closely resembles and embodies the ideals of public reason is the Supreme Court. The Supreme Court is political (in the sense of political liberalism) but does not engage in politics. This is to say, its arguments are based on shared political values and not controversial metaphysical views and it stands above the contestatory melee of partisan politics and advocacy (in a well-ordered society, anyway).

In contrast to the Supreme Court, Rawls identifies civil society and the background culture as the domain in which deliberation is released from the restrictions of public reason (Rawls, 2005, p. 444). Here we argue, advocate, justify from our many perspectives. And it is here that we can introduce novel, controversial, and radical ideas that are as yet not shared. Deliberation, justification, and arguments in this domain are not private but, he says, social. Thus it would appear that the proper place to discuss the difference principle and property-owning democracy is not the Supreme Court or the floor of the legislature but in civil society at large and within and through the social movements that emerge from civil society. From this view, then, Rawls's ejection of the difference principle from public reason radicalizes it and pushes it into everyday politics, perhaps even onto the barricades.

Rawls's acknowledgment that there is no overlapping consensus on social justice means that the social (and political) processes that might bring about such an overlapping consensus are still in play. Equality is a deeply embedded and abiding political value in liberal democratic culture. Rawls believed that if we thought through our commitment to equality it should lead us to something like the difference principle and therefore something closer to property-owning democracy. But we are not there yet, partly because we are also captured by another set of ideas that cross-cut egalitarianism.

Erik Olin Wright, in an issue of *Politics and Society* devoted entirely to egalitarian proposals for redesigning initial distribution rather than redistributing market outcomes, acknowledges that there is only weak interest in such egalitarian schemes among the public. He attributes this lack of interest to the presence of an alternative political ethos that has come to dominate the public sphere: "instead of a political ethos in which the basic well-being of all citizens was seen as part of a collective responsibility, the vision [has become] one in which each person took full 'personal responsibility' for their own well-being" (Wright, 2004, p. 4). The ethos of "personal responsibility" has roots within "ideas that are latent within our political culture" just as much as the ethos of collective responsibility.

With such dual loyalties within the public culture, we cannot (as judges and legislators) impose the difference principle and property-owning democracy even if, like Rawls, we are convinced that justice demands such a revamping of our distributive priorities. The ethos of "personal responsibility" cannot be dismissed as unreasonable the way, for example, opponents of civil rights could be judicially overruled and defeated in the court of public reason. In the end, then, Rawls's refusal to make the difference principle a non-negotiable component of justice within political liberalism serves to politicize economic justice, not to take it off the agenda. It throws economic justice back into the political mix to be fought and argued over with passion and commitment. Although the development of Rawls's ideas from *A Theory of Justice* to *Political Liberalism* points in the direction of a repoliticization of economic justice, activism was never on Rawls's personal agenda. He was an egalitarian and he thought that, deep down, so were we all. Egalitarianism was the reasonable not the revolutionary conclusion to draw. But what may have seemed philosophically reasonable in 1971 is now unquestionably politically radical in the 2010s.

By placing questions of redistribution outside of public reason, Rawls invites egalitarians to develop political and public agendas in addition to philosophical ones. This move calls for a public debate about where our shared commitments to equality lead us with regard to economic justice. Rawls's initial articulation of egalitarianism in the 1970s spawned an industry of creative political philosophy devoted to working through and working out many of the finer points of social and economic equality. In retrospect, it seems that this industry was premature. The philosophical debates within egalitarianism theory of the 1980s and 1990s have had little traction in the real world of politics. The problem has not been that, for the most part, they have been working within the philosophical bounds of a well-ordered society. The problem has been that the very premise of that well-ordered society – a shared public commitment to egalitarian principles of redistribution – has been absent. Rawls's clear acknowledgment in his political phase that questions of social justice are very much unresolved in the public culture is an invitation to liberals to move from political philosophy to public discourse. The take-home message is that a Rawlsian commitment to egalitarianism points to the need to develop arguments that persuade the public and contribute to the direction in which public culture moves and develops. The political or public reason turn in Rawls calls for a whole new debate about egalitarianism that is more political, more engaged, and more critical of existing distributive schemes than the debates that have thus far characterized Rawlsian scholarship.

Notes

1. For a similar reading of Rawls, see Kymlicka (2002), and Krouse and McPherson (1988).
2. Even in the post-9/11 atmosphere of heightened concern for security, Americans still value civil liberties in poll after poll. Davis and Silver (2004), for example, examine whether Americans prefer security against terrorist attacks over the protection of civil liberties. Overwhelming majorities thought that when it came to taking such measures as investigating nonviolent protestors (92%), racial profiling (82%), conducting searches without a warrant (77%), or monitoring communications (66%), civil liberties should be preferred over protecting security.
3. In *The American Ethos*, McClosky and Zaller (1984) cite earlier work (Westie, 1965) showing that nearly all people (98%) agree that "everyone in America should have equal opportunities to get ahead" and "Children should have equal education opportunities." See also Bartels (2008, p. 130) for public opinion data showing that Americans have deep commitments to equal opportunity.
4. Public opinion data indicating the weakness of support for the difference principle is often indirect since the difference principle itself is not usually the subject of inquiry. Feldman and Steenbergen (2001, p. 659), however, note that when it comes to helping the least advantaged members of society, Americans are motivated by humanitarian, not egalitarian, values: "If egalitarianism was the driving force behind public attitudes toward welfare, we would expect Americans to express greater support for redistributive policies since these most clearly contribute to equality. In fact, Americans overwhelmingly reject such policies, expressing support instead for policies that are much more tenuously associated with the goal of a more equal society (e.g. support for homeless shelters)." Page and Jacobs (2009) as well as Bartels (2008) also note that egalitarian values (which are clearly present in American public opinion) do not translate into, nor are they strongly connected to, support for principles or policies of egalitarian redistribution.
5. Thus Rawls in *Political Liberalism* asks: "How is it possible for there to exist over time a just and stable society of free and equal citizens, who remain profoundly divided by reasonable religious, philosophical, and moral doctrines?" (Rawls, 1993, p. 4).
6. It can be argued – and indeed a number of contributions to this volume do argue (Thomas, Chapter 5; Williamson, Chapter 14) – that a defense of property-owning democracy can be tied back to the first principle (for which there is deep cultural support) rather than the difference principle. This is no doubt true, but the first principle could also be compatible with many far less egalitarian schemes of distribution, it seems to me. Thus while it is possible to get to property-owning democracy by bypassing the difference principle, only the difference principle (or something like it) points to a radically different way to think about redistribution.
7. Thus Rawls writes: "The difference principle explicates the distinction between treating men as a means only and treating them also as ends in themselves. To regard persons as ends in themselves in the basic design of society is to agree to forgo those gains which do not contribute to their representative expectation. By contrast to regard persons as means is to be prepared to impose upon them lower prospects of life for the sake of higher expectations of others" (Rawls, 1971, p. 180).
8. Rather than aggregates, one is forced to make pairwise comparisons. Obviously this is not possible with every single individual in society, so, instead, one works with "representative individuals" of groups. "Representative individuals" is not a form of aggregation. How one decides on the description of representative individuals – that is, how one would decide what constitutes the least well off in society – is also widely debated. See Richardson and Weithman (1999).

9. Feldman and Steenbergen (2001) report that a 1992 survey of citizens in New York State shows that 81% of respondents agree that "Incomes cannot be made more equal since people's abilities and talents are unequal."
10. For example, the 1993 General Social Survey asked this question: "Some people think America should promote equal opportunity for all, that is, allowing everyone to compete for jobs and wealth on a fair and even basis. Other people think America should promote equal outcomes, that is, insuring that everyone has a decent standard of living and that there are only small differences in wealth and income between the top and bottom in society. Which do you favor: promoting equal opportunity or promoting equal outcomes?" Of the respondents, 84% answered "promote equal opportunity" (Davis, Smith, and Marsden, 2003).

References

Arneson, R.J. (1993) Equality, in *A Companion to Contemporary Political Philosophy* (eds R. Goodin and Pettit P.), Blackwell, Oxford.
Barry, B. (2001) Equality, in *Encyclopedia of Ethics*. Routledge, New York.
Bartels, L.M. (2008) *Unequal Democracy: The Political Economy of the New Gilded Age*. Princeton University Press, Princeton.
Cohen, J. (1989) Democratic equality. *Ethics*, 99, 727–751.
Cohen, J. (2002) The pursuit of fairness. *Boston Globe*, Dec. 1, 2002: D1.
Davis, D.W. and Silver, B.D. (2004) Civil liberties vs. security: Public opinion in the context of the terrorist attacks on America. *American Journal of Political Science*, 48, 28–46.
Davis, J.A., Smith, T.W., and Marsden, P.V. (2003) *General Social Surveys, 1972–2002: Cumulative File* (Computer file). 2nd ICPSR version. Chicago, IL: National Opinion Research Center [producer], 2003. Storrs, CT: Roper Center for Public Opinion Research. University of Connecticut/Ann Arbor, MI: Inter-university Consortium for Political and Social Research [distributors].
DiQuattro, A. (1983) Rawls and left criticism. *Political Theory*, 11, 53–78.
Feldman, S. and Steenbergen, M.R. (2001) The humanitarian foundation of support for social welfare. *American Journal of Political Science*, 45, 658–677.
Freeman, S. (2007) *Rawls*, Routledge, London.
Hochschild, J. (1981) *What's Fair? American Beliefs about Distributive Justice*, Harvard University Press, Cambridge, MA.
Krouse, R. and McPherson, M. (1988) Capitalism, property-owning democracy, and the welfare state, in *Democracy and the Welfare State* (ed. A. Gutmann), Princeton University Press, Princeton, pp. 157–185.
Kymlicka, W. (2002) *Contemporary Political Philosophy: An Introduction*, Oxford University Press, Oxford.
Lane, R.E. (1962) *Political Ideology: Why the American Common Man Believes What He Does*. The Free Press, New York.
McClosky, H. and Zaller, J. (1984) *The American Ethos: Public Attitudes toward Capitalism and Democracy*, Harvard University Press, Cambridge, MA.
Meade, J. (1964) *Efficiency, Equality, and the Ownership of Property*, Allen and Unwin, London.
Nagel, T. (1991) *Equality and Partiality*, Oxford University Press, Oxford.
Page, B. and Jacobs, L. (2009) *Class War? What Americans Really Think about Economic Inequality*, University of Chicago Press, Chicago.
Rawls, J. (1971) *A Theory of Justice*, Harvard University Press, Cambridge, MA.
Rawls, J. (1993) *Political Liberalism*, Columbia University Press, New York.
Rawls, J. (2001) *Justice as Fairness: A Restatement*, Harvard University Press, Cambridge, MA.

Rawls, J. (2005) The idea of public reason revisited, in *Political Liberalism*. Expanded Edition. Columbia University Press, New York.

Richardson, H. and Weithman, P. (eds) (1999) *The Philosophy of Rawls: A Collection of Essays, Volume II: The Two Principles and their Justification*, Garland Publishers, New York.

Scheffler, S. (1992) Responsibility, reactive attitudes, and liberalism in philosophy and politics. *Philosophy & Public Affairs*, 21, 299–323.

Westie, F.R. (1965) The American dilemma: An empirical test. *American Sociological Review*, 30, 527–538.

Wright, E.O. (2004) Introduction. *Politics and Society*, 32.

2
Property-Owning Democracy
A Short History

Ben Jackson

The rise to prominence of the term "property-owning democracy" in late twentieth-century political discourse and political theory is, on the face of it, a confusing and contradictory story.[1] Political theorists following in the footsteps of John Rawls alighted upon the idea of a property-owning democracy in the 1980s and 1990s as a nonsocialist model for the advancement of egalitarian distributive objectives. In the same period, intellectuals and politicians associated with the rise of neoliberalism, in particular those attached to the Thatcher government in the UK, sought to foster a property-owning democracy that was indifferent to a significant widening of income and wealth inequalities and was explicitly intended to undermine the electoral base of egalitarian politics. But these two versions of this fertile objective were not as distinct as they might appear, since both had in fact grown from the same historical root. The phrase "property-owning democracy" was first used by British Conservatives in the 1920s. It was then transmitted into academic political theory by the British economist James Meade. But in the course of its migration into the political theory of Rawls and his successors, property-owning democracy acquired much more radical connotations than had been entertained by its initial Conservative sponsors, as it merged with a broader, more explicitly egalitarian political tradition that emphasized the need for significant state-sponsored redistribution of existing property entitlements.

This chapter gives an account of this tangled conceptual history, and draws out some of the implications of the historical narrative for contemporary debates. In particular, it locates the genesis of the egalitarian model of property-owning democracy in two episodes in the history of political thought: in the rise of commercial republican thinking in the late eighteenth and early nineteenth centuries and in the mid-twentieth-century high tide of the socialist critique of capitalism. The underlying aim of this historical inquiry is to reconstruct the context in which James Meade developed his thinking on property ownership, and by extension to shed light on the appropriation of Meade's ideas by John Rawls and later political theorists. The bulk of the discussion will therefore focus on the British political debates about capitalism and socialism that played an important role in shaping Meade's political economy. My conclusion will be that the history of the property-owning democracy ideal should give pause to those contemporary egalitarians who seek to present the redistribution of private property as a clear practical *alternative* to either the welfare state or socialism.

Property-Owning Democracy Before Socialism: The Rise of Commercial Republicanism

The claim that private property ownership promotes the necessary independence of mind and social stability for the responsible exercise of political power has been a long-standing theme in Western political theory. However, this argument has usually been employed as a justification for class-stratified participation in political decision making rather than as the basis for a radical reconsideration of the existing distribution of property rights. With the gradual emergence of ideas of popular sovereignty and civic equality, though, the leading edge of the radical political theories of the eighteenth and early nineteenth centuries began to reshape traditional arguments about property ownership. Radicals of this period argued that a much larger citizenry could be entrusted with political power and that this widening of the status of citizenship should in turn be underwritten by a much wider diffusion of private property. The earliest versions of this form of argument, articulated for example by such pre-commercial renovators of classical republicanism as James Harrington and Jean-Jacques Rousseau, were agrarian and austerely critical of commerce and luxury. Such authors envisaged a community predominantly made up of small-scale agricultural producers, each with sufficient property (i.e., land) to be economically independent of one another and hence independent of each other's wills, but with none possessing such a large concentration of property as to enable domination of the political process or severe hierarchies of social status. As Rousseau argued: "Do you, then, want to give the state stability? Bring the extremes as close together as possible; tolerate neither very rich people nor beggars." Famously, he added that no citizen should "be so very rich that he can buy another, and none so poor that he is compelled to sell himself" (Rousseau, 1997 [1762], p. 78).[2]

Rousseau himself did not offer a particularly detailed account of how to go about achieving this condition of relative economic and civic equality, although he did advocate the taxation of luxury goods, and, along with other pre-commercial republicans such as Harrington, also supported some form of agrarian law. Modeled on what was believed to be the practice at one time in the Roman republic, such legislation aimed to limit the amount of land that any one individual could hold (Harrington, 1992 [1656], pp. 33, 100–114; Nelson, 2004, pp. 48–126, 188–193). These proposals, and the underlying republican hostility to the impact of concentrated wealth on politics, subsequently exerted a powerful hold on the thinking of the American revolutionaries, notably Thomas Jefferson (Nelson, 2004, pp. 195–233; Beckert, 2008, pp. 71–80). All of these pioneering republican theorists assumed that, in the largely agricultural polities they envisaged, regulations governing the inheritance of land should be sufficient to break up excessively large concentrations of wealth and to ensure that a basic minimum of property was allotted to the poorest citizens.

The advent of commercial society – or capitalism, as it would come to be known – precipitated a new departure in thinking about property relations. While Rousseau had sternly opposed the corruption and materialism of commerce, Adam Smith eloquently elaborated on its social benefits and on the growing social interdependence that was a result of the new industrial organization of production. Increasingly, the ideal of a free community of equally placed, independent peasant proprietors appeared sociologically implausible, not to say anachronistic. It was gradually superseded by a commercial republican vision that embraced a dynamic and expanding capitalist economy, and its highly differentiated division of labor, but which also envisaged a role for a democratic state in distributing resources to all members of the community as a means of securing the material conditions of their equal citizenship. Thomas Paine, who had been influenced by Smith, blazed this trail in the late eighteenth century with two striking, and incendiary, works: *Rights of Man, Part Two* (1792) and *Agrarian Justice* (1797).[3]

Paine was relatively sympathetic to commercial interests and directed most of his critical fire against the aristocracy in *Rights of Man*. His tone had changed somewhat by the time he penned *Agrarian Justice*, which expressed a palpable revulsion toward the moral depredations of a civilization that rendered some fabulously wealthy while others starved in the streets. In both works, Paine made the pioneering proposal that the rise of representative government should bring with it a new social commitment to individual rights to material resources, furnished by the state through a system of taxes and transfers. Paine argued that to enable citizens to possess the independence and security required to exercise their political duties, it was necessary to provide them with material support "not of the nature of a charity, but of a right" (Paine, 1995 [1792], p. 296). According to Paine in *Rights of Man*, such social rights should include benefits for the children of the poor, conditional upon attendance of the children at school; old age pensions; funding for universal education; the provision of a basic capital endowment for every newborn baby and newly married couple; and a scheme whereby the state would act as an employer of last resort in London (to take account of the extreme poverty fostered by the unprecedented anonymity of the metropolis). These measures would be funded by the progressive taxation of wealth (Paine, 1995 [1792], pp. 292–311). In *Agrarian Justice*, Paine put the case for a universal endowment of capital for every person, male and female, reaching the age of 21, as well as the payment of an annual pension to those over 50, to be funded through the taxation of inherited wealth. Paine argued that the accumulation of private property was "the *effect of society*," as opposed to the result of individual initiative and thrift, and concluded that every property owner should therefore return at least part of their holdings to the community that had facilitated their gains (Paine, 1995 [1797], pp. 419–425, 428, emphasis in original).

Although Paine's ideas are often cited as pioneering examples of proposals for a "property-owning democracy," it is intriguing that a number of them – pensions, child benefit, education, perhaps even the state as an employer of last resort – fit just as comfortably under the more traditional heading of the "welfare state." Paine's reason for advocating pensions was, after all, "to provide against the misfortunes to which all human life is subject" (Paine, 1995 [1792], p. 322). This point is missed, for example, by Ackerman and Alstott (1999, pp. 181–182) in their influential invocation of Paine. This is an early indication of a theme I will return to later in this chapter, namely that presenting a "property-owning democracy" as a superior alternative to a "welfare state" (or even, as I will demonstrate, as an alternative to "socialism") can be misleading.

This point aside, Paine certainly deserves recognition as the proponent of a pioneering and resonant republican vision that sought to break up large concentrations of property and disperse individual property rights through the use of the progressive taxation of wealth and state-sponsored redistribution. Paine's vision was carried forward in later nineteenth-century debates by a succession of theorists and political actors. For example, in Britain the early social radicalism of British Jacobins such as John Thelwall in time resurfaced in the demands of the "social Chartism" of the 1850s and 1860s for "the democratic and social republic," and indeed even found expression in some of John Stuart Mill's impassioned opposition to inherited wealth, particularly in land. Although broadly "Paineite" in emphasis, these ideological currents also retained an agrarian character, with land reform or even nationalization occupying a key role in their programs, alongside other reforms designed to promote social rights such as compulsory education, profit sharing, and the taxation of inherited wealth (Thompson, 1991, pp. 172–176, 200–203; Finn, 1993, pp. 86–92, 112–115, 132–134, 138–141, 267–273; White, 2009a). But this preoccupation with the monopolization of land was soon to be eclipsed in the radical mind by the threat posed to liberty and equality by the monopolization of capital. "Republican" solutions to this problem were to face searching scrutiny from radicals who suggested that an entirely new model of ownership was more suitable for the twentieth century.

Property-Owning Democracy at the Socialist High Tide (i): Progressive Conservative Origins

The assumptions that had underpinned Paine's commercial republicanism were therefore questioned as the nineteenth and early twentieth centuries unfolded. Brutally summarized, for many radicals the republican aspirations of individual independence and property dispersion increasingly seemed to stand in tension with the lived realities of capitalist economic development. Fresh ideological challenges were posed by the rise of larger units of production, owned and managed by a distant and powerful capitalist elite, and by the increase in social interdependency that resulted from highly complex industrial development, urbanization, and population growth. Despotism and domination was seen by radicals to stem from the unaccountable power of capitalists rather than aristocrats or landlords, while republican ideas about dispersing small-scale ownership as a means of fostering individual independence began to appear anachronistic in the context of a capitalist economy. Instead, radicals proffered a new ambition of asserting democratic collective control over the powerful productive forces that now seemed to be an inescapable feature of a modern economy. In other words, commercial republicanism was displaced on the left by the rise of socialism (McIvor, 2009, pp. 254–260).

As I have already mentioned, the phrase "property-owning democracy" was in fact coined by a British Conservative, who hoped to adapt Conservatism to the arrival of a mass working-class electorate by proposing the diffusion of individual property ownership as an ideological alternative to the collective ownership defended by socialists. A version of this idea, although not the precise phrase, had earlier been floated in British political debate by the sometime Liberal MP and Catholic social theorist Hilaire Belloc in *The Servile State* (1912). Influenced by Catholic social doctrine, especially Pope Leo XIII's 1891 encyclical *De Rerum Novarum*, Belloc argued that the early twentieth-century capitalist combination of political freedom for all with economic freedom for the minority who owned the means of production caused serious social instability and injustice. But Belloc rejected one possible solution to this problem, namely the nascent ideas for centralized social welfare provision (somewhat in the vein of Tom Paine) propounded by his former colleagues in the Liberal Party and by Fabian socialists such as Sidney and Beatrice Webb. In Belloc's view, the introduction of state welfare would lead directly to the enslavement of the working class, since reforms that aimed at guaranteeing the economic security of workers could only be implemented in return for the state increasing the level of scrutiny and control it exercised over their behavior. The arrival of these measures, Belloc argued, signaled a reversion from a society of freely contracting individuals to one grounded on status. If this vision was implemented, society would eventually be legally divided into discrete groups of owners and workers, with quite different rights and duties adhering to each (Belloc, 1912, pp. 3–4, 13–27, 97–98, 140–145, 155–183). Two plausible options remained, according to *The Servile State*:

> If you are suffering because property is restricted to a few, you can alter that factor in the problem *either* by putting property into the hands of the many, *or* by putting it into the hands of none. There is no third course. In the concrete, to put property in the hands of "none" means to vest it as a trust in the hands of political officers. (Belloc, 1912, p. 99, emphasis in original)

Belloc was therefore skeptical of this latter collectivist solution since it would hand vast and unaccountable power to the minority who would exercise political control over the means of production. The only attractive option, he argued, was to ensure a wider dispersion of individual property holdings among the population.

However, Belloc offered no concrete account of how his "distributive state" could be brought into being, instead restricting himself to drawing attention to the many advantages of a wider diffusion of property over its concentration in a few hands. The later interwar political activism of the "distributist" movement that tried to popularize Belloc's ideas, including the writings of Belloc's ally G.K. Chesterton, filled in some further details, advocating for example employee share-ownership, agricultural smallholdings, the break-up of large landed estates, schemes to turn unemployed workers into a new peasantry, and a general preference for small shops and enterprises over retail chains and large corporations (possibly expressed through the tax system). Belloc and the distributists were wary of using the power of the state to promote this agenda, however, and believed themselves to be chiefly engaged in the reform of moral values. They hoped that in due course this ethical change would lead to society reforming itself through the voluntary decisions of individuals (Corrin, 1981, pp. 125–147).

A more precise agenda along these lines was sketched a few years after Belloc's book by the Scottish Conservative politician Noel Skelton. Skelton was the first to use the phrase "property-owning democracy," giving it a debut in an influential series of articles in the *Spectator* in 1923, which were then reprinted as a book, *Constructive Conservatism*, in 1924. Skelton remains an enigmatic and neglected figure; it is not possible in this brief discussion to do justice to the subtlety of the analysis that led him to advocate a property-owning democracy (for further discussion, see Williamson, 2004; Ron, 2008, pp. 172–179; Torrance, 2010). He wrote in the wake of the Bolshevik revolution and presented his ideas as an explicit response to the appeal of socialism to a newly enfranchised British working class (on this political context, see Jarvis, 1996). The advent of socialism, Skelton noted, had significantly widened the scope of political debate. Previous political battles between Liberals and Conservatives had been like pre-1914 military engagements: fought on a narrow front by small professional armies. But the new conflict with socialism was analogous to the all-encompassing total war that the world had just endured. "Socialism fights on the broadest of fronts," politicizing vast areas of civil society previously deemed exempt from public debate. In this new era, "envelopment and the crushing defeat successful envelopment achieves form the danger against which Conservatism must guard in the great battles ahead." A rigorous and popular ideological alternative would therefore have to be offered if the Conservative lines were not to be overwhelmed (Skelton, 1923a, p. 746).[4]

Skelton's diagnosis of the fundamental issue to be addressed in this new era was similar to Belloc's (and may well have been influenced by *The Servile State*):

> For the mass of the people – those who live mainly by the wages of industry – political status and educational status have outstripped economic status. The structure has become lopsided. It is therefore unstable. Until our educated and politically minded democracy has become predominantly a property-owning democracy, neither the national equilibrium nor the balance of life of the individual will be restored. (Skelton, 1923b, p. 789)[5]

Like Belloc, Skelton also rejected the notion that public ownership represented a solution to this problem: "what everybody owns, nobody owns" (Skelton, 1923b, p. 789). Private property ownership, Skelton maintained, was essential both for the development of individual character and for the stability of the state:

> So deeply, indeed, has Conservatism felt the importance of this relation that in the past it was wont to maintain that only those who possessed private property should exercise political functions. That doctrine has now this new and pregnant application – that since, today, practically all citizens have political rights, all should possess something of their own. (Skelton, 1923b, p. 790)

Skelton identified four concrete policy proposals that followed from his analysis: first, the encouragement of profit sharing and, eventually, some form of co-partnership in modern industrial production. By co-partnership, Skelton meant that workers in enterprises would eventually receive some of their remuneration in the form of shares in the firm and, "as the workers become capitalists, 'seats on the board,' either for the domestic internal government of the concern, or for its general direction, very naturally follow." Second, Skelton advocated the expansion of agricultural smallholdings to diffuse landownership more widely. Third, he wanted to introduce cooperative principles into larger agricultural concerns, although he refrained from giving precise details of what this commitment might entail. Finally, Skelton endorsed the use of the referendum as a constitutional device to invoke popular opinion to overrule any parliamentary decisions that might threaten the new democratic constitutional settlement or the existence of private property rights (Skelton, 1923c, pp. 837–838).

Although these measures gave an indication of how Skelton's property-owning democracy would look in practice, there was still significant ambiguity about how far he was willing to take his stated objective of widening property ownership. There was certainly no intention to secure an egalitarian distribution of individual property rights, although presumably some narrowing of the class inequalities of the 1920s would have followed from his program. Similarly, and like Belloc, Skelton was reluctant to endorse a significant role for the state in bringing about his favored reforms. His articles suggested that he was in favor of Conservative politicians exercising moral suasion over the community, or perhaps the use of legislation to create incentives for changes to the economy, but certainly not in favor of compelling enterprises to undertake co-partnership schemes. Such proposals, Skelton said, "offer a means of economic, social and national progress which the state cannot dole out with a spoon" (Skelton, 1923c, p. 837). This anxiety about allotting too forceful a role for the state presumably also accounted for the failure of Skelton to mention any role for the taxation of wealth in his scheme. Fundamentally, Skelton's aim was to address what he saw as the legitimate economic grievances felt by the working class, and the consequent political and industrial instability, by creating "a real identification of interest between capital and labour" that would in effect lead workers to think more like capitalists (Skelton, 1923c, p. 837).

Skelton himself did not reach the front rank of British politics; he died of cancer in 1935 having served as a junior minister at the Scottish Office from 1931. However, by then his slogan of a "property-owning democracy" had been taken up by the Conservative Party leader, Stanley Baldwin, as he tried to carve out a rhetorically consensual, but firmly anti-socialist, Conservatism for the 1930s. Perhaps more significantly, Skelton's ideas influenced a younger generation of progressive Conservative politicians, including eminent figures such as Anthony Eden and Harold Macmillan, later to be leading players in the post-1945 remodeling of the Conservatives as a "One Nation" party and both Prime Ministers during the peak of the Party's emollient dalliance with Keynesianism, the welfare state, and trade unionism (Williamson, 1999, pp. 180–182; 2004). The phrase "property-owning democracy" first came to widespread public notice in Britain as a result of a famous speech by Anthony Eden to the 1946 Conservative Party conference. Eden called for "a nation-wide property-owning democracy," distinguishing between the socialist understanding of property, "where everyone must rely on the State for his job, his roof, his livelihood," and the Conservative view "that the ownership of property is not a crime or a sin, but a reward, a right and a responsibility that must be shared as equitably as possible among all our citizens" (Ramsden, 1995, p. 141; Eden, 1947, p. 420). Eden's ideas were picked up by other Conservative politicians, notably the party leader, Winston Churchill, and the creation of a property-owning democracy became an important ideological theme for the Conservatives as they sought to recover from the loss of the 1945 general election and to adapt to the new welfare state and nationalized industries introduced by the 1945–1951 Labour government.

In practice, though, Conservative politicians were often unclear about exactly *how* property ownership was to be more widely diffused and, like Skelton, they certainly did not propose to equalize private property holdings. The imaginative proposals originally entertained by Skelton were neglected, and party policy in the 1950s increasingly focused on home ownership as the principal means of fostering a society where everyone possessed at least a small amount of property (Ramsden, 1995, pp. 141–142, 175, 211, 255–256; Weiler, 2003, pp. 360–361). This postwar narrowing of the Conservative vision of a property-owning democracy further attenuated the already limited scope of Skelton's ideas but also opened the way for other ideological entrepreneurs to appropriate and radicalize his agenda.

Property-Owning Democracy at the Socialist High Tide (ii): Liberals and Labour Revisionists

While the Conservatives of Skelton's era were keen to characterize the British left, and socialists in particular, as crude collectivists in their attitude toward property ownership, this was of course a rhetorical caricature of a much more complex, and ideologically heterogeneous, political tradition. It is of particular significance in this context that an important strand of the British left's political thought blended the republican ambition of ensuring a more equitable distribution of private property to promote individual citizenship with the later socialist insistence on the need for collective control of the productive process.[6]

Before World War II, for example, important New Liberal and socialist writers distinguished between justifiable and socially harmful or unjust forms of private property. In an influential discussion of the nature of property rights, the New Liberal theorist and publicist Leonard Hobhouse drew on what he regarded as the Aristotelian idea of private property as necessary for the expression of individual personality. He argued that this position, properly understood, mandated the redistribution of private property, so that every citizen was able to access the personal freedom that was conferred by property ownership. In Hobhouse's view, the morally objectionable form of property that should be subject to collective control was not indeed capital ownership per se, but "property for power" as contrasted with "property for use." With this distinction, Hobhouse sought to differentiate between the ownership of relatively small amounts of property that conferred "control of things" and hence "gives freedom and security" for an ordered individual life, and the ownership of relatively large amounts, which gave "control of persons through things" and "gives power to the owner" (Hobhouse, 1994 [1913], pp. 180–181, 195–196, 198). According to Hobhouse, the legitimacy of this latter form of property was undermined not only because it endowed the owner with the power to exploit those who owned nothing, but also by the fact that it enabled the rich to avoid work altogether (Hobhouse, 1912, p. 17; Hobhouse, 1994, pp. 181, 191). Hobhouse's view was famously echoed by his New Liberal colleague J.A. Hobson, in his distinction between "property" and "improperty" (1918, pp. 28–32; 1929, p. 144),[7] terminology that the leading socialist intellectual R.H. Tawney in turn drew on in his book, *The Acquisitive Society* (1921). In that work, Tawney argued that certain forms of capital income were justifiable so long as they were *functional*, that is, related to genuine productive effort on the part of the individual or necessary to maintain economic efficiency. Functional wealth included productive private property that was used by its owners and a certain amount of income from interest (since savings could represent a genuine sacrifice on the part of the individual). Other forms of capital income, notably large inheritances, were considered *functionless* and could justifiably be taxed or bought out by the state (Tawney, 1937 [1921], pp. 58–59).[8] For egalitarians such as Tawney or Hobhouse, then, private property, when fairly distributed, was actually very desirable, since it advanced both freedom and equality.

This objective was coupled in the British left's political imagination with a keen awareness of the great, unaccountable power exercised by the owners of large capitalist enterprises and a desire to subject these concentrations of property to collective democratic control, whether through the use of progressive taxation of income and capital; the promotion of countervailing industrial power through strong trade unions; the outright state ownership of industries; or the promotion of alternative forms of public ownership such as workers' cooperatives, profit sharing, enterprises jointly controlled by workers and capitalists, syndicalism, and guild socialism. This latter idea, associated in particular with the work of G.D.H. Cole, sought to deflect Belloc-style worries about the "slavery" that would result from public ownership by envisaging an economy of worker-managed firms regulated by the state to protect consumer interests, but otherwise granted considerable associational autonomy and internal democracy (Cole, 1917, 1920; Stears, 1998). Cole was a keen student of Rousseau as well as Marx (Cole, 1913, 1935, 1950; Lamb, 2005). Guild socialism was a bold attempt to marry the idea of self-governing communities of independent citizens with the social complexity, interdependence, and necessary economies of scale fostered by the advent of industrial production.

All of this accumulated ideological capital was therefore at the disposal of a later generation of British liberals and socialists when Baldwin and, especially, Eden placed a property-owning democracy at the forefront of Conservative rhetoric and statecraft in the 1930s and 1940s. Like all such suggestive political slogans, the phrase itself became the subject of lively ideological debate as rival political formations attempted to claim ownership of it by integrating it into their own electoral appeals. Two of the strands of this ideological contest deserve particular attention since they provide a fairly precise political and intellectual context for the emergence of James Meade's thinking.

One strand was associated with the Liberal Party, in electoral retreat by the postwar period, but determined to regain the ideological initiative. As Stuart White (2009b) has shown, from the 1930s onwards, certain intellectuals and activists associated with the Party sought to carve out a distinctive Liberal ideological space that focused on securing a wider dispersion of property and power, as opposed to the concentration of property in either state or capitalist hands purportedly favored by the Labour and Conservative parties respectively. White suggests that leading Liberal publicists such as Elliot Dodds, as well as prominent Liberal politicians such as Jo Grimond, saw this agenda as a means of promoting a classically New Liberal combination of values. These Liberals regarded property dispersion as crucial for the realization of individual independence and autonomy, as well as for the advancement of the cooperative community that they thought was a necessary condition for the development of moral personality. To that end, they proposed an ambitious agenda of social and economic reform encompassing moves toward co-partnership and profit sharing in industry; worker involvement in industrial decision making (with some limited sympathy for industrial democracy); and the progressive taxation of capital, especially inherited wealth. Later, by the 1970s and 1980s, this Liberal agenda widened further to include the redistribution of capital via the introduction of universal capital endowments and a basic income scheme, by which juncture James Meade himself had become directly involved in internal party discussions (he had earlier given evidence to a Liberal Party committee on co-ownership in the late 1940s).

As with Skelton's proposals, however, this strand of Liberal thinking remained ambiguous about how far the power of the state should be deployed to implement these reforms, with some oscillation in official party policy, for example, between voluntary and compulsory variants of the co-partnership schemes. In addition, a minority of the exponents of these proposals explicitly entertained them as substitutes for, rather than as supplementary to, the welfare state institutions that were cemented into British public policy in the 1940s, in effect hoping that a diffusion of private property would obviate the need for extensive social insurance schemes (Wiles, 1957; White, 2009b, pp. 169, 171, 174, 181–182). Indeed, a number of figures later to be associated with the neoliberal right made their debut in public debate in the course of these Liberal Party discussions. The economists Arthur Seldon and Arthur Shenfield, later to be stalwarts of the Mont Pèlerin Society and the influential neoliberal think tank the Institute of Economic Affairs (IEA), worked closely with Dodds on his "Ownership for All" ideas in the late 1930s and 1940s. They helped to draft party policy documents on the subject and, in Shenfield's case, stood as a Liberal parliamentary candidate. Dodds's own thinking was also influenced by the proto-neoliberal theorists of the 1930s such as Wilhelm Röpke and Walter Lippmann (Seldon, 1990, pp. 34–35, 208; 2004 [1952], pp. 10–16; Sloman, forthcoming; Jackson, 2010). Meanwhile, other economists later associated with the IEA, such as Graham Hutton and Alan Peacock, were active in the 1950s in trying to water down the elements of the Liberal program that involved state compulsion (White, 2009b, p. 183, n6).

A second strand of postwar thinking about a property-owning democracy unfolded within the Labour Party and in particular among the group of intellectuals and politicians located on the right of the Party who were dubbed the "revisionists."[9] Labour politicians such as Hugh Gaitskell, Anthony Crosland, and Douglas Jay, along with allied economists such as Nicholas Kaldor, Arthur Lewis and, at times, James Meade, sought to downplay the importance of nationalization to the achievement of socialist objectives and instead to focus the Labour Party's attention on social policy and the distribution of property as the primary fields for egalitarian advance in the 1950s and 1960s. Meade offered the first glimpse of the emerging revisionist agenda in a memorandum produced for the Labour Party Research Department in 1948. As head of the Economic Section at the Cabinet Office from 1946 to 1947, Meade had been frustrated by certain aspects of Labour's economic strategy, and once out of government he articulated a liberal socialist alternative to the economic planning initially prioritized by Clement Attlee's administration. According to Meade, three strands of economic policy were necessary to achieve Labour's goals: Keynesian demand management rather than direct state intervention in the market; the public ownership of monopolies, but with a substantial private sector open to market forces; and, crucially, "a matter which in my opinion has been much neglected," the redistribution of private property:

> If private property were much more equally divided we should achieve the "mixed" citizen – both worker and property owner at the same time – to live in the "mixed" economy of public and private enterprise. The ownership of private property could then fulfill its useful function of providing a basis for private enterprise and for individual security and independence without carrying with it the curse of social inequality as it now does. (Meade, 1948a, pp. 2–3)

These were early, perhaps even influential, statements of what was to become a widespread revisionist sentiment. Like the Conservatives, Labour revisionists also aspired to create a property-owning democracy, but while the Conservatives said little about reducing the large wealth inequalities that stratified Britain, revisionist exponents of this idea explicitly sought to appropriate and radicalize wider property ownership as the most plausible route to advancing egalitarian ideals.

The revisionists' understanding of a property-owning democracy contested the highly partisan contrast between Conservative and Labour models of property ownership described by Eden in 1946. They argued that to pose a choice between a Conservative-sponsored defense of private property and a Labour-enforced socialization of property was a false dichotomy. On the contrary, the ideal society pictured by Labour was one in which private property was distributed much more equally between individuals, and in which the state and groups in civil society also held a certain amount of social property earmarked for collective purposes. The provision of a strong welfare state and the use of progressive income taxation were certainly indispensable components of this social vision, but formed only one element of a radical egalitarian program aimed at both fostering wider individual property ownership and encouraging alternative forms of social ownership.

The revisionists proposed to realize this vision through three strands of policy. First, they wanted to introduce much more strongly progressive taxation of wealth, in particular focusing on the reform of inheritance tax, so as to tax the beneficiary rather than the estate, and on the introduction of a graduated annual tax on property over a certain exemption limit. Second, they canvassed various measures to promote equal access to marketable skills and a greater dispersion of individual property holdings, notably plans to introduce nonselective state secondary education and a scheme proposed by Douglas Jay to widen individual share ownership through a state-sponsored national unit trust (as opposed to promoting share ownership via institutions in the City of London). Finally, they planned to expand the amount of property held in social ownership by establishing state investment funds that would acquire substantial shareholdings in private industry in order to divert their revenues to redistributive transfers and public services and as a means of reducing the capital gains that would otherwise accrue to the wealthy (Crosland, 1956, pp. 307–308, 404, 516, 496; Jay, 1962, pp. 235, 290–294; Jackson, 2005, pp. 425–437). Although frequently portrayed as advocates of a "Keynesian welfare state" route to equality, the revisionists' aim was not simply to create safeguards against certain social risks (though they certainly saw this as an important goal), but to create a community of free and equal citizens not subject to the economic and political domination of a wealthy minority.

The revisionist version of a property-owning democracy was therefore more egalitarian and much less inhibited about harnessing the power of the state than the Conservative or Liberal variants of the same idea. However, the Liberals did place greater emphasis than the Labour revisionists on the importance of ensuring greater worker participation in the management of industry, a theme that was largely neglected in the revisionist literature. This silence may partly be accounted for by the deeply rooted distinction within the culture of the British labor movement between "political" questions, the province of the Labour Party, and "industrial" matters, which were the exclusive preserve of the trade unions. In the 1950s and 1960s, for example, it was generally believed on the right of the British labor movement that trade union collective bargaining represented the most appropriate form of industrial democracy (on this cultural divide, see Howell, 2002, pp. 93–98, 194–221, 404–407; Ackers, 2007). But this silence also reflected the revisionists' rather limited interest in fostering greater opportunities for democratic self-government beyond the institutions of Westminster parliamentary democracy and participation in the internal life of political parties and trade unions. In summary, then, two strands of thinking about property ownership emerged on the postwar British left: a Liberal strand hesitant about deploying the power of the state but committed to wider participation in industry and democracy, and a Labour strand that was confident about using the state to equalize property ownership but shied away from embracing a more participatory model of industry and democracy.

Property-Owning Democracy at the Socialist High Tide (iii): James Meade

It is in this context – debates about capitalism and socialism in Britain between the interwar period and the 1950s – that the property-owning democracy advocated by James Meade should be located. Throughout his life, like many left-wing British intellectuals, Meade's politics variously placed him within, or somewhere between, the Liberal and Labour parties, depending on the latest iteration in the shifting ideological profiles of those two venerable political institutions. Meade took his undergraduate degree in politics, philosophy, and economics at Oxford University in 1930, his choice of subject motivated by a desire to contribute to the elimination of the mass unemployment of that era. He also participated in the intellectual left milieu in the university, joining the Labour Club and the socialist student discussion group overseen by G.D.H. Cole. Upon becoming a fellow in economics at Hertford College, Oxford in 1930, Meade was almost immediately drawn to the work of Keynes and became one of his key allies and interlocutors, as well as a staunch public advocate of Keynes's economic theory and policy prescriptions. Recruited into government service as an economist in the Cabinet Office during World War II, Meade played an important role in ensuring Keynes's ideas became absorbed into the mainstream of the British state's economic policy. Unlike Keynes himself, Meade was an instinctive egalitarian. As I noted earlier, when he returned to academia at the London School of Economics in 1947, he was dissatisfied with the aspects of the economic strategy pursued by Labour in government after 1945 that relied on economic planning rather than Keynesian demand management, but he was politically and intellectually close to the generation of younger Labour politicians who had trained as economists in the 1930s, such as Hugh Gaitskell and Douglas Jay, and who were instrumental in marrying Keynesian economics to egalitarianism in Labour Party policy making.

In addition to his technical work in economy theory, in the 1950s and 1960s Meade produced a series of interventions in public policy discussions intended to persuade the left of the virtues of a "liberal-socialist" synthesis that relied on the free play of the price mechanism supported by Keynesian demand management, and not central planning, to allocate resources. But Meade recognized that although the use of the price mechanism would protect certain important individual liberties and promote efficiency, it would also, if left to its own devices, result in unacceptable poverty and inequality. He therefore proposed a significant role for the state in ensuring a more equal distribution of income and wealth through the progressive taxation of wealth; the introduction of co-partnership between labor and capital in place of traditional capitalist firms; and the development of state investment funds that would take a significant stake in private industry in order to use the capital returns to fund a basic income for all citizens (Meade, 1948b, 1993 [1964]; Durbin, 1985, pp. 95–100, 103–106, 110, 136–144, 149, 194–198; Atkinson, 1996; Howson, 2000, 2004; Ron, 2008, pp. 179–183).

As suggested in the remarks by Meade quoted earlier, he attributed particular significance to securing a more egalitarian distribution of property, for reasons that harked backed to republican ideals:

> A man with much property has great bargaining strength and a great sense of security, independence, and freedom and he enjoys these things not only vis-à-vis his propertyless fellow citizens but also vis-à-vis the public authorities. He can snap his fingers at those on whom he must rely for an income; for he can always live for a time on his capital. The propertyless man must continuously and without interruption acquire his income by working for an employer or by qualifying to receive it from a public authority. An unequal distribution of property means an unequal distribution of power and status even if it is prevented from causing too unequal a distribution of income. (Meade, 1993, p. 41)

This passage is drawn from Meade's monograph, *Efficiency, Equality and the Distribution of Property* (1964), the text Rawls subsequently drew upon in *A Theory of Justice* (1999 [1971], pp. xiv–xvi, 241–242; 2001, pp. 135–140; Krouse and McPherson, 1988, pp. 79–106). In this work, Meade himself used the term "property-owning democracy" for the first time.[10] He set out four analytically distinct egalitarian strategies: a trade union state that relied on a strong labor movement to equalize wages and conditions; a welfare state that employed high direct taxes on incomes to fund generous social benefits; a property-owning democracy; and socialism.

Meade thought that the welfare state and trade union strategies would be ineffective if pursued on their own or pushed too far: the high rates of income tax required to fund social benefits would at some point impede economic efficiency and collective bargaining would eventually become inflationary. Moreover, both the welfare state and strong collective bargaining would leave untouched grave inequality in the ownership of property. Meade therefore recommended a hybrid egalitarian strategy as the way forward from the welfare state, combining measures to equalize private property holdings with an increase in the amount of the economy under social ownership (Meade, 1993, pp. 38–68). In effect, this was an analytical reconstruction of the debates about equality that had preoccupied British liberals and socialists from the 1930s onward. Meade combined elements from both the liberal and socialist strands of this discussion, marrying the revisionists' explicit egalitarianism and confidence in the power of the state with the liberal emphasis on fostering greater worker participation within industry.

Given Meade's emphasis on the importance of pursuing policies drawn from both the socialist and property-owning democracy egalitarian strategies, it is curious that Rawls and some of his successors alighted solely on the property-owning democracy strand of Meade's thinking. The choice that Rawls posed between a liberal socialist regime and a property-owning democracy was not one that Meade himself accepted. Indeed, given the scope of his proposals, it is arguable that Meade's own view was much closer to Rawls's understanding of a liberal socialist regime than a property-owning democracy.[11] Meade also regarded the introduction of an unconditional basic income as an integral part of his egalitarian vision, a measure that Rawls was more hesitant about (Freeman, 2007, pp. 229–230). In his later work, Meade continued to develop the egalitarian agenda he had laid out in the 1950s and early 1960s. In the final and most developed version of his proposals, Meade envisaged an economy almost entirely made up of firms that allocated incomes via profit-sharing agreements with their employees; a community fund that owned 50% of the nation's productive assets; and the use of the dividends and capital gains from these socially owned assets to fund an unconditional basic income to all citizens (Meade, 1975, 1989). In the 1980s, Meade was active in promoting these ideas within the Social Democratic Party that had broken away from Labour in 1981, and which allied itself to, and then merged with, the Liberal Party shortly afterward (White, 2009b, pp. 172, 179–180). But by then a different, although not completely unrelated, vision of a property-owning democracy was being introduced into British political debate by Margaret Thatcher.

Property-Owning Democracy After Socialism? Rawlsian and Neoliberal Lineages

It should now be clear why property-owning democracy emerged at the end of the twentieth century as a slogan for both the neoliberal right and for political theorists and policy entrepreneurs of the left. One important strand of thinking on this issue was initially generated from within the British Conservative Party, but later drew sustenance from a section of the Liberal Party and neoliberal political theory. These sponsors envisaged property-owning democracy as a means of averting socialism by converting at least some of what was perceived to be a class-conscious, unionized proletariat into individual, small-scale capitalists likely to feel solidarity with the interests of larger property owners. This version of the idea was not intended to be egalitarian but to foster greater personal responsibility and, ultimately, to diminish the legitimacy of the state's efforts to redistribute economic resources and interfere with market-generated property entitlements. In this vein, Margaret Thatcher and her allies explicitly picked up Eden's language about property-owning democracy as they privatized public-sector assets, enabling tenants in public housing to purchase their homes and individuals to buy shares in previously nationalized industries. The aim of these and similar policies was explicitly anti-egalitarian and indeed both income and wealth inequalities in Britain increased in the course of this restructuring program (Howell, 1984; Green, 2006, pp. 83–101, 129–131; Offer, 2008).

But a second strand of thinking, which can be traced back to Rousseau and Paine, and which was nurtured for many years in the British liberal socialist tradition, envisaged a property-owning democracy as a means of fostering civic equality rather than the dominance of a wealthy minority and of ensuring a more equal distribution of freedom and economic security. As this tradition evolved, it encompassed not only efforts to equalize individual property holdings but also the expansion of the social ownership of property and greater worker participation in the governance of industry. Rawls's adoption of a property-owning democracy can therefore be seen as an appropriation of elements of this tradition (White, 2002; Dagger, 2006, pp. 151–161).

How does this historical narrative help us to orientate the contemporary discussion about a property-owning democracy? Acquaintance with the history of the idea can help us to identify some dangers lurking within recent political theoretical and public policy debates. In particular, the presentation of a property-owning democracy as a systematic *alternative* to the welfare state or socialism is at variance with the historical exposition of the idea, unless the property-owning democracy that is desired is of the sort recommended by Conservatives and neoliberals. We have seen, for example, that the tendency to read Paine as an exponent of universal capital grants excludes from the discussion the various proposals that he advocated that would now be classified under the heading of the welfare state. Meanwhile, the analytical distinctions made by Meade between different egalitarian policy regimes were not in fact intended to represent a definitive practical choice. Rather, Meade presented four ideal types that can all be drawn on when designing egalitarian social institutions. In any actually existing democratic polity, egalitarians would be best advised to pursue a plurality of egalitarian strategies, varying the emphasis between each of the elements according to contingent political circumstances. Meade himself, taking as a background assumption the strong British welfare state and trade union movement of the 1950s and 1960s, recommended a mixture of both the strategies of socialism and property-owning democracy as the way forward. This more complex view of egalitarian strategy prompts two cautionary observations about contemporary attempts to promote the property-owning democracy agenda.

First, we should be wary of attempts to present a property-owning democracy as a way of replacing the welfare state or, arguably, even as the single most important strategy for advancing economic redistribution in Anglo-American capitalism today. Rawls himself seems to have believed that, in order to maintain a decent social minimum, a property-owning democracy would require income redistribution, full employment, and universal social services alongside the redistribution of property, although there remains room for debate over whether he nonetheless underestimated the amount of ex post income redistribution that would be required in a society with a more egalitarian distribution of assets (Krouse and McPherson, 1988, pp. 94–99; Freeman, 2007, pp. 227–231). However, these points have not always been clearly recognized by subsequent advocates of the property-owning democracy ideal. Bruce Ackerman and Anne Alstott, for example, sent out mixed messages about the welfare state in their agenda-setting book *The Stakeholder Society* (1999). While they noted the success of the American welfare state in its mid-twentieth-century heyday (and supported the preservation of what remained of it by the end of the century), they also found themselves inexorably drawn into "third way" rhetoric that pictured their "stakeholding" proposals for asset redistribution as offering a path forward from the purported failures of both neoliberalism *and* the welfare state. This rhetoric lured Ackerman and Alstott into advancing a caricature of the welfare state: they sketched a historically inaccurate account of it as a utilitarian project; asserted that the welfare state agenda had been fully tried and found wanting; and portrayed the objectives of the welfare state in residualist terms as focused on "providing the weak with a decent minimum." Fundamentally, they averred, "the point of stakeholding is to liberate each citizen from government" (Ackerman and Alstott, 1999, pp. 8–9, 15–16, 21–24, 182–183, quotes at 8, 9).[12]

This sort of language underestimates how successful the welfare state has been as an egalitarian strategy and concedes too much to its opponents. Given the very substantial social gains reaped by the Nordic welfare states, there is a case for seeing the strengthening of the welfare state in Britain and the United States as a more important egalitarian priority than measures to redistribute property (Bergmann, 2006). This point can be pressed further: if the major forms of individual property ownership that could plausibly be equalized in contemporary capitalist societies are home ownership and shares in private companies, then, as the financial crisis of 2008 has made clear, this will inevitably involve the exposure of individuals to significant financial risk. It is therefore crucial to secure individuals against such risks through collective social welfare provision if the property-owning democracy strategy is to be pursued.

Second, a close examination of Meade's writings suggests that the stark choice Rawls posed between a property-owning democracy and liberal socialism signified a departure from Meade's own views. Meade in fact advocated both: greater collective capital ownership *and* the equalization of private property holdings. Indeed, we should be clear that the leftist tradition of thinking examined in this chapter has been historically distinguished from its right-leaning counterpart by an acceptance that the scale and social interdependency of modern industrial production is such that, if the aim is to prevent a small class from controlling both the means of production and democratic political life, then it is necessary to exercise collective democratic control over the economy and not just to diffuse individual ownership more widely.[13] The work of James Meade and his predecessors suggests that, if the progressive property-owning democracy agenda is to be advanced, difficult questions about collective ownership and the structure of the capitalist firm must remain part of the conversation.

Notes

1. I am grateful to Christopher Brooke, Gregg McClymont, Martin O'Neill, Zofia Stemplowska, and Stuart White for comments on an earlier version of this chapter, and to the Leverhulme Trust for financial support during the completion of the final draft.
2. The words by Rousseau are quoted, alongside helpful critical discussion, in Rawls (2007, pp. 244–248, quotes at p. 247). See also White (2000).
3. For a more detailed discussion of the rise of this commercial republicanism, see Stedman Jones (2004, pp. 16–63).
4. Another military analogy had previously been widely discussed by late nineteenth- and early twentieth-century Conservatives, particularly by the Conservative Prime Minister Lord Salisbury, namely the aim of strengthening "the ramparts of property," which in essence meant defending the larger owners of private property from expropriation by fostering an electoral defensive shield made up of smaller property owners (Offer, 1981, pp. 148–160, 405–406).
5. This passage is also notable for being the first occurrence of the phrase "property-owning democracy."
6. The following paragraph draws on my discussion of this egalitarian tradition in Jackson (2007).
7. See also Freeden (1986, pp. 258–266).
8. For a systematic theoretical defense of this functional theory of property rights, partially inspired by authors such as Hobhouse and Tawney, see White (2002).
9. This and the following two paragraphs draw on my discussion of Labour revisionism in Jackson (2005).
10. By using the phrase, Meade was clearly alluding to contemporary British political debates. For example, he had recently read and commented on a draft of Douglas Jay's book *Socialism in the New Society*, which contained a chapter entitled "A Property-Owning Democracy" (Jay, 1962, pp. viii, 290–294).
11. Rawls did, however, indicate that he thought worker-managed firms compatible with his idea of a property-owning democracy (2001, p. 178); see also the chapter by Hsieh in this volume.
12. For a similar attempt to associate the welfare state with utilitarianism, see Freeman (2007, pp. 224–225). The diversity and complexity of the thinking behind the welfare state has been documented by, for instance, Harris (1992) and Freeden (2003).
13. Partially inspired by James Meade, this point has also been advanced in contemporary debates by Robin Blackburn (1999, 2005).

References

Ackerman, B. and Alstott, A. (1999) *The Stakeholder Society*, Yale University Press, New Haven.

Ackers, P. (2007) Collective bargaining as industrial democracy: Hugh Clegg and the political foundations of British industrial relations pluralism. *British Journal of Industrial Relations*, 45, 77–101.

Atkinson, A.B. (1996) James Meade's vision: Full employment and social justice. *National Institute Economic Review*, 157, 90–96.

Beckert, J. (2008) *Inherited Wealth*, Princeton University Press, Princeton.

Belloc, H. (1912) *The Servile State*, T.N. Foulis, London.

Bergmann, B. (2006) A Swedish-style welfare state or basic income: Which should have priority? in *Redesigning Distribution* (ed. E. O. Wright), Verso, London.

Blackburn, R. (1999) The new collectivism: Pension reform, grey capitalism, and complex socialism. *New Left Review*, 233, 3–65.

Blackburn, R. (2005) Capital and social Europe. *New Left Review*, 34, 87–112.

Cole, G.D.H. (1913) "Introduction" to J.-J. Rousseau, *The Social Contract and Discourses*, J.M. Dent, London.

Cole, G.D.H. (1917) *Self-Government in Industry*, G. Bell & Sons, London.

Cole, G.D.H. (1920) *Guild Socialism Restated*, Leonard Parsons, London.

Cole, G.D.H. (1935) *What Marx Really Meant*, Victor Gollancz, London.

Cole, G.D.H. (1950) Rousseau's political theory, in G.D.H. Cole, *Essays in Social Theory*, Macmillan, London.

Corrin, J.P. (1981) *G.K Chesterton and Hilaire Belloc: The Battle Against Modernity*, Ohio University Press, Athens.

Crosland, C.A.R. (1956) *The Future of Socialism*, Jonathan Cape, London.

Dagger, R. (2006) Neo-republicanism and the civic economy. *Politics, Philosophy and Economics*, 5, 151–173.

Durbin, E. (1985) *New Jerusalems*, Routledge, London.

Eden, A. (1947) A nation-wide property owning democracy, in A. Eden, *Freedom and Order: Selected Speeches 1939–46*, Faber and Faber, London.

Finn, M. (1993) *After Chartism: Class and Nation in English Radical Politics, 1848-1874*, Cambridge University Press, Cambridge.

Freeden, M. (1986) *Liberalism Divided*, Oxford University Press, Oxford.

Freeden, M. (2003) The coming of the welfare state, in *The Cambridge History of Twentieth-Century Political Thought* (eds T. Ball and R. Bellamy), Cambridge University Press, Cambridge.

Freeman, S. (2007) *Rawls*, Routledge, London.

Green, E.H.H. (2006) *Thatcher*, Hodder Arnold, London.

Harrington, J. (1992 [1656]) *Commonwealth of Oceana* (ed. J.G.A. Pocock), Cambridge University Press, Cambridge.

Harris, J. (1992) Political thought and the welfare state 1870–1940: An intellectual framework for British social policy. *Past and Present*, 135, 116–141.

Hobhouse, L.T. (1912) *The Labour Movement*, T.F. Unwin, London.

Hobhouse, L.T. (1994 [1913]) The historical evolution of property, in fact and in idea, in L.T. Hobhouse, *Liberalism and Other Writings*, Cambridge University Press, Cambridge.

Hobson, J.A. (1918) *Democracy After the War*, Allen & Unwin, London.

Hobson, J.A. (1929) *Wealth and Life*, Macmillan, London.

Howell, D. (1984) The property-owning democracy: Prospects and policies. *Policy Studies*, 4, 14–21.

Howell, D. (2002) *MacDonald's Party: Labour Identities and Crisis, 1922–1931*, Oxford University Press, Oxford.

Howson, S. (2000) James Meade. *Economic Journal*, 110, 122–145.

Howson, S. (2004) Meade, James Edward (1907–1995), *Oxford Dictionary of National Biography*, Oxford University Press, Oxford. Online edn, January 2008: http://www.oxforddnb.com/view/article/60333 (accessed February 8, 2011).

Jackson, B. (2005) Revisionism reconsidered: Property-owning democracy and egalitarian strategy in post-war Britain. *Twentieth Century British History*, 16, 416–440.

Jackson, B. (2007) *Equality and the British Left: A Study in Progressive Political Thought, 1900–64*, Manchester University Press, Manchester.

Jackson, B. (2010) At the origins of neo-liberalism: The free economy and the strong state, 1930–47. *Historical Journal*, 53, 129–151.
Jarvis, D. (1996) British Conservatism and class politics in the 1920s. *English Historical Review*, 111, 59–84.
Jay, D. (1962) *Socialism in the New Society*, Longman, London.
Krouse, R. and McPherson, M. (1988) Capitalism, "property-owning democracy" and the welfare state, in *Democracy and the Welfare State* (ed. A. Gutmann), Princeton University Press, Princeton.
Lamb, P. (2005) G.D.H. Cole on the general will: A socialist reflects on Rousseau. *European Journal of Political Theory*, 4, 283–300.
McIvor, M. (2009) Republicanism, socialism and the renewal of the left, in *In Search of Social Democracy: Responses to Crisis and Modernisation* (eds J. Callaghan, N. Fishman, B. Jackson, and M. McIvor), Manchester University Press, Manchester.
Meade, J. (1948a) Next steps in domestic economic policy. Archive of the Labour Party Research Department, Labour History Archive, People's History Museum, Manchester, RD 201, November 1948; later published in *Political Quarterly*, 20 (1949), 12–24.
Meade, J. (1948b) *Planning and the Price Mechanism: The Liberal-Socialist Solution*, Allen & Unwin, London.
Meade, J. (1975) *The Intelligent Radical's Guide to Economic Policy*, Allen & Unwin, London.
Meade, J. (1989) *Agathotopia: The Economics of Partnership*, Aberdeen University Press, Aberdeen.
Meade, J. (1993 [1964]) *Efficiency, Equality and the Ownership of Property*. Reprinted in J. Meade, *Liberty, Equality and Efficiency*, Palgrave, Basingstoke.
Nelson, E. (2004) *The Greek Tradition in Republican Thought*, Cambridge University Press, Cambridge.
Offer, A. (1981) *Property and Politics, 1870–1914*, Cambridge University Press, Cambridge.
Offer, A. (2008) British manual workers: From producers to consumers, c.1950–2000. *Contemporary British History*, 22, 537–571.
Paine, T. (1995) *Rights of Man, Common Sense and Other Political Writings* (ed. M. Philp), Oxford University Press, Oxford.
Ramsden, J. (1995) *The Age of Churchill and Eden, 1940–57*, Longman, London.
Rawls, J. (1999 [1971]) *A Theory of Justice*, rev. edn, Oxford University Press, Oxford.
Rawls, J. (2001) *Justice as Fairness* (ed. E. Kelly), Belknap Press, Cambridge, MA.
Rawls, J. (2007) *Lectures on the History of Political Philosophy*, Harvard University Press, Cambridge, MA.
Ron, A. (2008) Visions of democracy in "property-owning democracy": Skelton to Rawls and beyond. *History of Political Thought*, 29, 172–179.
Rousseau, J.-J. (1997 [1762]) *The Social Contract* (ed. V. Gourevitch), Cambridge University Press, Cambridge.
Seldon, A. (1990) *Capitalism*, Basil Blackwell, Oxford.
Seldon, A. (2004 [1952]) Liberalism and liberty: The diffusion of property, in *The Collected Works of Arthur Seldon, Volume 2: The State is Rolling Back* (ed. C. Robinson), Liberty Fund, Indianapolis.
Skelton, N. (1923a) Constructive Conservatism II: The new era. *Spectator*, May 5, 1923.
Skelton, N. (1923b) Constructive Conservatism III: Problem and principle. *Spectator*, May 12, 1923.
Skelton, N. (1923c) Constructive Conservatism IV: Democracy stabilised. *Spectator*, May 19, 1923.
Skelton, N. (1924) *Constructive Conservatism*, W. Blackwood, Edinburgh.

Sloman, P. (forthcoming) The Liberal Party and Economic Policy, 1929–64. Unpublished DPhil thesis, Oxford University.
Stears, M. (1998) Guild socialism and ideological diversity on the British left, 1914–26. *Journal of Political Ideologies*, 3, 289–305.
Stedman Jones, G. (2004) *An End to Poverty? A Historical Debate*, Profile, London.
Tawney, R.H. (1937 [1921]) *The Acquisitive Society*, Victor Gollancz, London.
Thompson, E.P. (1991 [1963]) *The Making of the English Working Class*, Penguin, London.
Torrance, D. (2010) *Noel Skelton and the Property-Owning Democracy*, Biteback, London.
Weiler, P. (2003) The Conservatives' search for a middle way in housing. *Twentieth Century British History*, 14, 360–390.
White, S. (2000) Rediscovering republican political economy. *Imprints*, 4, 213–235.
White, S. (2002) *The Civic Minimum*, Oxford University Press, Oxford.
White, S. (2009a) Reclaiming the republican roots of social democracy. Unpublished paper, Oxford.
White, S. (2009b) "Revolutionary liberalism"? The philosophy and politics of ownership in the post-war Liberal Party. *British Politics*, 4, 164–187.
Wiles, P. (1957) Property and equality, in *The Unservile State* (ed. G. Watson), Allen & Unwin, London.
Williamson, P. (1999) *Stanley Baldwin: Conservative Leadership and National Values*, Cambridge University Press, Cambridge.
Williamson, P. (2004) Skelton, (Archibald) Noel (1880–1935), *Oxford Dictionary of National Biography*, Oxford University Press, Oxford. Online edn, January 2008: http://www.oxforddnb.com/view/article/40226 (accessed February 8, 2011).

3

Public Justification and the Right to Private Property
Welfare Rights as Compensation for Exclusion

Corey Brettschneider

Regardless of the light in which [the rich] tried to place their usurpations, they knew full well that they were established on nothing but a precarious and abusive right, and that having been acquired merely by force, force might take them away from them without their having any reason to complain. Even those enriched exclusively by industry could hardly base their property on better claims. They could very well say: "I am the one who built that wall; I have earned this land with my labor." In response to them it could be said: "Who gave you the boundary lines? By what right do you claim to exact payment at our expense for labor we did not impose upon you? Are you unaware that a multitude of your brothers perish or suffer from need of what you have in excess, and that you needed explicit and unanimous consent from the human race for you to help yourself to anything from the common subsistence that went beyond your own?"

Rousseau, Discourse on the Origin of Inequality

The right to private property is among the most fundamental in liberal theory.[1] For many liberals the idea of the state is grounded in its role as a protector of private property. Thus liberal theory is often characterized by negative liberties designed to protect individuals from the intervention of both the state and their fellow citizens. In contemporary literature, this concern has led some liberals – or, more specifically, libertarians – to defend a "minimal state" which has the sole role of protecting private property (Nozick, 1974; Epstein, 2003). According to this view, the existence of property is morally and conceptually prior to the justification of the state.

If the liberal state is justified by its ability to protect property, the modern welfare state is often justified by its ability to meet needs. According to a view commonly referred to as "welfarism," the very fact that needs exist implies there is a moral obligation to meet them (Walzer, 1983). Furthermore, because the state is best able to meet these needs, it has an obligation to provide a safety net for all individuals. Thus, in contrast to some liberal or libertarian conceptions, which defend negative liberties that protect property as fundamental to politics, the welfarist conception posits an active role for the state in meeting needs through redistribution. Accordingly, the welfare conception is often thought to be at odds, in principle, with the libertarian focus on protecting property through negative rights.

In this chapter, I present a third way of thinking about the relationship between property and welfare. Although I recognize that there is a distinction between welfare rights and property rights, I argue that both types of rights are normatively interdependent.[2] Private property is often considered independent of politics. But given the coercive nature of the right to exclude, which is inherent in the institution of the right to private property, I contend that this right must have political justification. Specifically, I suggest how a contractualist account of justification might be used to legitimize the right to property. Drawing on the work of T.M. Scanlon and John Rawls, I invoke the criterion of reciprocity to argue that such a justification should treat all citizens as free and equal (Scanlon, 1998; Rawls, 2005).[3] I thus aim to use a broadly Rawlsian account of public justification to theorize the role of private property in a legitimate democracy.

The main challenge in offering a public justification of the institution of private property is to address the interests of those excluded from ownership. This is a particularly important problem for an account of property-owning democracy. On Rawls's view of property-owning democracy, it is essential that there be widely dispersed ownership of "real property" or ownership of land (Rawls, 2001). As he writes, "background institutions must work to keep property and wealth evenly enough shared over time to preserve the fair value of the political liberties and fair equality of opportunity over generations" (Rawls, 2001, p. 51).[4] Though property-owning democracy is concerned with spreading the distribution of property, it still assumes and coercively enforces private ownership (Rawls, 1999). Since real property involves the right to exclude, this assumed right must be justified to the excluded.

In this chapter, I give an account of how this challenge of justifying private property to the excluded can be met. I argue that private property can be justified only in regimes in which basic material rights are guaranteed to all members of society. Specifically, private property regimes are not justifiable unless they exist in states that secure some form of a basic welfare right. On my account welfare rights are not charity or supererogatory gifts of property owners. Rather, the right to welfare is a basic requirement of political legitimacy and states must provide resources to individuals in order to secure such rights. My ambition is to show that such rights are one necessary condition for justifying private ownership and that those subject to the right to exclude are compensated through basic material rights to welfare. I leave aside the question of whether a more egalitarian distribution of wealth than the one I defend is necessary in a just society, or what other rights are sufficient for a legitimate society. I also leave aside the question of what would suffice for a complete justification of private property. I contend only that if private property is justifiable, welfare rights constitute one necessary condition for their legitimacy.

My aim is thus more limited in several senses than a full-fledged argument for property-owning democracy. Instead, I hope to provide some of the foundations for such an argument by appeal to the necessary conditions to justify property ownership in a legitimate democracy. In this sense, my project is analogous to Rawls's own less ambitious hopes for political liberalism as opposed to a theory of justice. On his account, the constitutional essentials for legitimacy do not require all the guarantees of justice; for instance, they do not require the difference principle.[5] Similarly, rather than make the full case for property-owning democracy, I focus here on the more minimal task of providing a justification for the legitimacy of widespread private ownership and an explanation of why such a justification must include a role for welfare rights. This minimal account, however, helps to solve a fundamental question associated with property-owning democracy.

My account therefore serves as a potential starting point for thinking about some of the more robust proposals for property-owning democracy. It emphasizes how we might link the value of widespread ownership to material rights for all citizens. This emphasis differs from state socialism, laissez-faire capitalism, and what Rawls calls welfare state capitalism. While laissez-faire capitalism embraces private ownership, it says nothing about the importance of welfare rights for all. State socialism attempts to secure welfare rights, but leaves no room for widespread private ownership. Welfare state capitalism allows private ownership, but it does not ensure that ownership is widespread. Therefore any account of property-owning democracy must provide a theoretical justification that explains why there is an important role for the state in both protecting private ownership, including the enforcement of the right to exclude, and ensuring that that ownership benefits all.

In addition to providing a justificatory basis for many of the basic ideas of property-owning democracy, I also aim to link the theory to its contractualist roots. As Ben Jackson points out in his history of property-owning democracy for this volume, the idea has a broader basis beyond Rawls's work, and begins with Rousseau as one of its early originators. I suggest in this chapter why Rousseau, like Rawls, serves as the inspiration for my account of the parity of property rights and welfare. Indeed, the epigraph that begins this essay is suggestive of the basic framework that I develop, though I base it on a more modern idea of contractualism. While my piece is normative and is an argument in contemporary political theory, I hope the link to Rousseau will make explicit how contemporary accounts of property and welfare can draw from an early founder of the ideal of property-owning democracy.

The argument proceeds in three stages. First, I demonstrate why the institution of private property fundamentally implicates an active role for state coercion in enforcing the right to exclude. Second, I argue that the burden for public justification is to demonstrate why there are reasons for the excluded person to accept her duty to respect others' property rights. Third, I claim that such an argument can be made plausibly only when welfare rights are guaranteed to all citizens. It is important to note that this chapter is not intended as a broad defense of contractualist theory, but as an application of the contractualist framework to the question of property.

Before I proceed, I want to clarify the limits of my argument in this essay. As both a moral and a political theory, contemporary contractualism has had a slew of defenders and critics from a variety of perspectives. This is not the place to offer another general defense of contractualist theory. Rather, I will stipulate that contractualism is a good way to legitimize state coercion, and then ask about how it might be employed in potentially justifying private ownership.

Contractualist Justification and Private Property

Central to a contractualist account of property is the notion that state coercion be justifiable to all reasonable citizens. Clearly it would be practically impossible for all citizens to agree to each and every institution, so contractualists like Rawls reject this literal interpretation of unanimity in justification. In this sense, Rousseau's desire for "unanimous consent" for ownership is an impossible requirement. But in a broader sense, however, unanimity is an ideal of inclusion for contractualists and a basis for thinking about how all citizens should be treated. This conception of unanimity is present in Rawls's "liberal principle of legitimacy": "our exercise of political power is fully proper only when it is exercised in accordance with a constitution the essentials of which all citizens as free and equal may reasonably be expected to endorse in the light of principles and ideals acceptable to their common human reason" (Rawls, 2005, p. 137). Justifiable state action must meet the minimal requirement of respecting all citizens' status as free and equal, and in this sense unanimity remains a moral and political ideal.

In order to elaborate how this broad ideal of unanimity in justification can be applied to the justification of private property, a specifically political version of the "contractualist" test implicit in John Rawls's principle of liberal legitimacy and explicit in T.M. Scanlon's account of moral justification is helpful (Scanlon, 1998). If we want to know whether a particular instance of coercion is justified we should ask: given a motivation to reach universal agreement, could citizens who view themselves as free and equal *reasonably* reject such an instance of coercion? In addition to treating all citizens as motivated to reach universal agreement in justifying coercion, this account of justification importantly stipulates that the perspective and point of view of each individual should be addressed in examining whether coercion respects citizens' status as free and equal. This account of public justification embraces what Rawls calls the criterion of reciprocity (Rawls, 2005, p. xliv). Citizens treat each other reciprocally insofar as they recognize that each person has equally valid interests to consider in the process of public justification and that to a reasonable extent they should be treated as autonomous. In return for the requirement that justification be addressed to each individual's particular point of view, therefore, reciprocity implies that those individuals must recognize the interests of their fellow citizens as free and equal.

For contractualists such as Rawls, citizens' status as members of liberal democratic polities requires that these values of equality and autonomy always be respected in the process of political justification.[6] To the extent that rights justify and limit coercion they too are the subject of such justification.

Now that I have elaborated on the meaning of contractualist justification I will proceed to examine how this account can potentially justify private property. The question of whether contractualist justification is relevant to private property hinges in part on the meaning of private property. The very use of the word "private" to describe property not held by the state suggests that ownership exists independently of politics and the state. This common understanding is reinforced by the fact that private law, of which the law of real property in land is a part, formally concerns conflicts between private parties seemingly without state involvement. Libertarians, moreover, often argue that far from depending on the state for its existence, private property is threatened most by state power. Arguably, the authors of the United States' Constitution perceived such a threat, as they sought to limit the state's ability to seize private property. In the literature of political theory, however, contractualism, a version of public justification, is usually regarded as limited to the concern to evaluate legitimate state coercion. Therefore, if this popular understanding of property as *private* were correct, private property would not require public justification.[7]

However, contrary to the understanding of *private* property as state-independent, private ownership does require state coercion. For this coercion to be justifiable, all citizens not only must have a duty to respect property rights, but they must have a particularly political duty that should be enforced by the state. I argue that if such a duty indeed exists, it should be established through public justification.

We can begin to establish the need for a public justification of private property by critically examining some conceptual understandings of property that suggest there is no need for such a political justification.

I want to begin with a view not seriously advocated by property theorists because responding to it is useful in developing the argument for why to extend public justification to property. One possible conception of private ownership underlying the view of property as private is that ownership only entails possession by some particular person over some particular object, so private ownership is not necessarily a political matter but rather a private one. Although one sometimes possesses property, however, possession is a very weak account of what it means to have a *right* to private property (Grey, 1980).[8] Many forms of ownership do not involve tangible resources that can be possessed. For example, if one owns a timeshare one does not possess any particular object. Likewise, although a labor contract has value it would be odd to claim its value is possessed like a thing. These modern forms of ownership suggest that ownership cannot rightly be understood as ownership primarily over physical things.

Most modern property theorists suggest that private property can be understood best as a bundle of rights. Property owners can take advantage of their property's fungibility (trade it for another resource of similar value), use the resource to produce more resources (as with farm land or rental property), or choose not to use it at all. What is at issue here is the owner's right to control a resource. I call these rights "vertical" rights of ownership because they fundamentally concern the owner's relationship to the resource that is owned. In contrast to these vertical rights, a series of "horizontal" rights are also necessary to the right to property. Unlike vertical rights, horizontal rights concern the relationship between the owner and other citizens instead of the relationship between the owner and the thing owned. The most fundamental horizontal right is the right to exclude. This right suggests that ownership depends, in large part, on one's ability to have exclusive control over resources. In order to have exclusive control, however, one must be able to exclude non-owners from intervening in decisions regarding one's property or from taking one's property.

The argument for understanding property as a bundle of rights rather than as possession is sufficient to dispense with the understanding of private ownership as solely a private relationship between an owner and a thing he or she *possesses*, such that the state is irrelevant to the right to private property. As I have argued, this account misunderstands the variety of rights involved in the right to private property and cannot account for complex modern forms of ownership, such as stocks, in which no tangible thing is possessed. Nor can it explain how one has a right to property not in one's possession. However, a more sophisticated understanding of property might accept that property is a bundle of rights and recognize that private ownership fundamentally requires a right to exclude, while maintaining that these rights need not be guaranteed by the state. For instance, some libertarians might suggest that owners in the state of nature could enforce the right to exclude, either independently or by banding together. If libertarian thinkers could successfully eliminate a role for the state in protecting private property, they would go a long way to showing that public justification is irrelevant to private property. An owner who toils on and successfully protects his or her property would not need to provide any reasons to non-owners for their exclusion. While the state might have a justificatory relationship with its citizens, private individuals would have no such relationship with each other. If owners owe any justification to non-owners, libertarians might argue that they merely must demonstrate that through their labor they cultivated property, and through their strength they exercise their right to exclude others.

A great deal of literature considers whether private property exists in nature. Holmes and Sunstein (1999) offer a critique of the libertarian notion of private property in their book *The Cost of Rights*. According to Holmes and Sunstein, an active state role is empirically necessary for the institution of property to exist.[9] Thus they note that private property relies on the contribution of taxes by citizens to pay for police to enforce property rights, as well as for courts and a legal system to help regulate them. Indeed, since Holmes and Sunstein challenge the idea that property could exist at all in a state of nature, one could see their view as a challenge to the libertarian contention that private property should be excluded from public justification. Because private property requires institutional enforcement, it cannot conceivably exist except in the context of the state. In light of this view, one could argue that the justification of private property must be publicly defensible.

This debate over private property's existence in the state of nature is among the most fundamental in political theory. But I need not prove Holmes and Sunstein's position correct and the libertarian thesis about natural ownership incorrect to argue that private property, and in particular the right to exclude, requires public justification. It suffices to note that contemporary ownership does rely on state enforcement of the right to exclude. Property owners today undeniably depend on state law enforcement agencies to protect their property by enforcing laws against theft, trespass, and other property crimes, and they rely on the state judicial and criminal justice system to punish violators and ensure that the law is implemented accurately. In addition to actively coercing those who violate the law, the state deters individuals from violating the right to exclude by the threat of force. Thus, even if property feasibly could exist in the state of nature, such an institution would be distinct from private property in the state.[10] Regardless of whether, or how, the right to exclude might be enforced in nature, private property in the contemporary state is distinctive because of the way the right to exclude is enforced. The question for political theory is how best to justify this coercion.

Fundamentally, the issue of whether the right to exclude is justified will rest on whether there is a duty on the part of all citizens to respect the boundaries of enforcement. On some accounts such a duty exists because a true moral theory suggests that all individuals have obligations to respect property rights. The appeal to truth to ground a duty to respect property is prominent in the liberal tradition. Lockean accounts, for instance, often appeal to the truth of natural law. A contractualist account, however, rejects such appeals to a comprehensive theory on the grounds that it fails to respect all citizens' status as free and equal.[11] To respect citizens' autonomy entails respecting their ability to form and to pursue their own conceptions of the good, and to respect their equality entails ascribing equal moral weight to the comprehensive doctrines that each individual endorses.[12] Given that citizens reasonably disagree about which moral theories or other comprehensive doctrines are true, therefore, respecting their interests as free and equal entails not imposing one particular comprehensive doctrine on individuals who endorse a different doctrine. The implication for politics is that the state should not enforce political duties that are justified by reference to theories that are metaphysical or claim to posit moral truth. Rather, they should invoke an account of political justification that appeals to all reasonable citizens. Such an account is one specifically of political morality, and avoids appeal to a comprehensive moral theory.

It is important to note that nothing in the argument for extending contractualist justification to property entails that natural law or other metaphysical understandings of the right to property are either false or incompatible with contractualism. Rawls is clear that contractualism should be a "wide view" that allows for the reinforcement of reasonable positions on the justification of coercion through comprehensive doctrines. In this way the account respects "reasonable pluralism," incorporating a plurality of reasonable comprehensive conceptions, arguments, and traditions. Therefore, while arguments based on comprehensive conceptions such as natural law cannot be a part of contractualist justification, nothing prevents such accounts from reinforcing the contractualist arguments I make here.[13] At the same time, a reasonable pluralism is not *any* pluralism of doctrines or positions on policy. The challenge in applying contractualism to justifications of private property is to use particular examples to work out which positions, such as those endorsed by various comprehensive doctrines, are reasonable and which are not.

In contrast to comprehensive theories of property rights, a contractualist account of justification appeals to a process of reciprocal reason giving that aims to recognize citizens' political status as autonomous and equal. This approach emphasizes the political status of individuals rather than their moral status as prescribed by some comprehensive doctrine. In Rawls's terms, contractualism concerns the "political conception of the person" rather than a "metaphysical doctrine of the person" (Rawls, 2005, p. 29). Thus, contractualism requires coercion to be justified by reasons that all reasonable citizens can endorse regardless of their general moral standpoints. Central to my own account of contractualism, which draws broadly from Rawls, is the concern to appeal to the three core values of autonomy, equality, and reciprocity in justification of coercive institutions (Brettschneider, 2007). As I stated earlier, my aim is not to offer a full defense of such justification but rather to begin an inquiry into its potential for justifying the institution of private property.

We are now in a position to address the question of why this particular theory of political justification is relevant to the institution of private property. If state coercion must be justifiable to all reasonable citizens, it follows that the right to exclude and the coercion necessary to enforce it must be justifiable to all reasonable citizens. To determine how best to pursue this justification, it is useful to return to Rousseau's example, cited at the opening of this chapter.

Rousseau imagines that a property owner is confronted by a potential trespasser. The owner can rationalize his sense of ownership over a particular object, but the potential trespasser wants to know what reasons the owner can offer for her, specifically, to respect the owner's right to exclude. This encounter is significant because it frames the justification of property as a problem that must be answered by reciprocal reasons between citizens. It is because the horizontal right to exclude imposes a duty on the excluded person that she is entitled to know why she should accept her exclusion. Moreover, because the state ultimately guarantees this exclusion, she is entitled to a reason that respects her status as a free and equal citizen. An answer to the excluded individual's challenge should address her in a manner that takes seriously the interests that stem from this status. Does she have a compelling reason to respect her duty to be excluded? Can she reasonably reject the right to exclude?

Focusing on the relationship between the owner and the potential trespasser highlights why it is that the right to exclude within a state cannot depend on the question of whether private property exists in nature. Regardless of whether property exists in the state of nature, the owner and the potential trespasser here face a conflict that ultimately depends on state enforcement of the right to exclude. If the state is to act legitimately it must enforce this right only if it can do so based on reasons that take each individual's interests seriously.

Before addressing the central question of how the state can justify the right to exclude based on such reasons, two clarifications are necessary. First, what exactly is meant by my claim that property exclusion is coercive? It certainly is not coercive in the sense that owners routinely assault non-owners for trespassing. My claim also clearly cannot require an omnipresent state that can physically restrain each individual who attempts to trespass on or take another's property. Instead, the coercive apparatus of the state is manifest in the real threat of coercive force that is present whenever an individual violates another's right to property. This threat is revealed graphically every time the state arrests and punishes offenders; indeed, property crime in contemporary states is among the most common reasons for state punishment and imprisonment. The question is whether such limitations on stealing and other forms of unlawful taking are justified.

Second, who specifically are the relevant parties to whom the justification of property exclusion must be given? The most obvious answer is that because all citizens are excluded from some property, each instance of exclusion must be justifiable to all citizens. However, the burden of justifying the institution of private property to the wealthy is much easier than justifying property to the least well off. Justifying private ownership and the right to exclude to the wealthy is easiest because the institution of private property serves their interests greatly. Namely, they own property and can use it to produce more goods or exchange it for goods useful to pursue their own conceptions of the good. Here private property promotes individual autonomy in a way that communal systems of property do not.

However, the real challenge for the theorist who seeks a public justification for exclusion is to justify exclusion to those with the least interest in respecting the boundaries of private property, namely the least well off, whose interests are served least by private ownership. Imagine that the potential trespasser in Rousseau's example owns nothing but the clothes on her back. The institution of private property does not serve the potential trespasser's interests as a free and equal citizen, so the owner cannot merely assert his ownership of the property to justify the coercion implicit in his exclusion of the potential trespasser. How, then, can the owner justify this coercion?

This question of how to justify exclusion to the least well-off members of society is my subject in the next part of this essay. I begin by asking whether the right to exclude could be justified to a person with minimal or no ownership. Ultimately, I argue that no satisfactory justification could be given to anyone who falls below the threshold established by a set of basic welfare rights. But before I articulate this argument, it is worth considering positions that accept the burden of providing justification to the excluded, but deny my contention that legitimate states must ensure welfare rights. In the rest of this chapter I shall use the term "minimal owner" to refer to a person whose level of ownership falls below a certain basic level of welfare, and shall refer to a person with a greater level of ownership simply as a "property owner." At times I also will express this distinction by contrasting "owners" with "the excluded."

One way to demonstrate that exclusion is justified to the minimal owner is to show that her exclusion from private property somehow serves her reasonable interests. One strategy prominent in the literature considering justifications of private property is to demonstrate that the act of excluding the minimal owner actually benefits her more substantially in the long run, despite its apparent detriment to her immediate interests. For instance, some defenders of libertarian views of private property appeal to the aggregate benefit that private ownership brings to society as a whole.

These thinkers invoke a familiar skepticism regarding the productivity of common ownership. According to their view, it is only when land and wealth are privately owned that they can be productive for the entire society. Private individuals who claim exclusive ownership over land and wealth can be confident that they will reap all of the benefits of their property increasing in value, so they have an incentive to use it as productively as possible. In contrast, individuals in a system where land and wealth are owned communally know that the benefits resulting from effort on their part to increase the value of the community's property will be spread among all members of society. The return on the individual's effort is much less in this system of common ownership, so she has less incentive to use her property productively. An implication of this argument is that since the benefits to society increase as more property is held privately, the government should not force individuals to reduce their level of ownership by imposing taxes.

Libertarians who embrace such reasoning contend that property ownership is not a zero-sum game in which society must divide up a given amount of wealth. Rather, private ownership increases the overall amount of wealth that exists in a society, and this aggregate increase in turn benefits all. To quote a common saying, "a rising tide raises all boats."[14]

However, the problem with this justification as stated is that it establishes a benefit to society as a whole without addressing the reasonable basic interests of all citizens, including their basic material needs. Specifically, it risks ignoring the interests of those citizens who are minimal owners. Even if the overall benefits to society are greater under a system of private ownership than under a system with no private ownership, minimal owners reasonably could reject such a scheme because their reasonable interests are sacrificed for the interests of others in society. These minimal owners have no reason that appeals to them for accepting the right to exclude. Consider the following exchange:

PROPERTY OWNER (PO): I accept the challenge of showing that those who are excluded from private ownership actually have their interests served. Society as a whole has more goods than it would if I left my gates open, as nobody would use my property productively if it were owned communally. Because I make my property useful, others have their interests served.

MINIMAL OWNER (MO): But to whom is the property useful?

PO: To society, which has more goods than it would if my gates were forced open. Property is not, as you have implied, a fixed amount of goods to be divided up, but rather is a positive-sum game that serves the interests of all. For instance, my trading partners have more now than they would otherwise, the school I give to has more resources, and the soup kitchen I give to can provide to those in need.

MO: I'll take you on your word as a matter of economics. But you slip quickly from "the aggregate wealth is increased" to "everybody has his interests served." You need to address your argument to me, standing at your gates. To ask me to be happy for others when I myself do not have my most basic interests served is to ask too much. I cannot sacrifice my most basic interests as a citizen for the good of the whole.

PO: Okay, I see your point. You want me to show you how my property ownership not only serves others but also helps to meet your reasonable interests. I accept the challenge. You could go to the soup kitchen or get your name on the list of the housing charity I support. You should be grateful for society's charity.

MO: Your desire for gratitude is the mistake here. I am entitled to have my reasonable basic interests met in exchange for respecting your right to exclude me from your property, because meeting my reasonable basic interests is the basis for justifying the right to exclude. My reasonable basic interests are understood best as rights, and meeting them is not charity.

In contrast to libertarian theories that attempt to defend private property as a right distinct from political justification, the property owner's argument here appeals to the interests of the propertyless person and is set in terms of public reason. The problem with the property owner's argument, however, is that it relies on an aggregate conception of interests (Smart and Williams, 1973; Mill and Bentham, 1987). Aggregate conceptions of interests can easily ignore entirely the interests of particular individuals and thus are incompatible with the ideal of justification to each individual citizen. Thus, the minimal owner could reasonably reject the legitimacy of state enforcement of the right to exclude, since her reasonable basic interests are not met.

Despite the failure of the utilitarian approach, the normative requirement of justification of property rights to excluded individuals can be met given certain guarantees for all citizens. Reciprocal reasons for the right to exclude could be given to all citizens if, for example, property owners were taxed at a level sufficient to guarantee that the reasonable basic interests of all citizens were met. In other words, in order for all individuals to have reason to respect the right to exclude the state would, at minimum, have to guarantee that no one was in the position of the minimal owner, and that all citizens had their reasonable basic interests met. For instance, those in the middle of the income distribution, who have fungible resources and whose reasonable basic interests are met, could not reasonably reject the right of their wealthier neighbors to exclude them from their property. The system that excludes a particular member of the middle-income distribution from the use of others' property also protects his right to exclude and respects his status as free and equal by ensuring that his reasonable basic interests are met and that he has resources to pursue his particular conception of the good. Though this member of the middle-income distribution might not be able successfully to realize particularly extravagant conceptions of the good, he does have some resources beyond those necessary for subsistence that he can use toward whichever conception of the good he chooses to pursue. Thus, my suggestion is that at a minimum in order for citizens to have a reason to respect the right to exclude, they would have to be granted some level of welfare rights that ensured them a basic level of ownership, defined by their reasonable basic interests. In contrast, those who fall below this level of ownership would have no good reason to respect the right to exclude.[15] It follows that the state that seeks to legitimize its role in protecting the right to exclude should guarantee that no one falls below this basic level of ownership.

Before I explain the nature of these rights and why they justify private ownership, it is worth considering one more objection to my view.[16] A critic could contend that I have set the burden of justification too high. Why cannot the legitimizing condition for the right to exclude simply be that the minimal owner suffers no loss as a result of her lack of ownership? For instance, those who seek to show that property ownership causes no detriment to minimal owners might argue that the absolute economic status of a minimal owner will not change after an owner has acquired property.[17]

As I have framed it, however, the question of political justification concerns why coercion itself is acceptable, not whether persons are worse off after coercion than they were before. A good justification of coercion will seek to legitimize it by appeal to the interests of those who it most adversely affects, and in particular by asking whether they reasonably can reject such coercion. In the case of property the excluded are the persons to whom such justification should be addressed. Therefore, the relevant question does not involve a comparison of pre- and post-coercion status, but rather asks whether the society can justify coercion by explaining how it is consistent with meeting people's reasonable basic interests. I have suggested that one can justify property rights by showing that they meet the needs of all citizens, not just of some subset of society. In societies that fail to guarantee all individuals' reasonable basic interests, there is reason for citizens reasonably to reject the right to exclude. Thus, the legitimacy of the institution of private property in such societies is called into question.

I began this article with Rousseau's challenge to the property owner to justify his ownership to all. I have argued that this challenge can be met if state enforcement of private property rights can be justified to the excluded by appeal to the fact that their reasonable basic interests are met. On my view, material rights to welfare compensate for exclusion. Although my argument is incompatible with some libertarian conceptions of the right to property, it is rooted firmly in the liberal tradition (Freeman, 2001). Consider the following argument made by John Locke, the paradigmatic defender of liberal property rights, regarding owners' obligation to ensure minimal owners' right to subsistence:

> We know God hath not left one Man so to the Mercy of another, that he may starve him if he please: God the Lord and Father of all, has given no one of his Children such a Property, in his peculiar Portion of the things of this World, but that he has given his needy Brother a Right to the Surplusage of his Goods; so that it cannot justly be denied him, when his pressing Wants call for it. And therefore no Man could ever have a just Power over the Life of another, by Right of property in Land or Possessions; since 'twould always be a Sin in any Man of Estate, to let his Brother perish for want of affording him Relief out of his Plenty. As *Justice* gives every Man a Title to the product of his honest Industry, and the fair Acquisitions of his Ancestors descended to him; so *Charity* gives every Man a Title to so much out of another's Plenty, as will keep him from extream want, where he has no means to subsist otherwise. (Locke, 1988, p. 170)[18]

This passage is striking for two reasons. First, Locke acknowledges that the institution of private property partly is justified by its ability to provide for the welfare of minimal owners. Second, and more fundamentally, Locke regards basic welfare claims as "rights" on the "title" of property owners. Even for Locke, then, property rights are justifiable in part because they provide for the basic needs of the least well off. However, I do not merely want to endorse Locke's understanding of the relationship between welfare and property. For instance, Locke is unclear about how welfare rights should be enforced. Although he claims that there should be penalties on owners who do not meet the basic needs of minimal owners, he never outlines a system of state provision. In contrast, I argue that the state should enforce welfare rights because they are necessary to legitimate the right of property, which itself depends on state enforcement.

Three Models of Welfare Rights

Material rights compensate for the right to exclude. But how should compensation be distributed? I suggest three proposals as reasonable attempts to implement legitimize welfare rights. All three proposals are crafted with the aim of inclusion required by contractualism and appeal to the reasonable interests of both the property owner and the person excluded from ownership.

The right to a job

One form that the welfare right entitlement might take appeals to the core value of reciprocity: the right to work for a just wage. Here the state does not confer the economic benefits directly, but rather the individual is entitled to the potential to accrue resources. Owners often acquire their property through labor. Therefore, if there is a right of the excluded, it should be parallel not in result, but in opportunity. The excluded should, then, have a right to work and thus to acquire property.

Although the right to a job is one of opportunity, it still requires the state to guarantee a positive right. In agrarian economies with an abundance of farmland and agricultural training for citizens from a young age, citizens would have endless opportunity for jobs and the ability to acquire resources. Thus, in the Lockean account of the state of nature, citizens' opportunity to work does not rely on a state to provide opportunity rights. Yet in modern economies no such commons exist, and labor is found not through farming, but in a diverse, modern economy. Given the economic facts of the business cycle, there are often not enough jobs available for all citizens to labor. But given that the state enforces the right to exclude and the right of private property, which creates the conditions that allow modern economies to function and requires a duty on the part of all citizens, there are obligations to ensure that all are provided basic opportunities to work. Therefore, in the absence of the market providing jobs, the state should ensure the existence of work opportunities.

The public policy proposals for guaranteeing the opportunity to work range from those that embrace New Deal style, state-sponsored work programs, to modern proposals for "fair workfare."[19] These latter proposals require the state to provide funding and payment in return for work adequate to meet basic needs, but also suggest the possibility of public/private partnerships in providing jobs. According to Amy Gutmann and Dennis Thompson in *Democracy and Disagreement*, income must be linked to a citizen's willingness to participate in society. The authors argue that those who are able-bodied but refuse to work should not retain the right to an income. At the same time, they point out that the government is obliged to provide work opportunities for them. As Gutmann and Thompson see it, the state has no responsibility to support those people who do not then work because they have not fulfilled their part of the mutual obligation between the citizenry and the state. They posit, "If they choose to spend their life surfing at Malibu, they cannot reasonably expect their fellow citizens to support them."[20] Reciprocity implies as much.

These proposals for the right to work best reflect the value of reciprocity. Any claim by non-owners to the results of others' labor would be unreasonable because it would not demand the same rights that owners have (that is, the right to gain property in exchange for something), but rather the results of the owners' efforts.[21] This would smack of resentment or envy. In contrast, a demand for a right to work would ask only that all citizens share the same opportunity to acquire resources, which would allow them to make autonomous decisions about the good life. Therefore, the right to work, given its parallel opportunities for property owners as well as the recipients of this right, is a reasonable demand, acceptable to all.

The right to in-kind resources to meet basic needs

While the right to a job appeals to the core value of reciprocity, the idea that welfare should be distributed in a manner that ensures that the basic needs of all are met appeals to the preconditions of all of the three core values. Before one is able to live an autonomous life or to regard oneself as an equal citizen, it is necessary that his needs for shelter, food, and health care are met. Rights of autonomy are worthless for the starving and homeless. One prevalent way of thinking about how to meet basic needs is through the in-kind distribution of resources, such as food stamps, health insurance, and housing vouchers. The in-kind resources are not fungible, but rather serve to give citizens the ability to meet their basic needs.

In a legitimate society, including one that embraces the right to a job, basic needs would have to be met for those who are unable to work, whether due to injury, age, or impairments. These citizens continue to be members of society and are subject to the duties of citizens, including those created by the right to exclude. But while the right to a job and the opportunity that comes with it might justify exclusion to able-bodied citizens, it does not for those who cannot work. Opportunities to work are meaningless for those who have no actual ability to do so. Therefore, the reasons for exclusion (based on the idea that everyone can work) which might be reasonably acceptable from the point of view of able-bodied citizens, are reasonably rejected by those who cannot work. In contrast, provisions for basic survival that are met through in-kind resources could potentially serve to justify the right to exclude. Although such citizens cannot themselves make use of the opportunities of the right to a job, they can be compensated for their exclusion when the state ensures them the preconditions of autonomy.

Although in my view any reasonable account of "fair workfare" should ensure that basic needs are met for those who cannot work, a harder question concerns whether those who chose not to work despite the guarantee of such an opportunity should also be guaranteed in-kind resources to meet basic needs. The argument for rejecting the extension of this right was suggested in the previous section: property owners could eschew the right of all citizens to receive in-kind resources on the basis that this would give them the results of labor without the parallel obligation of work. I have suggested that this is an understandable claim, but I also want to point to a reasonable response.

Two points support the compatibility of this implementation of in-kind benefits to all (even those who can work yet chose not to) with contractualism. First, the argument for such a welfare right stems from the idea that all citizens' status as free and equal should not be contingent upon their participation in the workforce. It should not be contingent upon any particular duty of citizens. Arguably, then, even if citizens flout their duty to work, they are still entitled to have their basic needs met because the poverty that would result from any other policy would create an underclass of citizens not viewed as equals. Such a circumstance would be unacceptable in a society in which coercion is justifiable because all persons are regarded as equal citizens.

The second reason to favor extending in-kind welfare to all is that this method is better able to accommodate reasons why individuals might have justifications, from their particular points of view, not to work. Among these reasons might be a decision on the part of individuals to contribute to society in ways besides working. Those activities deemed work by the market are not the sole way individuals can contribute to society. Some might choose to add to society through taking care of children, or through other forms of unpaid domestic work. Others might pursue art or writing despite the lack of monetary compensation.

The right to a basic income

A proposal for enacting welfare rights into policy through guaranteed minimum incomes for all appeals more directly to the core value of autonomy than do proposals for in-kind benefits. If the argument of the previous section is correct, that those unable to work – or even those able to work – are entitled to have their basic needs met, the manner in which these needs are met should itself reflect this core value. Specifically, advocates of a basic income, or a basic stake, offer an alternative to in-kind distribution that allows citizens flexibility in how to use the resources allocated to them, or in other words offers fungibility. Defenders of a basic income have contended that in-kind resources unduly limit autonomy in deciding how to use resources to meet one's life plan. For instance, while some citizens might choose to allocate a large amount of their resources to health care, others might wish to increase the standard of their housing beyond the level preferred by their fellow citizens. In contrast to in-kind distributions, basic income allows citizens autonomy in determining how best to meet their basic needs.

Additionally, the argument for basic income more directly parallels the appeal to the value of autonomy that suggested why private ownership was justifiable in terms of the core values in the first place. I suggested that private ownership was more justifiable than centralized control over resources because it empowered individuals to make their own life choices about how best to use resources. Similarly, basic income schemes take control over resources out of the hands of the state and place it into the hands of citizens.

Among the proposals for distributing resources in a manner that enhances autonomy, those of Philippe van Parijs (1991) and Carole Pateman (2004) propose a minimum basic income for all citizens. Bruce Ackerman and Anne Alstott (1999) suggest giving every citizen an $80,000 lump payment on their eighteenth birthday. Both proposals aim to ensure basic welfare, but at the same time empower citizens' ability to make autonomous decisions about how best to meet their welfare.

In deliberations about these proposals, several concerns arise in addition to the basic one of whether able-bodied workers should receive such benefits. One issue concerns whether income should be structured so as to ensure that it is not wasted at one point. The lump sum payment, in particular, carries this risk. In contrast, an annual basic income would ensure that citizens continually had the means to meet their needs. Another point concerns the amount that must be provided in such an income. Citizens will differ about what counts as a basic means. Furthermore, some will suggest that the payment should provide citizens with wealth that goes beyond basic needs and allows them to pursue life plans beyond the most rudimentary.

The Proposals as Reasonable Alternatives

My ambition here is not to offer a specific policy proposal for implementing the right to welfare. Rather I have pointed to three views of how to implement this right, all of which are reasonable applications of the contractual test and the values of public justification. Regimes that respect one version of these policies could therefore be said to offer reasonable attempts to guarantee welfare rights. Moreover, in debates about implementing welfare rights it is plausible to think that some hybrid view would emerge – some combination of a right to work, a right to in-kind distributions of resources, and a right to income – that together could form a legitimate welfare right.

Regardless of how the right is met, one further issue concerns how to guarantee basic welfare without bringing a stigma upon recipients. The idea that welfare is a basic right, not charity, entails that policy should be designed not to ostracize or penalize those who receive it. In distributions of in-kind entitlements, for instance, policy makers would do well to combine the requirement that these resources not be stigmatized with the assurance that the identities of those who receive them remain anonymous.[22]

Although none of these three reasonable proposals are a full-fledged endorsement of Rawls's notion of property-owning democracy, it is worth pointing to how each of them realizes its general ideals and at least partially solves a puzzle that accompanies his theory. One of Rawls's concerns in his account of property-owning democracy is to ensure that real property ownership is widely distributed and not consolidated in the hands of a few. He criticizes welfare state capitalism for permitting "very large inequalities in the ownership of real property" (Rawls, 2001, p. 138). But, as I have demonstrated, the wide but not universal distribution of real property in property-owning democracy raises a question of how the right to exclude can be justified to those excluded from ownership. I have suggested how such an account can be justified by an appeal to the benefits to the excluded, and I have argued that widespread ownership need not mean that all citizens in a property-owning democracy must themselves possess real property. For instance, given the option, some might choose to rent rather than buy a house. Yet, I have argued, if actual property ownership is not extended, it is still important that all citizens in a property-owning democracy reap the benefits of a private property system. All three of my proposals can account for this requirement. I have therefore aimed to theorize how the right to exclude, which is a fundamental aspect of property-owning democracy, can be justified by satisfying each of the three proposals.

In addition to addressing the question of how the right to exclude can be justified in a property-owning democracy, it is also worth pointing out how each of the proposals has a general resonance with the idea of property-owning democracy for the recipients of welfare rights who might not own real property. The third proposal, for a basic income, offers a similar kind of fungibility as is often associated with real property to those who are non-owners. This fungibility provides for parity between the free use of private property and the free use of income. Of course, much more needs to be said about the appropriate level of guaranteed income, but, as theorists such as Van Parijs have argued, if the level were set beyond basic needs, this would give the recipients the freedom to pursue their own ideas of the good. The first proposal, for a right to a job, would ensure widespread access to the kinds of "human capital" that Rawls associates with property-owning democracy when he calls for "the widespread ownership of productive assets" (Rawls, 2001, p. 139). The right to a job would guarantee citizens a stake in the economic world.[23]

The second proposal, for in-kind resources, may lack the choice often associated with private property and may seem the most distant from property-owning democracy. However, even in a property-owning democracy, some citizens will have basic needs such as health care that cannot be met through work or through widespread property ownership. When citizens cannot exercise the ability to work, or when the cost of meeting basic needs such as health care exceeds the resources of citizens, property-owning democracy should secure these basic needs. Even though welfare provision might not itself resemble property, it might serve to justify the right to exclude, which is necessary to a private property regime. In sum, I take all three of these reasonable proposals to be consistent with the basic aims of property-owning democracy. All three proposals show how widespread ownership can be compatible with the material interests of all citizens.

Objections

My claim that a right to welfare is a necessary condition to justify private property is open to the objection that it is overly statist. One could argue that citizens' needs should be met through voluntary gifts to charity in the context of free markets, and not through state protection. I call this the "objection from free markets."

The objection from free markets fundamentally is about the best method for securing basic rights and, as such, does not really challenge my view. I acknowledge that private ownership protected by the state could lead, in many instances, to the guarantee of welfare rights for some citizens. Those who are employed by property owners and have salaries to cover basic needs may not need help from the state. Indeed, I have acknowledged that private ownership, in contrast to a system of common ownership, likely would increase the number of people covered in this way. But when I considered the utilitarian claim that benefits only need be secured in the aggregate, I stressed that it is insufficient for even *most* citizens to have these rights secured. Rather, these rights must be extended to *all* citizens. I do not rule out the possibility that this can be achieved through the free market. Indeed, for private contributions to secure welfare rights for all would achieve the core values better than a system of state provision of welfare rights. In non-ideal circumstances where this is not achieved, however, the state has an obligation to rectify the failure of the market. In this sense, the state's role can be understood as providing a safety net to secure basic welfare rights, though it need not provide welfare rights directly in each instance.

This formulation of the state as a guarantor of last resort resembles its role in securing negative rights. For instance, rights to exclude often are upheld by individuals of their own volition, especially in stable states. In this case, the state does not secure property rights through continual threats. Rather, private persons simply acknowledge their obligations as citizens. In instances where there is a breakdown in respect for these duties, however, the state plays a role in sanctioning violators. Similarly, when private persons ensure that welfare rights are provided to all through charitable contributions or the market, the state need not intervene to ensure those rights. When welfare rights are not provided for in this way, however, the state has a role in taxing and distributing resources to ensure that all citizens' welfare rights are met.

Another form of the "statist" objection appeals to concerns about the relationship between a right to welfare and autonomy. This position maintains that a state role in creating a safety net increases state power in a way that undermines the very independence and autonomy of citizens. According to this objection, to make the state the guarantor of welfare rights would be self-defeating because independence means independence from the state. Another way to put the point is to claim that there is a fundamental inconsistency between the enforcement of the right to private property and the right to welfare. Although private property enhances independence, a right to welfare undermines it. I offer two responses to this view.

First, minimal owners depend either on the market to provide them with a salary or, in the worst cases, on the charity of private individuals. The question, then, is not whether state-guaranteed welfare rights make citizens dependent, but whether they create greater conditions of dependence than otherwise would exist. I believe that a right to welfare could be structured in a manner that would make citizens less dependent on the government than they otherwise would be on charity or the marketplace (Katz, 2001). While charity workers can stipulate conditions for those who receive benefits – religious observance, for instance – a right to welfare is ensured on the basis of one's citizenship and without requirements that infringe unreasonably on individual life choices. Compared to charity, therefore, welfare rights give citizens more independence and autonomy than they otherwise would have.

In addition to making citizens more independent than often allowed by charities, the right to welfare protects citizens from a dangerous form of dependence on the market. If one is at the complete mercy of an employer for subsistence, one might have to accept degrading work assignments or deal with humiliation and harassment without complaint. In contrast, the right to welfare allows citizens to choose to work, but protects them from the economic need to accept debasing work that undermines their status as free and equal.

Second, as Holmes and Sunstein point out in *The Cost of Rights*, it is not obviously true that securing positive rights requires more state action than protecting negative rights, or the right to be free from coercion. Indeed, given the number of people in prison for property-related crimes, the state perhaps is most active when enforcing the right to exclude. A large and active police force is necessary even when property rights are conceived of solely as the right to be free from intervention by the state or from other citizens. After all, the police in such a regime will need to protect the wealthy from the minimal owners. It is not clear that the right to welfare would require more state action than would an exclusively negative right of property owners to be free from theft and other forms of coercion. While the right to welfare might require a state agency to ensure a basic income for all, distribute in-kind resources, or guarantee the availability of work, this likely would be a bureaucracy more benign than the police. Moreover, even if one takes the perspective of those who fear any increase in state power as a loss for individual autonomy, on balance the creation of agencies to support a right to welfare could reduce the size of the state. For instance, if such agencies led to a reduction in the crime rate, as some have suggested they might, the level of state action could decrease, not increase.[24]

Another version of the free-market objection argues that if citizens were provided with adequate education and health care, the market could secure basic income for all. According to this view, the empirical reason why individuals lack income in society is that they lack basic education and health care, which are the necessary conditions for playing a role in the market. Here I offer the same response that I did to the original objection from free markets: if the free market economy can meet the basic needs of all without state intervention, then so much the better. But if it fails to do so, the state has an obligation to function as a safety net.

Conclusion

The concepts of property and welfare often are considered separately in political theory. I have argued that although they are indeed conceptually distinct, their justifications are related. Private property is not about a relationship between an owner and the thing that she owns. Its meaning also stems largely from the rights it confers owners to exclude others from their property. Because of the coercive nature of property and in particular the right to exclude, property rights must be justifiable to the persons who are excluded from ownership. The best way to justify this exclusion to minimal owners is to demonstrate how it is part of a legal regime that ensures that their reasonable basic interests are met as well. When understood in terms of contractualist justification, therefore, the notion of private property partially should be reformulated to entail that material resources be given to those who lack them.

We are now in a position to understand how the property owner in Rousseau's example can reply to the minimal owner who stands at his gates. Rousseau imagines his hero challenging the property owner who attempts to exclude him from ownership. Rousseau's hero declares: "Do not listen to this imposter. You are lost if you forget that the fruits of the earth belong to all and the earth to no one!" (Rousseau, 1987, p. 60). In response, the property owner could argue: "It is by allowing private ownership that the 'fruits of the earth' best can be cultivated and guaranteed for all."

Notes

1. For discussion about this paper, I thank Amy Gutmann, Stephen Macedo, George Kateb, Alon Harel, John Tomasi, David Estlund, and Eric Posner. An earlier version of this paper was published as Chapter 6 of Democratic Rights: The Substance of Self-Government (Princeton University Press, 2007). In addition, another version of this paper will be published as part of a symposium in the journal Law and Ethics of Human Rights. For excellent research assistance and substantive comments, I thank Minh Ly.
2. My view thus is different from attempts to defend welfare rights as property rights, for example Reich (1964).
3. A debate exists over whether there is a distinction between reasonable rejection and reasonable acceptance by agents. For a good discussion of Scanlonian justification in the context of democratic theory, see Chambers (1996, chapter 6). For a good discussion of contractualism in a political context, see Moon (1993).
4. In his preface to the revised edition of *A Theory of Justice*, Rawls explains that "the background institutions of property-owning democracy, with its system of (workably) competitive markets, tries to disperse the ownership of wealth and capital, and thus to prevent a small part of society from controlling the economy and indirectly political life itself." See Rawls (1999).
5. Rawls notes that "though a social minimum providing for the basic needs of all citizens is also an essential, what I have called the 'difference principle' is more demanding and is not" Rawls (2005, pp. 228–229).
6. For present purposes I am willing to accept the implied limitation here on contractual theory that it offers justification only within liberal democratic societies and to leave aside the quite separate and wider issue of whether the theory offers a universal account of justification.
7. While such justification might be necessary if the state tried to take property, an obvious form of coercion, it would not at core be required to justify private ownership itself. Such ownership would exist independently of the state.

8. Grey refers to the "possession" view as a "layman's" view of ownership. For a similar view, see Leif Wenar (1998).
9. Liam Murphy and Thomas Nagel similarly argue that government and taxes are necessary for the market to function. They conclude, "It is therefore logically impossible that people should have any kind of entitlement to all their pretax income" (Murphy and Nagel, 2002). Their argument reinforces my contention that private property must be legitimated with reference to a more general political justification.
10. Samuel Freeman (2001) suggests that libertarianism is best understood as a feudal view that offers no justification for the state. But even if private ownership might be enforced without the state, many modern libertarians claim that the state does have a role in protecting private property. Thus, they still must give an account of state ownership.
11. For a good discussion and critical examination of this literature see Moon (1991).
12. The "capacity for a conception of the good" is one of the two "moral powers" that Rawls ascribes to free and equal citizens. See Rawls (2005, p. 19).
13. One argument for the compatibility of natural law and contractualist justification is found in David Gray Carlson (1994). Carlson contends that the ideal of free and equal citizenship can be justified by reference to both natural law and contractualist accounts. Samuel Freeman (2000) usefully suggests how natural law views, such as those of John Finnis and Robert George, are distinct from but still reinforce contractualist accounts to the extent that they affirm public reason.
14. For an extension of this reasoning to an argument against the welfare state see David Schmidtz's argument in Goodin and Schmidtz (1998).
15. For Holmes and Sunstein, one justification for basic welfare stems from the need to keep poor citizens from rebelling. Such a conception would set the level of welfare in a manner dependent on citizens' willingness to resist the law. But on my view the burden for the property owner is not to keep the minimal owner from storming the gates. Rather, it is a moral challenge to justify the institution of private property to the minimal owner qua free and equal citizen.
16. I would like to thank Leif Wenar for suggesting that I respond to this objection.
17. Alternatively, they could argue that there is a benefit compared to the state of nature. Both Locke (1988) in *Two Treatises on Government* and Hobbes (1985) in *Leviathan* argue in this way.
18. Locke did not seek to ensure this right through taxation, yet he arguably saw a role for the state in the guarantee of welfare rights. Specifically, he suggested that the state should fine parishes that failed to secure basic welfare for the poor. See his "An Essay on the Poor Law" (Locke, 1997, p. 198). It should also be noted that one of Locke's conditions for the legitimate appropriation of land in the *Second Treatise of Government* was that there be "enough, and as good left" for other individuals (Locke, 1988, p. 291). Thus, Locke held that a person's acquisition of land was legitimate only if it did not prevent others from meeting their basic needs.
19. Shklar (1991); Gutmann and Thompson (1996).
20. Gutmann and Thompson (1996, p. 280). The distinction between work and contribution is also relevant to the current debate over workfare. In the United States, unconditional state aid in the form of Aid to Families with Dependent Children (AFDC) has been replaced with a new welfare act, Temporary Assistance for Needy Families (TANF), which has had the major result of requiring recipients to either find work in the private sector or agree to work for state agencies. Critics argue that TANF requires work in return for benefits that are, in fact, below a livable wage, and thus demands cheap labor from the poor in an unjust and coercive manner. For a detailed analysis of the distinction between AFDC and TANF see the report by Vee Burke for the Congressional Research Service (CRS), at: http://digitalcommons.ilr.cornell.edu/cgi/viewcontent.cgi?article=1063&context=key_work

place&sei-redir=1#search=%22Vee%20Burke%20Welfare%20Reform%3A%20An%20Issue%20Overview%22 (accessed September 17, 2011).
21. I owe this point to comments made by Donald Moon at the Young Scholar Conference.
22. Examples include distributing basic income through checks that are mailed to the recipients' homes, as opposed to requiring visits to a central office, and distributing food stamps through debit cards.
23. Rawls lists employment as one of the primary goods: "Lacking a sense of long-term security and the opportunity for meaningful work and occupation is not only destructive of citizens' self-respect but also of their sense that they are members of society and not simply caught in it. This leads to self-hatred, bitterness, and resentment" (Rawls, 2005, p. lvii).
24. That a state guarantee of the right to welfare will lead to a reduction in the crime rate arguably is implicit in Holmes and Sunstein's contention that a state guarantee of basic subsistence is necessary to provide incentives for the poor to engage in social cooperation and to obey the law. See Holmes and Sunstein (1999, pp. 189–203). Without such voluntary self-restraint by the poor, a far larger and more powerful state would be necessary to protect property rights. For a discussion of several explanations of the relationship between a right to welfare and decreased crime, see Van Parijs (1992).

References

Ackerman, B. and Alstott, A. (1999) *The Stakeholder Society*, Yale University Press, New Haven.
Burke, V. (2003) "IB93034: Welfare Reform: An Issue Overview." Congressional Research Service. http://digitalcommons.ilr.cornell.edu/cgi/viewcontent.cgi?article=1063&context=key_workplace&sei-redir=1#search=%22Vee%20Burke%20Welfare%20Reform%3A%20An%20Issue%20Overview%22 (accessed September 17, 2011).
Brettschneider, C. (2007) *Democratic Rights: The Substance of Self-Government*, Princeton University Press Princeton.
Carlson, D.G. (1994) Jurisprudence and personality in the work of John Rawls. *Columbia Law Review*, 94 (6), 1828–1841.
Chambers, S. (1996) *Reasonable Democracy*, Cornell University Press, Ithaca, NY.
Epstein, R. (2003). *Skepticism and Freedom: A Modern Case for Classical Liberalism*, University of Chicago Press, Chicago.
Freeman, S. (2000) Deliberative democracy: A sympathetic comment. *Philosophy & Public Affairs*, 29 (4), 371–418.
Freeman, S. (2001) Illiberal libertarians: Why libertarianism is not a liberal view. *Philosophy & Public Affairs*, 30 (2), 105–151.
Goodin, R.E. and Schmidtz, D. (1988) *Social Welfare and Individual Responsibility*, Cambridge University Press, Cambridge.
Grey, T.C. (1980) The disintegration of property, in *Nomos XXII: Property* (eds R. J. Pennock and J. W. Chapman), New York University Press, New York, pp. 69–86.
Gutmann, A. and Thompson, D. (1996) *Democracy and Disagreement*, Belknap Press, Cambridge, MA.
Hobbes, T. (1985) *Leviathan*, Penguin Books. London.
Hobhouse, L.T. (1964) *Liberalism*, Oxford University Press, New York.
Holmes, S. and Sunstein, C. (1999) *The Cost of Rights: Why Liberty Depends on Taxes*, W.W. Norton, New York.
Katz, M.B. (2001) *The Price of Citizenship: Redefining the American Welfare State*, Metropolitan Books, New York.

Locke, J. (1988) *Two Treatises of Government* (ed. P. Laslett), Cambridge University Press, Cambridge.
Locke, J. (1997) An essay on the poor law, in *Locke: Political Essays* (ed. M. Goldie), Cambridge University Press, Cambridge, pp. 182–200.
Marshall, T.H. and Bottomore, T. (1992) *Citizenship and Social Class*, Pluto Press, Concord.
Mill, J.S. and Bentham, J. (1987) *Utilitarianism and Other Essays* (ed. A. Ryan), Penguin Books, New York.
Moon, J.D. (1991) Constrained discourse and public life. *Political Theory*, 19 (2), 202–229.
Moon, J.D. (1993) *Constructing Community: Moral Pluralism and Tragic Conflicts*, Princeton University Press, Princeton.
Murphy, L.B. and Nagel, T. (2002) *The Myth of Ownership: Taxes and Justice*, Oxford University Press, New York.
Nozick, R. (1974) *Anarchy, State, and Utopia*, Basic Books, New York.
Pateman, C. (2004) Freedom and democratization: Why basic income is to be preferred to basic capital, in *The Ethics of Stakeholding* (eds K. Dowding, J. De Wispelaeure, and S. White), Palgrave Macmillan, London.
Rawls, J. (1999) *A Theory of Justice*, rev. edn, Harvard University Press, Cambridge, MA.
Rawls, J. (2001) *Justice as Fairness: A Restatement* (ed. E. Kelly), Harvard University Press, Cambridge, MA.
Rawls, J. (2005) *Political Liberalism. Expanded Edition*, Columbia University Press, New York.
Reich, C. (1964) The new property. *Yale Law Journal*, 73, 733–787.
Rousseau, J.-J. (1987) Discourse on the origin of inequality, in *The Basic Political Writings: Discourse on the Sciences and the Arts, Discourse on the Origin of Inequality, Discourse on Political Economy, On the Social Contract*. Hackett Publishing Company, Indianapolis.
Scanlon, T. (1998) *What We Owe to Each Other*, Belknap Press, Cambridge, MA.
Shklar, J. (1991) *American Citizenship: The Quest for Inclusion*, Harvard University Press, Cambridge, MA.
Smart, J. J. C. and Williams, B. (1973) *Utilitarianism: For and Against*, Cambridge University Press, Cambridge.
Van Parijs, P. (1991) Why surfers should be fed: The liberal case for an unconditional basic income. *Philosophy & Public Affairs*, 20 (2), 101–131.
Van Parijs, P. (1992) Competing justifications of basic income, in *Arguing for Basic Income* (ed. P. Van Parijs), Verso Books, New York.
Walzer, M. (1983) *Spheres of Justice: A Defense of Pluralism and Equality*, Basic Books, New York.
Wenar, L. (1998) Original acquisition of private property. *Mind*, 107 (428), 799–819.

4

Free (and Fair) Markets without Capitalism
Political Values, Principles of Justice, and Property-Owning Democracy

Martin O'Neill

Introduction: Rawls Against Capitalism

It is a striking and underappreciated fact that John Rawls saw his theory of justice as leading to a fundamental critique of familiar forms of capitalism.[1] Especially in the writings of the final phase of his career, Rawls was at pains to point out that his theory of justice was inconsistent with traditional forms of capitalism, even when capitalism was combined, as it typically has been to different degrees in the various democratic states of Europe and North America, with relatively generous welfare states. Thus, although Rawls has often been read, by both his supporters and opponents, as providing a philosophical justification for the traditional welfare state, he in fact held the view that the general type of socioeconomic regime that he called "welfare-state capitalism" (henceforth, WSC) was structurally inconsistent with the achievement of social justice.

Rawls's hostility to the capitalist welfare state and his advocacy of more radical forms of socioeconomic organization are perhaps the most striking aspects of the revised presentation of his theory of justice in his book *Justice as Fairness* (Rawls, 2001; henceforth, *JF*).[2] Rawls's judgment that the realization of justice required a comprehensive reimagining of our familiar institutions seemed to come into greater focus in his latter years. One may speculate that this sharpening of Rawls's critical stance toward the institutional structure of capitalism was in part precipitated by the disappointments and reversals of real-world politics in the 1980s and 1990s. Such an explanation at least suggests itself when one reads Rawls's condemnation, written in 1998, of American civil society being "awash in meaningless consumerism" (Rawls & Van Parijs, 2003). From the standpoint of the 2010s, one can have little reason not to endorse Rawls's contempt for "the large banks and the capitalist business class whose main goal is simply larger profit" and whose desire is only for "economic growth, onwards and upwards, with no specific end in sight" (Rawls & Van Parijs, 2003, p. 9). Clearly, a just society could not be one in which the political agenda and the structure of economic life were determined, as they are frequently determined now in many countries, by these sectional capitalist interests.

So, if not capitalism, even tempered by a welfare state, what is the alternative? Rawls gives the names "property-owning democracy" (henceforth, POD) and "liberal socialism" to his two alternative socioeconomic systems, designed in explicit contrast to the capitalist welfare state. Rawls's alternative socioeconomic regimes look for a way of structuring patterns of ownership and control within the economy that is comprehensively different to that found in capitalist welfare states. This surprising and radical element of Rawls's theory has, so far, received insufficient attention, and there is thus a striking need both to understand the nature of Rawls's institutional proposals, and to assess their soundness and cogency.

In this chapter, I aim to investigate whether Rawls's hostility to welfare state capitalism is well motivated within the terms of his theory, and to examine whether he is right to think that even a generous welfare state would be unable to "realize all the main political values expressed by the two principles of justice" (*JF*, p. 135). In so doing, my aim is to pay special attention to the relationship between the institutional arrangements of the basic structure of society, and the ways in which Rawls aims to respect the values of liberty and equality through his two principles of justice.

I will begin, in the next section, by outlining Rawls's reasons for rejecting the institutional arrangements characteristic of WSC. I then go on to look at the institutions and policies that are characteristic of the "property-owning democracy" that Rawls advocates. I shall not discuss liberal socialism in the same detail, for a number of reasons. First, Rawls himself spends less space outlining the structure of a "liberal socialist" regime than he spends discussing POD, and there is therefore more to discuss with regard to POD.[3] Second, Rawls's remark that the choice between liberal socialism and POD should be decided on the basis of a "society's historical circumstances, . . . its traditions of political thought and practice, and much else" (*JF*, p. 139) firmly suggests that POD is the more plausible choice for societies (such as those of Western Europe and North America) that have latterly been capitalist. Third, this volume is centrally concerned with POD rather than other possible alternatives to capitalism.[4] Fourth, it may well be that POD and liberal socialism actually have a great deal in common. Given that Rawls describes liberal socialism as involving "a property system establishing a widespread and a more or less even distribution of the means of production and natural resources" (Rawls, 2007, p. 323) one may speculate that there would be, in effect, little real difference (other than in the specification of *formal* property relations) between a liberal socialist regime and some variant of POD. Both are centrally concerned, as we shall see, to put effective control over a broad range of productive resources into the hands of all citizens within a democratic society.

Having outlined the structure of property-owning democracy I shall go on, in the following sections, to discuss Rawls's reasons for supporting POD over WSC, in terms of the different elements of his two principles of justice, and in terms of Rawls's understanding of the place that the values of liberty and equality occupy within his theory of justice. In the penultimate section, I look at the respects in which WSC and POD are "ideal types" of social organization, and say something about their relation to real policy options. I conclude by suggesting that, whilst Rawls has good reason to prefer POD over WSC, some elements of his critique of WSC are more robust than others.

Rawls's Critique of "Welfare State Capitalism"

It is hard to resist the view that the real-world political institutions that have done most to advance the cause of social justice are those associated with the welfare state. Progressive taxation, the redistribution of wealth, and the public provision of goods like health care and education are all policies that are associated with those societies that come closer than others to the Rawlsian standard of justice. It might thus seem perverse for a liberal egalitarian theorist with the substantive commitments of Rawls to draw back from full support of the best existing institutional mechanisms for improving the material condition of the worst off, and for raising the levels of opportunity and social mobility within society. The pressing question, therefore, is why Rawls should be so hostile to the (seemingly beneficent) institutions of welfare state capitalism.

The short answer to this question is that, notwithstanding the capacity of those institutions to advance some way toward satisfying the demands of justice, Rawls identifies a number of structural limitations on the capacities of the institutions of welfare state capitalism. He views these structural constraints as preventing WSC from ever advancing sufficiently close to the goal of full social justice. Rawls holds that WSC unavoidably "violates the principles of justice" (*JF*, p. 137) in the following respects:

> Welfare-state capitalism ... rejects the fair value of the political liberties, and while it has some concern for equality of opportunity, the policies necessary to achieve that are not followed. It permits very large inequalities in the ownership of real property (productive assets and natural resources) so that the control of the economy and much of political life rests in few hands. And although, as the name "welfare-state capitalism" suggests, welfare provisions may be quite generous and guarantee a decent social minimum covering the basic needs, a principle of reciprocity to regulate economic and social inequalities is not recognized. (*JF*, pp. 137–138)

This is a daunting and comprehensive charge sheet against WSC. Put briefly, we can list Rawls's criticisms of WSC as falling under the following headings, (a)–(c):

a. WSC fails to guarantee the fair value of the political liberties, as "the control of the economy and of much political life rests in few hands." (*JF*, p. 138)

Hence, there is a violation of Rawls's first principle of justice, which demands not only that all citizens be provided formally with "a fully adequate scheme of equal basic liberties, which scheme is compatible with the same scheme of liberties for all" (*JF*, p. 42), but also that each citizen be guaranteed the *fair value* of the political liberties (i.e., those liberties – such as liberties of thought, speech, assembly, and political participation – that are social preconditions for the pursuit of democratic politics, such that they "ensure the opportunity for the free and informed application of the principles of justice to [the basic] structure and to its policies by means of the *full and effective* exercise of citizens' sense of justice" [*JF*, pp. 112–113, my italics]).[5] It seems clear from Rawls's remarks here that, with regard to his first principle of justice, he denies *not* that WSC could provide the formal protection of the equal basic liberties, but that WSC would be able to protect the *fair value* of the political liberties. Thus, while a WSC regime may be able to satisfy the first principle of justice in a weak or superficial sense, it cannot provide genuine satisfaction of the demands of that principle because it is unable to deliver to citizens the real underlying value of the deployment of their liberties in the political sphere.

In addition to this failing, the charge sheet continues when we move on from the realization of the values of democracy and political liberty to the realization of the values of individual liberty and equality:

> b. WSC cannot do enough to achieve equality of opportunity. (Thereby leading to a violation of the first part of Rawls's second principle of justice.)

We should bear in mind here that Rawls's standard of equality of opportunity is a highly demanding one, such that it is required "not merely that public offices and positions be open in the formal sense, but that all should have a fair chance to attain them" (*JF*, p. 43), where what Rawls means by a "fair chance" is that "those who have the same level of talent and ability and the same willingness to use these gifts should have the same prospect of success regardless of their social class of origin" (*JF*, p. 44). Thus, even a socioeconomic regime that is impeccably free of traditional forms of racial or gender discrimination (such as an idealized version of a capitalist welfare state) could find itself falling far short of the requirements of this principle insofar as it failed to do enough to decouple individuals' life chances from their social background. Moreover, just as welfare state capitalism fails to give individuals a "fair chance" of success, so too it fails to embody the egalitarian demand for a principle of economic reciprocity:

> c. WSC is incapable of institutionalizing a "principle of reciprocity," such as the difference principle, instead managing only to guarantee a "social minimum." (This is a violation of the second part of Rawls's second principle of justice.)

The criticism here is not only that WSC does not realize the difference principle (which Rawls sees as the highest expression of a "principle of reciprocity"), but that it fails to get anywhere close to this standard, through failing to take the egalitarian value of reciprocity sufficiently seriously in economic life. Reciprocity demands that "gains to those more advantaged must [also] benefit those least advantaged" (see Freeman, 2007b, p. 481), whereas in WSC, or in any regime that provides a (mere) social minimum (however generous), we have the situation where gains to those most advantaged of a system of social cooperation can float free of the standing of the less advantaged, thus violating this requirement of reciprocity.[6]

Thus, overall, and put simply, Rawls sees the institutional structure of WSC as being unable to meet the demands of any of the three elements of his principles of justice. Thus, Rawls's conclusion is that the achievement of any part of his principles of justice is impossible whilst we retain the sort of "welfare state capitalist" institutions with which we are familiar. This is a bleak prognosis indeed for a writer who has commonly been read as the defender par excellence of the welfare state. Rawls's prognosis regarding the impossibility of achieving his principles of justice under familiar socioeconomic institutions raises the question of what the institutional realization of the two principles of justice might actually look like. It is to that question that we now turn.

Rawls (and Meade) on the Aims and Features of "Property-Owning Democracy"

Rawls's pessimism about the possibilities of WSC regimes leads him to adopt the institutional and policy recommendations of a "property-owning democracy," which, as we've seen, he strikingly describes as "an alternative to capitalism" (*JF*, p. 136). In both his name for this socioeconomic regime and in a great deal of its content, Rawls here follows the example of the Nobel Prize-winning Cambridge political economist James Meade, who used the term "property-owning democracy" to describe his own political proposals, developed in his important (but now relatively neglected) 1964 book *Efficiency, Equality and the Ownership of Property*, for moving beyond the limitations of the traditional welfare state.[7]

Meade's proposals can be seen as having two main strands, one concerned with taxation and the other with redistribution (Meade, 1964, pp. 40–65, 75–77). First, with regard to taxation, Meade advocated the aggressive taxation of capital transfers between generations where, in distinction from standard forms of inheritance taxation, the system of transfer taxation would be designed so that transfers would attract broadly similar rates of taxation, whether they were realized through inheritance or by means of gifts *inter vivos*.[8] Second, Meade advocated the redistribution of that capital on a broadly egalitarian basis, alongside increased state spending on the broad development of human capital through publicly funded education and training. Significantly, Meade saw questions of the distribution of *human* capital as being absolutely essential to our understanding of distributive justice, for, as he put it, "Earning power depends upon education and training, and education and training involve the investment of scarce resources in those who are educated and trained. This represents an important form of capital and of property; and a considerable part of the earnings of the educated and trained is in fact a return on the capital invested in their education" (1964, p. 30).[9]

Alongside his emphasis on the (re-)distribution of human capital, Meade's interest in the redistribution of wealth looked not only to simple cash transfers, but also to the advocacy of the widespread dispersal of ownership and control over productive resources. He endorsed the "encouragement of institutional forms (such as profit-sharing schemes,[10] the instalment purchase of municipal houses by their tenants,[11] and the development of suitable investment trusts[12]) which would make easier and more profitable the accumulation of small properties" (1964, p. 76). Meade's emphasis on the redistribution of *wealth* rather than just the redistribution of *income* is one of the most distinctive elements of his view, and his interest in wealth redistribution was characterized as much by the wish "to encourage the accumulation of property by those with little" as by the accompanying aim of obliterating intergenerational concentrations of family wealth (1964, p. 59). In pursuing these ends, one of the striking features of Meade's version of property-owning democracy was its pluralism regarding useful means, marshaling a number of distinct policy mechanisms, including the tax system, direct transfer payments, education policy, housing policy, industrial policy, and government intervention in the financial markets, in pursuit of a unified and integrated political goal.

Rawls's POD shares a great deal in terms of the structure and ambitions of Meade's proposals, departing from Meade significantly only in its avoidance of certain eccentricities of Meade's model with regard to family policy,[13] and in putting a greater emphasis on the democratic dimension of POD. Rawls's aim, with the delineation of a POD of such structural similarity to that of James Meade, was to construct a social system that would remedy the multifarious shortcomings of WSC regimes, thereby allowing the realization of all parts of his two principles of justice.

The key to understanding Rawls's "property-owning democracy" is that it should be seen as a socioeconomic system delineated with an explicit focus on the satisfaction of the two principles of justice, and thereby also with an explicit focus on the significance of the political values of liberty, equality, and democracy. It therefore "guarantees the basic liberties with the fair value of political liberties and fair equality of opportunity, and regulate[s] economic and social inequalities by a principle of mutuality, if not by the difference principle" (*JF*, p. 138). Like WSC, it allows private property in productive assets (*JF*, pp. 138–139) (unlike Rawls's other favored socioeconomic alternative, "liberal socialism"). However, unlike WSC, under POD (as with Meade's version of property-owning democracy), the basic structure of society and its background institutions "work to disperse the ownership of wealth and capital, and thus to prevent a small part of society from controlling the economy and indirectly political life as well" (*JF*, p. 139). POD ensures "the widespread ownership of productive assets and human capital," and hence (following Meade) it makes use of varieties of (what we might call) *ex ante* redistribution (i.e., redistribution of the capital that individuals bring to the market) as opposed to *ex post* redistribution associated with WSC.[14] As Rawls describes the aims of POD:

> The intent is not simply to assist those who lose out through accident or misfortune (although that must be done), but rather to put all citizens in a position to manage their own affairs on a footing of a suitable degree of social and economic equality. The least advantaged are not, if all goes well, the unfortunate and unlucky – objects of our charity and compassion, much less our pity – but those to whom reciprocity is owed as a matter of political justice among those who are free and equal citizens like everyone else. (*JF*, p. 139)[15]

We should thus understand POD as a socioeconomic system with at least the three following central aims, 1–3:

1. *Wide dispersal of capital*: The *sine qua non* of a POD is that it would entail the wide dispersal of the ownership of the means of production, with individual citizens controlling substantial (and broadly equal) amounts of productive capital (including both human and nonhuman capital).

As Rawls puts it, "welfare-state capitalism permits a small class to have a near monopoly on the means of production. Property-owning democracy avoids this, not by the redistribution of income to those with less at the end of each period, so to speak, but rather by ensuring the widespread ownership of productive assets and human capital (that is, education and trained skills) at the beginning of each period, all this against a background of fair equality of opportunity" (*JF*, p. 139). Note here that Rawls very much shares Meade's interest in putting a *variety* of productive resources into the hands of each citizen, including their own trained productive capacities as well as the "external" means of production.

2. *Blocking the intergenerational transmission of advantage*: A POD would also involve the enactment of significant estate, inheritance, and gift taxes, acting to limit the largest inequalities of wealth, especially from one generation to the next.

3. *Safeguards against the "corruption" of democratic politics*: A POD would seek to limit the effects of private and corporate wealth on politics, through campaign finance reform, public funding of political parties, public provision of forums for political debate, and other measures to block the influence of wealth on politics (perhaps including publicly funded elections) (see *JF*, pp. 149–150).

Policies of type 3 should be viewed as being in place with an eye on the protection of the fair value of the political liberties, and are therefore closely connected with creating a regime that is in accord with the first principle of justice. Policies of type 1 and 2 should, in contrast, be viewed as providing the means for institutionalizing the demands of Rawls's second principle of justice. Through a combination of all three kinds of policies, Rawls has thereby specified a social system that has the capacity to overcome the structural limitations of WSC in delivering a fully just set of socioeconomic arrangements.[16]

Putting the Democracy into Property-Owning Democracy: POD and the Fair Value of the Political Liberties

I shall now turn to the assessment of Rawls's claims for the superiority of POD over familiar forms of welfare state capitalism. To take Rawls's principles in the order of their lexical priority, I want to begin with an assessment of Rawls's claim that a POD can deliver the equal basic liberties, with the requisite protection of the fair value of the political liberties, whereas WSC cannot do so. Specifically, I want to assess Rawls's claim that WSC "rejects the fair value of the political liberties, and … permits very large inequalities in the ownership of real property (productive assets and natural resources) so that the control of the economy *and much of political life rests in few hands*" (*JF*, pp. 137–138, my italics). My concern here is that Rawls's argument for the necessity of POD in order to secure the fair value of political liberties may be unsuccessful and, at the very least, it can be shown to depend on some controversial claims in political sociology. Rawls's argument on this point is, at any rate, rather too rapid, and in need of further support. Therefore, my claim is that enacting a POD may not be a necessary condition for securing Rawls's first principle of justice.

My contention is that Rawls's argument is too rapid on this point because he provides insufficient support for the claim that control of political life must always go hand in hand with control of unequal amounts of productive resources. In a number of places, Rawls identifies a close relationship between the two forms of power or control. For example, Rawls talks of POD as working "to prevent a small part of society from controlling the economy, and indirectly, political life as well" (*JF*, p. 139). Now, I have no wish to deny the claim that, under really-existing political arrangements in contemporary liberal democracies, economic power is often freely converted into political power. And neither do I wish to deny that this process of the "corruption" of politics undermines the possibility of each citizen enjoying the fair value of the political liberties. (When I talk about the "corruption" of politics by inequalities in wealth, I do not mean corruption only in the gross literal sense whereby the wealthy effectively buy the allegiance of politicians. I also have in mind milder forms of "corruption," whereby the aims of the democratic process are thwarted, and the political liberties of some citizens are rendered "merely formal," by the wealthy having a greater effective capacity than others to take part in political activity and influence political outcomes.)[17] My concern, rather, is that it may well be possible to pursue policies that prevent the conversion of economic power into political power, without waiting for the adoption of the full range of economic policies associated with a POD.[18]

It is somewhat curious that Rawls does not here fully pursue the alternative avenue of examining whether the fair value of the political liberties could be guaranteed (even under a broadly WSC regime) through mechanisms *other* than egalitarian dispersal of productive wealth: for example, through campaign finance reform or the regulation of political speech. In his comparison of WSC and POD, Rawls does not consider strategies whereby the political sphere can be *insulated* from the economic sphere, even under the conditions of background inequality associated with a WSC-type regime. But we may have reason to think that it is not impossible that a capitalist welfare state with highly concentrated ownership of the means of production could still enact such policies of "insulation." For present purposes, my concern is not to test the plausibility of the *insulation strategy*, but simply to highlight its possibility. G.A. Cohen, for one, emphasized the significance of this possibility in his *Rescuing Justice and Equality* (2008), where he says:

> I do not think, and I do not think that Rawls thought, that ensuring the people's opportunities to hold office and exercise political influence are substantially independent of their socioeconomic position requires substantially equal material holdings. I believe that un-American experience shows that election regulation, of a sort that Rawls would endorse, can produce political democracy under a wide inequality of income and wealth. (Cohen, 2008, p. 385)

Rawls's position is especially puzzling when one sees, in his discussion of the fair value of the political liberties (*JF*, pp. 148–150), that he actually *does* advocate, as Cohen says he does, precisely the kind of policies that I mention here for insulating the economic and political spheres from one another. Rawls makes use of just such a strategy in rebutting the common charge of socialists and radical democrats "that the equal liberties in a modern democratic state are in practice merely formal" (*JF*, p. 148).[19] Yet, if Rawls believes that these sorts of "insulation" policies would be sufficient to counter this sort of challenge from more radical forms of egalitarianism, then it is difficult to see why such strategies could not also be harnessed in defense of the possibility of satisfying the first principle of justice even under WSC.[20] We might say that Rawls is in two minds about the "insulation strategy" for protecting the fair value of the political liberties; and it thus seems difficult to make sense of Rawls's claim that POD solves the problem of political corruption, whereas WSC cannot.

Alternatively, we might approach the question from the other direction, so to speak, and question Rawls's claim that POD really is capable of solving problems of political "corruption" with which WSC is structurally unable to cope. With regard to Rawls's engagement with the criticisms of socialists and radical democrats, it is important here to note the limits to how far one can go, within the constraints of a POD, in securing the fair value of the political liberties by means of reallocating ownership and control of economic resources. Many socialists and radical democrats hold that unless there is state ownership (or at least effective state control) of the means of production, and therefore of investment decisions, democratic politics will be unacceptably constrained by the structural power of capital to limit state action (i.e., by virtue of its threat advantage in removing economic investment).[21] Fully accepting this line of argument would suggest that private ownership of the majority of productive assets is inconsistent with ensuring the fair value of the political liberties, and that hence the only acceptable socioeconomic regime is liberal socialism rather than either POD or WSC. If this socialist "structural constraint" argument works, then POD and WSC are, so to speak, in the same boat, as regards failing to meet the demands of Rawls's first principle.

As we have seen, it is clearly not Rawls's view that, in terms of the achievement of the first principle of justice, liberal socialism is itself superior to *both* POD and WSC. It nevertheless seems plausible to think that this "structural constraint" argument is likely to be the most important issue on which the plausibility of Rawls's response to his socialist critics will turn. A sketch of a Rawlsian response to this worry might begin by stressing that the value of democratic self-direction is not absolute, and must always be balanced by the sometimes countervailing value of individual liberty in the economic sphere. Such a line of argument would stress that any proposal which secured the complete autonomy of the democratic sphere from economic "structural constraints" only at the price of excessively truncating citizens' economic liberties would have thereby failed to strike a satisfactory balance between these various competing political values. For our present purposes, though, the salient point is just this: that POD and WSC may have more in common than Rawls seems to realize, both with regard to what they can do, and with regard to what they cannot do, to insulate democratic politics from economic life.

Therefore, while specific kinds of political solutions are no doubt needed to fight problems of political corruption, the policies that are needed (that is, type 3 policies, of the sort described above) could be available under WSC as well as under POD. Indeed, a WSC regime would be unable to enact such policies only if WSC is understood in its "worst case" form – as something of a "straw man" regime type (as it indeed sometimes appears to be in Rawls's presentation). Otherwise, it is difficult to see how a concern for preserving the fair value of the political liberties mandates an institutional choice of POD (including type 1 policies) over WSC, at least in the absence of a more developed argument. Such an argument might be advanced by pointing toward the real-world ineffectiveness of type 3 policies in guaranteeing broad equality of political influence in the absence of the eradication of inequalities in economic power. But such an argument would need to make use of controversial claims in political sociology, and would for that reason need to be made carefully. It is not sufficient simply to assume that economic power and political power must always go together, with inequalities in the latter being inevitable whenever inequalities in the former have not been eradicated.

When one considers the commitments of Rawls's view, there would seem to be an internal tension in his treatment of the connection between economic and political power. One might even worry that Rawls is here losing sight of the malleability of the rules of property ownership, and placing too much emphasis on the formal powers of ownership. After all, on Rawls's view the specification of the rules of property are not given in advance of the workings of the basic structure of society, but are specified by that basic structure itself.[22] Thus, it is open to our political institutions to specify, for example, that corporate funds cannot be used for political purposes, or that wealthy individuals can only direct a limited amount of their property toward the funding of political campaigns, as the entitlements of those property holders are themselves a matter of political determination, and are to be determined with reference to the demands of justice. Rawls's approach to thinking about the conventionality of relations of property ownership suggests that there are a number of ways in which we might hope to prevent the bad political consequences of the unequal division of economic power without our options being constrained only to the single political option, entailed by POD, of eradicating those economic power inequalities themselves.

Thus, with regard to the protection of the fair value of the political liberties, it would seem that the argument for preferring POD over WSC is to some degree incomplete. (Also incomplete is the argument that Rawls would need to make *against* the claim, associated with Joshua Cohen and others, that liberal socialism is, with regard to securing the fair value of the political liberties, superior to POD.) Rawls has not shown that the fair value of the political liberties can be secured only under POD, and the view that this should be the case in fact stands in tension with some of the other commitments of his theory. We should therefore conclude that, while a POD is plausibly a type of regime that could do well in terms of institutionalizing Rawls's first principle of justice, Rawls does not give us sufficient reason to conclude that his first principle could not also be satisfied, through the use of alternative political strategies, under WSC.[23]

Power, Opportunity, and Control of Capital: POD and Fair Equality of Opportunity

I want now to turn to the connection between Rawls's principle of fair equality of opportunity (henceforth, FEO) and his support for a property-owning democracy. As is well known, on Rawls's view, FEO is subordinated in importance to the first principle of justice (including the requirement on securing the fair value of the political liberties), but is lexically prior to the difference principle (Rawls, 2001, p. 43). As in the case of Rawls's argument for POD over WSC on the basis of securing the first principle of justice, I will suggest that Rawls's argument for POD over (some form of) WSC on the basis of achieving FEO is equally contestable, and generates a similar menu of intriguing but unresolved theoretical issues.

To begin with the uncontroversial: what is surely beyond dispute is that any institutional regime that aims to preserve fair equality of opportunity over time needs to have a keen concern for limiting the influence of social background on individual life chances. On Rawls's view, FEO is achieved when the influence of social factors on the capacity of individuals to achieve particular social positions is neutralized, such that "those who have the same level of talent and ability and the same willingness to use these gifts should have the same prospects of success regardless of their social class of origin" (*JF*, p. 44). This goal can only plausibly be achieved when type 2 policies – such as the various forms of inheritance and gift taxes proposed by Meade, which seek to block the intergenerational transmission of advantage – are enacted. Thus, we should accept the claim that type 2 policies are a *necessary* element of any socioeconomic regime that seeks to satisfy the FEO principle. Nevertheless, this is not equivalent to accepting the claim that FEO can be achieved only given the acceptance of a full-blown property-owning democracy. For one might take the view that the enactment of a range of type 2 policies (alongside other institutional elements, such as an excellent system of public education) could be sufficient to achieve FEO, without needing to go as far as embracing a full POD regime, together with its type 1 policies involving the broad dispersal of (human *and* nonhuman) productive capital. Thus, one may agree that type 2 policies are a necessary means toward the goal of FEO, whilst denying that FEO can be achieved only under the full institutionalization of a property-owning democracy.[24]

One immediate objection to this suggestion would be that type 1 and type 2 policies are so intertwined that it does not make sense to talk of pursuing either in isolation. But, while it is certainly true that the two types of policies are often likely to go together, and to be mutually supporting, it is not true to say that type 2 policies cannot be pursued without enacting type 1 policies. For example, a socioeconomic regime that prevented the intrafamilial transmission of wealth across generations could still allow substantial inequalities in the ownership of productive resources within each generation. Consider, for example, the policies associated with the "stakeholder grant" scheme advocated by Bruce Ackerman and Anne Alstott (1999), whereby all young adults would receive a one-off capital grant of $80,000, funded by aggressive inheritance taxation. Although superficially similar to POD, such a scheme, if taken in isolation, with its "starting gate"[25] characteristics, would be fully consistent with the emergence of inegalitarian concentrations of capital that would be inconsistent with the type 1 policy goals associated with a full-blown POD.[26]

In making this suggestion that POD may not be the only way to satisfy FEO, I am taking issue with the account of these issues that has been developed by Samuel Freeman. On Freeman's view, achieving FEO entails that there exist "real opportunities for all income classes to control capital and their means of production" (Freeman, 2007a, p. 107).[27] On Freeman's interpretation of FEO, which he presents as "conjectural" and as what might be considered a "friendly amendment" (2007b, p. 135) to the strict Rawlsian version of FEO, citizens of all socioeconomic classes (hence, *all citizens*) must possess a real (ongoing) opportunity to control productive capital. As Freeman puts it, FEO can be seen as generating "a positive duty ... to create for all citizens *a fair and adequate opportunity for control* over their means of production and working conditions" (2007b, p. 135). If FEO were, indeed, to entail this demand, then the role of type 1 policies (for the dispersal of productive capital) in safeguarding FEO would be clear.

However, Freeman's account in fact appears to depart significantly from Rawls's own interpretation of FEO, not least with regard to what is meant by an "opportunity" in the relevant sense. What is claimed under Rawls's FEO is simply that the likelihood of any particular individual attaining any particular occupational position within society should be a function of their effort and ability and *not* of "their social class of *origin*" (*JF*, p. 44, my italics). Rawls's full characterization of the requirements of FEO in *Justice as Fairness* makes clear that the requirement is more modest than in the "conjectural" version of FEO described and endorsed by Freeman. As Rawls puts it, "supposing there is a distribution of native endowments, those who have the same level of talent and ability and the same willingness to use these gifts should have the same prospects of success regardless of their social class of origin" (*JF*, p. 44). Note that the characterization of FEO here is in terms of (lifetime) *prospects*. The *opportunities* that Rawls's principle of FEO ranges over are thus the opportunities of individuals with given social backgrounds to come to membership of any of the full range of occupational positions that exist within society. They are, so to speak, *lifetime* opportunities enjoyed by individuals, regardless of their initial social background. This is a significantly different idea to that involved in Freeman's use of the term "opportunities," which he uses to describe the *ongoing* powers and capacities for control of the means of production possessed by individuals once they have already come to occupy a particular social position.

Under Rawls's FEO, there can exist highly concentrated control over the means of production, as long as all citizens have an equal lifetime opportunity to come to adopt a position of power and control over productive resources. By contrast, on Freeman's view, FEO is satisfied only when everyone has the *ongoing* potential to control productive capital (and hence only when type 1 policies of capital dispersal are being pursued). These two versions of FEO are, therefore, significantly different to one another. On the more modest reading of FEO, which I here endorse as characterizing Rawls's own view, FEO can be satisfied as long as everyone, regardless of social class of origin, has the *lifetime* opportunity to come to a position of control over productive capital. Moreover, as this more modest reading of FEO can be satisfied even when the actual distribution of control over productive capital takes an inegalitarian or hierarchical form, it can be satisfied in the absence of any type 1 POD policies. It is thus my contention that, on the most faithful reading of the FEO principle, it cannot be said uniquely to mandate a POD-type socioeconomic regime, even though there is of course nothing about a POD that is inconsistent with the achievement of FEO. Indeed, one can imagine a WSC-type regime, with an inegalitarian distribution of positions of control over productive capital, which nevertheless satisfied the FEO principle. Such a regime would need to enact robust type 2 policies, in terms of breaking down capital transfers *between* generations, but it would not need to transform itself all the way into a POD, through broadly dispersing control of capital *within* each generation.[28]

Before moving on to discuss the relationship between POD and the difference principle, it is worth first pausing to consider another dimension of the relationship between POD and fair equality of opportunity. The argument above is concerned with the distribution of nonhuman productive capital, and suggests that type 1 policies of capital dispersal are not mandated by the strict (or narrow) reading of FEO that Rawls himself endorsed, certainly with regard to control over "external" factors of production. The story is more complicated, though, when we turn to the case of *human* capital.

Here, Meade's remarks about the various functions of education, both as means of self-development and as a form of economic investment, come back to mind. A state that took seriously its obligations under FEO, even under its strict or narrow *lifetime* version, would presumably be obliged to provide individuals with the educational opportunities that would allow them to develop their native talents and abilities to their fullest extent, so that individuals' lifetime opportunities to occupy various occupational positions within society would be a function of those talents and abilities, rather than of morally arbitrary factors such as their family background. In pursuing such policies, the state would also thereby be pursuing policies that worked toward the broader dispersal of human capital within society; that is to say, the institutional background required by FEO would directly enact type 1 policies of capital dispersal with regard to *human* capital, even though the justification for such policies would be in terms of promoting individual self-development, rather than in terms of the advocacy of capital dispersal per se. (On the more expansive or "conjectural" *ongoing* version of FEO, this derivate commitment to pursuing type 1 policies would be correspondingly expanded to include the generous provision of *ongoing* opportunities for training and further education, and not just the provision of education for citizens up until working age.) Thus, it is not quite true to say that FEO does not mandate any policies of type 1, as such policies are mandated in a restricted sense, with regard to the development of human capital; instead, one should say that there is no direct line of argument from FEO to POD's comprehensive embrace of type 1 policies ranging over all varieties of productive capital.[29]

Power, Status, and Self-Respect: POD, the Difference Principle, and the Value of Equality

I want now to focus on the role of POD-type policies and institutions in realizing the second part of Rawls's second principle: namely, the difference principle, which states that inequalities in the distribution of social primary goods are justifiable only when they are of benefit to the least advantaged members of society. In discussing POD and the difference principle, my aim is to link the discussion to Rawls's elaboration of the value of equality, and especially to Rawls's account of the connection of the value of equality with power, domination, and self-respect. The previous two sections have registered some of the problems with regard to Rawls's argument for the necessity of POD and the inadequacy of WSC. In this section, where I turn to the difference principle, my conclusion is far more positive, for it is here, I suggest, that the strongest justification for the adoption of POD can be found.

In his "Comments on Equality" (*JF*, §39), where Rawls specifies the diversity of reasons which we have for regulating economic inequalities, he emphasizes that we should care about inequality in part because of its effects with regard to status, power, domination, and self-respect.[30] To start with power and domination, Rawls claims that:

> A second reason for controlling economic and social inequalities is to prevent one part of society from dominating the rest.... This power allows a few, in virtue of their control over the machinery of state, to enact a system of law and property that ensures their dominant position in the economy as a whole. (*JF*, pp. 130–131)

With regard to status harms, Rawls tells us that:

> A third reason [for regulating social and economic inequalities] brings us closer to what is wrong with inequality in itself. Significant political and economic inequalities are often associated with inequalities of social status that encourage those of lower status to be viewed both by themselves and by others as inferior. This may arouse widespread attitudes of deference and servility on one side and a will to dominate and arrogance on the other. These effects of social and economic inequalities can be serious evils and the attitudes they engender great vices. (*JF*, p. 131)

Bearing in mind these ways in which inequality can be a great evil can help to make sense of the reasons why the redistributive functions of WSC cannot be adequate to rectify the harms of an inegalitarian society. For, whilst inequalities of income can straightforwardly be rectified through a process of *ex post* redistribution through transfer payments (as in a capitalist welfare state), matters become more complex and troublesome if we consider the kinds of social inequality that may generate status harms (thereby undermining the self-respect of "low status" individuals), or which may lead to unacceptable forms of power or domination. These kinds of social inequality are far less likely to be remediable by means of the *ex post* redistribution of income.

To take an example, let us assume that society is structured in such a way that all decisions about economic investment and production are made by a small, high-status group who constitute something like a ruling class or economic elite. This dominant class gets to decide to a considerable degree how society is to be structured, and what the variety of jobs and social roles within that society is likely to be. Now, if we enact within this society the kind of "transfer based" *ex post* redistribution associated with many WSC-type mechanisms, we may presumably be able to create a society in which income is equalized (or "maximined") across the dominant and subordinate social classes. But we will nevertheless be completely unable to enact a redistribution of *power*, or of *status*, within this society by any plausible *ex post* mechanism, given that the shape of the society in terms of its productive relations, and the distribution of roles within the economy of that society, will still be a matter of decision by the dominant group. Only *ex ante* mechanisms, which challenged the ruling group's position of dominance by, for example, granting more control over productive capital to others, will be able to head off inequalities of wealth, inequalities of power (thereby preventing relations of domination), and their associated inequalities of status (thereby preventing the erosion of self-respect of the subordinate group). Thus, we may plausibly think that a "redistributive" *ex post* realization of the difference principle would fail to address some of the ways in which inequality is bad, because of its inability to address inequalities that result from the way in which social production is organized (rather than merely addressing inequalities that result from the distribution of the social product itself).[31]

This example is designed to suggest that the *ex post* redistribution of resources (e.g., in the form of transfer payments that constitute income streams) will be insufficient to address certain kinds of deep-seated social inequalities. But, in addition to this claim, one might go further, and contend that the *ex post* redistribution of resources may be actively counterproductive with regard to certain forms of social inequality. This is because the recipient of "welfare" payments may come to see himself as a passive beneficiary, rather than as a free and equal individual with his own valuable plan of life, and of equal standing with his or her fellow citizens. The recipient of such *ex post* transfers may experience these transfers as the *source* of his diminished status, and thereby as the mechanism that undermines his self-respect. Here, again, a reordering of social relations of production would seem to be the only way of making sure that all of the severe harms of inequality are eradicated.

An individual who lives in a social and economic environment that she plays some part in fashioning, and who engages her capacities as an agent with a conception of the good and an ability to cooperate with others in productive social relations, will be provided with the "social bases of self-respect," to use Rawls's phrase. In other words, citizens situated in this way will "have a lively sense of their worth as persons and ... be able to advance their ends with self-confidence" (*JF*, p. 59). Only by making sure that the structure of the economy is such as to broadly disperse control over productive resources, therefore, can we ensure that all citizens are able to have this "lively sense" of their own agency, and in so doing to head off the possibilities of harmful inequalities of power and status. In this way, the institutions of a property-owning democracy should be able to overcome problems of domination and social inequality in a way that the institutions of a capitalist welfare state are structurally incapable of doing. In so doing, as Rawls puts it in his discussion of Marx's critique of the division of labor under capitalism, "the narrowing and demeaning features of the division should be largely overcome once the institutions of property-owning democracy are realized."[32]

Given these clarifications, the egalitarian argument for POD-type arrangements becomes clear. The aim of the kind of radical socioeconomic reorganization characteristic of a property-owning democracy (and, especially, through its type 1 policies involving the wide dispersal of capital) is to realize the value of equality through *ex ante* compression of objectionable economic inequalities. A property-owning democracy aims to do this through the organization of economic life in a way that reduces the likelihood of social domination or of loss of status. Therefore, satisfaction of the difference principle, when viewed as ranging *not only* over income, but also over wealth in productive capital, as well as over the social primary goods of (a) the powers and prerogatives of offices and positions of authority and responsibility, and (b) the social bases of self-respect (see, e.g., *JF*, §17), plausibly mandates a move toward greater dispersal of control over productive resources.

If this line of argument is successful, then we have a clear demonstration of why policies of type 1 would be necessary if we are to create a fully just society. Insofar as such policies are characteristic of a POD, we therefore have an argument for the superiority of a POD to WSC-based regimes, which do not pursue similar policies. Thus, when we focus on the difference principle and the value of equality, we have good reason to endorse Rawls's argument for the superiority of a system of social organization that disperses control of productive resources over a system which concerns itself (as in the capitalist welfare state) primarily with matters of *ex post* economic redistribution.

Before concluding this section, I shall first deal with two possible lines of objection. One objection, relatively superficial in character, can easily be generated by my use of the contrast between *ex post* and *ex ante* redistribution. This contrast, which is mine rather than Rawls's, was suggested by Rawls's contrast between "the redistribution of income at the end of each period, so to speak ..." and "ensuring the widespread ownership of productive assets and human capital ... at the beginning of each period" (*JF*, p. 139). Both my talk of *ex post* versus *ex ante* policies, and Rawls's talk of discrete "periods" of economic production, might be thought to embody a naive and unsustainable picture of the economy as a sort of board game, like Monopoly, with discrete temporal phases, and a stop-start character. Neither Rawls nor I need be committed to such an outlandish model, and I take it that neither he nor I fail to see that the economy is an ongoing dynamic system, whereby the end of one period is always the beginning of another and where, as one might put it, one man's *ex post* is another man's *ex ante*.[33] Instead, this kind of "temporal" talk should be viewed as metaphorical and, as such, as potentially illuminating. What is intended is simply the contrast between (re-)distribution that looks to the productive resources that individuals are able to bring to the market, and redistribution that looks only to the streams of income that individuals have available for private consumption. I hope that this metaphorical use of temporal terms helps to shed light on this contrast, and that the dangers of over-literal interpretation do not render it unhelpful.[34]

A second objection to this part of my argument might be that I have misinterpreted the role of the "social bases of self-respect" in Rawls's overall argument. According to this rival interpretative view, one should see the difference principle as ranging only over the social primary goods of income and wealth, with powers and prerogatives of positions of authority and responsibility being distributed by the FEO principle, and with the social bases of self-respect being secured by the operation of the two principles of justice taken together. On this view, securing the social bases of self-respect is a holistic achievement of the principles of justice working in tandem, and it is a kind of category mistake to see the social bases of self-respect as among the distribuenda that fall under the purview of the difference principle.

There are two useful lines of response to this objection. First, even if its central point is granted, it remains of great importance to emphasize that the difference principle should be seen as operating over *wealth* (and hence over ownership of productive resources, among other things) as well as over *income*. Hence, the redistribution of income streams characteristic of the transfer payments of WSC would not be adequate for satisfying the difference principle viewed as also ranging over wealth. Second, though, it seems to me to be a more plausible and faithful reading of Rawls's view to see the social bases of self-respect (as well as powers and prerogatives of positions of authority and responsibility) as being among the residual concerns of the difference principle, even if they are goods that are also the concern of other elements of the principles of justice. This is because, insofar as one sees the difference principle as an attempt to realize the value of equality, one sees that part of the underlying justification of the difference principle is that it is able to address concerns relating to power, domination, and status. It would thus be unnatural to truncate the difference principle, and cut it free arbitrarily of its underlying normative justification, if it were treated too narrowly as ranging only over the goods of income and wealth. Thus, although I have in previous sections taken issue with some of the arguments regarding the justification of POD offered by Samuel Freeman, here at least I am very much in agreement with Freeman who, in his discussion of the difference principle, enjoins us to view it as ranging over a comprehensive index of the social primary goods. As Freeman puts it, "the relative well-being of the least-advantaged is determined by an index of primary goods, including not simply their share of income and wealth, but also their opportunities for powers and positions of office, non-basic rights and liberties, and the institutional bases of self-respect. The difference principle is the criterion for the just distribution of these primary goods as well" (Freeman, 2007b, p. 113).

Welfare State Capitalism and Property-Owning Democracy: Ideal Types, Public Policy, and Real Politics

Having assessed POD and WSC in terms of Rawls's principles of justice, I would now like to step back in order to highlight the status of POD and WSC as "ideal types," and to examine their somewhat complex relationships to real political regimes, and to particular institutional and policy options. Given the separability of policy types 1, 2, and 3, it is plausible to think that the best way of understanding POD is as a complex amalgam, composed of a set of different varieties of policy, each with a different underlying aim. This is significant if we consider the possibility of social arrangements that enact some, but not all, of the elements associated with POD, as when we consider, for example, WSC regimes which nevertheless enact type 2 and/or type 3 policies (as discussed above). There is perhaps a sense in which Rawls bestows a false unity on the idea of POD as a form of social organization, speaking as he does as if WSC and POD were each indivisible packages of policies. If we think more in terms of the particular kinds of *policies and institutional structures* that might be required in order to achieve social justice, then Rawls's discussion in terms of general *regimes* might come to seem overly schematic.

There is a related worry that Rawls's version of WSC is presented as something of a "straw man" position. WSC, according to Rawls, is a rather minimalist, unintrepid, and toothless version of a welfare state. We should resist the temptation, therefore, to think that Rawls's "WSC" refers unproblematically to really existing welfare states. The significant gains for social justice that have been made by welfare state regimes, such as the Swedish Social Democrat (SAP) governments of the postwar era, or the postwar Labour government in the UK, were typically made not only by the enactment of the narrow range of policies which Rawls associates with WSC regimes, but by a range of policies that include some which belong within Rawls's specification of the policies of a property-owning democracy. We might therefore conclude that Rawls's "WSC" is roughly equivalent to the subclass of "liberal" welfare states (as opposed to "conservative/corporatist" or "social democratic" welfare states) as identified by Gøsta Esping-Andersen in his book *Three Worlds of Welfare Capitalism* (1990).[35] It certainly does not characterize all societies that have answered to the description of being a "welfare state."

Real-world examples do much to blur the starkness of Rawls's contrasts between regimes. Whereas Rawls characterizes WSC as being interested only in *ex post* redistribution, the vigorously egalitarian education policies that have been pursued by a variety of European social democratic governments can very much be understood as generating mechanisms for the egalitarian *ex ante* distribution of human capital. Thus, even if the traditional welfare state has not done a great deal to disperse nonhuman capital (as in a POD), it would be unfair to conclude that traditional welfare state strategies take no interest in the *ex ante* distribution of productive assets.

Given these worries, we should bear in mind the potential distortions that can enter our thinking if we do not remember that POD and WSC are only *ideal types* of regime. All the policy elements of POD need not stand or fall together, and nor are they all inconsistent with a broadly WSC-based set of political arrangements. It might therefore be potentially misleading to present POD and WSC as competitor positions. Rather, one might view them more as staging posts on a broader continuum of policies that might be enacted in the pursuit of social justice. POD-type measures can be viewed as useful extensions of, rather than replacements for, the welfare state. This is very much the way that James Meade thought about the policies and politics of POD. As Meade put it: "These measures are needed, for the most part, to supplement rather than to replace the existing Welfare-State policies" (Meade, 1964, p. 75, my italics).

Moreover, despite his negative assessment of WSC, we should not lose sight of the fact that Rawls himself endorses many central aspects of the traditional welfare state. For example, Rawls is committed to policies such as universal health care and disability cover, which are very much part of the traditional range of policies associated with *ex post* WSC approaches.[36] It would be difficult to see how such traditional "welfare state" functions of redistributive *ex post* social insurance could be replaced with analogous *ex ante* policies. So, insofar as Rawls wishes to give the label "property-owning democracy" to the set of socioeconomic institutions which would realize the two principles of justice, one must thereby conclude that such a POD needs to contain many elements which replicate, rather than in all cases replacing, significant elements of the traditional welfare state.

Thus, for a number of reasons, one should be cautious with regard to Rawls's overly schematic typology of "regime types." POD and WSC are not simple rivals, each with its own indivisible internal coherence. Rather, each of these Rawlsian regimes represents an amalgam of possible policies and institutional arrangements. Accordingly, plausible institutional and policy menus will typically draw from across these Rawlsian regimes, and the adoption of elements of a property-owning democracy need not involve the wholesale rejection of traditional welfare state mechanisms.

This point about the fuzzy borders between POD and WSC connects to a related point about political strategy, with regard to the process of political change and the transformation of socioeconomic regimes. Taking, as an example, the problem of securing the fair value of the political liberties, it is significant that "type 3" policies can be advocated for enactment under near-to-current conditions, rather than making sense only given the thoroughgoing "regime change" that would be involved in full enactment of a POD. We need not think that there is no hope of reducing the influence of money in politics until we can achieve an egalitarian reordering of the productive relationships of our economies. Given this, insofar as we endorse principles of justice that are broadly similar to those identified by Rawls, we may welcome the "fungibility" of the set of policies characteristic of a POD as holding out the hope that some of the aims of a POD, in terms of achieving and securing social justice, can be achieved within the constraints of (something like) WSC.

Conclusion – Liberty, Equality, and Property-Owning Democracy

The argument of this chapter has suggested that the best reasons for supporting a property-owning democracy are connected to the difference principle, rather than to the fair value of the political liberties, or to fair equality of opportunity. The difference principle, when viewed as ranging over the full range of social primary goods, can be institutionalized only under conditions associated with POD (or something rather like it), whereas fair equality of opportunity and the fair value of the political liberties could plausibly be achieved under a variety of different socioeconomic regimes. One might put the same point in a different way by saying that Rawls's best reasons for advocating a POD are grounded in the value of equality rather than the values of liberty and democracy. Here, my view parts company from Rawls himself, who clearly took the view that WSC was inconsistent with each of the separate elements of his principles of justice (*JF*, p. 137). I also diverge to some degree from the view of Samuel Freeman, whose view would seem to be that the best reasons for adopting POD over WSC are based on securing the fair value of the political liberties, and on securing fair equality of opportunity, and who correspondingly downplays the significance of the difference principle in determining our selection of POD over WSC, in choosing a just socioeconomic regime (Freeman, 2007b, pp. 133–135, 224–226; also Freeman, 2007a, pp. 105–198). On my account of these issues, neither of the elements of Rawls's principles of justice that are lexically prior to the difference principle are sufficient to determine the case in favor of POD.

As against Rawls and Freeman, my claim is that many of the aims of a property-owning democracy (e.g., relating to the aims advanced by type 2 and type 3 policies) can be achieved under a capitalist welfare state, even with a relatively inegalitarian distribution of productive resources. In terms of egalitarian strategy, this is potentially good news, as it means that we have more options than the single option of agitating for systemic "regime change." Those with a concern for social justice can also pursue more piecemeal methods for moving toward satisfaction of the principles of justice. Nevertheless, Rawls is surely right in claiming that a truly just society, which satisfies the difference principle, as well as the other (lexically prior) elements of his theory of justice, will require the increased dispersal of productive resources characteristic of a property-owning democracy. Systemic regime change, away from the traditional institutions of welfare state capitalism, is surely necessary if Rawls's principles of justice are to be fully institutionalized. It is impossible to conclude in any way other than by saying that Rawls's hostility to capitalism (in anything like its current form), and his determination to find an alternative to it, on the basis of his deep commitment to the possibility of achieving social justice, was cogent and entirely well motivated. Our hope for the achievement of social justice cannot coherently be a hope for merely incremental change within a political economy dominated by "the large banks and the capitalist business class" (Rawls and Van Parijs, 2003, p. 9 in online version). Instead, as Rawls knew, it must be a hope for something transformatively better.

Notes

1. This chapter draws upon, and has evolved as a descendant of, an earlier article on this subject (O'Neill, 2009b). For comments on various versions of this chapter, or for useful discussion on the issues with which it is concerned, I am grateful to Derek Bell, Paul Bou-Habib, Luc Bovens, Corey Brettschneider, Chris Brooke, Thom Brooks, Tom Christiano, Matthew Clayton, the sadly late Jerry Cohen, Gijs van Donselaar, Bob Goodin, Axel Gosseries, Nien-hê Hsieh, Waheed Hussain, Peter Jones, Gerald Lang, Mary Leng, Graham Long, Dominic Martin, Keir Martin, Kieran Oberman, Shepley Orr, Philippe Van Parijs, Jonathan Quong, Ingrid Robeyns, Miriam Ronzoni, David Rose, David Schweickart, Raj Sehgal, Hillel Steiner, Zofia Stemplowska, Alan Thomas, Antoon Vandevelde, Alex Voorhoeve, Jack Vromen, Thomas Wells, Steve de Wijze, Andrew Williams, Thad Williamson, and Jonathan Wolff. I am also grateful to audiences at the 2007 APSA meeting in Chicago; at a "Priority in Practice" Workshop at University College London; at the Jepson School of Leadership Studies at the University of Richmond, Virginia; at the Erasmus Institute for Philosophy and Economics at Erasmus Universiteit Rotterdam; at the Lovanium Seminar in Ethics and Public Policy at the Katholieke Universiteit Leuven; at an AHRC Workshop on Egalitarian Theories of Justice at the University of Exeter; and at a workshop of the Newcastle Ethics and Legal & Political Philosophy group at Newcastle University.
2. Although the most systematic discussion of the contract between "welfare-state capitalism" and "property-owning democracy" comes in Rawls's *Justice as Fairness* (2001), there is also a sustained discussion of property-owning democracy in Chapter 5 of Rawls's *A Theory of Justice* (1971), especially section 43, and again in the Preface to the French edition of *A Theory of Justice* (reproduced as the preface to the revised (1999) edition of *A Theory of Justice*, see especially at pp. xiv–xvi).
3. Rawls's development of his idea of "liberal socialism" is very brief, and it receives much less attention than POD in *Justice as Fairness*. Rawls does claim, though, that a "liberal socialist" regime could meet the demands of the two principles of justice in the same way as does a POD (see *JF*, p. 138). Rawls envisages "liberal socialism" as involving a number of competing, democratically controlled firms operating within "a system of free and workably competitive markets" (ibid.), and retaining free choice of occupation. See also Rawls's remarks on Marx in his *Lectures on the History of Political Philosophy* (2007), where he describes the central features of liberal socialism (pp. 322–323). For a number of liberal socialist proposals along the broad lines envisaged by Rawls, see Cohen (1989a, pp. 25–50); Miller (1989); Roemer (1994a, 1994b); Schweickart (1993, 2002); Alperovitz (2004); and Nove (1983). See also Archer (1995). For a mid-twentieth-century precursor of more recent forms of market socialism, see Durbin (1940). Rawls himself has a footnote (*JF*, p. 136, fn3) to the discussion of various versions of (what may be described as) liberal socialism in Elster and Moene (1989); that collection contains proposals for institutional alternatives to capitalism by, among others, Karl Ove Moene, Alec Nove, and John E. Roemer.
4. Although see the chapter in this volume by David Schweickart for a comparison of Rawls's POD to Schweickart's own version of liberal socialism, which he calls "economic democracy," and the chapter by Gar Alperovitz for discussion of the comparison between POD and the (broadly) liberal socialist view endorsed by Alperovitz, based around his idea of a "pluralist commonwealth."
5. On the "fair value" of the political liberties, see Rawls (2001, pp. 148–150, §45). In according significance to the fair value of the political liberties, Rawls is in large part responding to Daniels (1975).

6. For an illuminating discussion of the place of the "principle of reciprocity" in Rawls's thinking, see Cohen (1989b).
7. See Meade (1964). Although Rawls is avowedly following Meade in his use of the term "property-owning democracy," the term had a prehistory even before Meade's book. The term originates with the Scottish Conservative and Unionist politician Noel Skelton (1880–1935), who sketched the earliest version of a "property-owning democracy" in a series of articles for the *Spectator* in 1923 (See Skelton (1924).). The term "property-owning democracy" was popular as a label used to describe a range of policies proposed by mid-twentieth-century British Conservatives, including Anthony Eden, especially around the time of the 1955 general election. In harnessing the term to genuinely progressive ends, Meade was, perhaps somewhat mischievously, appropriating the language of his political opponents. On the genealogy of the term "property-owning democracy," see Ron (2008) and Jackson (2005). For an interesting and influential source, influenced by Skelton's thinking, see Harold Macmillan (1938). At any rate, none of the uses of the term that come before Meade's have much, if any, bearing on the content of Rawls's particular POD proposals. For a comprehensive excavation of the history of property-owning democracy before Rawls, see Ben Jackson's chapter in this book. (As an interesting aside, Skelton, who died in 1935 just before the general election of that year, is one of the few individuals ever to have been re-elected posthumously to the House of Commons.)
8. For, as Meade puts it, "If death duties are to be used seriously as an instrument for the equalization of properties, it is essential that gifts *inter vivos* should be taxed in the same way as bequests at death" (1964, pp. 54–55).
9. Meade continues: "Of course expenditure on education cannot be treated simply as any other form of productive capital investment. It confers benefits quite apart from the fact that it increases the future commercial earning power of the educated. It enables the educated person to enjoy a fuller life quite apart from any increase in his money income which it may bring; ... But education does undoubtedly have value to the educated person as a straightforward commercial investment. It increases the productivity and economic value of the person educated" (1964, p. 31).
10. By which Meade is referring to employee share schemes "whereby workers can gain a property interest in business firms" (1964, p. 59).
11. It will not escape the notice of British readers that this bears a striking similarity to a policy pursued with notable success by Mrs Thatcher in her first administration, by means of the 1980 Housing Act, which gave council tenants the right to buy their houses at attractively low prices. The policy was extraordinarily popular, and played a substantial role in Thatcher's electoral success in the 1980s. Some readers of a progressive outlook may take this association with Thatcher's policies to be to the detriment of property-owning democracy. To others, this may serve as evidence that a property-owning democracy of the sort advocated by Meade is able admirably and successfully to integrate a range of particular policies that have traditionally been associated with a range of distinct positions at different points on the ideological spectrum. (On Thatcher's privatization of council housing, see Campbell (2003); Green (2006); and McSmith (2010).)
12. What Meade has in mind here, with regard to "suitable investment trusts," includes "financial intermediaries in which small savings can be pooled for investment in high-earning risk-bearing securities" (1964, p. 59), thereby bringing the benefits of investment in financial instruments to all members of society.
13. Meade described himself as a proponent of "eugenics" (1964, pp. 63–65), although his proposals regarding family policy are less troubling than this label might imply. He was mainly concerned, on the one hand, uncontroversially, to ensure the widespread availability, to all sections of society, of effective contraception (p. 64), and, on the

14. other hand, and more idiosyncratically, to provide tax incentives for those with high incomes to have more children (ibid.). What is most troubling about this strange corner of Meade's view is that he seems to suggest that those who are "rich [and] successful" are also "intelligent," in distinction to the "poor, unsuccessful and unintelligent" (ibid.).
14. I shall come back to the language of *ex ante* versus *ex post* distribution below.
15. Rawls's insistence that the fundamental aim of his account of justice is not the rectification of accident or misfortune immediately suggests an important contrast with "luck egalitarian" views of distributive justice, although this is not a contrast I shall pursue here. For fuller discussion, see Freeman (2007b, pp. 111–142).
16. For other elaborations of the policies integral to a POD, see Krouse and McPherson (1988). Rawls describes himself as being indebted to the discussion of Krouse and McPherson (2001, p. 135). See also Freeman (2007b, pp. 112–115, 132–136, 219–235); and Freeman (2007a, pp. 10–11, 75–109).
17. See Rawls (2001, §45 and esp. p. 149).
18. Indeed, a number of writers take exactly this approach to the problem of the corruption of politics by economic inequalities. See, for example, Walzer (1983), Kaus (1992), and Sandel (2000).
19. Here Rawls is explicitly responding to the criticisms of his first principle developed by Norman Daniels in "Equal Liberty and the Unequal Worth of Liberty" (1975).
20. See, for example, Cohen (1989a). For a socialist critique of Rawls, see Schweickart (1979). See also DiQuattro (1983) and Christiano (2010).
21. Alternatively, we might draw the conclusion that Rawls thinks that the insulation strategy can be effective only when used in tandem with the strategy of wealth dispersal. But, if so, this is a substantive assumption in political sociology that requires rather more in the way of support. Absent an account of why the insulation strategy, if pursued on its own, must always fail, it seems reasonable to give more of the benefit of the doubt to such "insulatory" policies. I am grateful to Waheed Hussain for pushing me toward greater clarity on this issue.
22. See Rawls's discussion of property rights at Rawls (2001, pp. 114–115). On the broadly Rawlsian view of property rights as conventional, see Murphy and Nagel (2002), and also O'Neill (2009a).
23. To be sure, this is not to show that POD might not, in fact, present a more structurally secure, and thereby stable, means for institutionalizing Rawls's first principle than that available under WSC. It is simply to say that, as things stand, (a) this case has not yet been made, and (b) even if POD did present a setting in which the institutionalization of the first principle might be more stable than under WSC, we should not be too quick to discount the possibilities of realizing Rawls's first principle under WSC. I am grateful to Thomas Wells and Miriam Ronzoni for pushing me to say more on this point.
24. Needless to say, even if it is true that FEO can be achieved without recourse to type 1 policies, this does not mean that it is easy to achieve FEO, given the political difficulties of enacting (even very limited versions) of type 2 policies. For a discussion of some of these difficulties in a US context, see Graetz and Shapiro (2005). With regard to the British context, see O'Neill (2007, pp. 62–71), and White, with Prabhakar and Rowlingson (2008).
25. On "starting gate" theories, see Dworkin (2000).
26. I am grateful to Antoon Vandevelde, Philippe Van Parijs, and Jack Vromen for pressing me to say more about the ways in which these two types of policies can be disentangled.
27. See also Freeman's discussion of POD and FEO in Freeman (2007b, pp. 135–136).

28. This is not to say that Freeman's arguments in favor of POD, on the basis of POD's ability to provide ongoing opportunities for control of productive resources, may not be independently plausible. It is simply to note that Freeman's argument on this point departs significantly from, and goes very much beyond, meeting the demands of Rawls's FEO principle. Freeman is right to characterize his view as a "friendly amendment" to Rawls's, but it is also an amendment with rather momentous implications as regards the choice between different socioeconomic regimes.
29. I thank Philippe Van Parijs for illuminating discussion of the relationship between FEO, POD, education, and human capital.
30. Here, Rawls seems to be following T.M. Scanlon. See Rawls (2001, p. 130, fn48). For Scanlon's account of the badness of inequality, see "The Diversity of Objections to Inequality" (Scanlon, 2003). See also Scanlon (2009). For a broader discussion of Rawls's and Scanlon's treatments of the badness of inequality, with regard the various conceptions of the nature and value of equality, see O'Neill (2008b).
31. For further development of the idea that a concern with equality, understood as ranging over a set of diverse social primary goods, leads to a concern for restructuring the organization and control of production itself, see O'Neill (2008a).
32. Rawls (2007, p. 321). Section on "Marx – His View of Capitalism as a Social System."
33. Although this is not to say that there might not be possible socioeconomic regimes that, for good reasons, did try to introduce this sort of "periodization" into economic life, for example through the periodic collection and then redistribution of tradable vouchers bestowing control over elements of the means of production, as in some versions of market socialism. (Although POD itself would not seemingly be likely to have this feature.) I am grateful to the late Jerry Cohen for bringing this point to my attention.
34. Mandle (2009, p. 169) similarly emphasizes that "The contrast between adjustments occurring at the beginning or end of each period is metaphor." But he also holds that, nevertheless, "the contrast reveals how Rawls thinks about the requirements of economic justice" (ibid.).
35. See Gøsta Esping-Andersen (1990), especially pages 26–29. On the political theory of "really existing" welfare states, see Goodin (2003) and Pierson and Castles (2006). On the postwar Labour governments in the UK, see Morgan (1984) and Hennessy (2006). On the evolution of Labour's political thought over the twentieth century, see Jackson (2007). On social democracy in Sweden, see Andersson (2006). On social democracy in general, see Przeworski (1986), Sassoon (1996), Moschonas (2002), Berman (2006), Meyer with Hinchman (2007), and Judt (2010).
36. See, for example, Rawls's endorsement of Norman Daniels's suggestions for state-funded health care (*JF*, pp. 175–176). Indeed, Rawls speaks of "a basic level of health-care provided to all" as one of "the main institutions of a property-owning democracy" (*JF*, p. 176). On Daniels's proposals, see his article "Health care needs and distributive justice" (1981); see also Daniels (1985) and (2007).

References

Ackerman, B. and Alstott, A. (1999) *The Stakeholder Society*, Yale University Press, New Haven, CT.
Alperovitz, G. (2004) *America Beyond Capitalism: Reclaiming Our Wealth, Our Liberty, Our Democracy*, John Wiley, Hoboken, NJ.
Andersson, J. (2006) *Between Growth and Security: Swedish Social Democracy from a Strong Society to a Third Way*, Manchester University Press, Manchester.

Archer, R. (1995) *Economic Democracy: The Politics of Feasible Socialism*, Clarendon Press, Oxford.
Berman, S. (2006) *The Primacy of Politics*, Cambridge University Press, Cambridge.
Campbell, J. (2003) *Margaret Thatcher: The Iron Lady*, Jonathan Cape, London.
Christiano, T. (2010) The uneasy relationship between democracy and capital. *Social Philosophy and Policy*, 27 (1), 195–217.
Cohen, G.A. (2008) *Rescuing Justice and Equality*, Harvard University Press, Cambridge, MA.
Cohen, J. (1989a) The economic basis of deliberative democracy. *Social Philosophy and Policy*, 6, 2–50.
Cohen, J. (1989b) Democratic equality. *Ethics*, 99 (4), 727–751.
Daniels, N. (1975) Equal liberty and the unequal worth of liberty, in *Reading Rawls: Critical Studies on Rawls' "A Theory of Justice"* (ed. N. Daniels), Basic Books, New York.
Daniels, N. (1981) Health care needs and distributive justice. *Philosophy & Public Affairs*, 10, 146–179.
Daniels, N. (1985) *Just Health Care*, Cambridge University Press, Cambridge.
Daniels, N. (2007) *Just Health: Meeting Health Needs Fairly*, Cambridge University Press, Cambridge.
DiQuattro, A. (1983) Rawls and left criticism. *Political Theory*, 11, 53–78.
Durbin, E. (1940) *The Politics of Democratic Socialism*, Routledge, London. (Reprinted as D. Reisman (ed.) (1994) *Theories of the Mixed Economy*, vol. 5, Pickering & Chatto, London.)
Dworkin, R. (2000) *Sovereign Virtue: The Theory and Practice of Equality*, Harvard University Press, Cambridge, MA.
Elster, J. and Moene, K.O. (eds) (1989) *Alternatives to Capitalism*, Cambridge University Press, Cambridge.
Esping-Andersen, G. (1990) *Three Worlds of Welfare Capitalism*, Princeton University Press, Princeton.
Freeman, S. (2007a) *Justice and the Social Contract: Essays on Rawlsian Political Philosophy*, Oxford University Press, New York.
Freeman, S. (2007b) *Rawls*, Routledge, New York.
Goodin, R.E. (2003) The end of the welfare state? in *The Cambridge History of Twentieth Century Political Thought* (eds T. Ball and R. Bellamy), Cambridge University Press, Cambridge.
Graetz, M.J. and Shapiro, I. (2005) *Death by a Thousand Cuts: The Fight Over Taxing Inherited Wealth*, Princeton University Press, Princeton.
Green, E.H.H. (2006) *Thatcher*, Hodder Arnold, London.
Hennessy, P. (2006) *Never Again: Britain 1945–1951*, 2nd edn, Penguin, London.
Jackson, B. (2005) Revisionism reconsidered: Property-owning democracy and egalitarian strategy in post-war Britain. *Twentieth Century British History*, 16 (4), 416–440.
Jackson, B. (2007) *Equality and the British Left: A Study in Political Thought, 1900–64*, Manchester University Press, Manchester.
Judt, T. (2010) *Ill Fares the Land*, Allen Lane, New York.
Kaus, M. (1992) *The End of Equality*, Basic Books, New York.
Krouse, R. and McPherson, M. (1988) Capitalism, "property-owning democracy," and the welfare state, in *Democracy and the Welfare State* (ed. A. Gutmann), Princeton University Press, Princeton.
Macmillan, H. (1938) *The Middle Way*, Macmillan, London. (Reprinted as D. Reisman (ed.) (1994) *Theories of the Mixed Economy*, vol. 4, Pickering & Chatto, London.)
Mandle, J. (2009) *Rawls's A Theory of Justice: An Introduction*, Cambridge University Press, Cambridge.

McSmith, A. (2010) *No Such Thing As Society: A History of Britain in the 1980s*, Constable & Robinson, London.
Meade, J. (1964) *Efficiency, Equality and the Ownership of Property*, George Allen & Unwin, London.
Meyer, T.with L. Hinchman (2007) *The Theory of Social Democracy*, Polity Press, Cambridge.
Miller, D. (1989) *Market, State and Community: Theoretical Foundations of Market Socialism*, Oxford University Press, New York.
Morgan, K.O. (1984) *Labour in Power, 1945–1951*, Oxford University Press, Oxford.
Moschonas, G. (2002) *In the Name of Social Democracy*, Verso, London.
Murphy, L. and Nagel, T. (2002) *The Myth of Ownership*, Oxford University Press, New York.
Nove, A (1983) *The Economics of Feasible Socialism*, George Allen & Unwin, London.
O'Neill, M. (2007) Death and taxes: Social justice and the politics of inheritance tax. *Renewal: A Journal of Social Democracy*, (15)4, 62–71.
O'Neill, M. (2008a) Three Rawlsian routes towards economic democracy. *Revue de Philosophie Économique*, (8) 2, 29–55.
O'Neill, M. (2008b) What should egalitarians believe? *Philosophy & Public Affairs*, (36) 2, 119–156.
O'Neill, M. (2009a) Enterprises et conventionnalisme: Regulation, impôt et justice sociale. *Raison Publique*, 10, 171–200.
O'Neill, M. (2009b) Liberty, equality and property-owning democracy. *Journal of Social Philosophy*, (40)3, 379–396.
Pierson, C. and F.G. Castles (eds) (2006) *The Welfare State Reader*, 2nd edn, Polity Press, Cambridge.
Przeworski, A. (1986) *Capitalism and Social Democracy*, Cambridge University Press, Cambridge.
Rawls, J. (1971) *A Theory of Justice*, Harvard University Press, Cambridge, MA.
Rawls, J. (2001) *Justice as Fairness: A Restatement* (ed. E. Kelly), Harvard University Press, Cambridge, MA.
Rawls, J. (2007) *Lectures on the History of Political Philosophy*, Harvard University Press, Cambridge, MA.
Rawls, J. and Van Parijs, P. (2003) Three letters on *The Law of Peoples* and the European Union. *Revue de Philosophie Économique*, 8, 7–20. Available online at: http://www.uclouvain.be/cps/ucl/doc/etes/documents/RawlsVanParijs1.Rev.phil.Econ.pdf (accessed September 7, 2011).
Roemer, J.E. (1994a) *A Future for Socialism*, Harvard University Press, Cambridge, MA.
Roemer, J.E. (1994b) *Egalitarian Perspectives: Essays in Philosophical Economics*, Cambridge University Press, Cambridge.
Ron, A. (2008) Visions of democracy in "property-owning democracy": Skelton to Rawls and beyond. *History of Political Thought*, (29)1, 89–108.
Sandel, M. (2000) What money can't buy: The moral limits of markets, in *The Tanner Lectures on Human Values, 21* (ed. G. B. Peterson), University of Utah Press, Salt Lake City. Available online at: http://www.tannerlectures.utah.edu/lectures/documents/sandel00.pdf (accessed September 7, 2011).
Sassoon, D. (1996) *One Hundred Years of Socialism: The West European Left in the Twentieth Century*, I.B. Tauris, London.
Scanlon, T.M. (2003) The diversity of objections to inequality, in *The Difficulty of Tolerance*, Cambridge University Press, Cambridge.
Scanlon, T.M. (2009) When does equality matter? Unpublished, Department of Philosophy, Harvard University. A version of February 2009 is available online via the Law School of the

University of California at Los Angeles: bit.ly/whenequality (accessed November 11, 2011).

Schweickart, D. (1979) Should Rawls be a socialist? A comparison of his ideal capitalism with worker-controlled socialism. *Social Theory and Practice*, 5, 1–27.

Schweickart, D. (1993) *Against Capitalism*, Cambridge University Press, Cambridge.

Schweickart, D. (2002) *After Capitalism*, Rowman & Littlefield, Lanham, MD.

Skelton, N. (1924) *Constructive Conservatism*, W. Blackwood, Edinburgh.

Walzer, M. (1983) *Spheres of Justice*, Basic Books, New York.

White, S. with R. Prabhakar and K. Rowlingson (2008) *How to Defend Inheritance Tax*, Fabian Society, London.

5
Property-Owning Democracy, Liberal Republicanism, and the Idea of an Egalitarian Ethos

Alan Thomas

Recent political philosophy has seen an upsurge of interest in republicanism and the suggestion that the republican tradition might offer new insights into a central concern of Anglo-American political philosophy, namely, egalitarianism (Dagger, 2006). Gerald Gaus has suggested that republicanism might be a source for a new, post-socialist account of distributive justice (Gaus, 2003, p. 64).[1] One question that I address in this chapter is how this claim relates to the most highly developed and widely accepted liberal form of egalitarianism, namely, Rawls's theory of justice.

I have previously argued that a fully satisfactory defense of Rawls's project, spanning his broader commitment to political liberalism as well as his more narrowly focused theory of justice, needs to add to his position elements from the superficially competing tradition of republicanism (Thomas, 2006, chapter 12). The resulting composite view, a liberal form of republicanism, seems to me to make the most sense of Rawls's overall commitments, even if some of those need to be selectively reinterpreted. In my view, then, there is significant convergence between one strand of the republican tradition and Rawls's work.[2] In this chapter I want to develop this argument further by demonstrating that a liberal-republican starting point is the most secure basis for Rawls's egalitarianism.[3] By "secure" here I mean something very specific: that *only* a basis in republicanism allows one decisively to address the most well-known critique of the content of Rawls's principles, namely, G. A. Cohen's critique of the difference principle. My aim is further to strengthen the case for this "liberal republican" reading of Rawls by arguing that without it, Cohen's critique cannot be answered.[4]

I am going to reinterpret Cohen's arguments against Rawls as an updated version of Marx's critique of liberalism in "On the Jewish Question" (Marx, 1844). I say "reinterpret" advisedly, as Cohen did not think that Marx's argument retained any force against Rawls's view.[5] Marx argued that classical liberalism gave all people formally equal status as citizens, expressed in terms of rights, but then permitted such high levels of material inequality that this merely formal notion was rendered practically ineffective. Marx's discussion is the canonical formulation of the claim that liberal "rights" merely mask exploitative social relations. In my view, Cohen's version of this critique ought be interpreted as follows: there is an inconsistency between the ethos of collective solidarity that is expressed by a society's adoption of Rawls's principles of justice and the special incentives that the second part of the second principle (the difference principle) permit.[6] Rawls permits departures from equality if those benefit the worst off. Cohen argues, however, that the attitude of those better-off, more talented, citizens who demand incentivization to market their labor at above the average reservation wage is morally no different from that of a kidnapper. They *make it the case* that they will not market their labor if not so incentivized. The only solution, Cohen urges, is a supplementary egalitarian ethos to compensate for this (inadvertent) internal inconsistency within Rawls's egalitarianism.[7] As I have noted, Cohen was exclusively focused on the corrosive impact that these incentives putatively have on the character of individuals; my complementary focus will be on the wider political dangers of the excessive concentrations of wealth in private hands that the unfettered operation of these incentives also seems to permit.

I will argue that appreciating the resources within Rawls's work for resisting these intertwined lines of critique leads one to endorse the specific form in which he saw his egalitarianism as being implemented, namely, a version of the property-owning democracy described by Cambridge economist James Meade.[8] This form of political economy has proved independently attractive to neo-republicans, too (Dagger, 2006). However, as I will show, this complete implementation of Rawlsian egalitarianism as a property-owning democracy is, in Rawls's view, subject to the democratic process. This has the consequence that any given society might choose not to adopt it. My conditional agreement with Cohen is this: if dispensing with the complete implementation of Rawls's view in a property-owning democracy (or in a market socialist regime) were permitted, then Cohen's critique of Rawlsian special incentives would be resurrected. But that would lead to the undermining of the fair value of the political liberties, in the face of substantial material inequality. This material inequality would allow the political domination of weaker agents by more powerful ones in precisely the way that Marx envisaged.

I therefore argue that a liberal republicanism that shares Rawls's fundamental commitment to effective political agency is a more secure basis for Rawls's own egalitarianism than Rawls's view taken alone. Rawls saw the threat from Marx's argument and put in place the "fair value proviso" for the political liberties to meet it. I will argue that this fail-safe device does not function as Rawls hoped that it would. The implementation of the republican value of freedom from domination will not compromise the fair value of the political liberties in the same way. Overall my aim is to argue that there is, indeed, a form of neo-republican political economy that should energize our commitment to equality.[9] However, it has been "hiding in plain sight"; it is Rawls's egalitarian view, but set in a novel context.

From Liberalism to Republican Liberalism

Political liberalism is a general, reflective account of politics underpinned by a distinctive contextualist epistemology (Rawls, 1971, 1993; Larmore, 1990; Thomas, 2006).

The defining problem for a political theory in the modern West is a deep-seated pluralism in reasonable comprehensive conceptions of the good. The basic aim of political liberalism is to specify a politicized conception of freedom and equality that is independent of any particular conception of the good as it is affirmable from within any such conception.

The recent work of Philip Pettit and Charles Larmore has demonstrated the extent to which political liberalism converges significantly with the superficially competing tradition of republicanism (Pettit, 1997, 1998, 2002, 2006; Larmore, 2001, 2004, 2008).[10] I say "superficially competing" as there are two distinct forms of republicanism discussed in contemporary political philosophy: an "Athenian" strand represented by Charles Taylor, Michael Sandel, and Richard Dagger, and a "Roman" strand represented by Skinner and Pettit. The former makes political participation part of the good life; the latter does not do so. Given that political liberalism argues that the modern problem of legitimacy in the face of pluralism cannot be solved by any political conception based on a single exclusionary conception of the good life, it is not surprising that it shares a common starting point with the Roman tradition of republicanism, whilst repudiating the Athenian tradition.

Norman Daniels points out that Rawls's most basic commitment is to "democratic equality," where the qualifier "democratic" picks out as important an aspect of his view, as does his more familiar emphasis on equality (Daniels, 2003; see also J. Cohen, 2003). Rawls's starting point is the implementation of an ideal, namely, how we express our nature as rational and reasonable beings in self-determination (but not the collective self-determination of the Athenian tradition of republicanism). We are interested in liberties, opportunities, and resources because our primary concern is effective political agency. This consists in the expression of our two moral powers, through our pursuit of our conception of the good, and through our standing as citizens in the context of a just society. Our standing as free and equal is understood as requiring, through justice as fairness, that those needs of ours have to be met that allow the exercise of our powers of rationality and reasonableness (Daniels, 2003, Cohen, 2003). In a well-ordered society, viewed as a single cooperative venture, it is mutually known that we have elected to express our standing as free and equal in a way that allows us to recognize each other's identical standing (Rawls, 1993, pp. 300–302). We acknowledge that other citizens are equal participants in the democratic determination of society: that is why, in agreeing on the principles of justice, we are securing the social basis of self-respect (Daniels, 2003). Daniels describes the relevant notion of equality thus: "Those who are worst off must continue to see themselves as worthy equals – in participation, in opportunity, and in the interest they have in pursuing their ends – or they will not be able to sustain their self-respect and thus their participation" (Daniels, 2003, p. 247–248).

This concept of democratic equality parallels the Roman republicans' belief in freedom as nondomination. Such freedom, the republican argues, is best secured under a regime of just law, constrained by a public process of democratic deliberation, in such a way that our commitment to these laws can be seen as expressive of an underlying norm of equal respect for persons (Larmore, 2004; Larmore, 2008, p. 183). Rawls noted the close parallel between his views and classical republicanism:

> At most there can be differences (with justice as fairness as a form of political liberalism) on matters of institutional design and the political sociology of democratic regimes. These differences, if there be such, are not by any means trivial; they can be extremely important. But there is no fundamental opposition because classical republicanism does not presuppose a comprehensive religious, philosophical or moral doctrine. Nothing in classical republicanism, as characterized above, is incompatible with political liberalism as I have described it. (Rawls, 1993, p. 205)[11]

Assuming that the general outline of Rawls's view is the more familiar, what are the main features of the less familiar republican tradition, in its Roman as opposed to Athenian form?

The republican believes in public-ness and self-government (Pettit, 1997; Dagger, 1997, 2006, p. 153). Self-government is not, however, the autonomous collective self-determination of the Athenian tradition, but the valuing of political participation as a means of prudently protecting each citizen's interests under a regime of just law. The identification of interests that the state will protect is itself a matter of free and open rational dialogue that requires two things: first, citizens able to reason collectively about the public good; second, a public willing to reshape the agenda of interests as society changes through time. The latter, in turn, requires free associations, civil society, and a public sphere (Thomas, 2006, chapter 12). For the republican, freedom under law requires a state (Larmore, 2004, 2008). The state makes law that is a precondition of freedom from arbitrary authority and is one source of our identification of the particular political community to which citizens owe allegiance. The republican citizen is identified with a particular regime of law, partly constitutive of the identity of a contingent, historically identifiable community.

One argumentative strategy in defense of republicanism notes that it has a clear-eyed view of the evils that come with the inception of a state. There are certain standing problems that all political views can recognize but which republicanism takes explicit measures to address: corruption, faction, and the abuse of political power in a form where some citizens come to dominate others. This notion of shared common evils is one powerful motivation for adopting republicanism, particularly given the modern history of the nation-state, with its unparalleled marshalling of resources and technology to pursue its goals.

In Rawlsian liberalism a concern for socioeconomic equality is lexically subordinated to the equal scheme of basic liberties; in the republican tradition a concern with economic inequality follows from the concern with freedom as nondomination. Economic inequality is of concern to republicans insofar as some citizens come to dominate others by the improper exercise of political power and insofar as it erodes the bonds of common citizenship (Dagger, 2006, p. 154). On any republican view, the state acts to preserve its self-governing citizens from arbitrary power (Pettit, 1997; Dagger, 2006). A concern with the potentially damaging role of private interests is also reflected in Dagger's argument that republicans will place a high instrumental value on the quality of public debate. He contrasts republicanism's sense of "public-ness" with that of merely private interests. However, he also notes that such institutional measures are only valuable, for the republican, if combined with a suitably wide distribution of civic virtue (Dagger, 2006, pp. 156–157).

Is there genuine convergence between political liberalism and Roman republicanism or simply a coincidence of general themes? The skeptic might note that one of the leading proponents of contemporary republicanism, Philip Pettit, emphasizes the differences between his views and those of Rawls throughout his book, *Republicanism* (Pettit, 1997). My view is the very opposite: that Pettit's view is only finally defensible if it incorporates aspects of Rawls's conception of justice as reciprocal fairness.

Pettit interprets Rawls as *solely* a theorist of negative liberty in a way that contrasts with Pettit's central organizing idea, which is that republicanism adds to Berlin's famous "two concepts" of liberty a third concept of liberty. This is the republican conception of freedom as nondomination. My view is that Pettit's contrast between his views and those of the political liberal are overdrawn. Furthermore, there is a lacuna in Pettit's defense of republicanism that can be filled in by supplementing what he says with considerations drawn from Rawls. According to Pettit, an individual enjoys freedom as nondomination when he or she enjoys the status of a free citizen who is robustly free from interference by the agency of another. However, in unpacking the distinction between the freedom-enabling "constraint" of law, and domination, Pettit makes essential reference to a person's interest or the idea of a common interest (Pettit, 1997, pp. 52–57). The wrong kind of interference with a person's choices or scope of action does not track the right interests; this is the crucial criterion for distinguishing freedom from domination. The latter notion, the idea of a common interest, is then explicated via the idea of a forum for the identification of interests (Pettit, 1997, pp. 187–202). It is the latter that offers a critical check on the identification of interests. With those interests established, the republican designs political institutions in such a way as to implement republican freedom as nondomination.

If that is the overall structure of Pettit's position then it involves a circular pattern of justification. It is true that Pettit's model of deliberative democracy represents the identification of an ideal, a critical check on forms of interference. It is, to use a metaphor, about the normative content of his theory and it is not about an institutional structure. But content and structure are interdependent in a republican theory in a way that introduces this circularity. One of the insights of the republican tradition as a whole, and Pettit's work in particular, is the emphasis on how institutions are not the instruments of normative policy causally responsible for its implementation (Pettit, 1997, pp. 106–107). They are, rather, constitutive of those normative policies via their implementation in institutional design. This does, however, raise an issue about how Pettit's contestatory model of democracy is to be designed in such a way that this inevitable circularity forms a virtuous, and not a vicious, circle of justification. The circularity is this: institutional design has a bearing on the identification of common interest; the latter determines what counts as freedom from arbitrary interference; freedom as nondomination is *implemented by* and *constitutes* institutional design (including the design of the contestatory forum). My diagnosis is that what is missing is a broader guarantee that the forum of contestatory democracy meets an independent standard of *being fair*. What guarantees that we have a virtuous and not a vicious circle here is the underwriting of the whole structure by an independent standard for the implementation of a fair procedure.

For this reason it seems to me that Pettit's republicanism can be appropriately supplemented by Rawls's theory of justice as reciprocal fairness. Whereas Pettit speaks of the common good, or of common interests, Rawls takes citizens to have two highest-order interests that shape their other interests. (This represents the priority of right over the good.) Their highest-order interest is in the full expression of their two moral powers of rationality and reasonableness. Operating under the constraints of the theory of legitimacy stated in *Political Liberalism*, the expression of these powers proceeds via the justification of a purely political doctrine, motivated by reasonable comprehensive conceptions of the good. This political doctrine takes the form of a model of citizenship. The connection with Pettit's ideas is that this model of citizenship represents a status. That status consists in being robustly free: in Pettit's terms, being an agent free from domination.

Suppose one takes Rawls's two highest-order interests as one's starting point in justification. The aim is then to construct an artificial device of representation, the original position, both to model and to give insight into our existing political ideas in such a way as to give rise to further, surprising, consequences. It is the whole model that expresses our conception of the free citizen, not a subpart within the model. The latter error is to confuse the standing of the parties in the original position with our standing as citizens, the people who use the model to gain insight into, and to explicate, our views on freedom, equality, and justice.

This contrasts with Pettit's approach: his interpretation of interests treats them as a good *within* the model of the original position. Given that he seeks only to establish that freedom from nondomination is an instrumental good, it suffices for him that it function as a primary good in Rawls's sense (Pettit, 1997, pp. 90–92). It is one of the goods chosen within the model of the original position on the same basis as all the other primary goods. (It is something you would want whatever else you wanted.) On the alternative view I am proposing here, we are not to see republican freedom as one primary good among others, established via application of Rawls's *thin* theory of the good. It is, on the contrary, one of those thick values that is implemented via Rawls's methodology, not a thin value represented within it as part of the original position. The whole device of the original position serves both to model, and to give insight into, our already existing political values, including freedom as nondomination. It does so in a way that avoids the concern about circularity that I have identified. We can do more than simply point to the contestatory forum and argue that whatever it identifies as a common avowable interest constitutes those interests. We can, instead, claim that this is true provided that the forum implements in its institutional design the independent value of fairness. We can identify the forum with the constitutional stage of Rawls's four-stage sequence of justification.

Supplementing Pettit's account with aspects of Rawls's view gives a different account of that in which freedom from domination consists. In his standard formulation, Pettit speaks of arbitrary interference as interference with choice that does not track a person's interests or the common good. However, he does on occasion use a different formulation: that arbitrary interference is unfair interference. That is, I think, precisely the point that, if articulated, would remove the circularity from his claims about the nature of avowable interests. However, that simply highlights the fact that Pettit is presupposing a theory of the nature of fairness. Rawls's conception of justice as reciprocal fairness can be used to explicate that idea in precisely the way that other critics of Pettit have emphasized. Both John Christman and Christopher McMahon have independently argued that Pettit's position presupposes a prior notion of fairness, even if not explicitly the Rawlsian conception of justice as fairness. (See also Christman, 1998, pp. 205–206; McMahon, 2005, p. 71.)

The position seems to me this. A synthesis of political liberalism and republicanism begins from the idea that our two moral powers are the basis of a derived political interest. That is the interest in being an effective political agent: of being able fully to express our moral powers. Effective political agency is expressed by a political ideal of citizenship as a status in which one is free from arbitrary domination. Republicanism supplies the theory of freedom; the conception of justice as fairness explains what it is for domination to be nonarbitrary. In its overall architectonic, this view is closer to Rawls; in its understanding of freedom as nondomination and of the constitutive role of institutional design it is closer to Pettit. In taking our most important political value to be effective political agency it seems to me to draw on both views. That is the kind of hybrid position that I refer to as liberal republicanism.

Perhaps we do not need to choose here. There is an irenic position that claims that there is no reason to see an incompatibility between Pettit's republicanism and Rawlsian political liberalism if the former offers insights on questions about which the second view is simply silent. Charles Larmore has recently given extended consideration to the compatibility, or otherwise, of his version of political liberalism and Pettit's republicanism and has broadened the discussion to include Rawls's views, too. He concludes that:

> Pettit's argument for aligning Rawls with the Hobbesian theory of freedom is unpersuasive. That does not mean . . . that we should abandon the idea of figuring out whether Rawls conceived of liberty as the absence of interference or as the absence of domination. Nonetheless, I believe not only that there emerges no clear-cut answer to this question, but also that we should not be surprised to come up with none. Only as a result of Pettit's own work are we in a position to formulate precisely the distinction between these two conceptions and to grasp their different implications. One might well expect that Rawls sometimes leaned toward the one, and sometimes toward the other. (Larmore, 2004, p. 111)

I think that is correct. Rawls noted that there can be more than one acceptable argument in support of his principles of justice. For example, he observed that "there can be . . . considerable differences in citizens' conceptions of justice provided that these conceptions lead to similar political judgements. And this is possible, since different premises can yield the same conclusion" (Rawls, 1971, p. 387–388). The question is whether Rawls's failure to draw the distinctions between three kinds of liberty that Pettit highlights marks sufficient reason to demarcate the two political theories as irreconcilably distinct. Larmore thinks not, and that seems to me a reasonable conclusion to draw.

I conclude that there is a deep convergence between political liberalism and republicanism. (Thomas, 2006, chapter 12) However, if political liberalism and republicanism share many features, one could also predict that they would share similar vulnerabilities. From the early reception of Rawls's views, critics from the political left argued that Rawls's priority of liberty was incompatible with the inequalities permitted by the difference principle.[12] The societies we live in are not Rawlsian, but we can generalize from them concerns we may continue to have even if our society was Rawlsian. One might, for example, observe that formal equality before the law can be undermined by individuals (whether persons or corporations) with very substantial socioeconomic power in a way that seems to substantiate Marx's critique of liberal rights. This is the threat that Michael Walzer describes in his theory of complex equality, constructed around the idea that domination in one sphere of goods ought not to be leveraged to generate domination in another sphere (Walzer, 1984). Money and power, he argues, are the two sphere-transcendent goods that are paradigmatically used to leverage domination in this way.

Importantly, as I will explain below, Rawls agreed. He seems to have found it very plausible to claim, as a generalization of political sociology, that without special protections for the political liberties the better off would act in concert to leverage their advantages over the worst off. The political process is, as Rawls put it, a "limited space," by which I take it he implies it is inherently competitive (Rawls, 1993, p. 328). The political liberties are particularly sensitive to "our social position and our place in the distribution of income and wealth" (ibid.). As I will describe in more detail below, the threat is either that the better off might make Rawls's theory unstable, by acting in concert to skew the political process toward their own interests, or that they might introduce an objectionable dependency into the theory by controlling the degree to which all other citizens are able to enjoy their liberties (all liberties, that is, not only the political liberties).

Rawls's response to this threat to the consistency of his view was fourfold: he introduced the "equal worth" of the entire scheme of basic liberties; he restricted this, practically, to the fair value of the political liberties; he made some policy suggestions, such as the state funding of political parties, that attempted to secure this fair value in a very restricted way; finally, and importantly for my discussion, he suggested that his entire package of views needed to be taken in the context of his complete political economy in the way that I will describe. However, as we shall see, the neo-Marxist concern about the overall structure of Rawls's position continues to attract adherents, notably G.A. Cohen, who argues that Rawls's remedies do not go far enough and, in fact, that Rawls inadvertently permits behavior that undermines the very ethos of collective solidarity on which his whole view depends.[13]

Before proceeding to exposit Cohen's critique in more detail, let me note at the outset that the republican shares a similar vulnerability. As Gerald Gaus insightfully notes, protection from domination via just law does not make the exercise of dominant power impossible: it simply makes it more costly (Gaus, 2003, p. 72). Some laws, such as pro-union legislation or anti-trust or anti-monopolistic legislation, directly undermines dominant economic positions, as Charles Larmore points out (Larmore, 2004, section 5). However, Larmore also stresses that most law is *not* like this: what troubles the republican is that some people have the capacity to dominate and law does not usually take that capacity away (Larmore, 2004.). It simply makes it costly to use it, but some very dominant actors might decide the cost was worth it. Larmore develops this point to argue that what matters for the republican is not sanctions per se, but what they express, namely a public and shared commitment to just law imposed by an impartially underwritten collective agency. That is importantly correct, but it also suggests that the republican, as much as Rawls, might want to take the preemptive step of undermining very dominant socioeconomic or powerful positions before they can arise. Thus both traditions are interested in the prospects for a liberal-republican political economy that *disperses* power and resources. Such an arrangement as preemptive dispersal thereby undercuts the capacities for domination that would otherwise accrue to very powerful agents who may attempt unjustly to leverage their domination in one sphere into another. But I should now deepen my description of why a neo-Marxist critique of Rawls seems compelling in the first place.

Cohen's Critique of Rawls

Several commentators have noted that Cohen's critique of Rawls is an updating of Marx's critique of liberalism, an interpretation that Cohen himself endorsed (Estlund, 1998; Sensat, 2003; Baynes, 2006; Cohen, 2008, pp. 1–2). Cohen focuses his critique not on the lexically prior basic liberties, nor on the first part of the second principle, guaranteeing equality of opportunity. He is concerned solely with the difference principle that permits departures from inequality insofar as they benefit the representative worst-off person and also permits any inequalities that do not worsen the position of the worst off even if they improve the position of the better off (Van Parijs, 2003).[14] Cohen, like some of Rawls's communitarian critics, argues that any political community that endorsed Rawls's two principles would show, by such endorsement, that it was committed to a high degree of social solidarity. However, the way in which Rawls permits inequalities inadvertently undermines this solidarity.

The thrust of Cohen's argument is directed at the behavior tolerated on the part of those who prove to be, in any given distribution, able by means of the natural lottery of both talent and the capacity for effort to make themselves better off in that distribution. They are legitimately incentivized not simply in a compensatory way (that is, for lengthy training or work that is particularly difficult) but also in the form of special incentives. Special incentives reflect their unwillingness to work unless they are rewarded either at, or above, the average level of reward. The problem, Cohen argues, is that the whole Rawlsian scheme is justified as one in which no member of a group is any more unequal than he or she need be, but in the scenario described these inequality-generating incentives are produced solely by the antisocial attitudes of the better off. They make it the case that they need to be incentivized in order to supply their labor; if they were not, they would withdraw it. But this is, morally, no different from the stance of a kidnapper. Rawls has, then, inadvertently permitted egoistic and selfish behavior that will corrode the ties of social solidarity, implicitly leading to the undermining of the very commitment to justice that selected the two principles in the first place.

I will call this latter argument Cohen's "overspill" argument: it involves some interpretative license, but it avoids the obvious rejoinder to Cohen that a society that implements Rawls's principles but lacks Cohen's ethos involves people acting wrongly, but not unjustly (Daniels, 2003). By extending some of Cohen's remarks about the idea of political community, we can explain why the problem he has identified would be more serious than a compromised acceptance of a society that was justly governed, but that contained many people whose commitment to justice was accompanied by other, selfish, motivations.[15] Cohen alleges that the internal inconsistency of Rawls's view would lead to a Rawlsian society unraveling over time, degenerating into an unjust one (Cohen, 2008, chapter 1, section III). However, Cohen further argues, this can be avoided if the citizens of that political community adopt an ethos of justice, located in their individual behavior and motivations, that compensates for this inadvertent loophole in Rawls's arguments. A society with such an ethos will be more just than one without as it will dispense with special incentives.[16]

Cohen's argument has been much discussed and I will not review those arguments here since I have done so elsewhere; for present purposes I want to isolate Cohen's main line of argument relevant to this paper (Thomas, 2005, forthcoming). It focuses on the scope of application of Rawls's theory of justice. One of Rawls's innovations was to apply his principle of justice to what he called the basic structure of society. Cohen argues that his motivation for this was poorly thought through, and was ambivalent between a focus on those structural features with a particularly deep impact on people's life chances, or those coercively imposed by the legal system. Moreover, Cohen continues, this institutional focus ignores the fact that "the personal is the political" and that Rawls's restricted focus tolerates "justice free zones" in our collective social life where the demands of social justice are simply discounted. (In particular, it is crucial for his overall argument that individual decisions to market one's labor on the labor market take place in such a "justice free zone.") The tainted incentives of the better off are simply exempted from the demands of justice by Rawls's institutional focus. As they continue to enrich themselves, even at no cost to the worst off, the incentive argument sounds less and less appealing: "Where the worst off are not too badly off, it looks more fanatical to assign absolute priority to their claims. But the stronger the case for ameliorating the situation of the badly off is, the more discreditable (if I am right) the incentive argument is on the lips of the rich" (Cohen, 1995b, p. 37). Cohen's case seems, then, superficially plausible. However, I think its real import is not that which Cohen suggests; there are resources within Rawls's egalitarianism for deflecting this critique, but only if one focuses not solely on the two principles but also on the exact form of a just political economy within which Rawls sought to implement them.

In pursuing this line of argument, one first needs to ask whether Rawls does really restrict the scope of his theory of justice solely to the basic structure. In answering this question one needs to bear in mind two points: Rawls does not believe that his principles apply everywhere. He is a normative pluralist and in that sense some parts of our lives are beyond justice. Parents do not commit an injustice if they do not regulate the distribution of resources between their children by those principles. Furthermore, there is a sense in which Rawls also believes that it is simply impossible for a person, no matter how motivated, to regulate every one of his or her economic transactions aiming solely to be just. Individual transactions are aggregated into a system whose scale, complexity, and emergent properties make that unfeasible. But, granted those two points, Cohen is still, in my view, mistaken about Rawls's views on the scope of justice (Thomas, forthcoming; see also Scheffler, 2005). Rawls applies his theory of justice to individuals via the basic structure: his structural focus is not a means of applying it to something other than individuals. His aim is not to make *all* our social relations, such as those in families, fair, but to make our relations *pervasively* fair, extending at least as far as individual decisions to market one's labor (Thomas, forthcoming).

What do I mean by pervasively fair? I mean that we can understand Rawls's remarks about the fact that one cannot directly regulate individual conduct in one of two ways: we can see individual transactions as simply indifferent to justice, with mechanisms located elsewhere to make the whole system of transactions just. An alternative reading argues that market transactions that presuppose justice are thereby made just, an interpretation strengthened by the observation that this is the *only* way that they can be made just (the feasibility argument). The first view permits those justice-free zones that require Cohen's compensatory ethos. The second view accuses Cohen of misinterpreting, as egoistic, economic behavior that is permissibly self-interested as it presupposes a commitment to justice. By so adjusting market transactions that their effects are rigged to be fair, we thereby show that we are presupposing justice, not discounting it. We acknowledge the demands of justice by committing ourselves to participation in a system with built-in systemic mechanisms that make the effects of transactions fair.

One ground for Rawls's approach is that he wants his rule of justice to be publicly specifiable, commonly known, and reflexively applied in a way that reflects his very broad understanding of the word "institution" (Williams, 1998).[17] However, these functional features of a rule do not change the fact that they ultimately apply to people; what they determine is that they apply to people in a certain way, that which Philippe van Parijs has called "motivation conscious institutional engineering" (Van Parijs, 2003, p. 230). Rawls's denial that individuals can, via their individual decisions, make a social process occurs in a particular context to make a specific point. That point is the implausibility of a libertarian account of justice given its neglect of the role of "background conditions" to individual transactions:

> The role of the institutions that belong to the basic structure is to secure just background conditions against which the actions of individuals and associations take place. Unless this structure is appropriately regulated and adjusted, an initially just social process will cease to be just, however fair and free particular transactions may look when viewed by themselves. (Rawls, 1993, p. 266)

This passage contains, in summary form, Rawls's best line of defense against Cohen (Thomas, forthcoming). The basic structure is constitutionally regulated: it establishes the values of a free community of equals within which individuals and associations may exercise their more particular liberties in the marketplace.

This line of response is very abstract and the best way to appreciate its force is to specify it in a particular way, namely, to show how Rawls's use of the idea of a property-owning democracy exemplifies this strategy of presupposing justice at the level of a society's complete property settlement. (This constitutes what Rawls called "adjusted" as opposed to "pure" procedural justice.) Cohen's critique can be undermined only if we focus on the specific form of its implementation in a property-owning democracy. I take it that it is no coincidence that, in his independent investigation of what could constitute a neo-republican political economy, Richard Dagger ends up endorsing a broadly similar set of proposals (but without addressing the question of its place in an overall scheme of justification that will be my focus below) (Dagger, 2006). I will now describe in more detail how this proposal is supposed to be worked out before turning to the different role that these ideas play in liberal and republican defenses of equality.

A Liberal Republican Political Economy

I noted above that there is independent interest in the idea of a neo-republican political economy (Gaus, 2003; Dagger, 2006). The idea is certainly worth exploring independently of the issue of the extent to which it allows one to address Cohen's concerns. Richard Dagger has argued that "There is enough agreement amongst neo-republicans to make a reasonably coherent conception of a civic economy possible; and second, that this conception will be attractive enough to appeal to anyone who is not already convinced that the market should rule in all matters or that it should figure in none" (Dagger, 2006, p. 152). This is a description that could equally have been applied to Rawls, who rejected free-market "laissez-faire" economic arrangements on the grounds that they permit morally arbitrary contingencies to determine competitive advantage and hence resource allocation. He also rejected a centralized command economy as a threat to the basic liberties, particularly the liberties of free association and choice of occupation. Unsurprisingly, the liberal republican concurs with both of these lines of reasoning. He or she will also concur with Rawls that once the basic liberties are in play it is important to secure their worth, but will disagree with Rawls that it is unrealistic to secure fair value for anything other than the political liberties.

The divergence between Rawls and the republican lies in how each view treats the kinds of economic inequality permitted by the difference principle. If such inequality can lead to accumulations of wealth that lead to domination and arbitrary power, such as when domination in one sphere is leveraged into domination in another, then the republican will seek to put protections in place to prevent such a capacity arising in the first place. For all these reasons (and others) Richard Dagger has concluded that a republican political economy will be, precisely, a Meade-style property-owning democracy of the kind that Rawls defended, a conclusion convergent with that of Stuart White (Dagger, 2006, p. 160; White 2003, and White in this volume). Freedom from arbitrary domination will be extended to the workplace; there will be a presumption in favor of workplace democracy and worker ownership; the nature of work must be consonant with, or at least not corrode, citizens' virtues (Hsieh, in this volume; O'Neill, 2008); economic decisions at the level of communities must be subjected to regulation; there must be substantial inheritance tax, a progressive taxation scheme of last resort, and a guaranteed basic minimum wage.[18]

The majority of these ideas are found in both Meade and in *A Theory of Justice* and they became an increasingly prominent part of Rawls's work up to and including *Justice as Fairness: A Restatement* (2001). Rawls is committed to the market and to private property, but he declares an official agnosticism over whether the means of production are to be privately or socially owned. However, if a capitalist society is one divided into a property-owning class and a class without property that is dependent solely on income from labor, then Rawls was never a capitalist (Krouse and McPherson, 1998, p. 80). In his ideal property-owning democracy, markets operate in a context structured pervasively by fairness. The state intervenes not only to supply public goods and to counter negative externalities but also to impose adjusted procedural justice. Some effects are the unintended outcomes of intended behavior; the vestigial (and comparatively unimportant) "invisible hand" part of Rawls's view is that the market, of its nature, decentralizes economic power and protects freedom of occupational choice. It does the former by protecting free association and free equality of opportunity and does the latter by giving rise to differential earnings (Rawls, 1971, p. 272).

But other effects are self-consciously engineered: the holdings of land and capital are widely dispersed; no sector dominates the control of resources; inheritance laws are strongly egalitarian; incentives are put in place for small savers; there is substantial public investment in the education system; and each citizen is given income from property and the opportunity to invest. The aim is to increase the supply of skilled labor and reduce dependence and exploitation in the labor market, with the effect that the residual incentives in the system can *all be viewed as compensatory* because their role has been transformed. In other words, with the full implementation of a property-owning democracy in place, the special incentives permitted by the difference principle that were the particular target of Cohen's critique have been significantly diminished. Paul Smith comments as follows:

> The idea that the equalization of property ownership would transform the labour market, by equalizing bargaining power and eliminating the economic coercion to accept drudge jobs at low pay and thus forcing employers to make all jobs attractive, all things considered, is crucial to Rawls's idea that, in a competitive labour market located in a just basic structure, income inequalities would tend just to compensate the costs of different jobs, that is, tend to equality, all things considered. (Smith, 1998, p. 225)

Rawls follows Meade in rejecting welfare state capitalism by equalizing property ownership prior to the corrective effects of progressive taxation or a guaranteed income. The consequences of this for Cohen's vestigial critique of Rawls are profound: "Economic equalization is more likely and reliably to be effected, as Rawls thinks, by institutions and policies that equalize bargaining power than by an egalitarian ethos restraining the exercise of unequal bargaining power (and egalitarian institutions and their distributional results are what, if anything, could produce an egalitarian ethos)" (Smith, 1998, p. 227).[19]

If we take Rawls's complete view, implemented so as to respect his lexically ordered principles of justice as fairness, then the special incentives to which Cohen objected are significantly reduced, even if not eliminated.[20] If both Rawls and the Roman republican can agree on this approach to egalitarianism, and I believe they should, why cannot the argument end there? I believe it cannot, not because of the content of their respective accounts of an egalitarian political economy (which are very similar) but because of the strategic rationale each can give for it. But before going into that issue in more detail, I should address the question whether Cohen has any rejoinder to the kind of view I have put forward to undermine his critique of special incentives.

In *Rescuing Justice and Equality* Cohen does consider this line of argument and responds to it (Cohen, 2008, pp. 386–387). Cohen objected that it is insufficient, as a response to his critique, to establish merely that special incentives will *tend* to be eliminated in a property-owning democracy. He endorses Krouse and McPherson's objection that Rawls does not prove that "in equilibrium the relative attractiveness of jobs will be equal, all things considered" because Rawls believes that natural endowments of talent will vary (Rawls, 1971, p. 305; Krouse and McPherson, 1998, p. 93). In my view this simply identifies points at which Cohen and Rawls are at cross-purposes: the aim of Rawls's view is to redress, not eliminate, inequality. Relatedly, Rawls's reference to the attractiveness of jobs concerns the attractiveness of the *job*. Its focus is not how attractive a job is to a given individual. That issue would be determined, on a case-by-case basis, by establishing how a person's talents determine a specific labor burden. Rawls simply has no interest in issues at that level of individual specificity: his justifications are always systemic and justified to representative classes of people and not to individuals.

Liberal and Republican Approaches to Effective Political Agency

I noted at the outset that I did not intend to introduce any artificial distance between political liberalism and republicanism since this paper is part of an ongoing project to develop their rapprochement. However, I do think that while both views exhibit similar strengths and vulnerabilities in how they conceive of the relative balance of liberty and socioeconomic justice, it is the republican component of liberal republicanism that offers a more secure context for Rawlsian justice. My argument, in summary, is that both Rawls's account of "ideal based" political theory and neo-republicanism are concerned with the citizens' effective political agency. However, Rawls's strategy threatens, inadvertently, to undermine this commitment from within by leaving the implementation of his property-owning democracy to the democratic process itself.

I have described the line of left-wing argument directed against Rawls that claims that the inequalities permitted under the difference principle will work, through time, to erode the fair value of the political liberties. (I have offered an interpretation of Cohen's critique of Rawls as the basis for a more specific development of that argument: untrammeled special incentives will lead to concentrations of private economic power that are a threat to the liberties.) I have explained how there are resources in Rawls's work to address it, but the neo-republican has a more direct argument to the same end. The primary goal of politics is to secure robust freedom under law and the values of participation, publicity in deliberation, and public virtue are all directed toward the defense of effective political agency. A distinctive form of neo-republican economy is capable of securing the conditions of effective political agency. That is a non-optional core to neo-republican policy. There is a very important substantive issue here: Rawls's ideal of democratic equality trades off the value of effective political agency against the democratic determination of which issues are to be settled by constitutional guarantees and which are to be subject to the legislative process (and potentially also judicial review). In order to explain my disagreement with Rawls over this issue I need to specify in some detail his account of the basic liberties and the potential threat to those liberties from the inequalities permitted by the difference principle.

The most complete account of the priority of the basic liberties occurs in Rawls's later work, notably in *Political Liberalism* (Rawls, 1993, lecture VIII). The parties in the original position select the basic liberties, and their priority, in an indeterminate form, knowing that they need to specify a more complete "fully adequate" scheme later in the process. Each justificatory stage proceeds in this way: the selection of a necessary but jointly insufficient set of conditions for the expression of our two moral powers (insufficient, that is, to determine the next justificatory stage). Overall we are trying to secure "the common and guaranteed status of equal citizens in a well-ordered democratic society" (Rawls, 1993, p. 335). Rawls's actual discussion of how what he calls the two basic cases of fundamental liberty have been worked out in the history of American constitutional law are, obviously, directly tied to that particular political tradition.[21]

Rawls explicitly states that the first principle of justice is to be "applied at the stage of the constitutional convention" (Rawls, 1993, p. 336). The parties to the original position now become the delegates in a way that reflects, solely, a change in their role: given a list of just and workable constitutions they select that one that is most likely to serve them best at the next, legislative, phase. The veil of ignorance is thinning at this point: this choice is made in the light of "general knowledge of how political and social institutions work, together with the general facts about existing social circumstances" (Rawls, 1993, pp. 336–337)

It is at this level of the institutional implementation of the first principle that the fair value proviso explicitly operates.[22] The constitution "is seen as a just political procedure which incorporates the equal political liberties and seeks to assure their fair value," and in this passage Rawls moves from process to product (Rawls, 1993). The constitution is implemented *as* guaranteed by the fair value proviso. This is hardly surprising given that the process was set up in such a way as to make this choice inevitable, but not wholly determinative of the next (legislative) stage. The difference principle does not appear until the third, legislative, phase:

> Although delegates have a notion of just and effective legislation, the second principle of justice ... is not incorporated into the constitution itself. Indeed, the history of successful constitutions suggests that principles to regulate economic and social inequalities, and other distributive principles, are generally not suitable as constitutional restrictions. Rather, just legislation seems to be best achieved by assuring fairness in representation and by other constitutional devices. (Rawls, 1993, p. 337)

This entire process is regulated by a special safeguard focused on the equal political liberties. They play a special role in "regulating the basic structure as a whole," a point that is crucial to understanding Rawls's treatment of their fair value. He identifies the key issue in this way: "Whether principles for the basic liberties and their priority are acceptable depends on the complementing of such principles by others that provide a fair share of (the material) means required for persons to advance their good" (Rawls, 1993, p. 325). This is Rawls's anticipation of the Marxist concern that "the basic liberties may prove to be merely formal" (Rawls, 1993, p. 325). The first distinction that he draws in addressing this concern is between a basic liberty and the *worth* of liberty (Daniels, 1989). Material inequality is to be interpreted not as a restriction on liberty, but on the worth of liberty, namely, "the usefulness to persons of their liberties" (Rawls, 1993, p. 326). Rawls then outlines how his view is supposed to work: given that the difference principle sanctions inequality, then of course it immediately follows that the worth of liberty varies across individuals as income and wealth are "all purpose" primary goods. If they are unequal, some people can realize their ends more effectively than others.

So some inequality in the worth of liberty comes with the territory, as it were. If justice as fairness is justified *at all* then some people's liberties are worth less than other people's. But this fact also comes with built-in compensation: a constitution secures equal basic liberties and equality of opportunity for everyone. The key question, then, is what happens when the difference principle is introduced? Certainly, one can conclude from the outset that Rawls's concern is one of degree. If one is to remain committed to justice as fairness at all, there is no reasonable goal of making the usefulness of everyone's liberties de facto equal. The issue, rather, is this: is the worth of some people's liberties impaired to an unacceptable degree, and for an unacceptable reason, once the inequalities permitted by the difference principle enter the frame? I think Cohen's argument gives us adequate reason to conclude that the answer to that will be "yes" (even if that is an argument he did not pursue against Rawls himself). Without the kind of macro-level restructuring of the holdings of capital that make the outcomes of market transactions fair, special incentives will have the kind of destructive impact on mutual solidarity that Cohen feared. They will, further, play a role in generating excessive concentrations of wealth and power in private hands. Those unfortunate consequences will eventuate unless background-adjusted procedural justice is in play. My concern is that it arrives too late in Rawls's sequence of justification.

Rawls clearly states that "it is beyond the scope of a philosophical doctrine to consider in any detail the kinds of arrangements required to insure the fair value of the equal political liberties" (Rawls, 1993, p. 327). But he notes their importance: without some set of measures of this kind "just background institutions are unlikely to be either established or maintained" (Rawls, 1993, p. 328). While it seems reasonable for Rawls not to go into details, he is at least prepared to indicate where he thinks the major threat to the fair value of the equal basic liberties lies in the following passage:

> One guideline for guaranteeing fair value seems to be to keep political parties independent of large concentrations of private economic and social power in a private-property democracy, and of government control and bureaucratic power in a liberal socialist regime. In either case, society must bear at least a large part of the cost of organizing and carrying out the political process and must regulate the conduct of elections. (Rawls, 1993, p. 328)

This passage indicates Rawls's main area of concern and his more specific discussions amplify it: he is particularly concerned with "fair and equal" access to political office in terms of both office holding and the conduct of elections.[23] Without the fair value proviso, the better off could certainly join forces to exercise a disproportionate influence: "we cannot be sure that the inequalities permitted by the difference principle will be sufficiently small to prevent this" (Rawls, 1993, p. 328). So, by Rawls's own lights, the fair value proviso has real work to do even in a Rawlsian society. He seems even more pessimistic about a non-Rawlsian society where there is no fair distribution of the "all purpose" means to pursue one's goals. This implies that Rawls believes that the better off usually *will* seek to leverage economic into political influence as a plausible generalization within political sociology.

It is at this stage of his argument that Rawls reveals why he only issues the fair value proviso for the political liberties, not the liberties as a whole: they regulate access to, and control of, the political process that in turn has implications for the regulation of the basic structure. So the threat is clear: in a non-Rawlsian society, the better off will have a tendency to exert undue influence over the political process in a way that will interfere with the operation of the regulation of the basic structure and hence background justice. Even in a Rawlsian society, where the worst off have equal liberties and their fair share of income and wealth, the "fair value" proviso has work to do.

So Rawls accepts that the unchecked operation of the difference principle will see the better off, acting in combination, leveraging their advantage to reduce the fair value of the political liberties to the less well off, by means of controlling access to the political process. In addition, this is a threat to the justice of the basic structure, introducing instability as a threat to the overall justification of justice as fairness. By an "overall justification" here, I mean the wider justification that takes into account the congruence of justice with the good and with the stability of a conception of justice.[24] The better off, when they act in concert, or when large concentrations of wealth develop, will not be public spirited when they take control of public office or the political process. Rawls does not explicitly state, but clearly implies, that they will act to further their narrow sectional interests.

I say the equal worth of *all* the basic liberties deliberately: I do think that there is a deeper point here that, uncharacteristically, Rawls has overlooked. Even if it is only reasonable to guarantee the fair value of the equal basic political liberties, *it is not solely those liberties that are threatened if that safeguard fails*. Because, recall, the grounds for prioritizing the political liberties was that they act as the gatekeeper for the regulation of the basic structure. When the liberties are undermined, and when the material inequalities permitted by the difference principle allow the better off to leverage their socioeconomic advantage to exert undue influence over political office and the political process, there is no reason to believe that their selfish pursuit of their own narrow interests will stop there. They will, of course, want to weaken the fair value proviso in order to maintain their ongoing advantageous control of the political process, but Rawls's disenchanted view of this kind of "soft despotism" suggests that this is not all that they will aim to do.

There are two issues here: the first concerns stability, the second an internal tension in Rawls's view. On the first view, if the envisaged process plays out, the operation of a generalization in political sociology will lead to a Rawlsian society ceasing to be Rawlsian. That will make the whole conception of justice as fairness unstable. On the second view, if the envisaged process plays out, the society will remain Rawlsian, but the failure of the fair value proviso will mean that equal basic political liberties will *not* imply a basic equal worth of all the liberties taken as a whole. This would be a systemic disadvantage to the worst off. Both options are a problem for Rawls, but the latter is the more serious problem.

But cannot Rawls easily reject the second problem? He might respond that the better off will not undermine the equal basic political liberties as a means to undermining the other basic liberties. That is because they are just as reciprocally protected by the equal basic liberties as any other person impartially considered. The better off will not act in a self-stultifying way against their own interests; they will not take away their *own* constitutionally guaranteed protections. So this argument lapses back into the first: the better off acting in concert would make a Rawlsian society unstable. After all, Rawls meticulously explains how the case for the priority for each of the basic liberties would be chosen in the original position by the parties solely concerned to advance the good of those that they represent (Rawls, 1993, pp. 310–318). Why would the better off act so as to undermine their own liberties? I do not think the issue is straightforward and can be so easily addressed.

It is of course true, as Rawls notes at the outset of the discussion, that if justice as fairness is justified at all then the *usefulness* of their liberties to the worst off is less than it is to those who are better off. But that is, as it were, a system-wide justification: it remains true that no one is any worse off than he or she need be compared to any other feasible arrangement. But, unfortunately, on the second scenario where the fair value proviso fails, the problem is that *how much* worse off the worst off are in making use of their liberties is under the political control of the better off. This is, for the republican, a form of objectionable dependence even if is, as it were, counterfactual. Whether or not a Rawlsian society remains Rawlsian has been put into the hands of the better off.

Furthermore, in this second scenario those positioned as the worst off are now systematically disadvantaged as a class. In the first, systemic, justification of justice as fairness the term "the worst off" is a non-rigid description that picks out those who happen to be in this relative position in any distribution. But in this second kind of systematic disadvantage, they are picked out as the group of people that they actually are. Those actually in that position can see the usefulness of their liberties eroded *exactly as Rawls said they would be* if the difference principle were to operate unchecked by the proviso in accordance with his very plausible principle of political sociology.

I would also add that I do not find it inconceivable that the better off, acting in concert, might act in a way that undermines the priority of liberty. After all, they might reason than if they sacrifice some loss of liberty for the sake of (for example) greater economic growth, then they might be more than adequately compensated, even if those who are worse off than them do worse in both respects.

Which argument do I want to pursue against Rawls? A combination of both arguments. It is a serious problem if, beginning from Rawls's own arguments, justice as fairness proves to be an unstable conception of justice. The failure of the fair value proviso leads to the better off gaining undue influence on the political process in a way that erodes the background fairness of society and also leads to a failure to implement justice as fairness. But even more damaging is the second line of concern: that within a society that remains fully Rawlsian, the operation of the difference principle and the failure of the fair value proviso leads the better off to gain undue influence over the political process, with two effects. The first is a republican concern about domination: that the better off control *how much* effectiveness the basic liberties of the worst off possess. The second concern is shared by liberal and republican alike as it concerns fairness: the better off are in a position to exploit their dominance selectively to reduce the effectiveness of the basic liberties. This affects everyone, but those who already worse off will suffer disproportionately more.

This all serves to highlight how very important the fair value proviso is to Rawls. Yet the positive proposals he puts forward to secure it are discouragingly thin. "Fair and equal access" to the political process means, in practical terms, the public funding of elections, restrictions on campaign contributions, and equal access to the media:

> How best to proceed is a complex and difficult matter; and at present the requisite historical experience and theoretical understanding may be lacking, so that we must advance by trial and error. But one guideline for guaranteeing fair value seems to be to keep political parties independent of large concentrations of private economic and social power in a private-property democracy, and of government control and bureaucratic power in a liberal

socialist regime. In either case, a society must bear at least a large part of the cost of organizing and carrying out the political process and must regulate the conduct of elections. (Rawls, 1993, p. 328)

Without these provisions Rawls believes that the political process will be held hostage by concentrated private economic power in the way that he has described. My reaction to this interpretation of the proviso is that given the plausibility and extent of the threat to his own view that Rawls identified, his proposals seem very weak and highly unlikely to achieve his own ends.[25]

The test, as always, is whether or not we have a "workable conception of justice which fits, on due reflection, our considered convictions" (Rawls, 1993, p. 327). It is hard not to conclude that Rawls's account seems both too much, and too little, focused on pressing concerns in the society with which Rawls was most familiar, namely the USA. It seems too much concerned with the political reality contemporaneous to Rawls because the wretched state of American democracy, which one insightful critic has described as a form of "inverted totalitarianism," seems at the very least served by urgent reform to the funding of elections and political parties along the lines of the fair value proviso (Wolin, 2008).[26] However, there seems a loss of perspective in the belief that this would *suffice* as an effective measure to make that society more Rawlsian. That optimism seems unrealistic from the perspective of other societies where the public funding of political parties and elections is taken as a matter of course. Those societies do not seem immune from the kind of threats to the fair value of the liberties that Rawls sought to address.

My judgment is that Rawls's identification of the threat to liberty by large concentrations of economic power in private, particularly corporate, hands is far more convincing than his ostensible remedy. He might reasonably ask how the republican intends to do better. My remedy is *not* one of the three alternatives that Rawls rejects: abandoning justice as fairness completely, abandoning the difference principle as one part of that overall view, or prioritizing some interest that requires additional protection over other interests.[27] The alternative view put forward here is not subject to any of Rawls's objections. The very same measures, of instantiating a republican political economy, in the form of a property-owning democracy, that we need to take to ensure that the operation of the difference principle does not corrode social relations in the way that Cohen identifies are the measures that will guarantee the equal worth of the liberties, without Rawls's version of the "fair value proviso."

Rawls's critique of the welfare state is directly relevant here (Rawls, 2001, pp. 137–140). One of the grounds on which Rawls believed that welfare state capitalism is objectionable is that it leaves the economy under the control of small groups that exercise disproportionate economic power.[28] One of its damaging consequences is to produce a demoralized underclass who do not have an equal chance of influencing the political process and hence have no say in their own fate. (Rawls adds that laissez-faire capitalism is even worse and a socialist command economy worse still.) If our only options as just political economies are a property-owning democracy or a democratic socialist regime, why are those considerations not deployed at this earlier stage in Rawls's argument in order greatly to strengthen the fair value proviso?

Am I, then, suggesting the alternative of guaranteeing the worth of *all* the basic liberties in a way that Rawls alleges is irrational, superfluous, or socially divisive? No, I am not. My republican response is, rather, to "cap" the inequalities permitted by the difference principle and to prevent large concentrations of wealth from arising in the first place. Those two aims are realized by a property-owning democracy. If those permissible inequalities under the difference principle are unchecked, then the political dangers that Rawls identifies are real. But his method of redress, the fair value proviso for the equal basic liberties, arrives too late from my point of view and is any case ineffective. (This exactly parallels the way in which welfare state redistribution struck the later Rawls as both too late and as ineffective in a just society.) The better strategy is to preempt these issues and, as a side benefit, to flatten out the inevitable difference in the usefulness of the liberties to citizens by flattening out permissible inequalities across the system as a whole.

The Republican Alternative

My concerns over Rawls's failure to protect the basic liberties, not simply the political liberties, reflects Cohen's influence. It reflects the *conditional* correctness of his argument, even if I have had to complement it with a more traditional Marxist concern over the compatibility of substantial material inequality and political liberty. My view is that inadvertently, in his attempt to secure the fair value of political liberty, Rawls has left that fair value hostage to democratic deliberation after the four-stage sequence is complete. Without an endorsement of the political economy of a property-owning democracy, morally tainted special incentives will be tolerated that will undermine the very basis of social solidarity that is expressed by our commitment to all three principles. (As Cohen's critics emphasize, those principles come as a holistically connected package.)[29] A democratic society might, then, choose to implement a property-owning democracy or it might not. If not, then we will not be able to rig the outcome of market decisions so as to make them fair, and Cohen's critique of Rawls will be back on track. That will lead either to a society that is justly governed, but not just throughout individual motivations, or, I have argued, to a society in which the very commitment to justice as fairness will be undermined. So whether Rawls's view is self-undermining depends on whether or not due democratic deliberation decides so to undermine it.

I submit that is an uncomfortable position for Rawlsians to occupy. The aim of the view was, above all, to allow those who are the worst off to remain free and equal citizens bound up in a system of mutual and reciprocal recognition even when material inequality is permitted. But on the uncomfortable option now before us, a society can democratically decide not to implement the full range of measures implicit in a property-owning democracy, such that adjusted procedural justice cannot be left to "take care of itself" (as Rawls hoped it would). Substantial material inequalities will thereby be permitted that undermine the fair value of political liberty. But that value ought to be non-negotiable: it is the practical expression not of a mere status, but of the exercise of a capacity, namely, our two moral powers. Rawls might have mistakenly believed that this option could be ruled out by his own version of Cohen's argument:

> Yet sometimes the circumstances evoking envy are so compelling that given human beings as they are, no one can reasonably be asked to overcome his rancorous feelings. A person's lesser position as measured by his index of objective primary goods may be so great as to

wound his self-respect: and given his situation we may sympathize with his sense of loss. Indeed, we can resent being made envious, for society may permit *such large disparities in these goods that under existing social conditions these differences cannot help but cause a loss of self-esteem* ... Since self-respect is the main primary good, the parties would not agree, I shall assume, to count this sort of subjective loss as irrelevant. (Rawls, 1971, pp. 534, 468, emphasis added)

In other words, excessive distance between the worst off and the better off will harm the self-respect of the former and self-respect is a primary good. But that argument is only available to Rawls *after* the background context of adjusted procedural justice is in play; as a response to Cohen, taken alone, it begs the very question at issue, namely, will the special incentives permitted under the difference principle make a just Rawlsian society unstable? Given a plausible generalization in political sociology that Rawls accepted, and given the weakness of the fair value proviso, it seems to me that it will. Rawls cannot allow this inadvertent inconsistency in his own principles; but he can only avoid it through the full implementation of his conception of justice in the kind of political economy exemplified by a property-owning democracy. Only that background prevents tainted special incentives arising in the first place.

The overall effect of Rawls's package of principles is to mitigate the effect of the natural lottery of talents, not to redress it. My concern is solely with the one component of Rawls's view that is non-negotiable, which is our standing as free and equal citizens, bound in a political community by mutual recognition and self-respect. The fair value of the political liberty is threatened to an unacceptable degree even within the range of mitigated inequalities unless the complete implementation of Rawls's scheme is adopted by a given society. However, in his irenic attempt to base a theory of justice on as wide a range of intuitions as possible, Rawls's first principle and first part of the second principle are secured in the constitution; the difference principle is introduced at the legislative phase (partly because their interpretation is subject to a great deal of reasonable disagreement and also because of Rawls's commitment to the institution of judicial review). But at that stage, without adjusted procedural justice, special incentives have been permitted in a way that erodes the quality of social relations and leads to damagingly large accumulations of economic power. That rebounds to threaten the basic liberties in just the way that Rawls feared. Rawls's measures to ensure fair value are clearly inadequate but then any other set of measures implemented at this stage are already in the business of "damage control," but not preemptive dispersion.

Can the republican, and *ex hypothesi* the liberal republican, do better? I believe that he or she can. The solution, in my view, is to return to the overall aim of securing our standing as free and equal citizens by eliminating arbitrary domination. If we prioritize the republican emphasis of the liberal-republican reading of Rawls, we can argue that the specific policies implemented after the four-stage sequence not be allowed to undermine, even via unintended side effects, the liberties specified and mutually adjusted during the constitutional stage of the sequence. We need to reconceive of the four-stage sequence, so that the fair value of political liberty is not undermined.

How is this result to be achieved? In Pettit's version of republicanism, his institutional focus is not derived from a prior, instrumental, concern with freedom as nondomination. He emphasizes that institutional design in the republican tradition is *constitutive* of nondomination. This is separate from his account of deliberative politics, the actual contested process by which we identify those "avowable common interests" that the state's implementation of a just regime of law is intended to track. It is a way of securing a "constitutional provision of non-domination" (Pettit, 1997, pp. 67–68, 95). That, in turn, reflects the most important, and distinctively republican, common avowable interest: "An outstanding matter of common interest amongst people is precisely the interest they each have in avoiding domination by others" (Pettit, 1997, p. 289).

My proposal, then, is that republicanism offers a more secure basis for the fair value of political liberty because whatever institutional measures are required for its implementation and protection are identical to those that secure freedom as nondomination. Freedom as nondomination is the republican's (and political liberal's) implementation of effective political agency. On that basis the implementation of a property-owning democracy can form part of the institutional design of a society, allowing the implementation of Rawls's two principles in a way invulnerable to Cohen's neo-Marxist critique.

It might seem to strain credulity to require such detailed macroeconomic policies as those implemented in Meade's property-owning democracy to take on the status of constitutional fundamentals. Agreed, but we do not have to present the issue in quite those terms. One can, instead, make a republican case for not simply the basic liberties and the priority of political liberty to the other liberties being a constitutionally secured fundamental, but also the fair value of political liberty itself. The question then is in what does that safeguard consist? We have good reason to place a positive right in the constitution not to welfare payments, but to an inalienable capital holding for each citizen to reduce his or her dependence on income from labor. We can then propose various institutional schemes for the realization of further republican values, such as wide dispersal of property, a scheme of employment subsidies, and so on. Taken together we might then seek single schemes of implementation that would jointly realize these values, of which, clearly, Meade's scheme would be one well-developed proposal.

The aim, then, is not to enshrine the Rawls/Meade view, in all its details, in the constitution but to put in the constitution what one might call a "task specification" for the legislative and executive phases: institutional structures that secure the fair value of political liberty not by giving everyone a right to welfare, but by giving everyone a right to an inalienable capital holding. Pettit believes that a good polity can secure freedom as nondomination alone in a way that excludes Rawls's package of lexically ordered principles; I think that is, as Charles Larmore has demonstrated, a mistake and I have agreed with this diagnosis (Larmore, 2004, 2008). Both political liberalism and republicanism share an evaluative commitment to equal respect for persons. But the republican strategy that Pettit follows seems to me, for the reasons I have given, to suggest a liberal-republican basis for Rawls's own egalitarian commitments more secure than that provided by political liberalism taken alone.

Conclusion

Political liberalism does not require supplementation by an "ethos of justice," as it already expresses one. What it does require is supplementation by a liberal republicanism that explains the priority afforded to the basic liberties in terms of the basic commitment to understanding freedom as nondomination. A corollary of this view is that the fair value of the political liberties reflects a basic commitment to effective political agency. Democratic politics cannot be allowed to be responsible for the undoing of this commitment by permitting substantial inequalities that permit the domination of the worst off by very powerful agents. Yet this commitment is threatened unless that which Cohen identifies as a "justice-free zone," in which special incentives are permitted, can be redescribed as presupposing, not discounting, the demands of justice. That requires a particular kind of political economy: a property-owning democracy. That requirement, then, is defended by the liberal republican as basic to the defense of effective political agency. The upshot is that the fair value of political liberty will have to be guaranteed in a constitution. A scheme of implementation for those goals that effectively realize it will constrain democratic deliberation. Only then will the basis of Rawls's two principles of justice be secure.[30]

Notes

1. Not a development, I should add, of which he approves!
2. In retrospect, some of the earlier discussions of the relationship between liberalism and republicanism generated more heat than light precisely because they were focused on whether one view was correct to the exclusion of the other. Such papers as Burtt (1993a, 1993b), Herzog (1986), and Patten (1996) all protested that attempting to write the history of political reflection, particularly in the American tradition, in a way that downgraded Locke and elevated "the Machiavellian moment," was implausible. Burtt and Herzog further argued that there were no resources in contemporary reflection for the recovery of republicanism, pointing to the role in the tradition of the all-powerful founder who imposes republicanism in a transformative way. Patten argued that republicanism added nothing to the content of the liberalism of Rawls and Dworkin (but he explicitly exempted Philip Pettit's work from his critique). More recent work, particularly that of Philip Pettit and Charles Larmore, has helpfully dropped this issue of mutual exclusion.
3. Taken together they confirm that a form of republicanism can say something novel about the justification for a view of distributive justice, but the content of that egalitarian theory is not novel: it is Rawls's original view, interpreted precisely as he intended it to be interpreted. I will argue that it is Rawls's fair value proviso that fails to protect the content of his principles in the way that he envisaged.
4. Early papers that argued for a rapprochement between liberalism and republicanism were Sunstein (1988) and Michelman (1988); those papers were not always sensitive to the distinction between the Athenian and Roman traditions within republicanism that are discussed further below. That distinction has been at the forefront of recent work; it separates, for example, such important statements of the republican tradition as and Pettit (1997) and Dagger (1997).
5. As Martin O'Neill reminded me, in Cohen (2008, p. 385) there is an "in principle" *agreement* with Rawls's view that material inequality is compatible with equal basic liberty and the fair value of the political liberties. I think this point needs to be handled carefully. Anyone sympathetic to a Rawlsian view has to believe that the kinds of inequalities permitted by the difference principle do not *automatically* undermine the basic liberties and their fair value, on pain of taking any Rawlsian view to be internally self-undermining *ab initio*. My argument here is that they do not do so only if a constitutional guarantee for an

egalitarian scheme is secured. (Rawls resisted placing such a guarantee within the constitution.) That egalitarian scheme will be very similar to a property-owning democracy; whatever the details, any such scheme must work to preempt the concentration of wealth in private hands by widely dispersing the ownership of capital. In that sense I, too, agree with Rawls "in principle" while disagreeing with the particular way in which he treated the fair value of political liberty. But I concede that Cohen seems exclusively focused on the personal vices that he thought Rawls's difference principle permitted and less concerned with the social impact of those vices on the fair value of the political liberties (and liberty as a whole).

6. I exercise some interpretative license here on the grounds that Cohen (2008, p. 45) is hostile to "soggy mega-Gemeinschaftlichkeit," invoking, instead, Rawls's notion of "ties of civic friendship" (ibid.) However, Rawls connects "civic friendship" to fraternity and solidarity, for example at Rawls (1999, pp. 90–91). In defense of my interpretation I would cite Cohen's contrast between "a *bargaining* conception and a *community* conception of social relationships" (2008, p. 82, emphases added). I discuss these issues further in Thomas (forthcoming).

7. Cohen's restriction of his critique to individual motivations means that the ultimate normative point of his critique of Rawls turns out to be that his egalitarian ethos will result in citizens accepting a very high taxation rate (Cohen, 2008, pp. 70, fn40, fn41). Cohen states in a footnote added for his 2008 book that "My use of the doctor example gives the false impression that the principal effect of an egalitarian ethos would be to induce agents to forego what they can get on the market. Such an ethos would indeed in certain circumstances have that effect, but a more important relevant effect of an egalitarian ethos *is to induce agents to accept very high rates of taxation*" (Cohen, 2008, p. 70, fn40, emphasis added). See also the discussion at (Cohen, 2008, pp. 122–123). This is consistent with Cohen's persistent misunderstanding of Rawls as a high-taxing welfare state theorist (for which see, for example, Cohen, 2008, pp. 123, 202–203). However, I hope that by connecting his critique to the traditional democratic socialist concern that high levels of inequality threaten liberty, the normative point of his critique can be made sharper than simply inducing Scandinavian levels of income tax within the (unchallenged) framework of the redistributive welfare state.

8. Strictly speaking, Rawls leaves it to the democratic process to select between a property-owning democracy or a form of market socialism as the only two kinds of political economy compatible with justice as fairness. A complete argument requires a demonstration of why a property-owning democracy is superior to market socialism; for reasons of scope I cannot go into that issue here.

9. So my conclusion harmonizes with that of Dagger (2006).

10. This is Larmore's avowed aim; Pettit's work, in my view, shows how this convergence is possible, but it is not his aim to demonstrate it. He tends to place artificial distance between his own view and Rawls's but, as Larmore shows, there is no real conflict here and Pettit is making more precise issues that are in Rawls simply indeterminate. As Larmore points out, Rawls had no reason to draw the sharper distinctions that Pettit draws (Larmore 2004, 2008).

11. It is ironic that Rawls notes in this passage that the only difference between his views and classic republicanism is the political sociology of democratic regimes, as my main aim here is to argue that these will, in fact, be identical.

12. In a prescient paper Arthur DiQuattro pointed out the interpretative errors on which some of the critiques depended: DiQuattro (1983).

13. However, as I have noted, Cohen did not extend his critique to address the concern that the levels of material equality permitted by the difference principle undermined the fair value of the liberties: "I do not think, and I do not think Rawls thought, that ensuring that people's

opportunities to hold office and exercise political influence are substantially independent of their socioeconomic position requires substantially equal material holdings" (Cohen, 2008, p. 385). But see footnote 5 above.

14. This is Rawls's understanding of an equal distribution where no one is any worse off than he or she need be and the requirement of efficiency has been taken into account.

15. As Daniels puts it: "we (and Rawls) can say that some such choices [i.e., those of antisocial incentive seekers] are *wrong but not unjust*. They might be just plain greedy or selfish, and there is nothing to stop anyone from raising these moral criticisms of such choices" (Daniels, 2003, p. 269, emphasis added). This is a particularly powerful ad hominem critique of Cohen as it works within his sharp dichotomy between "the political" (restricted in the scope of justice to the basic structure) and "the personal" (including personal decisions to market one's own labor). That dichotomy is challenged in Thomas (forthcoming). On Daniels's view Cohen's critique of Rawls misfires because the scenarios he describes involve a just society that contains other ethically objectionable motivations, but the demands of justice have been fully met.

16. It must be conceded that this critique seems more effective against the Pareto arguments of the first edition of *A Theory of Justice*, arguments from which Rawls tactically withdrew in subsequent revisions (Rawls, 1971, 1999).

17. He takes the term to refer to "a public system of rules which defines offices and positions with their rights and duties, powers and immunities, and the like" (Rawls, 1971, p. 5). He gives as examples "games and rituals, trials and parliaments, markets and systems of property. An institution may be thought of in two ways: first as an abstract object, that is, as a possible form of conduct expressed by a system of rules; and second, as the realization in the thought and conduct of certain persons at a certain time and place of the actions specified by these rules" (Rawls, 1971, p. 55). See also the discussion of the basic structure in Rawls (1993, lecture VII).

18. This list requires some caveats that I have omitted for the purpose of exposition here. First, Dagger is unhappy with the emphasis on inheritance tax if this interferes with the justice of the family (Dagger, 2006). Second, whether or not a Rawlsian scheme is best implemented via subsidies paid to those who occupy the worst-off representative group (such as unskilled workers) or via a guaranteed minimum wage has been interestingly discussed by Van Parijs (2003). It seems to me that a republican would offer further arguments for the former option than those considered by Van Parijs: if workplaces have been democratized then they are a further context for the exercise of civic virtue and it is better for all citizens to have the opportunity to so participate than not.

19. Smith goes on to add, "There is a certain irony in the fact that it is the liberal Rawls who conceives economic equalization effected by a structure of institutions to equalize economic bargaining power and it is the Marxist Cohen who conceives equalization effected by morality restraining the exercise of unequal power" (Smith, 1998, p. 227). That I have, on behalf of republicanism, extended Cohen's argument to Marx's traditional concern about the threat that material inequality posed to the liberties in a way contrary to Cohen's own intentions simply deepens this irony.

20. Just as Smith comments that under the fully implemented scheme "income inequalities ... tend to equality" (Smith, 1998, p. 225), my claim is not that special incentives are eliminated. They are, however, significantly reduced and that, combined with the claim that individuals in a Rawlsian society presuppose justice in their decisions to market their own labor, suffices to address Cohen's concerns.

21. This reflects the methodological precept on page 293: "a list of the basic liberties can be drawn up in two ways: One way is historical, we survey the constitutions of democratic states

and put together a list of liberties normally protected, and we examine the role of these liberties in those constitutions which have worked well." So we can assume that Rawls is discussing the American constitutional tradition either because it is his own, or because he thinks it has "worked well" in securing the basic liberties.

22. "In sum, then, the constitution specifies a just political procedure and incorporates restrictions which both protect the basic liberties and secure their priority" (Rawls, 1993, p. 339).
23. He draws an interesting analogy between this fair value proviso and the first part of the second principle guaranteeing fair equality of opportunity: "This notion of fair opportunity parallels that of fair equality of opportunity in the second principle of justice" (Rawls, 1993, p. 327). Stephen Wall comments, "A fair opportunity to achieve some good is realized when all persons, who are equally talented and equally motivated, have an equal chance to acquire it" (Wall, 2006, p. 248).
24. Not only is stability an important value for Rawls; the basic liberties are involved in a special way with securing it (Rawls, 1993, p. 316).
25. I have already noted that Cohen does not share this concern; for a similarly optimistic endorsement of an "insulation" strategy that protects the fair value of the liberties from material inequalities, see the chapter by O'Neill in this volume.
26. Wolin means something precise by "inverted totalitarianism." "Although the concept of totalitarianism is central to what follows, my thesis is not that the current American political system is an inspired replica of Nazi Germany's [totalitarianism]" (Wolin, 2008, p. ix). Wolin contrasts the total mobilization of society by the state in conventionally totalitarian regimes with an inverted form of totalitarianism that is "only in part a state-centered phenomenon. Primarily it represents the political coming of age of corporate power and the *political demobilisation of the citizenry*" (Wolin, 2008, p. x, emphasis added).
27. Rawls gives these three arguments against protecting the fair value of all liberty, not just the political liberties, in *Political Liberalism* (1993, p. 329). He alleges that the proposal is either irrational, superfluous, or divisive.
28. For an insightful discussion of Rawls's critique of welfare state capitalism see Martin O'Neill's chapter in this volume (Chapter 4).
29. As emphasized by Smith (1998), Estlund (1998), Daniels (2003), Van Parijs (2003), Tan (2004), and Baynes (2006) in the course of developing their respective critiques of Cohen.
30. I am grateful to Kathryn Brown for her help with this chapter and to both Stuart White and Richard Dagger for very kindly taking some trouble to send me offprints of their papers. In both cases I learnt a very great deal from their work. My indebtedness to Charles Larmore's recent work on the convergence between his own political liberalism (and Rawls's parallel theory) and republicanism should be apparent throughout. I am grateful both to Charles and to the editors of this volume, Martin O'Neill and Thad Williamson, for very helpful comments on this chapter that greatly improved the final result.

References

Baynes, K. (2006) Ethos and institution: On the site of distributive justice. *Journal of Social Philosophy*, 37, 182–196.
Burtt, S. (1993a) The politics of virtue today: A critique and a proposal. *American Political Science Review*, 87, 360–368.
Burtt, S. (1993b) Civic virtue and self-interest. *The American Political Science Review*, 89, 147–151.

Christman, J. (1998) Review of Philip Pettit: *Republicanism: A Theory of Freedom and Government. Ethics*, 109, 202–206.
Cohen, G.A. (1995) Incentives, inequality and community, in *Equal Freedom* (ed. S. Darwall), University of Michigan Press, Ann Arbor, pp. 331–398.
Cohen, J. (2003) For a democratic society, in *The Cambridge Companion to Rawls* (ed. S. Freeman), Cambridge University Press, Cambridge, pp. 86–138.
Cohen, G.A. (2008) *Rescuing Justice and Equality*, Harvard University Press, Cambridge, MA.
Dagger, R. (1997). *Civic Virtues: Rights, Citizenship, and Republican Liberalism*, Oxford University Press, Oxford.
Dagger, R. (2006) Neo-republicanism and the civic economy. *Philosophy, Politics and Economics*, 5, 151–173.
Daniels, N. (1989) Equal liberty and unequal worth of liberty, in *Reading Rawls: Critical Studies on Rawls' A Theory of Justice* (ed. N. Daniels), Stanford University Press, Stanford, pp. 253–281.
Daniels, N. (2003) Rawls's complex egalitarianism, in *The Cambridge Companion to Rawls* (ed. S. Freeman), Cambridge University Press, Cambridge, pp. 241–276.
DiQuattro, A. (1983) Rawls and left criticism. *Political Theory*, 11, 53–78.
Estlund, D. (1998) Liberalism, equality, and fraternity in Cohen's critique of Rawls. *Journal of Political Philosophy*, 6, 99–112.
Gaus, G. (2003) Backwards into the future: Neorepublicanism as a postsocialist critique of market society. *Social Philosophy and Policy*, 20, 59–91.
Herzog, D. (1986) Some questions for republicans. *Political Theory*, 14, 473–493.
Krouse, R. and McPherson, M. (1998) Capitalism, "property-owning democracy" and the welfare state, in *Democracy and the Welfare State* (ed. A. Gutmann), Princeton University Press, Princeton, pp. 79–106.
Larmore, C. (1990) Political liberalism. *Political Theory*, 18, 339–360.
Larmore, C. (2001) A Critique of Philip Pettit's republicanism. *Nous: Philosophical Issues*, 11, 229–243.
Larmore, C. (2004) Liberal and republican conceptions of freedom, in *Republicanism: History, Theory, and Practice* (eds D. Weinstock and C. Nadeau), Frank Cass, London, pp. 96–119.
Larmore, C. (2008) The meanings of political freedom, in *The Autonomy of Morality*, Cambridge University Press, Cambridge, pp. 168–195.
Marx, K. (1844) On the Jewish question. *Deutsch-Französische Jahrbücher*.
McMahon, C. (2005) The indeterminacy of republican policy. *Philosophy & Public Affairs*, 33, 67–93.
Michelman, F. (1988) Law's republic. *Yale Law Journal*, 97 (8), pp. 1493–1538.
O'Neill, M. (2008) Three Rawlsian routes towards economic democracy. *Revue de Philosophie Économique*, 8, 29–55.
Patten, A. (1996) The republican critique of liberalism. *British Journal of Political Science*, 26, 25–44.
Pettit, P. (1997) *Republicanism: A Theory of Freedom and Government*, Oxford University Press, Oxford.
Pettit, P. (1998) Reworking Sandel's republicanism. *Journal of Philosophy*, 95, 73–96.
Pettit, P. (2002) Keeping republican freedom simple: On a difference with Quentin Skinner. *Political Theory*, 30, 339–356.
Pettit, P. (2006) The determinacy of republican policy: Reply to McMahon. *Philosophy & Public Affairs*, 34, 275–283.
Rawls, J. (1971) *A Theory of Justice*, Harvard University Press, Cambridge, MA.
Rawls, J. (1993) *Political Liberalism*, Columbia University Press, New York.

Rawls, J. (1999) *A Theory of Justice*, rev. edn, Harvard University Press, Cambridge, MA.

Rawls, J. (2001) *Justice as Fairness: A Restatement*, Harvard University Press, Cambridge.

Scheffler, S. (2005) The division of moral labour. *Proceedings of the Aristotelian Society Supplementary Volume*, supplementary volume 79, 229–253.

Sensat, J. (2003) Classical German philosophy and Cohen's critique of Rawls. *European Journal of Philosophy*, 11 (3), 314–353.

Smith, P. (1998) Incentives and justice: G.A. Cohen's egalitarian critique of Rawls. *Social Theory and Practice*, 24 (2).

Sunstein, C. (1988) Beyond the republican revival. *Yale Law Journal*, 97, 1539–1590.

Tan, K.-C. (2004) Justice and personal pursuits. *Journal of Philosophy*, CI, 331362.

Thomas, A. (2005) The permissibility of prerogative grounded incentives in liberal egalitarianism. *Ethics and Economics*. Online: https://papyrus.bib.umontreal.ca/jspui/handle/1866/3337 (accessed September 9, 2011).

Thomas, A. (2006) *Value and Context: The Nature of Moral and Political Knowledge*, Clarendon Press, Oxford.

Thomas, A. (forthcoming) Cohen's critique of Rawls: A double counting objection. *Mind*.

Van Parijs, P. (2003) Difference principles, in *The Cambridge Companion to Rawls* (ed. S. Freeman), Cambridge University Press, Cambridge, pp. 200–240.

Wall, S. (2006) Rawls and the status of political liberty. *Pacific Philosophical Quarterly*, 87, 245–270.

Walzer, M. (1984) *Spheres of Justice: A Defense of Pluralism and Equality*, Basic Books, New York.

White, S. (2003) *The Civic Minimum: On the Rights and Obligations of Economic Citizenship*, Oxford University Press, Oxford.

Williams, A. (1998) Incentives, inequality and publicity. *Philosophy & Public Affairs*, 27, 3, pp. 225–247.

Wolin, S. (2008) *Democracy Incorporated: Managed Democracy and the Specter of Inverted Totalitarianism*, Princeton University Press, Princeton.

6

Property-Owning Democracy and Republican Citizenship

Stuart White

Introduction

The liberalism of John Rawls and republicanism are widely seen as distinct, indeed opposing, conceptions of political society. Some political theorists have recently begun to challenge this interpretation, pointing to some important affinities between Rawls's thinking and republicanism (De Francisco, 2006; see also Buttle, 1997).[1] In this chapter I seek to push this reorientation of perspective a step further by developing one very specific argument which links Rawls's conception of justice as fairness with a republican conception of citizenship: there is good reason to think that a society which enacts just economic arrangements, as Rawls conceives them, will also require an active, participatory form of democratic citizenship.[2]

I shall proceed as follows. The first section takes a preliminary look at the Rawls and republicanism issue. It draws out the proposed contrast between Rawls's and republican conceptions of citizenship, and argues that this contrast is exaggerated. Justice as fairness, and political liberalism more generally, is not republican as a matter of fundamental principle. But Rawls holds out the possibility that its fundamental principles might turn out to support a republican model of citizenship in the light of researches into the sociology of democratic societies.

The following sections then present an argument in support of a specifically republican elaboration of justice as fairness. At the heart of the argument lies an attempt to bring together two discussions of the social psychology of "democratic" societies: Rawls's discussion of how citizens in a just society develop an effective sense of justice, rendering their public conception of justice stable; and Tocqueville's discussion of the ills of democratic personality. The argument begins by bringing into focus two features of Rawls's theory of the just society. The first feature is Rawls's claim that a just society will be a "property-owning democracy" in which conventional welfare state policies are complemented (or perhaps to some extent replaced) by institutions which work to disperse the ownership of both of human and financial capital. The second feature is Rawls's emphasis on the "stability" of conceptions of justice (that is, their ability to win and sustain the loyalty and commitment of citizens). The question I pose is: Is there any reason to think that the material conditions of life in a property-owning democracy will create a problem for the stability of justice as fairness?

I then proceed to suggest that Alexis de Tocqueville's analysis of the social psychology of democratic societies offers some reasons to think that there could well be such a problem. A Rawlsian property-owning democracy arguably represents a perfect embodiment of "democracy" in Tocqueville's sense, and Tocqueville famously argues that the economic conditions of democratic life engender ills of individualism and materialism. If Tocqueville is correct, then there is reason to question whether citizens in a property-owning democracy will develop an effective sense of justice, and thus whether justice as fairness, as expressed in the institutions of property-owning democracy, will be stable.

However, Tocqueville also identified methods of combating the ills of democratic personality, not the least of which is the devolution of public responsibilities with a view to drawing citizens into participation in political life. If correct, Tocqueville's claim about the formative effect of political participation is one that would feature in the reasoning of parties in the "constitutional convention" stage of Rawls's hypothetical social contract; it would give the parties reason to embody a republican understanding of their political liberties in the design of their political structures. I go on to consider some objections to, and limitations of, my argument. The conclusion draws out from the discussion some wider lessons for both republican and liberal political theory.

The Republicanism of Rawls's Liberalism: An Open Question

Many political theorists who self-identify as republicans regard Rawls as a theorist of liberal citizenship, as opposed to the republican form of citizenship they favor. Variations on this theme can be found, for example, in the writings of Michael Sandel, Quentin Skinner, and David Miller (Sandel, 1996; Skinner, 1998; Miller, 2000). My first goal in this paper is to explain why I think that the relationship between republicanism and Rawls's type of liberalism is much more open than this standard contrast suggests. To begin with, however, we need to make the proposed contrast itself clear.

The contrast is helpfully set out by David Miller. A "liberal" conception, Miller writes, sees citizenship "as a set of rights enjoyed equally by every member of the society in question." He adds: "Although citizens enjoy equal political rights, nothing is said about how zealously they are supposed to exercise them" (Miller, 2000, p. 44). By contrast, the republican conception "conceives the citizen as someone who plays an active role in shaping the future direction of his or her society through political debate and decision-making" (Miller, 2000, p. 53). Miller sees Rawls as firmly on the liberal side of this liberal–republican contrast:

> What, for Rawls, does it mean to be a citizen? . . . A citizen is just someone who subscribes to a certain set of principles . . . a citizen is not conceived as being an active participant in politics: although political rights are included in the first principle of justice, so by definition a citizen is someone who has the right to participate, all that is actually required of him or her is

acknowledgement of the principles of justice. So long as one can adopt the citizen perspective in thought, one may live an entirely private existence ... (Miller, 2000, p. 46)

Having set out the contrast between republican and Rawlsian liberal conceptions of citizenship, let me now explain why I think it is overstated.

To begin with, the contrast may underplay the significance of the idea of natural duty in Rawls's liberalism, a point emphasized by Alan Patten in an important response to republican critics of Rawls (Patten, 1996).[3] Rawls argues that the "most important" of our natural duties is the "natural duty ... to support and to further just institutions" (Rawls, 1999, pp. 293–294).[4] What do we have to do to fulfill this natural duty? It is plausible to think that to fulfill the duty we have to, say, exercise our right to vote with a view to promoting just policies. Moreover, if there is a derivative duty to vote, then is there not also, perhaps, a related derivative duty to keep informed about public affairs so that, when the time comes, one is able to exercise the vote in accordance with the duty to support and further just institutions? As Rawls says, "everyone, and not only those in public life, is meant to have political views concerning the common good" (Rawls, 1999, p. 413; see also Cohen, 2003, p. 102). Now when Miller writes that the Rawlsian citizen is only required to "adopt the citizen perspective in thought" he does not mean to exclude the activities of voting and informed deliberation. But these activities define an important and nontrivial level of political participation, one that does set an important limit on how far citizens "may live an entirely private existence."

My second reservation with the standard contrast derives from the distinction that Rawls himself makes between what he calls "classical republicanism" and "civic humanism." The former is "the view that if the citizens of a democratic society are to preserve their basic rights and liberties, including the civil liberties which secure the freedoms of private life, they must also have to a sufficient degree the 'political virtues' and be willing to take part in public life" (Rawls, 1993, p. 205). The latter is "the view that man is a social, even a political, animal whose essential nature is most fully realized in a democratic society in which there is widespread and vigorous participation in political life" (Rawls, 1993, p. 206). Crucially, on the latter view, "[p]articipation is not encouraged as necessary for the protection of basic liberties ...", but "is seen as the privileged locus of the good life" (Rawls, 1993, p. 206). Being grounded in a very specific conception of the good life, civic humanism fails to take seriously the "reasonable pluralism" that Rawls believes any public philosophy for a free society must accept. But with respect to classical republicanism, Rawls comments:

> At most there can be differences [with political liberalism] on matters of institutional design and the political sociology of democratic regimes. These differences, if there be such, are not by any means trivial; they can be extremely important. But there is no fundamental opposition because classical republicanism does not presuppose a comprehensive religious, philosophical or moral doctrine. Nothing in classical republicanism, as characterized above, is incompatible with political liberalism as I have described it. (Rawls, 1993, p. 205)

To clarify, I think Rawls is saying something like this: Classical republicanism is committed, by definition, to a particular sociological thesis about the importance of active political participation to the maintenance of just social institutions. Political liberalism as such does not contain this sociological thesis. But political liberalism does not necessarily deny this thesis; and, if one accepts it, then, as a political liberal, one might well have to accept the institutional implications that the classical republican draws from it. This is why the classical republican and political liberal differ "*[a]t most*" about "matters of institutional design and the political sociology of democratic regimes": the difference – "if there be such" – is contingent on the political liberal not accepting a specific sociological thesis and a related institutional prescription, but there is nothing inherent in the core philosophy of political liberalism which makes disagreement on this point inevitable. Political liberalism is, in this sense, open to the possibility of republicanism. As Rawls states in *Justice as Fairness*, "justice as fairness is perfectly consistent with classical republicanism" (Rawls, 2001, p. 142).[5]

Some might still question whether political liberalism really is consistent with "classical republicanism." In particular, a critic might claim that a Rawlsian liberalism simply can't entertain a republican commitment to active political participation as a norm of citizenship because this would violate the liberal commitment to "neutrality." This, in essence, is the argument of Michael Sandel. In his *Democracy's Discontent*, Sandel presents "liberalism" as based on a "voluntarist" notion of liberty which celebrates the freely choosing individual (Sandel, 1996). Liberty, in this sense, requires that the state be neutral between different conceptions of the good. Neutrality, in its turn, means that the liberal state can have no "formative project" aimed at fostering the character or virtue of its citizens. Taking a stand in favor of the politically active mode of citizenship is precisely the sort of thing that the neutrality-minded liberal state, or "procedural republic," cannot do as it would infringe on the (voluntaristic) liberty of the individual.

The weakness in this argument, as applied to Rawls's liberalism, is its failure to distinguish between neutrality of effect and neutrality of justification (Farelly, 1999; Mulhall and Swift, 2003, pp. 472–473). As we have seen, when Rawls discusses the possible consistency of political liberalism with republicanism, he focuses on the issue of the kind of rationale or justification being offered for promoting political participation and associated virtues. There is, on Rawls's view, a troubling departure from neutrality if the justification appeals to a particular "civic humanist" conception of the good life, but not – or at least, not *necessarily* – if the justification is that political participation and associated virtues are necessary or important to secure just institutions.[6] To be sure, a policy that promotes political participation will have an unequal effect or impact on different conceptions of the good, burdening those who really want strongly private existences. But since Rawls's liberalism is not committed to neutrality of effect as such, this is not a problem. Rawls's view is that liberal states may and should do all sorts of things that violate neutrality of effect provided they have good (enough) justice-based reasons for doing so.

Thus, I feel able to come back to the claim that political liberalism is indeed open to the possibility of republicanism. My aim in the remainder of this chapter is to outline a version of the sociological argument for classical republicanism – an argument for why the political liberal, or at least the political liberal who supports justice as fairness, should indeed accept a sociological thesis about the importance of political participation to the maintenance of just social institutions, and accordingly support a republican prescription for political institutions. When Rawls comments on this possibility he remarks:

"Machiavelli in *The Discourses* is sometimes taken as illustrating classical republicanism ... A more appropriate example from our standpoint here would be Tocqueville in *Democracy in America*."[7] Rawls does not elaborate on this remark; but I shall set out one possible elaboration below.

Property-Owning Democracy

Justice as fairness holds that for a society to be just in its economic arrangements they must satisfy fair equality of opportunity and the difference principle. Economic arrangements are also constrained by justice as fairness to preserve the fair value of citizens' political liberties. What kind of economic arrangements will meet these conditions? Rawls argues that there are two types of economic system that serve to meet them. One is "liberal socialism" in which "the means of production are owned by society" but "economic power is dispersed among firms, as when, for example, a firm's direction and management is elected by, if not directly in the hands of, its own workforce" and "firms ... carry on their activities within a system of free and workably competitive markets" (Rawls, 2001, p. 138). However, Rawls gives more attention to a second possibility, a system which he calls (borrowing the label from the British economist James Meade) a "property-owning democracy" (Meade, 1964). I shall focus on property-owning democracy in this chapter. This is the system that Rawls gives most attention to, perhaps because he believes that the choice of economic systems must be attentive to the history and context of a society and he thinks that property-owning democracy is more attuned to the history and context of most Western democratic societies (Rawls, 1999, p. 242; Rawls, 2001, 139).[8]

Rawls is at pains to emphasize, particularly in his later work, that property-owning democracy is quite different to what he terms "welfare-state capitalism." Rawls draws out the contrast as follows:

> One major difference is this: the background institutions of property-owning democracy work to disperse the ownership of wealth and capital, and thus to prevent a small part of society from controlling the economy, and indirectly, political life as well. By contrast, welfare-state capitalism permits a small class to have a near monopoly of the means of production.
>
> Property-owning democracy avoids this, not by the redistribution of income to those with less at the end of each period, so to speak, but rather by ensuring the widespread ownership of productive assets and human capital (that is, education and trained skills) at the beginning of each period, all this against a background of fair equality of opportunity. The intent is not simply to assist those who lose out through accident or misfortune (although that must be done), but rather to put all citizens in a position to manage their own affairs on a footing of a suitable degree of social and economic equality. (Rawls, 2001, p. 139)

Stating the basic idea in very schematic terms, a property-owning democracy is a republic of educated property holders. One naturally thinks of images of society as a community of artisans or farmers, though these specific images obviously have a somewhat anachronistic flavor to them. Rawls is envisaging a suitably modernized, updated equivalent of these historic social ideals.

Setting out property-owning democracy in more detail, Rawls identifies the following features, stressing the illustrative character of what he is saying (Rawls, 1999, pp. 243–250):

1. A background political system that respects the basic liberties, both personal and political.
2. An educational system that helps to secure fair equality of opportunity: "... the government tries to insure equal chances of education and culture for persons similarly endowed and motivated either by subsidizing private schools or by establishing a public school system."
3. Anti-discrimination and related laws to help secure fair equality of opportunity.
4. A minimum income guarantee secured through "family allowances and special payments for sickness and employment or more systematically by such devices as a graded income supplement (a so-called negative income tax)" (Rawls, 1999, p. 243).[9]
5. Taxation of wealth transfers: the government should enact some form of taxation of gifts and inheritances, perhaps including a capital receipts tax, so as to "gradually and continually to correct the distribution of wealth" so that inequalities in inheritance "are to the advantage of the least fortunate and compatible with liberty and fair equality of opportunity" (Rawls, 1999, p. 245).
6. An expenditure tax: to raise revenues to meet social justice expenditures, the government employs a tax on income but giving full tax exemption to the share of income that is saved; there is a case for making this a proportional rather than a progressive tax.
7. Further taxation for provision of public goods subject to the (very demanding) condition that the tax arrangements are such that everyone, or just about everyone, is willing to consent to the resulting "tax public goods" package.

Clearly, there is a debate to be had about whether these institutions really would suffice to satisfy justice as fairness. Recent work in this vein has stressed ideas such as universal capital grants and the idea of "community funds" to provide revenue streams for public benefits in addition to the items on the above list (Ackerman and Alstott, 1999; Holtham, 1999). But I am not sure these differences of detail will have a large effect on the argument which follows and so – provisionally – I put them aside.

Justice and Stability

From the institutions that give expression to justice as fairness, I turn now to one of the considerations that Rawls argues supports it: the value of stability.[10]

Stability, in Rawls's sense, refers to the capacity of a conception of justice, and of the institutions through which it is manifested, to win and sustain the warm support of the citizens who live under this conception of justice and its associated institutions. Stability is linked in Rawls's discussion with the acquisition of a "sense of justice": an understanding of the public principles of justice and a disposition of support for them that inclines people to want to enact them in legislation and to comply with just legislation:

> One conception of justice is more stable than another if the sense of justice that it tends to generate is stronger and more likely to override disruptive inclinations and if the institutions it allows foster weaker impulses and temptations to act unjustly. The stability of a conception depends on a balance of motives: the sense of justice that it cultivates and the aims that it encourages must normally win out against propensities toward injustice. To estimate the stability of a conception (and the well-ordered society that it defines), one must examine the relative strength of these opposing tendencies. (Rawls, 1999, p. 398)

In Rawls's view, when considering the conception of justice suitable for society we must consider its relative stability in this sense: "a strong point in favour of a conception of justice is that it generates its own support" (Rawls, 1999, p. 154). The parties in the original position are, therefore, required to bring the value of stability to bear on the choice they face between justice as fairness on the one hand and the principle of average utility on the other. Rawls argues that the parties have good reason to regard justice as fairness as more stable than the principle of utility. His basic argument for this claim appeals to what we can call the law of reciprocity: a putative psychological law according to which people tend to feel affection and goodwill toward that which – or those who – affirms their good. Given this psychological law, the issue becomes one of whether people living under the respective conceptions of justice are more likely to feel that their good is affirmed by justice as fairness or by the principle of average utility. Rawls is in no doubt that justice as fairness wins this contest. In essence, this is because nobody's basic freedom or economic well-being is jeopardized under justice as fairness but the same cannot be said for the principle of average utility.[11] Under the latter principle, some people may be called upon to accept a loss of basic freedoms and/or a deprivation of basic economic well-being for the sake of maximizing average welfare. For this sort of arrangement to be stable, a psychological law of reciprocity will not suffice. People must be capable of an extreme, self-abasing form of altruism.

The law of reciprocity is clearly pivotal to the stability argument and it will prove helpful for later discussion to unpack Rawls's thinking on this in more detail. Rawls's full explanation of how people come to acquire a sense of justice pictures moral development proceeding in three stages. In stage one, which we might term *family reciprocity*, the child growing up in a just society experiences parental love and responds to this by growing to love and care for her parents. In the second stage, which we may term the *extension to wider society*, the child growing up in a just society gradually enters a wider social world in which she experiences other citizens following the rules of this society. As they comply with these rules "with evident intention," and the rules work to her benefit, she experiences others as showing her goodwill and concern and, in accordance with the law of reciprocity, she wishes to return this, developing "ties of friendly feeling and trust" for her fellow citizens (Rawls, 1999, p. 429). The third stage of development may be termed the *extension to principles*. At this stage, the individual reflects on the underlying principles that shape the rules that she and others comply with. She understands that these are the basis on which the compliance she experiences and practices works for the good of all. Seeing the principles as affirming her good, and that of others for whom she has come to care, she comes to regard the principles themselves with loyalty and affection. She now possesses a sense of justice: a disposition to support her society's principles of justice and, as suggested in the passage quoted above, a disposition that is strong enough that it normally outweighs temptations to act unjustly on the basis of self-interest. Putting the point with a touch of dramatic exaggeration: the principles of justice become akin to a friend or family member for whom she cares and to whom she has loyalty.[12]

Two features of Rawls's account need to be highlighted. First, for the law of reciprocity to operate as we move out of the family sphere into the wider community, it is vital that the citizen does have a clear perception of how her own good is in fact sustained by the efforts and contributions of her fellow citizens. There must be a perception of there being something significant there to reciprocate. Let's call this the *perception assumption*. Secondly, it is crucial to Rawls's account that the sentiments of fellow feeling generated through the law of reciprocity be strong (enough) relative to the temptations of self-interest, which may incline individuals either to defect from the established terms of cooperation if they think they can get away with it or to try to renegotiate the terms of cooperation so that they are personally more favorable but less just. Let us call this the *balance of motives thesis*.

Having now set out Rawls's conception of property-owning democracy, which gives concrete institutional expression to the principles of justice as fairness, and the stability argument which he makes in support of these principles, I end this section by posing the question that we shall explore in the next: Is there any reason to think that the social conditions of a property-owning democracy might obstruct the development of a sense of justice, and so call into question the stability of justice as fairness?

Tocqueville on the Ills of Democratic Personality

One possible source of insight into this question is provided by Alexis de Tocqueville's *Democracy in America* (Tocqueville, 2003), of course first published in the nineteenth century. Part of Tocqueville's aim in this work is to chart and explain the social psychology of a democratic society that has emerged without the encumbrance of a feudal past. This is with a view to evaluating the long-term prospects of democratic society, in particular for individual freedom. It is widely understood that by "democratic society," Tocqueville does not mean only a society with the institutions of political democracy. "Democracy," in Tocqueville's usage, embraces the political, social, and economic spheres. It is a form of society characterized by such things as equal rights of political participation, the absence of ascriptive class hierarchies, and a moderately (though far from fully) equal distribution of wealth. Wealth is spread so that, while there is inequality, each individual or household has a high degree of independence. Thus, Tocqueville talks of democracy as a form of society in which "distinctions of class are blurred and privileges abolished ... patrimonies are divided up and education and freedom spread" (Tocqueville, 2003, p. 617).

Democracy, in Tocqueville's sense, can be understood as an "ideal type" to which the actual America he saw was an approximation (at least for white males). What would a society look like if it were to fit more closely the ideal type? A plausible answer, I think, is that it would look a lot like a Rawlsian property-owning democracy. For this is a vision of a society in which there is an absence of ascriptive status hierarchies ("distinctions of class are blurred and privileges abolished"); universal political enfranchisement ("freedom spread"); a wide spread of wealth ("patrimonies are divided up"); and equality of opportunity in education ("education ... spread").[13]

If this is so, then provided that the America Tocqueville analyzed was sufficiently democratic for him to acquire genuine insight into the nature of democratic society, Tocqueville's analysis of the ills of democratic personality might have relevance to assessing the stability of justice as fairness as manifested in the institutions of a property-owning democracy. It may be that Tocqueville's analysis gives us some insight into the social psychology that is likely to obtain in a property-owning democracy, and that we can draw some lessons from this as to how far the citizens of a property-owning democracy are likely to develop a sense of justice in the way that Rawls's account of stability supposes.

In volume 2 of *Democracy in America*, Tocqueville diagnoses at least two ills of democratic personality, *individualism* and what we may term *materialism*. Let us start with individualism. Famously, Tocqueville defines individualism as "a calm and considered feeling which persuaded each citizen to cut himself off from his fellows and to withdraw into the circle of his family and friends in such a way that he thus creates a small group of his own and willingly abandons society at large to its own devices" (Tocqueville, 2003, p. 587). It "is democratic in origin and threatens to grow as conditions become equal" (Tocqueville, 2003, p. 588). Tocqueville explains this as follows:

> As social equality spreads, a greater number of individuals are no longer rich or powerful enough to exercise great influence upon the fate of their fellows, but have acquired or preserved sufficient understanding and wealth to be able to satisfy their own needs. Such people owe nothing to anyone. They are used to considering themselves in isolation and quite willingly imagine their destiny as entirely in their own hands.
>
> Thus, not only does democracy make men forget their ancestors but also hides their descendants and keeps them apart from their fellows. It constantly brings them back to themselves and threatens in the end to imprison them in the isolation of their own hearts. (Tocqueville, 2003, p. 589)

Looking closely, individualism seems to have both a cognitive and an affective element: it arises "from wrong-headed thinking rather than from depraved feelings. It originates as much from defects of intelligence as from the mistakes of the heart" (Tocqueville, 2003, p. 588). Affectively, it consists in a strong attachment to the circle of family and friends and a high degree of indifference to the lot of the wider society: the democratic citizen "abandons society at large to its own devices." Cognitively, it consists in an exaggerated, mistaken sense of independence. Economic self-sufficiency, based on moderate wealth, generates a sense that one is radically self-reliant, needing one's fellow citizens very little. The democratic citizen loses sight of the essential interdependency of social life and, thus, of how his own well-being depends crucially on the efforts and contributions of others. Through what seems to be a reverse operation of Rawls's law of reciprocity, the cognitive error seems to underpin the affective orientation. If one fails to see that one's well-being does in fact depend crucially on the efforts and contributions of others then, seeing nothing to reciprocate, one naturally assumes that one "owe[s] nothing to anyone." Other people's well-being is their affair, as yours is entirely your own, and not something about which one need concern oneself.

In terms of Rawls's account of how a sense of justice emerges, individualism seems to put into question what I have termed the perception assumption, that is, the assumption that if citizens receive certain benefits from the cooperative efforts of others under just institutions, they will also *perceive* these benefits. Tocqueville's analysis suggests that people living in a property-owning democracy may not in fact perceive, or fully perceive, the benefits that others provide through their dutiful compliance with the rules of a just social order. Whereas Rawls expects us, as citizens, to work with a picture of the social world as a "cooperative" venture, Tocqueville argues that the economic conditions of a democratic society will incline individuals to a very different picture of their social world. What comes to mind is an "islandic" conception of society. Each family views itself an island, self-sufficient unto itself, doing its own thing, tackling its problems in its way. Each family-island is aware of the fact that there are many surrounding islands. But those are *other* islands. They are separate ventures from our family-island venture. They work for the success of their ventures as we work for the success of ours. We don't wish them ill, but since we see their efforts as pertaining to their ventures, which are wholly separate from ours, we see no reason of *reciprocity* to care much about them.

Let us now turn to materialism. I use the term here to refer to what Tocqueville calls the Americans' love of "comfort" and "physical pleasures." According to Tocqueville, in a democratic society, "[a]ll men are preoccupied with the need to satisfy the slightest of their bodily needs and to provide for the little conveniences of life" (Tocqueville, 2003, p. 616). The moderate wealth holders that make up democratic society are focused, almost obsessively, with incremental material advance. This is because every person lives in a state where they cannot take affluence for granted but in which affluence is also a reasonable hope. Moderate wealth holders are spurred on at once by the hope of gain, perhaps considerable gain, and by the fear that what they have already won may slip away. As Tocqueville explains it:

> when distinctions of class are blurred and privileges abolished, when patrimonies are divided up and education and freedom spread, then the poor man's imagination conceives the desire to obtain comfort and the rich man's mind is overtaken by the fear of losing it. A lot of modest fortunes spring up. Their owners have enough physical comforts to have a liking for them but not enough to be content. They never win them without effort or indulge them without anxiety. (Tocqueville, 2003, p. 617)

In terms of Rawls's account of how citizens develop a sense of justice, materialism can be expected to strengthen the temptations on the part of many citizens toward defection from just terms of social cooperation and toward efforts at renegotiating for more favorable terms that take society away from justice.

So Rawls's account of how citizens will develop a sense of justice under property-owning democracy seems challenged from two quarters. On the one hand, individualism will weaken the extent to which the law of reciprocity works to build attachment to the welfare and interests of one's fellow citizens. It will make citizens less other-regarding. At the same time, materialism can be expected to strengthen the extent to which people feel the need to prioritize their own interests. Putting the two forces together, we are then left to wonder whether the balance of motives thesis (the thesis that a reciprocity-based sense of justice will outweigh self-interested desires to depart from justice for personal advantage) is likely to hold. It seems at least plausible that the typical citizen's concern for others, based on the law of reciprocity, will not be strong enough to outweigh temptations to defect or renegotiate in the direction of injustice. Insofar as justice as fairness is institutionalized through property-owning democracy, this implies that justice as fairness may not be as stable a conception of justice as Rawls thinks.

Is there a way to rescue the stability of justice as fairness as embodied in the institutions of a property-owning democracy?

The Republican Response

Tocqueville claimed not only to have identified some ills of the democratic personality but to have identified some ways of addressing them: "The Americans," he writes, "have exploited liberty in order to combat that individualism which equality produced and have overcome it" (Tocqueville, 2003, pp. 592–593). By "liberty" here Tocqueville means what we ordinarily think of as republican liberty, the liberty constituted by participating in government so that government becomes a form of self-rule. The Americans have secured liberty in this republican sense by devolving decision making to the local level. The state at the center forces its citizens to be free, in the republican sense, by refusing to monopolize decision-making power. Participation in local government in turn combats both the cognitive and affective problems of democratic personality:

> As soon as communal affairs are treated as belonging to all, every man realizes that he is not as separate from his fellows as first imagined and that it is often vital to help them in order to gain their support... When the public is in charge, every single man feels the value of public goodwill and seeks to court it by attracting the regard and affection of those amongst whom he is to live.
>
> Many of the emotions which freeze and shatter men's hearts are then forced to withdraw and hide away in the depths of their souls. Pride conceals itself; scorn dares not show its face. Egoism is afraid of itself. (Tocqueville, 2003, p. 592)

In other words, participation in local political bodies makes citizens more aware of their interdependence, so correcting the illusion of self-sufficiency generated by the wide dispersion of moderate wealth. Rawls's law of reciprocity then has more opportunity to take effect. At the same time, such participation forces citizens to argue in terms of public interests and common goods and this shapes individuals' preferences so that they genuinely have more concern for these interests and goods.[14] On this basis, Tocqueville asserts what we may here term the *Tocqueville thesis*: "... I affirm that, to combat the evils produced by equality, there is but one effective remedy, namely political freedom [that is, republican freedom, implying active participation in politics]" (Tocqueville, 2003, p. 595).[15]

Tocqueville's argument was taken up, of course, by John Stuart Mill. Echoing Tocqueville's analysis of individualism, Mill comments on "how little there is in most men's ordinary life to give any largeness either to their conceptions or to their sentiments" (Mill, 2001, p. 233). But involving the individual in political decision making allegedly expands both the mental and moral horizons of the individual. As with Tocqueville, Mill sees participation in "local administrative bodies" as the main vehicle for this "public education of the citizens" (Mill, 2001, p. 378). More recently, Stephen Elkin has reiterated the argument (Elkin, 2006, pp. 180–82; see also Burtt, 1993, p. 366). Even more recently, work on new systems of "empowered participatory governance" in tackling crime, managing schools, regulating use of the environment and other tasks have pointed to the potential formative effects of these systems as part of their justification (Cohen and Sabel, 1997; Fung and Wright, 2003; Cohen and Fung, 2004; Fung, 2004). One place we might look for relevant evidence concerning the Tocqueville thesis is in the burgeoning literature on "social capital," particularly given the role that Tocqueville's work plays as a key historical reference point in this literature. Social capital is, of course, a complex term, but in one of its core senses it refers to norms of generalized trust and reciprocity that facilitate social cooperation in the political and other spheres. As such, we can regard it as at least a rough proxy for the attitudes which we associate with the moderation of democratic individualism. If not equivalent to an effective sense of justice, social capital, in this sense, is plausibly seen as necessary for its cultivation. So what does the empirical research on social capital tell us? Is it consistent with the Tocqueville thesis?

Unfortunately, and despite the status of Tocqueville in the social capital literature, not a lot of empirical research has looked at how the design of political institutions affects social capital (Lowndes and Wilson, 2001; Hooghe and Stolle, 2003).[16] Robert Putnam's *Bowling Alone*, for example, briefly argues the Tocquevillian thesis that strong local government will assist the development of social capital (Putnam, 2000, p. 513). But the focus of the book's empirical research lies elsewhere, as indeed it does in Putnam's earlier *Making Democracy Work* (Putnam, 1994). Some of the recent research into the determinants of social capital is, however, supportive of the Tocqueville thesis (Freitag, 2006). That said, we should be wary of uncritically celebrating localization or decentralization as a specific means to greater participation and its alleged Tocquevillian benefits. There might be many other ways of promoting such participation. And decentralization is unlikely to produce the envisaged benefits in all contexts, for example if the local decision-making units, reflecting patterns of strong residential segregation by class or by race, are socially homogeneous and hence provide few opportunities for people to cooperate in decision-making with people unlike themselves (Putnam, 2000, p. 513; Macedo, 2005, pp. 73–86).

If the Tocqueville thesis is correct, then there is an obvious implication for our argument above about the stability of justice as fairness under property-owning democracy: the way to combat the stability problem is to complement the economic institutions of property-owning democracy with political institutions that embody republican liberty.

Developing the point in terms of Rawls's theory we might imagine that at the "constitutional convention" stage of the hypothetical social contract the parties are asked to make a basic choice between more or less republican interpretations of the political liberties guaranteed under Rawls's first principle of justice.[17] On the one hand, they can opt for a "liberal" model of the political liberties – in Miller's sense of the word, one which treats political participation as something which citizens should be free to involve themselves with as much or as little as they like. On the other hand, they can opt for a republican interpretation of the political liberties: that is, one which treats political participation as an important civic duty and which requires political institutions to encourage performance of this duty. The idea is not, of course, that all citizens ought to be political *activists*, people for whom politics is the central, self-defining activity of their lives. Rather, the idea is that whatever is central and self-defining to people in their private lives should not be to the exclusion of some minimally decent level of civic and political engagement.[18]

Rawls famously imagines that once the parties in the original position have chosen the principles of justice to regulate their society, they then move to a "constitutional convention" in which they choose their society's political structures in accordance with the agreed principles of justice (Rawls, 1999, pp. 172–174). As in the original position, the parties to the convention are assumed to have and to use all relevant general sociological knowledge. If Tocqueville's sociology is correct, they will take this sociology into account in selecting between liberal and republican interpretations of the political liberties. Given a commitment to the economic institutions of a property-owning democracy, the parties will have good reason to favor the republican interpretation. In this way, commitment to a republican form of citizenship can quite plausibly emerge out of Rawls's hypothetical social contract.[19]

Some Objections

We have seen how a liberal theory of justice like Rawls's may need to be complemented by a republican theory of citizenship stressing the importance of widespread active participation in political life. However, there are a number of ways in which the marriage of liberal justice and republicanism outlined here might be challenged.

One issue here is that unlike Tocqueville's model of a democratic society, a Rawlsian property-owning democracy does have a role for a sizeable welfare state. Might this not be a source of solidarity lacking in Tocqueville's democracy, one which addresses the ills of individualism and/or materialism, so making republican liberty unnecessary as a response to the stability problem? Second, it might be possible to realize justice as fairness through institutions other than those of a property-owning democracy and these institutions might not generate the same problem of stability. As noted, Rawls himself refers us to the alternative of liberal socialism. Third, there might be forms of property-owning democracy or liberal socialism (or some hybrid) in which economic life itself has a strongly associational character which works to temper the ills of democratic personality. Individualism is tempered, we might imagine, by participation in workers' cooperatives or in industry-wide producer associations or "guilds."[20] (See the chapter by Hussain in this volume.) Rawls anticipates this line of thought when he comments that property-owning democracy is compatible with "Mill's idea of worker-managed cooperative firms" and that the political liberal might conceivably have a preference for a worker-managed form of property-owning democracy because of its formative effects (Rawls, 2001, pp. 176, 178–179; see also Dahl, 1985, pp. 94–107; O'Neill, 2008). If these associational devices suffice to counter the ills of democratic personality, then there will be no need for the republican response suggested above.

These are all good points, but there are also good reasons to think that these points do not count decisively against our argument. To begin with, one can reasonably question whether merely adding a welfare state (a phrase which, of course, itself covers a very wide range of institutional possibilities) to the other institutions of a property-owning democracy will necessarily combat individualism and/or materialism. It seems just as possible that the otherwise uncorrected ills of democratic personality might undermine or constrain the welfare state. Or else, closer to Tocqueville's own anxieties about "under what new features despotism might appear in the world," the civic disengagement produced by individualism and materialism might lead the state to expand its regulatory power, producing a particular form of welfare state that is an expression of state paternalism rather than citizen solidarity (Tocqueville, 2003, p. 805). Even where a welfare state is initially generated by citizen solidarity, over time it may come to be perceived by citizens influenced by individualism and materialism as an alien, arbitrary imposition by a remote state. This is one reason why there is at present in many welfare states such interest in so-called "co-production" in which welfare providers come together with those they serve to design and deliver services. Here, we see glimpses of an argument that runs something as follows: the welfare state will be overwhelmed by individualism and/or materialism unless it takes a relatively participatory form. Republican citizenship is here being called in to come to the aid of the welfare state.

Similarly, in a liberal socialist system, worker cooperatives might become subject to what Martin Buber saw as a collective egoism which works against an effective sense of justice (Buber, 1948, p. 68). The same might apply to the corporations, unions, or guilds of an associative form of liberal socialism or property-owning democracy. In all of these cases – the welfare state, workers' management, syndicalism or corporatism – the proposed institutions could conceivably help to combat the problems of individualism and/or materialism. But this does not necessarily mean that they will suffice in this respect. There could well be a need for republican liberty to complement these other institutions in addressing these problems, as, indeed, they might be necessary to complement the contribution of republican liberty. They might conceivably all be important parts of the formative project by which a democratic citizenry seeks to insure itself against the ills of democratic personality.

Conclusion: Lessons for Republicans and Liberals

We can now see one, clear line of argument for why it may be necessary to conjoin a liberal theory of social justice with a republican conception of citizenship. Liberal justice demands certain institutions in the economic sphere, for example those of a property-owning democracy. But a Tocquevillian sociology suggests that these institutions may engender certain ills of democratic personality: individualism and materialism. These ills could undermine the stability of the economic institutions which realize liberal justice. However, a Tocquevillian sociology also suggests one way of countering these ills, and thereby rescuing the stability of liberal justice: republican citizenship. The argument as I have presented it is far from conclusive; there are too many contestable empirical steps in the argument for it to be so. But I think it is logically coherent and, in empirical terms, credible. In concluding, I want to consider what wider lessons we might draw out from this discussion.

First, what lessons might self-styled republicans take from our discussion? The main lesson, I think, is to end the war with philosophical liberalism. As we noted above, contemporary republican political theory repeatedly defines itself in terms of unflattering contrasts with (what is taken to be) liberal political theory. This chapter has not considered all of these alleged contrasts, but it has certainly shown that one of the more widespread contrasts, in terms of active and passive conceptions of citizenship, is misguided. Republicans need to be more careful in their characterizations and criticisms of liberalism, and less reliant on liberalism as an "Other" against which the virtue of republican political theory can be defined.

The main lesson I want to draw out for liberals is the need to think in richer sociological terms about the problem of stability in a just state. Rawls's treatment of stability is suggestive, but it cannot be considered the final word on the subject. Even if the specifically Tocquevillian critique of Rawls's account of stability presented in this chapter turns out to be unfounded, there may be other sociologies that do point to problems with Rawls's account. To this extent contemporary liberal political theory needs to be, or to become, sociological as well as philosophical; and, in this respect, regardless of the specific conception of citizenship it endorses, it needs to become much more like republican political theory.

Notes

1. De Francisco's paper is extremely helpful in pointing to republican elements in Rawls's thought, and includes a discussion of the issue of stability which is central to this chapter. This chapter does not range as widely as De Francisco's in terms of drawing out Rawls's republicanism but focuses in depth on one particular argument linking liberal justice to republican citizenship through the concern for stability.
2. I use the term "republicanism" in this chapter *only* to refer to a conception of *citizenship* that holds that citizens ought to participate in political life and should be encouraged by public action to participate. The term might also be used to refer to a particular conception of *legitimacy*, one which sees the legitimate exercise of political authority as resting on inclusive political processes that seek a common good; or to a particular conception of *freedom*, one which stresses the importance of dependency or domination, as opposed to actual interference, as conditions which limit an individual's freedom. For the record, I think that Rawls's understanding of what we are doing when we seek to develop a theory of justice is deeply influenced by the republican conception of legitimacy, but I do not pursue this point here. For further discussion, see De Francisco (2006).
3. Patten effectively shows how Quentin Skinner and Charles Taylor fail to establish a philosophically significant distinction between the republicanisms they favor and the liberalisms of thinkers such as Rawls and Ronald Dworkin.
4. According to Rawls, this duty has "two parts: first, we are to comply with and to do our share in just institutions when they exist and apply to us; and second, we are to assist in the establishment of just arrangements when they do not exist, at least where this can be done at little cost to ourselves" (Rawls, 1999, pp. 293–294).

5. At pp. 142–145 of this text Rawls restates the contrast between civic humanism and classical republicanism drawn in *Political Liberalism*. He comments (2001, p.144): "Between classical republicanism ... and the liberalism represented by Constant and Berlin, there is no fundamental opposition ... Here they may be differences in weighing competing political values; but this is importantly a matter of political sociology and institutional design. Since classical republicanism does not involve a comprehensive doctrine, it is also fully compatible with political liberalism, and with justice as fairness as a form thereof."
6. I am not sure that Rawls, or a Rawlsian liberal, would want to dismiss neutrality of effect as altogether irrelevant. In particular, if a policy has a neutral justification in terms of justice, but the gain to justice is small, and the non-neutrality of impact is large, then I suspect a Rawlsian liberal would probably not wish to endorse the policy. Imagine a case, for example, where state promotion of a specific religion would generate attitudes conducive to (slightly) greater social justice, and it is proposed to promote this religion on these grounds. The argument for this policy satisfies neutrality of justification, but I think the policy's non-neutrality of impact, as between different comprehensive ethical doctrines, would still give a liberal great concern. However, it does not follow from this that a liberal need eschew any kind of "formative project" to shape citizen character in a way that is supportive of justice.
7. See Rawls (1993, p. 205, n37). The reference to Machiavelli is repeated in Rawls (2001, p. 144, n13) though without the following comment about Tocqueville.
8. When one looks at Meade's model of a property-owning democracy in its most developed form the contrast with liberal socialism becomes somewhat blurred. Meade assumes that a large proportion of society's productive assets are publicly owned, providing the state with an important source of revenue to finance a universal social dividend. See Meade (1989).
9. Rawls almost certainly intends to write "payments for ... unemployment" here rather than "employment."
10. Since my focus in this paper is largely on what follows from within a Rawlsian framework, I take it provisionally as given that stability is an important value in considering what is just. However, even if one were to show that stability is in fact irrelevant to the question of what is truly, fundamentally just, the discussion would still have relevance in considering what sort of political institutions might need to complement the economic institutions of a property-owning democracy.
11. "When the two principles are satisfied, each person's basic liberties are secured and there is a sense defined by the difference principle in which everyone is benefited by social cooperation. Therefore we can explain the acceptance of the social system and the principles it satisfies by the psychological law that persons tend to love, cherish, and support whatever affirms their own good. Since everyone's good is affirmed, all acquire inclinations to uphold the scheme." See Rawls (1999, pp. 154–155).
12. Rawls reiterates this account of a "reasonable moral psychology" in Rawls (2001, pp. 195–197).
13. In an essay discussing what Rawls means when he says that his theory of justice is intended "for a democratic society," Joshua Cohen emphasizes how Rawls understands the term "democracy" in Tocquevillian fashion to refer to a kind of egalitarian society and not just to a kind of political system. Rawls's enterprise can be understood, in part, as an attempt to work out what principles must govern the ordering of a society if society is to be truly democratic in the Tocquevillian sense. See Cohen (2003, pp. 95–100).
14. Contemporary theorists of deliberative democracy frequently argue that public deliberation will have this effect. See, for example, Cohen (1997, pp. 76–77), Elster (1997, pp. 11–19), and Miller (2000, pp. 15–18).

15. Cheryl Welch summarizes Tocqueville's view thus: "Only participatory democracy – vigorous local self-governing groups – can provide a context in which individuals will be forced to interpret their private interests in a publicly useful manner." See Welch (2001).
16. As the co-editors of one fairly recent collection of essays put it: "One of the most interesting questions from the political science perspective … concerns the conditions and influences that facilitate, maintain, or even destroy those aspects of social capital that benefit society at large. It is rather puzzling that this question is seldom explicitly addressed." See Hooghe and Stolle (2003, p. 5).
17. On the constitutional convention stage of the hypothetical social contract, see Rawls (1999, pp. 172–174).
18. Here I endorse the general spirit of Gerry Stoker's call for a more participatory democratic system, but one in which the demands of participation are suited to a "politics for amateurs." See Stoker (2006, pp. 149–162).
19. Loren King has recently identified a related argument (King, 2005). He argues that the parties in the original position have reason to adopt a federalist form of political organization as a means of handling reasonable disagreement about the policies and institutions required by the principles of justice. The argument developed here shares with King's an emphasis on the possible merits of political decentralization, but the rationale is fundamentally about promoting political participation for its educative effects rather than finding a fair way to cope with reasonable disagreement about principles of justice.
20. There is of course a long tradition of thought about this possibility with which a longer discussion could engage, including Hegel's and Durkheim's respective discussions of corporatism. For a contemporary statement, with an emphasis on formative effects, see Cohen and Rogers (1995), especially the closing essay, "Solidarity, Democracy, Association" (pp. 236–267).

References

Ackerman, B. and Alstott, A. (1999) *The Stakeholder Society*, Yale University Press, New Haven.
Buber, M. (1948) *Paths in Utopia*, Routledge and Kegan Paul, London.
Burtt, S. (1993) The politics of virtue today: A critique and a proposal. *American Political Science Review*, 87, 360–368.
Buttle, N. (1997) Liberal republicanism. *Politics*, 17, 147–152.
Cohen, J. (1997) Deliberation and democratic legitimacy, in *Deliberative Democracy: Essays on Reason and Politics* (eds J. Bohman and W. Rehg), MIT Press, Cambridge, MA, pp. 67–91.
Cohen, J. (2003) For a democratic society, in *The Cambridge Companion to Rawls* (ed. S. Freeman), Cambridge University Press, Cambridge, pp. 86–138.
Cohen, J. and Fung, A. (2004) Radical democracy. *Swiss Journal of Political Science*, 10, 23–34.
Cohen, J. and Rogers, J. (1995) *Associations and Democracy*, Verso, London.
Cohen, J. and Sabel, C. (1997) Directly-deliberative polyarchy. *European Law Journal*, 3, 313–342.
Dahl, R.A. (1985) *A Preface to Economic Democracy*, University of California Press, Berkeley.
De Francisco, A. (2006) A republican interpretation of the late Rawls. *Journal of Political Philosophy*, 14, 270–288.
Elkin, S. (2006) *Reconstructing the Commercial Republic: Constitutional Thought after Madison*, University of Chicago Press, Chicago.
Elster, J. (1997) The market and the forum: Three varieties of political theory, in *Deliberative Democracy: Essays on Reason and Politics* (eds J. Bohman and W. Rehg), MIT Press, Cambridge, MA, pp. 3–34.

Farelly, C. (1999) Does Rawls support the procedural republic? A critical response to Sandel's *Democracy's Discontent*. *Politics*, 19, 19–25.

Freitag, M. (2006) Bowling the state back in: Political institutions and the creation of social capital. *European Journal of Political Research*, 45, 123–152.

Fung, A. (2004) *Empowered Participation: Reinventing Urban Democracy*, Princeton University Press, Princeton.

Fung, A. and Wright, E.O. (2003) *Deepening Democracy: Institutional Innovations in Empowered Participatory Governance*, Verso, London.

Holtham, G. (1999) Ownership and social democracy, in *The New Social Democracy* (eds A. Gamble and T. Wright), Blackwell, Oxford, pp. 53–68.

Hooghe, M. and Stolle, D. (2003) Introduction: Generating social capital, in *Generating Social Capital: Civil Society and Institutions in Comparative Perspective* (eds M. Hooghe and D. Stolle), Palgrave Macmillan, Basingstoke, pp. 1–18.

King, L. (2005) The federal structure of a republic of reasons. *Political Theory*, 33, 629–653.

Lowndes, V. and Wilson, D. (2001) Social capital and local governance: Exploring the institutional design variable. *Political Studies*, 49, 629–647.

Macedo, S. (ed.) (2005) *Democracy at Risk: How Political Choices Undermine Citizen Participation, and What We Can Do About It*, Brookings Institution Press, Washington, DC.

Meade, J. (1964) *Efficiency, Equality and the Ownership of Property*, Allen and Unwin, London.

Meade, J. (1989) *Agathatopia: The Economics of Partnership*, University of Aberdeen, Aberdeen.

Mill, J.S. (2001) Representative Government [1861], in J.S. Mill, *Utilitarianism, On Liberty, Considerations on Representative Government*, Dent, London, pp. 187–428.

Miller, D. (2000) Citizenship and pluralism, in *Citizenship and National Identity*, Polity Press, Cambridge, pp. 41–61.

Mulhall, S. and Swift, A. (2003) Rawls and communitarianism, in *The Cambridge Companion to Rawls* (ed. S. Freeman), Cambridge University Press, Cambridge, pp. 460–487.

O'Neill, M. (2008) Three Rawlsian routes towards economic democracy. *Revue de Philosophie Économique*, 8 (2), 29–55.

Patten, A. (1996) The republican critique of liberalism. *British Journal of Political Science*, 26, 25–44.

Putnam, R.D. (1994) *Making Democracy Work: Civic Traditions in Modern Italy*, Princeton University Press, Princeton.

Putnam, R.D. (2000) *Bowling Alone: The Collapse and Revival of American Community*, Simon and Schuster, New York.

Rawls, J. (1993) *Political Liberalism*, Columbia University Press, New York.

Rawls, J. (1999) *A Theory of Justice: Revised Edition*, Harvard University Press, Cambridge, MA.

Rawls, J. (2001) *Justice as Fairness: A Restatement*, Harvard University Press, Cambridge, MA.

Sandel, M, (1996) *Democracy's Discontent: America in Search of a Public Philosophy*, Harvard University Press, Cambridge, MA.

Skinner, Q. (1998) *Liberty before Liberalism*, Cambridge University Press, Cambridge.

Stoker, G. (2006) *Why Politics Matters: Making Democracy Work,*: Palgrave Macmillan, Basingstoke.

de Tocqueville, A. (2003) *Democracy in America* [1835, 1840], (trans. G.E. Bevan), Penguin, Harmondsworth.

Welch, C. (2001) *De Tocqueville*, Oxford University Press, Oxford.

Part Two

Interrogating Property-Owning Democracy: Work, Gender, Political Economy

7

Work, Ownership, and Productive Enfranchisement

Nien-hê Hsieh

In the revised edition of *A Theory of Justice*, John Rawls writes that of the two items he would handle differently if he "were writing *A Theory of Justice* now," one would be "to distinguish more sharply the idea of a property-owning democracy … from the idea of a welfare state" (1999b, p. xiv).[1] Rawls seems concerned to correct what he takes to be a serious misperception – namely, that an economic regime in which a small minority owns the means of production can qualify as just. For Rawls, if there is to be private ownership of the means of production, justice requires the widespread distribution of productive assets and human capital over time, something that property-owning democracy, but not welfare state capitalism, aims to achieve.[2]

In explaining the choice of property-owning democracy over welfare state capitalism, Rawls emphasizes the significance for the least advantaged in owning productive assets. Under welfare state capitalism, a decent standard of living for the least advantaged is secured through the redistribution of income (Rawls, 2001, p. 139). Rawls contrasts this with the approach under property-owning democracy:

> The intent is not simply to assist those who lose out through accident or misfortune (although that must be done), but rather to put all citizens in a position to manage their own affairs on a footing of a suitable degree of social and economic equality.
>
> The least-advantaged are not, if all goes well, the unfortunate and unlucky – objects of our charity and compassion, much less our pity – but those to whom reciprocity is owed as a matter of political justice among those who are free and equal citizens along with everyone else. Although they control fewer resources, they are doing their full share on terms recognized by all as mutually advantageous and consistent with everyone's self-respect. (2001, p. 139)

For Rawls then, it seems that justice requires individuals to be able to support themselves to some degree through economically productive activity and that considerations of self-respect inform the terms of that activity (Freeman, 2007b, p. 229).[3]

To further our understanding about property-owning democracy, in this chapter I explore what we have reason to conclude about the terms on which individuals ideally engage in economically productive activity in a just society. Specifically, I explore what we can infer from Rawls's claim that property-owning democracy satisfies the requirements of justice whereas welfare state capitalism does not, and from what Rawls writes about participation in economically productive activity more generally. The picture that emerges is one in which considerations about work play a role in the choice of an economic regime from the perspective of justice as fairness, perhaps more so than is often held to be the case.[4] On this view, full "productive enfranchisement" – that is, being able to participate in economically productive activity on terms consistent with citizens' self-respect – not only requires that people have work, but also requires that certain conditions be met with regard to the content, governance, and status of work.

As a point of clarification, by "work" I mean a person's mental or physical activity within the formal economy that contributes to the production of some good or service to be sold in the market. To be clear, this definition excludes a variety of productive activities, including care for children by parents or volunteer activities. The focus in this chapter is on activities most readily amenable to regulation by public rules and related to the earning of income.[5] In addition, this definition leaves open the desirability of such activities, even though the term "work" is often associated with toil and drudgery. As defined here, an activity need not be boring, undesirable, or devoid of meaning to qualify as work. Work can be just as much a "calling" – that is, "directed towards accomplishing goals which tie in with larger goals in the community and world."[6] What matters is that it contributes to the production of some good or service to be sold in the market within the context of the formal economy.

The chapter is organized as follows. In the first section, I examine the role that widespread ownership of productive assets plays in the choice of property-owning democracy. I argue that if the widespread ownership of productive assets matters in the choice of property-owning democracy for reasons relating specifically to economic production, it matters not only because it enables the least advantaged to participate in economic production, but also because it involves them in specific ways. In the following section, I focus on the way in which the widespread ownership of productive assets helps to ensure opportunities for meaningful work. I then look at the way in which the widespread ownership of productive assets helps to protect workers against arbitrary interference at work. In both cases, the ownership of productive assets is relevant because it reduces the extent to which individuals depend upon their labor for income. Because widespread ownership of productive assets is not the only means to reduce the extent to which individuals depend upon their labor for income, I go on to explore ways in which the widespread ownership of productive assets affects the status of work in the context of economic production as a way to understand better the choice of property-owning democracy.

Why Asset Ownership?

In *The Law of Peoples*, Rawls writes that for a society to qualify as just, it must "serve as employer of last resort through general or local government, or other social and economic policies" (1999a, p. 50). The reason, according to Rawls, is that "the lack of a sense of long-term security and of the opportunity for meaningful work and occupation is destructive not only of citizens' self-respect, but of their sense that they are members of society and not simply caught in it" (1999a, p. 50). Here Rawls makes explicit the idea that is implicit in his account of property-owning democracy, which is that a just society requires all citizens to have the ability and opportunity to participate in some form of economically productive activity.

In the account of property-owning democracy, widespread ownership of productive assets is presented as one way to help ensure the participation of all citizens in economically productive activity. However, widespread ownership of productive assets is not the only way to do so. For example, as Rawls suggests above, the state itself may employ citizens who otherwise are unable to find work, or the state may provide subsidies to private firms to hire citizens.[7] Given these alternatives, the question arises as to whether the ownership of productive assets matters in the context of economically productive activity for reasons other than simply enabling participation in such activity.[8]

Furthermore, there is reason to believe that even with the widespread distribution of productive assets, the state must serve as employer of last resort to ensure that all citizens have an opportunity to participate in economically productive activity insofar as their participation is meant to be a significant source of income. For the least advantaged, in the absence of an employer of last resort, participation in economically productive activity would require self-employment of some sort on the part of those unable to find work. This raises two issues. First, if these individuals are unable to find employment, is there good reason to assume there will be greater success for them in the context of self-employment? Second, by requiring individuals to invest their productive assets in their place of employment, self-employment brings with it a degree of financial risk that seems unreasonable to ask the least advantaged to bear. Hence, there is reason to doubt that widespread ownership of productive assets is adequate on its own to ensure participation by all citizens in economically productive activity. Society still needs to serve as employer of last resort.

Accordingly, one may ask whether ownership of productive assets affects citizens' participation in economically productive activity in a way that matters from the perspective of justice as fairness. This is not to deny that widespread ownership of productive assets may matter from the perspective of justice with respect to considerations that lie outside of the realm of economic production, such as realization of the fair value of political liberties (Cohen, 1989, p. 28).[9] Rather, the point is this. If there are alternatives to widespread ownership of productive assets that promote participation in economically productive activity and if ownership of productive assets is not adequate to ensure participation by all citizens, what about the choice of property-owning democracy depends upon the role of productive assets in economically productive activity? If widespread ownership of productive assets is relevant, it seems reasonable to expect it should be relevant with respect to its immediate context, which is economic production.

One answer that may be given is that widespread ownership of productive assets enables workers to exercise greater control in decision making within the enterprises in which they work (Freeman, 2007b, pp. 225–226).[10] Although Rawls makes explicit that there is no basic right to worker control of the means of production (2001, p. 114), in *Justice as Fairness* he writes that it is "a major difficulty" that the account of justice as fairness "has not considered the importance of democracy in the workplace and in shaping the general course of the economy" (2001, p. 178). Various arguments have been made that a just economic regime requires some form of "workplace democracy" – a system in which workers have at least equal say in the management and governance of the enterprises in which they work as do the providers of capital.[11]

For example, it is has been argued that justice as fairness grounds a principle of self-determination that applies not only to the state but to other social organizations, including economic enterprises (Young, 1979). Participation by workers in the management and governance of economic enterprises also has been defended on grounds that the distribution of positions of power and authority in economic life is subject to the difference principle (O'Neill, 2009).[12] Less direct lines of argument are concerned with the likely effects that features of economic production have on the functioning of democratic institutions or the realization of basic rights and liberties in noneconomic domains. As alluded to above, one such argument holds that workplace democracy is needed to limit the undue influence of capitalists on the state and to realize the fair value of political liberties (Cohen, 1989, p. 28). Another such argument holds that workplace democracy is needed to ensure the development of psychological conditions important for citizens in a just society – such as the sense that social institutions are open to reform.[13]

Without explicit institutional guarantees for workplace democracy, however, there is reason to doubt that widespread ownership of productive assets on its own is adequate to provide workers, and especially the least advantaged, with the required degree of control. In contemporary economies, much economic production occurs in the context of large-scale economic enterprises. If the ownership of productive assets is distributed equally, it is likely that any given enterprise will be owned by a large number of shareholders, each with a relatively small share of ownership. Under such circumstances, the share of ownership for any one worker is unlikely to be great enough to grant her the degree of effective control that Freeman suggests is required for property-owning democracy to satisfy the requirements of justice as fairness. More generally, if an individual exercises control as a worker by way of her status as an owner, she exercises no more control than someone who owns shares in the enterprise and does not work there. The only way, it seems, for workers to possess an effective degree of control by way of ownership is through ownership in small and medium-sized enterprises. Just as in the case of self-employment, however, from the perspective of the diversification of risk, it is undesirable for workers to invest their financial capital heavily in the enterprises in which they work.[14]

The question remains as to what about the choice of property-owning democracy depends upon the role of widespread ownership of productive assets as it relates specifically to the economic activity. In what follows, I argue that we can better understand the choice of property-owning democracy if we focus on the ways in which considerations about the content, governance, and status of work matter from the perspective of justice as fairness.[15]

The Content of Work: Meaningful Work

In the philosophical literature on work, one question that arises about the content of work is whether a highly specialized division of labor precludes work that qualifies as meaningful (Hsieh, 2008a). Although the term "meaningful work" is sometimes used to refer to work that is meaningful from an individual's own point of view, most commentators have in mind an objective conception of what such work involves. Specifically, they have in mind work that requires the exercise of judgment, initiative, and intellect on the part of workers and that allows workers a great deal of discretion in how the work is done.[16] For example, on one interpretation of Karl Marx's critique of the division of labor, meaningful work is required to respect a worker's claim to self-realization (Elster, 1986). Another argument is Aristotelian in nature. On this argument, meaningful work is required to overcome the division of labor that relegates some workers to the role of executing what they themselves have not conceptualized (Murphy, 1993).

Rawls seems to share these concerns. In *A Theory of Justice*, Rawls describes the division of labor in a just society. He writes that in a just society "the worst aspects of this division can be surmounted: no one need be servilely dependent on others and made to choose between monotonous and routine occupations which are deadening to human thought and sensibility" (1999b, p. 464). Rawls concludes, "the division of labor is overcome not by each becoming complete in himself, but by willing and meaningful work within a just social union of social unions in which all can freely participate as they so incline" (1999b, p. 464). Like the commentators cited above, Rawls has in mind an objective conception of meaningful work. Meaningful work is the opposite of monotonous and routine work, and it involves the exercise of intellect and is not deadening to human sensibility. For Rawls, the concern is that the lack of opportunity for meaningful work is damaging to citizens' self-respect.

Because Rawls does not say much more about this, it will help to summarize an account that makes sense of his concern (Moriarty, 2009). As defined by Rawls, self-respect involves two aspects. The first is a sense of one's own worth and worth in pursuing one's conception of the good or life plan. The second is the confidence to advance one's own ends (Freeman, 2007b, p. 482). For Rawls, to have a sense of worth in pursuing one's conception of the good, the conception of the good must satisfy the Aristotelian Principle, according to which it must "call upon [one's] natural capacities in an interesting fashion" (Rawls, 1999b, p. 386). Work that does not qualify as meaningful – that is, work that is "monotonous and routine" and "deadening to human thought and sensibility" – fails to satisfy this requirement, and does not support a citizen's sense that her conception of the good is worth carrying out. As Moriarty (2009) points out, in modern economies, it is reasonable to assume that many people work full-time over the course of most of their life. Participation in work is, in other words, "*mandatory* and *extensive*" (Moriarty, 2009, p. 453).[17] Because of the dominant role that work plays in the course of people's lives, there is good reason to hold that work is likely to play an important role in one's conception of the good such that the lack of opportunity for meaningful work is harmful to citizens' self-respect.[18]

By focusing on the role that meaningful work plays in Rawls's account of justice, we are better able to understand the choice of property-owning democracy with respect to the role that widespread ownership of productive assets directly plays in economic activity. Under welfare state capitalism, most individuals depend upon their labor for income. Whether work is meaningful may be a factor in choosing an occupation, but if an individual is completely dependent on her labor for income, whether work qualifies as meaningful is likely to be less significant as a factor in her choice. In contrast, under property-owning democracy, the meaningfulness of work can play a larger role in the choice of occupation. By reducing the degree to which the least advantaged depend upon labor for their income, property-owning democracy makes it easier for them to consider the meaningfulness of work in their choice of work (Hsieh, 2009, p. 406).

The Governance of Work: Protection against Arbitrary Interference

In addition to the content of work, an important area of inquiry in the philosophical literature on work concerns the governance of work – that is, the allocation of decision-making rights within the workplace (Hsieh, 2008a). As discussed above, the case for choosing property-owning democracy is sometimes explained on grounds that widespread ownership of productive assets results in workplace democracy, but there is reason to doubt that widespread ownership of productive assets alone is adequate to grant workers the required degree of control.

In this section, I argue that we can better understand the relevance of widespread ownership of productive assets if we adopt a view under which workplace democracy matters not so much for worker control, but for realizing a basic right to protection against arbitrary interference at work. On this view, even if widespread ownership of productive assets does not result in workplace democracy, it still achieves the same aims associated with worker democracy – namely, protection against arbitrary interference at work.[19]

To begin, it will help to explain briefly what counts as arbitrary interference at work. Successful operation of an economic enterprise is likely to require the scope of decision making to encompass decisions that result in substantial interference in the lives of workers. First, there are decisions that either direct a worker to perform specific tasks or specifically limit the actions that a worker may take within the context of her employment. Second, there are decisions that relate to general features of her employment, such as working conditions, compensation, or promotion. Third, there are decisions that are not made directly about the worker, but nevertheless affect her. Examples include decisions about what a company produces or decisions to relocate a company's operations. If little or no justification can be given for these instances of interference in terms of the workers' interests upon whom the interference is visited, then workers are subject to arbitrary interference in significant areas of their lives. When speaking of arbitrary interference, I have in mind severe forms of arbitrary interference – severe both in terms of the impact of the interference on the interests of those on whom it is visited and in its arbitrariness because there is little or no justification for it in terms of the interests on whom it is visited.[20]

In Rawls's account, for something to be accorded the status of a basic right, it must be counted among the social bases of self-respect, which are "those aspects of basic institutions normally essential if citizens are to have a lively sense of their worth as persons and to be able to advance their ends with self-confidence" (2001, p. 59). A number of features about work give us reason to place protection against arbitrary interference at work among the social bases of self-respect. As noted in the previous section, there is reason to hold that participation in work is "mandatory and extensive" (Moriarty, 2009, p. 453). Of particular concern is that the interference under consideration is visited by the decision of one individual on another individual within the context of an institutionally sanctioned decision-making procedure. To visit arbitrary interference on another individual is to treat her as though her interests and judgments do not matter.[21] As such, arbitrary interference means treating an individual as lacking in standing or in worth. It is treating another individual without respect. To lack protection against such interference is to be placed in a position in which it is permissible, by virtue of the basic structure, to be treated by another individual as lacking in standing or in worth. It is difficult to imagine situations more damaging to developing a sense of self-worth and self-confidence than to be in such a position.[22] In turn, I argue that just as there is a basic right to personal property on Rawls's account, so too should there be a basic right to protection against arbitrary interference at work.

One way to protect workers is through legal regulations, such as safety standards, that proscribe the range of interference that can be visited upon workers in the course of economic activity. Another way to protect workers is to guarantee a right to exit from their place of work. In response to a managerial directive, the worker is free to leave. There are limits, however, to the desirability and efficacy of either approach. As discussed above, the need for discretion seems to be a fundamental feature of economic activity. There is a limit to how much the discretion of managers can be restricted before the very nature of what makes economic enterprises valuable in the first place is undermined. With regard to exit, if what distinguishes economic enterprises is the exercise of discretion, unless a worker is to avoid working in an economic enterprise altogether, she remains subject to the capacity for arbitrary interference.[23] In addition, recall that the case for property-owning democracy gives us reason to hold that having work matters for self-respect, so there is a significant cost from exiting work altogether.

Workplace democracy provides one way to meet this challenge. By allowing workers to vote on managerial decisions that result in severe forms of interference, workers are able to protect themselves against arbitrary interference. The protection accorded by workplace democracy is especially important when the cost to pursuing external remedies is prohibitively expensive or when the interference is difficult to rectify *ex post*. In this manner, it appears that we arrive at an argument for workplace democracy that is grounded in a liberal egalitarian account of justice.

Widespread ownership of productive assets represents a further way to help protect workers against arbitrary interference at work. By reducing the degree to which individuals are dependent upon their labor for income, property-owning democracy helps to reduce the extent to which individuals are subject to the capacity for arbitrary interference at work. In contrast, under welfare state capitalism, even if workers enjoy a high standard of living they remain dependent upon their labor for their income. Accordingly, by acknowledging a basic right to protection against arbitrary interference at work, we are better able to understand the choice of property-owning democracy with reference to the way in which widespread ownership of productive assets affects economic activity.

The Status of Work: Workers as Property Owners

The account thus far is consistent with what James Meade (1964) – from whom Rawls adapted the concept of "property-owning democracy" – took to be the defining feature of such an economic regime. According to Meade, the "essential feature" of property-owning democracy is a reduction in the degree to which economic need drives the choice of work (1964, p. 40).[24] As discussed thus far, by reducing the importance of remuneration as a criterion for occupational choice, greater ownership of productive assets makes it easier for individuals to choose work that qualifies as meaningful. In a similar manner, with respect to the governance of work, by reducing the reliance on their labor for income, greater ownership of productive assets means that individuals are better positioned to avoid being subject to arbitrary interference at work.

There are, however, other ways in which to reduce the extent to which individuals depend upon their labor for income. One way, for example, is through the provision of a government-guaranteed stipend, or "basic income" (Van Parijs, 1995). In turn, the question may be asked whether there are ways in which the widespread ownership of productive assets matters in the context of economically productive activity beyond reducing the reliance on labor for income. In what follows, I take up this question.

The first point to note is that the income generated by privately owned capital differs from a government-guaranteed grant in a way that seems relevant from the perspective of justice as fairness.[25] The difference is this. In the case of a government-guaranteed grant, the recipient depends on the specific decision of the state. The recipient lacks a degree of independence and security that is enjoyed by the owner of capital. Insofar as the ability of workers to seek meaningful work or to avoid arbitrary interference at work depends in part on the independence and security associated with the income not associated with her labor, then it seems that a government-guaranteed grant does not reduce the reliance of individuals on their labor income in the same way as in the case of widespread ownership of capital.

Second, in an economic regime in which the means of production are privately owned, the widespread ownership of productive capital reflects an ideal about sharing the burdens of work in a way that welfare state capitalism does not. Work carries with it the association of being performed out of necessity, whether at the individual level or at the level of society as a whole. That is, it is difficult to imagine a society without work. In a private property regime with a highly unequal distribution of productive resources, it is likely that a small group of citizens will be able to avoid work, whereas the vast majority of citizens will not. In such a society, even if political equality and a high standard of living can be sustained, the fact remains that there will be a group of people who are free to enjoy an even higher standard of living without having to work at all. In contrast, in a society with widespread ownership of productive assets, this is unlikely to be the case. If work is something that can hardly be avoided as a society, perhaps it is only fair that the most advantaged members of society can't afford not to work.

This point can be put another way. Although capital contributes to economic production in the sense that without it, output would be lower, there is a sense in which the contribution of capital itself is not a productive activity in a way that work is. As stated by Joan Robinson, "*owning* capital is not a productive activity" (1942, p. 18). To be certain, there is mental and physical activity involved in deploying capital, but this activity is not the basis on which the capital owner receives a return on her investment. In contrast, even if work is not burdensome, work involves the direct contribution of a person's time and effort toward the production of some good or service. In ensuring there is no class of individuals who can afford not to work, property-owning democracy expresses a certain ideal of equality with regard to the nature of contribution expected from each individual.

Third, the widespread ownership of productive capital protects against a certain kind of status inequality that may arise under welfare state capitalism in the context of economically productive activity. One way to organize the participation of individuals in economically productive activity is through the employment relationship. In the employment relationship, employers possess residual rights of control – that is, employers have the right to make decisions about matters that are left undecided in the context of the employment relationship. In this manner, the employment relationship privileges the interests of employers with respect to matters that are undecided prior to entering into the relationship. Although labor can hire capital, under welfare state capitalism, many citizens are likely to work as employees hired by owners of capital without being owners of capital themselves. In the context of economically productive activity, there is likely to be a group of citizens whose interests are privileged as owners of capital and a group of citizens whose interests are not.

The widespread ownership of productive assets may be said to protect against this kind of status inequality by ensuring no one group of citizens is privileged in this manner. It should be noted that this inequality is not necessarily addressed through the redistribution of income after the production process. The inequality under consideration is within the context of economically productive activity. Furthermore, there is a sense in which this inequality of status is even more basic than any inequality in the distribution of offices or positions of authority within the economic sphere. It is about the question of whose interests are served in the context of contractual incompleteness in the production process. That the interests of capital are likely to have a certain kind of priority under a capitalist regime should not come as a surprise. The widespread distribution of productive assets in such a regime helps to ensure against there being a group of citizens who are only on one side of the relationship.

Although these last two points are expressed in terms of equality, they also may be understood as expressing the ideal of fraternity, which "involves a sense of civic friendship and some degree of social solidarity, as well as equality of social respect and a lack of deference and civility" (Freeman, 2007b, p. 198). Freeman explains that

> one way to understand the difference principle is as an institutional expression of the value of fraternity; for it requires that no one gain at other's expense, that departures from equality of income and wealth as well as powers and positions or office must benefit everyone, and that citizens enjoy greater advantages only if they are to the benefit of others who are less well off. (2007b, p. 198)

In a similar manner, property-owning democracy may be understood as an expression of the ideal of fraternity within the context of economically productive activity.

To be clear, the aim of this section is not so much to provide independent grounds on which to argue that work represents a distinctive contribution from the perspective of justice as fairness or that the employment relationship involves an objectionable kind of status inequality. Rather, the point is that if we accept these claims, we can better understand the choice of property-owning democracy with respect to the role that widespread ownership of productive assets plays in the context of economic production. Insofar as this gives us reason to accept these claims, then full productive enfranchisement concerns not only the content and governance of work, but also considerations about the status of work.

Conclusion

Central to the choice of property-owning democracy over welfare state capitalism is the aim of property-owning democracy to promote the widespread ownership of productive assets. As I have argued in this chapter, just why this feature is relevant from the perspective of justice as fairness is not always obvious, at least with respect to the way that ownership of productive assets affects the participation of citizens in economically productive activity. There are, of course, arguments as to why the widespread ownership of productive assets is relevant for noneconomic considerations, such as the role that asset ownership plays in ensuring the fair value of political liberty for citizens. However, if widespread ownership of productive assets is relevant, it seems reasonable to expect it should be relevant with respect to its immediate context, which is economic production.

In this chapter, I have argued that the widespread ownership of productive assets is relevant in part because it reduces the extent to which individuals depend upon their labor for income. This aspect of the widespread ownership of productive assets is relevant because it helps to support two claims of citizens: the opportunity for meaningful work and a basic right to protection against arbitrary interference at work.

Because there are means to reduce the extent to which individuals depend upon their labor for income that need not involve widespread ownership of productive assets, I also explored ways in which the widespread ownership of productive assets affects the status of work in the context of economic production. Property-owning democracy, I have argued, expresses a certain ideal of equality with regard to the nature of contribution required at the level of society as a whole. It also expresses a certain ideal of equality of protecting against a kind of status inequality within the productive process. Insofar as the choice of property-owning democracy gives us reason to accept this interpretation of the case for property-owning democracy, then full productive enfranchisement concerns not only the content and governance of work, but also considerations about the status of work.

Liberal egalitarianism has been criticized for paying insufficient attention to questions about economic production. In the words of Iris Marion Young (2006), questions about justice have been considered largely from within a "distributive paradigm" – that is, an interpretation about questions of justice as questions about the allocation of rights, goods, and opportunities among citizens (2006, p. 91). If the account in this chapter is correct, many of the resources for moving beyond this distributive paradigm are present in Rawls's account of property-owning democracy and in the account of justice as fairness. By moving beyond this distributive paradigm and thinking more about justice in production, the hope is that we will be that much closer to realizing what justice demands.

Notes

1. I thank Martin O'Neill and Thad Williamson for their comments and support in writing this chapter. In addition, I thank the Wharton Legal Studies Research Program for funding this research and the Harvard University Program in Ethics and Health for providing a hospitable working environment. All errors remain my own.
2. Welfare state capitalism, as defined by Rawls, "permits a small class to have a near monopoly of the means of production" (2001, p. 139). In contrast, property-owning democracy seeks to ensure "the widespread ownership of productive assets and human capital (that is, education and trained skills) at the beginning of each period, all this against a background of fair equality of opportunity" (2001, p. 139). For a more detailed discussion, see Rawls (1999b, pp. 234–242). See also Krouse and McPherson (1988) and Freeman (2007a).
3. "Rawls thinks that part of being an independent person with a sense of self-respect is to be in a position to provide for oneself while working in a job that itself is not demeaning and does not undermine self-respect" (Freeman, 2007b, p. 229). Self-respect, according to Rawls, is "perhaps the most important primary good" (Rawls, 1999b, p. 386).
4. For a helpful discussion of the lack of attention paid to questions about economic production among liberal proponents of justice, see Young (2006).
5. In this chapter, I leave aside questions about the division of labor within the household and between the sexes.
6. In addition to callings, Gregory Pence distinguishes two categories of work: laboring and workmanship. "Laboring," Pence writes, "is generally: (1) repetitious, (2) not intrinsically satisfying, (3) done out of necessity; labor also involves (4) few higher human faculties, and (5) little choice about how and when the work is done." Workmanship is differentiated from laboring by the following: "(1) use of higher human faculties, (2) some intrinsic satisfaction in the activity itself, (3) some degree of choice about when work is done and how, (4) pride of the worker in the products of work" (2001, pp. 93–94).
7. For a proposal along these lines, see Phelps (1997).
8. Note that Rawls does not regard working in a job of "last resort" as inconsistent with citizens' self-respect. In contrast, Elster (1988) raises an objection to government-provided work along these lines.
9. By "realizing the fair value of political liberties" is meant that "citizens similarly gifted and motivated have roughly an equal chance of influencing the government's policy and of attaining positions of authority irrespective of their economic and social class (Rawls, 2001, p. 46).
10. Under property-owning democracy, "workers normally can control real capital and their work conditions, whether as private owners or as members of unions or worker cooperatives" (Freeman, 2007b, p. 226).
11. For two surveys, see Cohen (1989) and Hsieh (2008a).
12. For some related arguments, see Clark and Gintis (1978), Schweikart (1978), and Peffer (1990, 1994).

13. This has been referred to variously as the "psychological support argument" (Cohen 1989, pp. 28–29), the "democratic character argument" (O'Neill, 2008, p. 31), and the "formative argument" (Hsieh, 2008a, pp. 85–86). An early version of this argument is found in Pateman (1970).
14. It may be thought that greater ownership of productive assets confers upon workers greater control over their lives at work insofar as they are in a better position to exit the enterprises in which they work. As discussed in later sections, given the need to exercise discretion within economic enterprises, there is a limit to the degree of control that workers are able to exercise through the use of exit. I thank Waheed Hussain for pressing me to raise this point earlier.
15. Parts of the following discussion are drawn from Hsieh (2005, 2008a, 2009).
16. For example, see Schwartz (1982), Arneson (1987), Bowie (1988), and Walsh (1994). A notable exception to this view is Van Parijs (1995), who argues that what counts as meaningful work is inherently subjective.
17. Moriarty's italics.
18. As Moriarty (2009) points out, this account is consistent with Rawls's requirement that specific conceptions of the good are not to form the basis for evaluating economic institutions or legislation. Although providing opportunities for meaningful work may have the effect of favoring conceptions of the good that include meaningful work, the purpose is not to promote a specific conception of the good, but rather to promote self-respect. Between Rawls's earlier and later work, there is some variation in how comprehensive these requirements of neutrality are taken to be. At a minimum, they apply to basic features of the constitution and justification for the use of the coercive power of the state. For helpful discussion, see Muirhead (2004). For another discussion of neutrality, see Kymlicka (2001). I thank Thad Williamson for pressing me to clarify this point.
19. The following discussion draws from a summary of the argument in Hsieh (2008a). The original argument is in Hsieh (2005). Following Philip Pettit's account of freedom as nondomination (1997), I call a regime that protects against arbitrary interference at work a regime of "workplace republicanism." I discuss the relation between this account and Philip Pettit's conception of freedom as nondomination in Hsieh (2005). I discuss the relation between workplace republicanism and workplace democracy in Hsieh (2008b). I thank Martin O'Neill for pressing me to clarify a number of points in this summary.
20. To be clear, an instance of interference can be arbitrary in this sense even if the interference follows from a decision that is justified in the context of the decision-making procedure internal to economic organizations. That is to say, I assume that it is possible to describe a decision-making procedure in a positive sense without reference to whether the economic regime that permits such a decision-making procedure is consistent with the principles of justice. As a further point of clarification, it should be noted that the lack of justification in terms of the worker's interests is understood only as a sufficient condition for the interference to be considered arbitrary.
21. Raz (1990) makes a similar point with respect to authority. He writes, "we have views of what interpersonal relations are morally acceptable. They involve mutual respect, reciprocity, etc. One-sided submission to the will of an authority seems to violate these precepts" (p. 16).
22. Consider an example given by White (2003) in which a worker says to himself, "I had better not go to those gay clubs any more because if my boss finds out he might sack me, and I will then be destitute. Instead, I had better go to the Young Conservative's Association to impress him" (p. 47).
23. There are also costs specific to exiting any one place of work. For discussions on what distinguishes economic enterprises and the role of discretion, see Coase (1937), Garrouste and Saussier (2005), and Williamson (2002).

24. According to Meade (1964), "the essential feature of this society would be that work had become rather more a matter of personal choice. The unpleasant work that had to be done would have to be very highly paid to attract to it those whose tastes led them to wish to supplement considerably their incomes from property. At the other extreme those who wished to devote themselves to quite uncommercial activities would be able to do so with a reduced standard of living, but without starving in a garret. Above all labour-intensive services would flourish of a kind which (unlike old-fashioned domestic service) might be produced by one man for another of equal income and status. Play-acting, ballet-dancing, painting, writing, sporting activities and all such 'unproductive' work as Adam Smith would have called it would flourish on a semi-professional semi-amateur basis; and those who produced such services would no longer be degraded as the poor sycophants of immoderately rich patrons" (pp. 40–41). Although Meade's conception of property-owning democracy involves a high degree of automation, the basic point remains the same – namely, that individuals need not take remuneration as the most important criterion for choosing work.
25. I thank Thad Williamson for highlighting the significance of this difference.

References

Arneson, R. (1987) Meaningful work and market socialism. *Ethics*, 97, 517–545.
Bowie, N. (1988) A Kantian theory of meaningful work. *Journal of Business Ethics*, 17, 1083–1092.
Clark, B. and Gintis, H. (1978) Rawlsian justice and economic systems. *Philosophy & Public Affairs*, 7, 302–325.
Coase, R. (1937) The nature of the firm. *Economica*, n.s. 4, 386–405.
Cohen, J. (1989) The economic basis of deliberative democracy. *Social Philosophy and Policy*, 6, 25–50.
Elster, J. (1986) Self-realization in work and politics: The Marxist conception of the good life. *Social Philosophy and Policy*, 3, 97–126.
Elster, J. (1988) Is there (or should there be) a right to work?, in *Democracy and the Welfare State* (ed. A. Gutmann), Princeton University Press, Princeton, pp. 53–78.
Freeman, S. (2007a) *Justice and the Social Contract*, Oxford University Press, Oxford.
Freeman, S. (2007b) *Rawls*, Routledge, London.
Garrouste, P. and Saussier, S. (2005) Looking for a theory of the firm: Future challenges. *Journal of Economic Behavior and Organization*, 58, 178–199.
Hsieh, N. (2005) Rawlsian justice and workplace republicanism. *Social Theory and Practice*, 31, 115–142.
Hsieh, N. (2008a) Justice in production. *Journal of Political Philosophy*, 16, 72–100.
Hsieh, N. (2008b) Workplace democracy, workplace republicanism, and economic democracy. *Revue de Philosophie Économique*, 9, 57–78.
Hsieh, N. (2009) Justice at work: Arguing for property-owning democracy. *Journal of Social Philosophy*, 40, 397–411.
Krouse, R. and McPherson, M. (1988) Capitalism, "property-owning democracy," and the welfare state, in *Democracy and the Welfare State* (ed. A. Gutmann), Princeton University Press, Princeton, pp. 79–106.
Kymlicka, W. (2001) *Contemporary Political Philosophy*, 2nd edn, Oxford University Press, Oxford.
Meade, J. (1964) *Efficiency, Equality and Ownership of Property*, Allen and Unwin, London.

Moriarty, J. (2009) Rawls, self-respect, and the opportunity for meaningful work. *Social Theory and Practice*, 35, 441–459.

Muirhead, R. (2004) *Just Work*, Harvard University Press, Cambridge, MA.

Murphy, J. (1993) *The Moral Economy of Labor: Aristotelian Themes in Economic Theory*, Yale University Press, New Haven.

O'Neill, M. (2008) Three Rawlsian routes towards economic democracy. *Revue de Philosophie Économique*, 8, 29–55.

Pateman, C. (1970) *Participation and Democratic Theory*, Cambridge University Press, Cambridge.

Peffer, R. (1990) *Marxism, Morality, and Social Justice*, Princeton University Press, Princeton.

Peffer, R. (1994) Towards a more adequate Rawlsian theory of social justice. *Pacific Philosophical Quarterly*, 75, 251–271.

Pence, G. (2001) Towards a theory of work. *Philosophical Forum*, 10 (1978–1979). Reprinted in *Philosophy and the Problems of Work: A Reader* (ed. K. Schaff), Rowman & Littlefield, Lanham, pp. 93–106.

Pettit, P. (1997) *Republicanism: A Theory of Freedom and Government*, Clarendon Press, Oxford.

Phelps, E. (1997) *Rewarding Work*, Harvard University Press, Cambridge, MA.

Rawls, J. (1999a) *The Law of Peoples*, Harvard University Press, Cambridge, MA.

Rawls, J. (1999b) *A Theory of Justice*, revised edn, Belknap Press of Harvard University Press, Cambridge, MA.

Rawls, J. (2001) *Justice as Fairness* (ed. E. Kelly), Belknap Press of Harvard University Press, Cambridge, MA.

Raz, J. (1990) Introduction, in *Authority* (ed. J. Raz), New York University Press, New York, pp. 1–19.

Robinson, J. (1942) *An Essay on Marxian Economics*, Macmillan, London.

Schwartz, A. (1982) Meaningful work. *Ethics*, 92, 634–646.

Schweickart, D. (1978) Should Rawls be a socialist? A comparison of his ideal capitalism with worker-controlled socialism. *Social Theory and Practice*, 5, 1–27.

Van Parijs, P. (1995) *Real Freedom for All: What (If Anything) Can Justify Capitalism?* Oxford University Press, Oxford.

Walsh, A. (1994) Meaningful work as a distributive good. *Southern Journal of Philosophy*, 32, 233–250.

White, S. (2003) *The Civic Minimum: On the Rights and Obligations of Economic Citizenship*, Oxford University Press, Oxford.

Williamson, O. (2002) The theory of the firm as governance structure: From choice to contract. *Journal of Economic Perspectives*, 16, 171–195.

Young, I.M. (1979) Self-determination as principle of justice. *The Philosophical Forum*, 11, 30–46.

Young, I.M. (2006) Taking the basic structure seriously. *Perspectives on Politics*, 4, 91–97.

8
Care, Gender, and Property-Owning Democracy

Ingrid Robeyns

In this chapter I ask what impact a regime shift from a capitalist welfare state to a property-owning democracy would have on gender justice and on caregivers and dependents.[1] Would property-owning democracy serve the interests of caregivers and their dependents better and would it be a more gender-just economic system than current forms of capitalism and the different varieties of the welfare state that we currently know?

As Ben Jackson's contribution to this volume makes clear, the term "property-owning democracy" has historically been used in a variety of ways, including proposals from both conservative and egalitarian strands (Jackson, Chapter 2). My analysis will focus only on the egalitarian versions of property-owning democracy, in particular on John Rawls's proposal (Rawls, 2001). An egalitarian property-owning democracy can be summarized as a socioeconomic regime that involves the private ownership of productive assets and a widespread distribution of human capital. In a property-owning democracy the background institutions aim at dispersing the ownership of wealth, thereby preventing a small group in society from controlling the economy, and indirectly political life as well (Rawls, 2001, p. 139).

My analysis will proceed as follows. In the first section I briefly sketch the empirical background of care work and gender relations in contemporary liberal democratic societies (especially Europe and North America). These empirical facts tend to be poorly known, but they provide us crucial information if we want to properly evaluate the gender and care effects of different socioeconomic regimes. The second section then draws on the literature on justice, care, and gender to sketch what properties a socioeconomic regime should have in order to properly account for care work and move toward gender justice. I will present a typology of care regimes that would meet the needs of caregivers, and describe how they differ in terms of their impact on the gender constellation, and also on the kind of social policies and institutions that they require. The following section then moves to answering the core question of this chapter: what are the effects of implementing a property-owning democracy on caregivers and

Property-Owning Democracy: Rawls and Beyond, First Edition. Edited by Martin O'Neill and Thad Williamson.
© 2012 Blackwell Publishing Ltd. Published 2012 by Blackwell Publishing Ltd.

dependents and on gender relations? I will argue that property-owning democracy would present some improvement for caregivers, dependents, and gender egalitarians in comparison with a capitalist society with weak labor market protection and public provision for care work. However, if we also want property-owning democracy to meet the needs of caregivers and make significant progress toward gender justice, an additional set of policies (not intrinsic to property-owning democracy) need to be added. In analytical terms, we need a philosophical and political-economic approach that conceptualizes "the economy" in terms of both production *and social reproduction*, and that incorporates an informed view on the nature of gender. Since both the policies required for a property-owning democracy in the strict sense and the policies aiming to provide gender justice and meeting the needs of care require significant redistribution and/or expenditures, this raises difficult questions about economic and political feasibility. Proponents of a property-owning democracy therefore need to investigate whether it is feasible to combine the social institutions and policies of a property-owning democracy with those of a decent care regime.

Care and Gender in Contemporary Capitalist Societies

Human beings are not born as capable, autonomous, individual adults who can provide and care for themselves. Rather, we are born as extremely vulnerable babies who are fully dependent on the care given to us by others. We cannot survive if we are not given dedicated, time-intensive attention and hands-on care in the first years of our lives, and we continue to be dependent on care work by others throughout our lives, possibly again becoming heavily dependent on hands-on care at old age or in periods of illness and disability. Some human beings remain dependent on full-time care throughout their lives, such as the severely disabled (Feder, 1999).

Part of the hands-on care for dependents is done by care workers who perform care work as a profession: nannies, elderly carers, disability carers, babysitters, and so forth. In addition to the hands-on care that is done by care workers, much of the care that dependents receive is unpaid work done by caregivers. These are generally relatives (parents or adult children), friends, neighbors, and volunteers. It is often, whether exclusively or partly, a labor of love: it is something that caregivers primarily do out of love, sympathy, and commitment for those who are dependent on them.[2] But the fact that it has these other-regarding motives does not mean that it is not "work," at least not in the loose sense in which we talk about "work" in daily life: it has to be done by someone, and it requires time, energy, skills, and dedication by the worker.[3] Care work is needed to keep our society and our economies going: without raising children, there won't be a next generation of workers to keep the economic system (whether capitalist or otherwise) going.

Care work takes different forms. In policy discussions the notion is invoked much more narrowly than in daily life, where it is used to include relational aspects of friendship, self-care, and care for animals and the natural environment. For present purposes I will focus on childcare, elderly care, care for the ill and for the disabled. Hands-on care is a large part of those forms of care, and we know from time budget studies that for persons with care responsibilities, this kind of care strongly competes in terms of time allocation with other types of work, especially paid work on the labor market. Put differently, people with care responsibilities for children, the elderly, and the disabled are very likely to be in a time-crunch if they are struggling to combine hands-on care with holding a job (independent of whether having a job is only motivated by the income it generates or also by other aspirations, such as playing a role in public life or developing a professional identity.)

About half the work that people do in postindustrial societies is unpaid work, which consists of unpaid care work and household work.[4] Adults spend much time on unpaid care work, and this represents a significant cost in terms of devoted time and lost opportunities to them. The cost of care work can be illustrated by Nancy Folbre's illuminating estimates of the cost of raising a child, based on US time budget data for 2000 (Folbre, 2008). The costs of raising a child fall into two main categories: expenditures and care work (which includes child-related household work). Annual per-child expenditures range from US$6700 per infant in families with three or more children to just over US$12,000 for teenagers in one-child families (Folbre, 2008, p. 74).[5] Yet the time cost of parental care is even bigger than the expenditures on children.[6] Parents, especially mothers, spend an extraordinarily large amount of time caring for their children, indeed often many more hours than they spend in paid work. A child with two parents present enjoys on average 32 hours a week of active parental care (with either or both of the parents present), whereas for children of single parents this amounts to 23 hours. Translating this into a monetary value is not straightforward, since there are different ways to put a monetary value on family care work. Under very modest assumptions,[7] the annual cost of parental family care in a two-parent two-child household is estimated to amount to US$13,352; in a one-parent family US$11,024 (Folbre, 2008, p. 130).

Care work is confronted with a problem in the structure of its costs, which other types of work do not face to the same degree. In most postindustrial societies, care work is expensive relative to other types of work, because it is highly labor intensive, and labor costs are increasingly more important in determining the relative cost of a product or service than other costs (such as capital costs, raw or intermediate material resources, or technology). Moreover, the Baumol effect (also known as Baumol's cost disease) can explain why in real terms the cost of care work (and thus the shadow-cost or the opportunity cost of unpaid care work) is going up over time. In many economic sectors, the productivity of workers increases with technological change and innovation: for example, a car mechanic in the UK has a much higher productivity than a century ago, thanks to the new technologies that she can use. Yet for workers in the care sector, the possibilities of labor productivity increases through technological innovation are very limited. However, if relative wages increase in other sectors (since productivity goes up), the wages of care workers will increase too, without the corresponding increase in productivity. Since productivity gains in care work are very hard to establish, care work will become increasingly expensive in comparison to other types of work.

A very harsh capitalist society, with only a very low minimum wage (or no minimum wage at all), with many poorly skilled people who have few options, and where the power balance between labor and capital strongly favors the latter, is probably an exception to the above analysis. Many states of the USA seem to qualify for this category. In those societies, care work is performed by poorly skilled people, who work for very low wages, and who cannot expect a wage increase if the productivity in the economy overall increases. If a society has a large army of unskilled and poor people who desperately need a job, then care services will be relatively cheap. This would make the cost of care, all other things being equal, cheaper for people buying those care services, but I do not see how one can regard such a societal arrangement as just at all. Such societies should be evaluated as unjust, since they allow hard-working people to remain poor while others, who are not harder working, to be excessively rich. I should therefore qualify my conclusion: In societies with social institutions guaranteeing all citizens access to education that qualifies them for minimally decent jobs, with procedures to safeguard that the balance of power between capital and labor remains minimally fair, and with labor market regulations or welfare state provisions which guarantee that those who work are not poor, we can expect that care work is expensive and will in relative terms become more expensive as the high-tech postindustrial economy continues to develop.

Thus, given the very limited possibilities of productivity increases, the relative unit cost of care work is increasing over time. If we add to this the increased predicted need of elderly care in many countries, due to the aging of the population and the longer longevity of the elderly, it should be clear that we should give the provision of care work a central place in the design of any future socioeconomic system. However, as I will argue throughout this chapter, care work and caregiving have been rather neglected in the discussion of alternative socioeconomic systems, and the scholarly debate on property-owning democracy is not very different in this respect.

Clearly, a society can choose to partly socialize the cost of raising children and caring for other dependents. Socializing these costs can be done by providing direct transfers to parents and other guardians of children, by providing free education, generously subsidized parental leave and other care leaves, and by providing public childcare facilities, or regulating and subsidizing private childcare facilities.

Yet what all societies have in common – whether the costs are socialized or not, and whether the wages for care workers are low or not – is that roughly half the work people do is unpaid work, and most of that unpaid work is care work (Goldschmidt-Clermont and Pagnossin-Aligisakis, 1996; Gershuny, 2000; Picchio, 2003). The large share of unpaid work in the total amount of work we do is a fact that needs to be taken on board when evaluating existing or developing alternative visions of welfare regimes and socioeconomic systems.

What does gender have to do with all this? I am taking a constructivist perspective on gender, whereby "gender" stands to "culture" as "sex" stands to "nature" (Robeyns, 2007). Gender refers to the differences between men and women that are socially constructed, rather than given by nature. Sally Haslanger (2000) defines gender in terms of the social positions that men and women occupy. A person belongs to a gender because she is thought to have certain bodily features that reveal her reproductive capacities. These bodily features function as markers for evaluating individuals as either men or women, and for justifying their respective social positions. Gender is thus a social category which has, in the dominant social discourse of most societies, two modes, man and woman.[8] Observations or imaginations of sexual characteristics serve as markers to classify individuals in different social positions. The social category "gender" thus becomes projected on the biological category "sex." The point about the concept of gender is that women and men are treated according to their social category (gender) for reasons that have nothing, or only tangentially, to do with their biological category (sex).

One of the dimensions of gender is that women are believed to be better at care work, are socialized into care work, and are encouraged and expected to care. Men are believed to be less good at caring, are often discouraged from caring, and are in some circumstances discriminated against if they want to care.[9] The result is that on average women do much more care work than men (Robeyns, 2007).

It is a very difficult and contested discussion as to *why* it is the case that women do so much more care work than men. Some point to nature, which would have given women a "natural advantage" to care, or which would give (the large majority of) women stronger desires or preferences to do unpaid care work rather than be employed (Becker, 1991; Hakim, 2000; Tooley, 2002). Other arguments point to the social norms of caring, which encourage women to care and discourage men from caring (Badgett and Folbre, 1999; Brighouse and Wright, 2008; Gheaus, 2008; Gheaus and Robeyns, 2011). In addition, in some countries the socioeconomic institutions such as the structures of the labor market or conditions for health care insurance discourage couples from sharing paid and care work equally. One could also develop an argument that care is socially undervalued and financially a risky choice, and men are rational by not wanting to spend too much time on care and moreover are in a bargaining position that helps them to follow this low-risk path – a behavior we also observe among those women who are in a bargaining position to do so, due to their stronger human capital or financial position.

Whatever the correct explanation, it stands beyond doubt that the notions of gender and care are deeply intertwined. Since women are so much more engaged with unpaid care work, they have a much higher stake in how our social and economic institutions value, protect, subsidize, and redistribute care work. Similarly, it is very unlikely that we can significantly move closer to a gender-just society without a shift to a socioeconomic regime that takes care work seriously, and reconsiders its status, reward, and redistribution (Okin, 1989; Bubeck, 1995; Wright, 2009).

The available empirical evidence shows that a division of labor in a household whereby one partner (generally the man) specializes in paid market work, and the other partner (generally the woman) specializes in unpaid household and care work, is risky for the latter. Specialization in unpaid care and household labor leads to substantial *economic risks*, especially financial risks at divorce (Bergmann, 1981). Empirical studies show that economic dependence on a breadwinner can have disadvantageous consequences in the case of marital breakdown. In the USA, women's standards of living decline between 13% and 35% after divorce, while men's standard of living increases by 11% to 13% (Peterson, 1996). In Britain, the mean net income after divorce increases slightly for men, whereas it decreases by 14% for women and 18% for children (Jarvis and Jenkins, 1999).[10] If the specialization in care and household work takes the form of not quitting the labor market completely, but of holding a small part-time job, then in most countries this comes at the cost of lack of (or much more limited) health benefits and pension insurance. Women who quit the labor market may plan to take a break for merely a few years and then return to the labor market, yet this comes at the cost of lower lifetime earnings: they are highly unlikely to return to the earnings which they could have earned had they stayed employed. A break away from the labor market thus has a depressing effect not just on immediate but also on *lifetime* earnings, even if the break is only for a few years.

Many people, including scholars, tend to downplay the size and importance of the care work that is done in society, and assume away the impact of gender on our lives, including the fact that care is a deeply gendered phenomenon.[11] Yet I believe it is very instructive to try to understand *why* gender, care, and the family remain so detached from normative discussions about justice and the evaluation of socioeconomic regimes. First, "the economy" is often equated with "markets" – whether they are labor markets, production markets, consumption markets, or investment markets. In addition, many economists and (to a somewhat lesser degree) econo-political philosophers still have a romanticized view that care work is not real work – rather, it is assumed to fall into the category of leisure activities. While such an assumption is often defended on the grounds of the parsimony of the model or a libertarian outlook on the world, it has caused great harm to the analysis of the unpaid economy, and has introduced a deep gender and care bias in the analysis of socioeconomic systems and theories of justice. Martha Nussbaum is thus right when she writes that

> care for children, elderly people, and people with mental and physical disabilities is a major part of the work that needs to be done in any society, and in most societies it is a source of great injustice. Any theory of justice needs to think about the problem from the beginning, in the design of the basic institutional structure, and particularly in its theory of the primary goods. (Nussbaum, 2006, p. 127)

The same can be said about any normative theory of a socioeconomic system including proposals for a property-owning democracy. The question we need to ask is: will property-owning democracy be a regime that is more gender just and will it better meet the needs of caregivers and their dependents than the alternative economic systems? And a closely related question is: if property-owning democracy is a regime that we have good reasons to endorse independent of our concerns for care work and gender issues, what is needed to create a care-supportive and gender-just version of property-owning democracy? To answer these questions, we now turn to an analysis of what is needed to move toward gender justice and provide more support for caregivers and dependents.

Supporting Care and Moving Toward Gender Justice

If we analyze the virtues and pitfalls of different socioeconomic regimes, then what features should those regimes have in order to be supportive for caregivers and dependents, while at the same time making societies more gender just?

Scholars have different views on how to do justice to (or: take proper care of) caregivers while at the same time reducing gender injustice (Robeyns, 2008; Wright, 2009). Although there are a variety of views, we could distinguish the following three ideal typical regimes for dealing with these issues.[12]

The first model is the *"full commodification of care" welfare regime*: all working-age adults should be encouraged to work full time, and the state should make provisions or encourage the creation of a market to make this possible for those adults who have care responsibilities. In this regime, there will be no incentives at all for not being employed on the labor market, whether it is because one needs to care or rather wants to surf in Malibu. Care should be commodified to a large extent, perhaps even to the largest extent possible. This does *not* imply that this care work should be left to the market, let alone to the unregulated market: the commodification of care could be either unregulated and unsubsidized, hence completely left to the working of the markets; or it could be regulated but unsubsidized, which would imply that the quality would be controlled but those in need of care (or their parents or family members) would pay the full cost of it; or the commodification of care could be both regulated and subsidized, in which case the quality would be controlled and the costs of care work would be (in part or completely) borne by taxpayers. Most defenders of this full commodification of care regime, such as the feminist economist Barbara Bergmann, plead for high-quality and highly subsidized public provisions for care (Bergmann, 1998, 2008).

The second model is the *family care welfare regime*, which strives for care to be done as much as possible by relatives or friends. A welfare state endorsing this model can support family caregivers in a variety of ways. For example the labor regulations could stipulate that parents are allowed to quit their jobs for three or five years when their children are young while being guaranteed that they have access to the same job upon their return. Or the state could implement generous tax breaks for parents of young children who do not earn an income of their own, thereby effectively supporting stay-at-home caregivers. The bottom line is that women and men who want to provide care by themselves should be financially supported in doing so.

The third model is the *combined welfare regime*, which combines elements of the commodification of care model and the family care model either synchronically, diachronically, or combined. The *diachronically combined welfare regime* endorses the family care welfare model when the child is a baby, and shifts to the commodification of care welfare model when the children become older. For example, a welfare state which endorses this model gives parents generously paid parental leaves when the child is younger than one year, but does not encourage (or even actively discourages) part-time work or nonparticipation in the labor market in other circumstances. For other types of care, similar provisions are made. The diachronically combined care model would provide for full-time paid leave when a child is ill or an older family member very seriously ill, for example by providing protected care leaves. The *synchronically combined welfare regime* provides incentives and support for continuous but only part-time allowances to care over a long period, for example by allowing parents to take one day a week parental leave for several years, or by structuring the labor market in such a way that there are plenty of high-quality part-time jobs of 12, 24, or 32 hours a week, with the same pro rata benefits and protection as full-time jobs.

How do these models fare on accounts of support for care needs and for tackling gender injustice? Of course, to a large extent this depends on the level of financial support in those regimes. If, for example, parental leave is a right for many consecutive years, but only at a very low lump-sum grant, then the support is extensive in time but limited in its level. Still, bracketing the issue of the level of the financial compensation for a moment, it is possible to make some general remarks on the effects of these models on care and gender issues.

Some feminists support the commodification of care model, and have argued for an extensive commodification of care work and household work (cooking, cleaning, etc.), since otherwise women will keep being pushed back into the domestic sphere, whether with a low or high reward and status. The commodification of care model may improve gender equality, but only if the working conditions of the (overwhelmingly female) workers who do the commodified care are good; otherwise it may only be an improvement for the financially better-off women. In addition, it is important to note that the style of this gender equality is "total androgyny, male style" as Barbara Bergmann (1998) has called it: men and women should roughly behave the same on the labor market, with women effectively becoming as oriented toward paid work as men are nowadays. In other words, this model evaluates gender equality in terms of being part of the world of commerce, exchange, and production. It leaves the labor market virtually untouched, since it does not require that firms and organizations reorganize their structures so as to take into account that many employees are workers who carry the ultimate responsibilities for dependents, and who may indeed also have a paramount need to spend time caring for those dependents.

The commodification of care regime implicitly assumes that all care work *can* be outsourced: it is believed that it does not matter who does the care work – whether it is done by a committed parent or parental figure, or a student in a gap year, or a nanny who will leave next year and who is terribly missing her own children a thousand miles away. This assumption can be attacked on two grounds. Firstly, there is ample evidence from development psychology that it does matter that children can spend enough time with their parents for their healthy development. Children want to be with their parents, and they actually need their parents (or other adults with whom they form years-long, stable, caring relationships) for a minimal time on a daily, weekly, monthly, and yearly basis. The exact quantification of this need is a matter of great dispute, but no one denies that children need to spend some time with their parents. Secondly, most parents want to spend some time with their children, and one could even argue that this is a need on their part. The commodification of care model does not, in general, recognize those needs. It rather only recognizes, or at least prioritizes, the needs by parents to earn a living and/or to be a working adult. Moreover, it is a model that few women and men actually want. As John Baker puts it, "an attempt to address the gendered division of labor by externalizing and commodifying care while pushing carers into paid employment runs against its members' deeply ingrained understandings of human relationships and frustrates their needs for love and care" (Baker, 2008, p. 6).

The family care regime takes the other extreme. It improves the rewards, and probably the social status, of family caregivers, and recognizes that care dependents (especially children) need time with their caregivers. But it does not recognize that there are benefits to both some dependents (especially children) and to the caregivers if the caregivers are also enabled to hold jobs, and if the dependents are able to be cared for by care workers (for example, children attending high-quality nurseries). Still, there are good arguments for giving children not only time with their parents, but also nonparental care (Gheaus, 2011). The benefits of qualitative nonparental care for children are well documented for all ages of certain groups of vulnerable dependents, and for older children of all social backgrounds. The main area of dispute is the balance of benefits and risks to children younger than one. A recent American study found that for working mothers who work under suitable circumstances, the net benefits are neutral, and indeed are positive for the subgroup of mothers who do not work more than 30 hours a week (Brooks-Gunn, Han, and Waldfogel, 2010).[13] Moreover, the proponents of the family care model tend to ignore the well-documented risks that the corresponding gender division of paid labor and work pose to women's quality of life and long-term vulnerabilities (Okin, 1989; Bergmann, 1998, 2008; Robeyns, 2001).

The mixed model endorses the claims that it is not desirable that all care is commodified, and that caregivers have a variety of needs, including needs to provide hands-on care, but also needs to do other types of activities, such as paid work. The mixed regime also accounts for some empirical findings from human capital studies in labor economics, which have demonstrated that the economic security and life-long income generation capacities of workers are best protected if they don't completely quit the labor market for too long. Political parties and groups that oppose the mixed models do this in most cases either based on a comprehensive notion of the good life (such as the earlier mentioned view of Barbara Bergmann that it would be better if we all behaved in the way most men are currently behaving on the labor market), or based on a world-view that prioritizes GDP growth and people's economic contribution above other goals, including those people's quality of life understood in a broader and not purely materialistic sense.

While all three models have their advocates and opponents, my understanding of the relevant scholarly literatures is that the mixed care regime succeeds best, all things considered, to balance all relevant interests. Clearly, the mixed care model comes in versions that accept some gender injustices in order to protect other relevant values, such as the freedom to choose one's own way of living, but also in more radical versions that do more to destabilize the gender order.

What lessons for the analysis of property-owning democracy can we learn from this brief sketch of the debate on care-friendly and gender-destabilizing regimes? First, it is instructive to see that there is a huge literature and an extensive debate on how a just and good society would deal with issues of care and dependency (a debate which I have only been able here to sketch in a rather brutish way). It is regrettable that most insights of this debate are missing in the discussion of socioeconomic regimes, where the implicit and nonanalyzed assumptions remain that (a) care work is not real work, and thus does not belong in a discussion of economic systems, and (b) women do more care work than men, but since this is what they choose we should not be morally or politically worried about that. I have only been able to briefly touch upon the enormous literature that criticizes, and in my view successfully demolishes, both assumptions, yet it is sobering to see that we haven't, in my view at least, made that much progress since the path-breaking publication on gender justice by Susan Okin (1989) over 20 years ago.

Second, the brief overview also shows that all of the models proposed to address the needs of caregivers and to reduce gender injustice require active intervention by the government. Moreover, all except the most minimalist model (being the commodification model, which regulates commodified care but does not subsidize it) require state intervention and financial redistribution. Indeed, many of the policies in these models require rather far-going labor market regulation (e.g., right to care for a sick child, right to parental leave) and are very costly. The lesson to take home is: reducing gender injustice to a significant degree and doing justice to caregivers costs a lot of money – for the simple reason that care work is very time intensive, and thus either requires a paid labor force doing that work, or else requires an unpaid caregiver to forgo her labor market income.

This brings us, finally, to the questions which this chapter aims to address: what would the impact of a regime shift from a capitalist welfare state to a property-owning democracy be on gender justice and on caregivers and dependents? Would a property-owning democracy serve the interests of caregivers and their dependents better and would it be a more gender-just economic system than current forms of capitalism and than the different varieties of the welfare state that we currently know?

The Consequences of Property-Owning Democracy for Gender and Care

Property-owning democracy is a socioeconomic regime that involves the private ownership of productive assets and a widespread distribution of human capital, whereby the background institutions aim at dispersing the ownership of wealth, thereby preventing a small group in society from controlling the economy. It is thus a market economy in which the distribution of different forms of capital is as equal as possible. Yet as Thad Williamson and Martin O'Neill (2009) note, the notion of property-owning democracy has not been extensively studied, and the general notion needs to be unpacked or translated in order to understand which social policies and institutions it would require in advanced postindustrialized societies.

Property-owning democracy is in many ways similar to the welfare state, since it also tries to protect the fair value of political liberties and protect the interests of the worst-off social class. Yet property-owning democracy is "a regime that broadens property ownership directly, rather than a welfare state dependent on large-scale *ex post* redistributions to limit inequalities" (Williamson and O'Neill, 2009, p. 4). Rawls (and others) believe that a property-owning democracy has a crucial advantage over a welfare state, in at least two respects. First, the welfare state with its focus on *ex post* redistribution does nothing to prevent a strong concentration of capital in the hands of a few, and this will lead to a disproportional influence in politics and hence a corresponding concentration of political power. Second, the welfare state regards the net recipients of financial redistributions as passive victims of socioeconomic injustice that needs to be rectified, rather than as agents of change. The intent of a property-owning democracy "is not simply to assist those who lose out through accident or misfortune (although that must be done), but rather to put all citizens in a position to manage their own affairs on a footing of a suitable degree of social and economic equality" (Rawls, 2001, p. 139).

How does this translate in terms of more concrete socioeconomic policies and institutions? O'Neill and Williamson neatly summarize these as follows:

1 Wide Dispersal of Capital: The *sine qua non* of a property-owning democracy is that it would entail the wide dispersal of the ownership of the means of production,

with individual citizens controlling productive capital, both in terms of human and non-human capital (and perhaps with an opportunity to control their own working conditions).
2   Blocking the Intergenerational Transmission of Advantage: A property-owning democracy would also involve the enactment of significant estate, inheritance and gift taxes, acting to limit the largest inequalities of wealth, especially from one generation to the next.
3   Safeguards against the Corruption of Politics: A property-owning democracy would seek to limit the effects of private and corporate wealth on politics, through campaign finance reform, public funding of political parties, public provisions of forums for political debate, and other measures to block the influence of wealth on politics (perhaps including publicly funded elections). (Williamson and O'Neill, 2009, p. 5)

What, if any, would be the gender effects, and the effects on caregivers, of those three sets of policies?

Let me start with the third effect, the Safeguards against the Corruption of Politics. We could expect this set of measures to have a gender effect, since women are less likely to be able to buy their way in politics. In a nutshell, there are many fewer wealthy women than wealthy men, and if the influence of wealth on politics is limited, then this should decrease the relative power of men in politics, and thus increase the power of women. The effects on caregivers are very difficult to predict: if a property-owning democracy triggered all sorts of radical and egalitarian virtues in people, and led to a more critical and self-reflective society which would embrace a caring and egalitarian ethos, then it may, in a very indirect way, also benefit caregivers since the injustice in the distribution of care and its reward and social status could be more democratically debated in society. But frankly, such a prediction would be a rather wild speculation; we don't know whether the policies and institutions that would aim at safeguarding the corruption of politics would make any tangible difference for caregivers.

The policies aiming at the Wide Dispersal of Capital would have three effects. First, they would have a slight, and only indirect, beneficial effect on gender justice and for caregivers. The effect would be indirect via the lesser degree of inequality in wealth, and thus, derivatively, in income from wealth. Women tend to hold much less financial wealth and other forms of nonhuman capital than men, and thus any additional redistribution would benefit women in this regard. Yet a redistribution of wealth would do nothing to accommodate caregivers in the sense of redistributing care between men and women, or improving the status and reward of caregiving.

The second possible effect of the policies aimed at a wide dispersal of capital would depend on the question whether or not property-owning democracy always comes with increased workplace democracy. *If* a property-owning democracy also *guaranteed* an opportunity to control one's working conditions, than that would be a major advantage for caregivers, since all versions of the mixed care regime models assume that the workplace adapts (to some extent) to the needs of the family, for example by offering a high-quality nursery on the site of the workplace, by introducing the rights to part-time work (on pro rata similar conditions), or by allowing flexible working hours or allowing workers to take time off to care for an ill dependent on short notice. This would not only benefit women. Some evidence seems to suggest, for example, that men who are legally entitled to parental leave are discriminated against if they take up that leave in comparison with men who do not (Albrecht, Edin, Sundström, and Vroman, 1999). Fathers also often claim on an anecdotal basis that they are confronted with social norms compelling them to not make use of their legal rights to parental leave. If workplaces were really democratic, then one would expect these injustices against male caregivers to wane over time. Hence a first conclusion that can be drawn is that those versions of a property-owning democracy that include a full-fledged version of workplace democracy as an *essential* aspect of property-owning democracy should be more beneficial for the needs of caregivers and gender justice compared with a property-owning democracy that does not regard workplace democracy as an essential element.

The third and final effect of policies aimed at a wide dispersal of capital are to a large extent similar to what we have learnt in the last decade from the gender analysis of an unconditional basic income or basic capital grant. If the wide dispersal of capital implies that everyone would, at some point in their lives, be given an unconditional stock of financial capital, or of other nonhuman capital which they could sell (like land, real estate, or stocks), then this capital stock could be used to generate an infinite income stream. Clearly, this will be a rather modest income stream, in all likelihood not enough to live on, let alone to raise a family. Yet in societies that do not have a commodification-of-care or a mixed care regime, the correspondent lack of public childcare facilities may imply that this modest income stream would de facto function as a basic income. As I have argued in detail elsewhere, a small, unconditional, basic income, in combination with the existing gender norms and gender expectations, would strengthen the gender division of labor and thus worsen gender injustice, since it gives a financial incentive to withdraw from the labor market which increases the economic vulnerability of people, especially in the long term when human capital has eroded (Robeyns, 2001). Since in a property-owning democracy all citizens have decent or high levels of human capital, this implies that all mothers who use the basic income which is generated by their property-owning democracy-sponsored capital will lose out in terms of their current and future earnings as well as their opportunities to flourish in the nonfamily sphere. Of course, if the specific rules of the property-owning democracy don't allow the possibility to turn one's property into an income stream then this problem won't occur – but in that case the property transfer also cannot contribute to lightening the burden of care for caregivers.

What about the second set of policies, those aiming at the Blocking of the Intergenerational Transmission of Advantage? Here, the same argument applies as for the Wide Dispersal of Capital: since women and especially caregivers are more concentrated at the bottom of the wealth distribution, there may be an indirect beneficial effect. However, it *may* be the case that a pitfall for caregivers lurks below the institutions that aim at blocking the intergenerational transmission of advantage. Whether this will be the case or not depends on whether the large inheritance and gift taxes that will be needed to reach this effect will come *on top of* large other forms of taxes, or rather *replace* these other forms of taxes (such as income tax, or consumption taxes). The reasoning is the following. In the previous sections of this chapter I have tried to show that the total package of social policies and institutions that are needed to meet the needs of caregivers is very expensive. In the second section I showed how costly caring is, especially if we do not want to engage in the use of commodified care which is paid an indecent wage. In the third section I explained that all defensible forms of care regimes demand a large package of public policies. For example, Barbara Bergmann calculated that the Swedish welfare state, which corresponds to a high-quality diachronically mixed care model, costs about 60% of Swedish GDP, and thus taxation on labor and other forms of income is among the highest in the world (Bergmann, 2008). The inheritance and gift taxes that are part and parcel of a property-owning democracy would presumably *not* be used to fund the policy package of a mixed care regime, since these taxes would be redistributed in order to spread the ownership of capital.

At best, a property-owning democracy would coexist with the policies of the various possible care regimes. But this would imply two instances of high-level taxation: high-level inheritance and gift taxes to encourage the wide dispersal of capital, and a high level of other types of taxes (labor taxes, consumption taxes) to fund the policies that are needed for a decent care regime. The crucial question is whether that is what proponents of a property-owning democracy had in mind, and whether that makes the property-owning democracy proposal less feasible. The answer to the latter question at least in part depends, I believe, on the context. Financial inequality is in some countries extraordinarily large whereas GDP per capita is high. In those countries the introduction of a mixed care welfare regime together with a redistribution of wealth would be economically more feasible than in more egalitarian countries, where the inequality in money passed on from one generation to the next is much smaller. The figures on the situation in the United States that are cited by Thad Williamson (Chapter 11 in this volume) are simply stunning, and I don't think many (if any) feminists would object to the redistribution he proposes. Yet in other countries, such as many European countries, taxation on labor and inheritance is already very high, and financial inequality much lower, which drastically limits the scope for moving toward a property-owning democracy without jeopardizing the policies that are part of the mixed care regime. By introducing plain statistics, Williamson's chapter should remind us that the final verdict on the gender- and care effects of the move from the current situation to a property-owning democracy will depend on what that current situation exactly looks like, in terms of (a) the current levels of economic inequality, (b) the current package of care-supporting policies, and (c) the political feasibility of introducing the taxation that is needed to establish a property-owning democracy and to fund those care-supporting policies that are still missing.

Conclusion

In this chapter I have developed a gender and care analysis of property-owning democracy in three steps. First, I have summarized some essential facts and figures regarding the nature and magnitude of care work and caregiving, and the nature of gender. Second, I have presented my reading of the literature on what gender justice and a proper acknowledgment of care would demand from socioeconomic regimes. The bottom line taken from that overview was that any defensible care regime will be financially very costly, and will require a mix of labor market regulations, social security provisions, and public services (such as nurseries and care institutions for the elderly and the disabled) which are funded, and controlled or provided, by the government.

Third, from Rawlsian political philosophy I have taken the standard conceptualization of a property-owning democracy, and have asked whether property-owning democracy, so understood, would enhance gender justice and protect the interests of caregivers and dependents.

From a gender and care perspective, the risks or potential negative effects of a property-owning democracy are limited to those constellations of property-owning democracy that allow citizens to turn their property into an indefinite income stream. If the property-owning democracy regulations allow citizens to use their capital to generate a basic income, then this could function as a financial incentive to withdraw from the labor market. Under those circumstances property-owning democracy would strengthen the gender division of labor, and thus strengthen gender injustice, rather than weakening it.

The benefits of a property-owning democracy are limited to the fact that women, as a group, are currently less politically powerful and less financially well off in comparison with men, and thus *any* redistributive policy will benefit women in this respect (and the same can be said for caregivers). However, it is important to see that a property-owning democracy does not give us the social policies and institutions that caregivers really need in any of the welfare models that I discussed above.

This should not really be a surprise if we look at property-owning democracy with the distinction between investment and consumption in mind. We could understand the shift from a capitalist welfare state to a property-owning democracy as a shift from a regime consisting primarily of redistribution of *consumption flows* (like in welfare benefits, and the provision of consumption services such as health care) to a regime that primarily redistributes *investment flows* (investments in all types of capital, such as human capital like education, and economic capital, like company co-ownership). The problem is that caregivers and dependents especially need a particular type of consumption flow, namely care provisioning in kind (child care, elderly care, etc.), financial support for care leaves, and regulations of the labor market that should make the combination of paid work and family care run more smoothly. The investment flows do not meet their needs as they should be met.

If proponents of a property-owning democracy care about gender justice and about meeting the needs of caregivers and their dependents, then they have to ask whether a property-owning democracy can be combined with traditional welfare state policies that are especially important for caregivers. It is unclear to me whether this is either economically or politically feasible. If a proponent believes it is possible, then a more detailed plan of such a property-owning *and* care-supporting democracy will be needed to analyze its viability. If it turns out that it is not possible to combine a property-owning democracy with a decent care regime, then we have to decide where our priorities should lie.

Notes

1. I am grateful to Anca Gheaus, Martin O'Neill, Anders Schinkel, and Thad Williamson for comments on an earlier version of this chapter, and to the Netherlands Organization for Scientific research (NWO) for research funding.

2. Obviously the distinction between paid care workers and unpaid caregivers is a categorical distinction that will not always entirely match reality. Some caregivers may be paid in an indirect way, for example by an exchange of favors or an intertemporal exchange of care (e.g., healthy grandparents caring for their grandchild who will in turn be cared for by those grandchildren or their parents when they are older and frail).
3. There may be a theoretical difficulty in conceptualizing care work such that it neatly fits a precise definition of "work" – but that problem would take us too far here, and its examination will have to await another occasion. In this chapter I will use "work" in a looser understanding. I thank Anca Gheaus for discussion of these issues.
4. I will not explicitly discuss household work in this chapter. To the extent that household work is done for people who cannot do this work themselves (young children, frail elderly, severely disabled, ill people), it falls under my discussion of care work. The household work that healthy adults do for themselves will not be considered here, since I believe that it is unclear to what extent it raises any normative issues for the analysis of socioeconomic systems, and a proper analysis of gender and care issues is much more urgent.
5. In a one-child family, the total cost of expenditures for a child during his or her entire childhood will amount to US$205,383. For a child in a family with three or more children, this decreases to just under US$128,000.
6. The time cost of parenting takes about 60 to 65% of this total cost.
7. Folbre argues that the replacement cost approach is the most appropriate way of valuing labor inputs: she recommends using the wage rate required to hire a replacement for the work done, rather than the actual or potential wage rate of the person doing the work. Folbre opts for a lower bound estimate. In her estimates she values the hours of active care by the hourly wages of an average childcare worker (US$7.43 in 2000, which is low compared to the median for all workers at US$13.74). For the passive care hours she uses the federal minimum wage. In both cases she assumes the presence of two children. She does not include sleeping time and overlapping parental time in these estimates.
8. One could argue that transsexuals or people with ambiguous sexual identities form other modes in this conceptualization of gender. Yet since this chapter is about the analysis of socioeconomic regimes and their treatment of caregivers and their dependents, it seems justified to focus on the most important categorical distinction at work in the distribution of care work – the categories of "men" versus "women."
9. The different norms for men and women can be clearly seen in European Union maternity and paternity leave legislation. See Foubert (2002) and Robeyns (2009).
10. While these studies are already somewhat older, and hence the exact percentages may have lowered somewhat, I see no reason to assume that the order of magnitude of these empirical findings would no longer be valid.
11. In Rawls's work on justice, and his discussion of property-owning democracy, this is not much different. In the 514 pages devoted to *A Theory of Justice*, Rawls ignores care and gender issues entirely – and despite the elaborate criticism of feminist scholars such as Susan Okin (1989) in her path-breaking book *Justice, Gender and the Family*. Rawls only offered a very brief section covering care, gender, and the family in *Restatement*. Moreover, while Rawls may have thought he adequately responded to his feminist critics in *Restatement*, many contemporary feminist economic and political philosophers still find his work inadequate or puzzling in its dealing with issues of care, gender, and the family. See, for example, Nussbaum (2006) and Robeyns (2010).
12. The models I present map rather closely to the three models defended by Nancy Fraser (1994) in her article "After the Family Wage: Gender Equity and the Welfare State." The model which Fraser favors corresponds to the "synchronically combined welfare regime" in my terminology.

13. Note that to the best of my knowledge no research is being done on the possible harm and benefits of fathers working full time, part time, and not being employed.

References

Albrecht, J.W., Edin, P.A., Sundström, M., and Vroman, S.B. (1999) Career interruptions and subsequent earnings: A reexamination using Swedish data. *Journal of Human Resources*, 34, 294–311.

Badgett, M.V. Lee and Folbre, N. (1999) Assigning care: Gender norms and economic outcomes. *International Labor Review*, 138, 311–326.

Baker, J. (2008) All things considered, should feminists embrace basic income? *Basic Income Studies*, 3, Article 6.

Becker, G. (1991) *A Treatise on the Family*, enlarged edn, Harvard University Press, Cambridge MA.

Bergmann, B. (1981) The economic risks of being a housewife. *American Economic Review*, 71, 81–86.

Bergmann, B. (1998) The only ticket to equality: Total androgyny, male style. *Contemporary Legal Issues*, 76, 75–86.

Bergmann, B. (2008) Basic income grants or the welfare state: Which better promotes gender equality? *Basic Income Studies*, 3, Article 5.

Brighouse, H. and Wright, E.O. (2008) Strong gender egalitarianism. *Politics and Society*, 36, 360–372.

Brooks-Gunn, J. Han, W.-J., and Waldfogel, J. (2010) First-year maternal employment and child development in the first seven years. *Monographs of the Society for Research in Child Development*, 75, 1–147.

Bubeck, D. (1995) *Care, Gender and Justice*, Clarendon Press, Oxford.

Feder, E.K. (1999) *Love's Labor: Essays on Women, Equality and Dependency*, Routledge, New York.

Folbre, N. (2008) *Valuing Children. Rethinking the Economics of the Family*, Harvard University Press, Cambridge, MA.

Foubert, P. (2002) *The Legal Protection of the Pregnant Worker in the European Community*, Kluwer Law International, The Hague.

Fraser, N. (1994) After the family wage: Gender equity and the welfare state. *Political Theory*, 22, 591–618.

Gershuny, J. (2000) *Changing Times. Work and Leisure in Post-industrial Societies*, Oxford University Press, Oxford.

Gheaus, A. (2008) Basic income, gender justice, and the costs of gender symmetric lifestyles. *Basic Income Studies*, 3, Article 8.

Gheaus, A. (2011) Arguments for nonparental care for children. *Social Theory and Practice*, 37(3), 483–509.

Gheaus, A. and Robeyns, I. (2011) Equality-promoting parental leave. *Journal of Social Philosophy*, 42 (2), 173–191.

Goldschmidt-Clermont, L. and Pagnossin-Aligisakis, E. (1996) Measures of unrecorded economic activities in fourteen countries. In United Nations Development Programme, *Background Papers for the Human Development Report 1995*, Oxford University Press, New York.

Hakim, C. (2000) *Work-Lifestyle Choices in the 21st Century*, Oxford University Press, Oxford.

Haslanger, S. (2000) Gender and race: (What) are they? (What) do we want them to be? *NOÛS*, 34 (1), 31–55.

Jarvis, S. and Jenkins, S. (1999) Marital split and income changes: Evidence for Britain. *Population Studies*, 53, 237–254.

Nussbaum, M. (2006) *Frontiers of Justice. Disability, Nationality, Species Membership*, Harvard University Press, Cambridge, MA.

Okin, S. (1989) *Justice, Gender and the Family*, Basic Books, New York.

Peterson, R. (1996) A re-evaluation of the economic consequences of divorce. *American Sociological Review*, 61, 528–536.

Picchio, A. (ed.) (2003) *Unpaid Work and the Economy. A Gender Analysis of the Standards of Living*, Routledge, London.

Rawls, J. (2001) *Justice as Fairness: A Restatement*, Harvard University Press, Cambridge, MA.

Robeyns, I. (2001) Will a basic income do justice to women?" *Analyse und Kritik*, 23 (1), 88–105.

Robeyns, I. (2007) When will society be gender just?, in *The Future of Gender* (ed. Jude Brown), Cambridge University Press, Cambridge.

Robeyns, I. (ed.) (2008) Should feminists endorse basic income? *Basic Income Studies*, 3, 3.

Robeyns, I. (2009) *Onzichtbare onrechtvaardigheden*. Inaugural lecture at Erasmus University, Rotterdam.

Robeyns, I. (2010) Gender and the metric of justice, in *Measuring Justice: Primary Goods and Capabilities* (eds H. Brighouse and I. Robeyns), Cambridge University Press, Cambridge, pp. 215–235.

Tooley, J. (2002) *The Miseducation of Women*, Continuum, London.

Williamson, T. and O'Neill, M. (2009) Property-owning democracy and the demands of justice. *Living Reviews in Democracy*, 1.

Wright, E.O. (ed.) (2009) *Gender Equality. Transforming Family Divisions of Labor*, Verso, London.

9
Nurturing the Sense of Justice
The Rawlsian Argument for Democratic Corporatism

Waheed Hussain

One of the most important and visible divisions in the world today is a division among market societies.[1] The United States, United Kingdom, Canada, and Australia favor a system that relies mainly on markets to coordinate the activities of individual workers and firms. European social democracies, on the other hand, favor a system that makes greater use of collective agreements between the organized representatives of labor and capital.

The tension between these different "varieties of capitalism" has come to occupy an important place in many social and political debates around the world. However, the literature on the implications of Rawls's political philosophy for economic life has paid relatively little attention to the differences between these regimes. One reason may be that Rawls himself thought that the principles of justice were compatible with a wide range of social arrangements, including both private property and socialist regimes. On his view, the choice between "property-owning democracy" and "liberal socialism" is mainly a practical question that has to be settled by looking at what sort of arrangement would best realize the goals of justice as fairness, given the traditions, institutions, and mix of social forces in a particular society (Rawls, 1999, pp. 242, 247–248).[2] If Rawls's theory is agnostic about the choice between a private property system and a socialist one, then it seems natural to think that it is also agnostic about the choice between different private property regimes.

My aim in this chapter is to show that Rawls's theory is not agnostic about the choice between different private property systems. Taken as a whole, the theory provides a moral argument in favor of the more "organized" or "corporatist" model associated with many European countries. The key to the argument is the moral ideal of stability. Political morality requires that our basic institutions should be stable "for the right reasons," that is, in virtue of a shared sense of justice. Liberal democratic institutions should be anchored in a liberal democratic spirit in the people. Rawls has a complex account of how just arrangements can achieve this kind of stability, and I argue that a democratic corporatist arrangement is more consistent with this account. So the principles of justice may be compatible with many private property systems, but considerations of stability favor the corporatist arrangement.

Two Forms of Property-Owning Democracy

In order to bring certain questions about the structure of the economy more clearly into focus, my discussion will center on two forms of property-owning democracy (POD). Call these a *liberal market POD* and a *democratic corporatist POD* respectively.

Both models are ideal types in the sense that they are abstract models and actual institutional arrangements can embody them to a greater or lesser degree. Both models are also PODs. This means that they both incorporate the central features of a just POD, including private ownership in the means of production, protections for the basic liberties, an education system designed to minimize the effects of class origin and family background, and a system of taxation and inheritance designed to break up large concentrations of wealth that might emerge in any generation.

Where the models differ from each other is in the way that they approach the task of coordinating economic activity. The liberal market POD relies mainly on markets to coordinate economic activity. Under this arrangement, firms are involved in a multidimensional competition with other firms to make a profit. Any widespread practices in economic life, such as the use of certain technologies or the predominance of certain compensation structures, would be mainly the result of competition between firms. By contrast, a democratic corporatist POD relies on markets but also makes extensive use of corporatist deliberation and rule making. Widespread practices in economic life under this arrangement may be the product of competition between firms, but they may also be the product of explicit rule making by the representatives of different groups involved in production.

Stated more formally, the democratic corporatist POD differs from the liberal market POD in two respects:

1. It fosters the formation of a limited number of secondary associations to represent the perspective of major segments of the population in various rule-making forums.
2. It takes steps to ensure that changes to the rules of economic competition come about through a process of deliberation and reasoned agreement among the relevant associations.

Under democratic corporatism, there would be a limited number of encompassing associations in each industry or sector of the economy to officially represent the perspectives of various groups who participate in production (such as workers and owners). These associations would meet regularly to establish the parameters for competition between firms. The process of establishing these parameters would be one in which representatives deliberate rather than bargain: that is, instead of negotiating strategically to further the interests of their constituents, parties would cooperate with each other to find standards and polices that all could accept as a reasonable framework for competition.[3]

The German "codetermination" system provides an imperfect, but helpful real-world illustration (Wiedemann, 1980, Vitols, 2001; Charkham, 2005). Under the laws of codetermination, large corporations must reserve half of the seats on their supervisory boards for labor representatives. Along with shareholder representatives, these representatives vote on a range of corporate policy issues, including the hiring and firing of executive officers. At the same time, the codetermination system empowers industry-wide unions, such as IG Metall and IG Chemie, to bargain on behalf of all the workers in their respective industries and to appoint representatives to the supervisory boards of all of the large corporations in them. These powers enable unions to engage manufacturing associations in corporatist bargaining processes that establish the ground rules for economic competition between firms. These ground rules cover a range of issues, including compensation, pensions, work hours, job training, and worker retention. For the German system to fully embody the democratic corporatist model, representative associations on both sides would have to be transparent and responsive to their memberships, and the decision-making process would have to take the form of deliberation rather than mere bargaining.

What makes democratic corporatism a form of "corporatism" is that – following Philippe Schmitter's famous definition – it relies on a limited number of corporate bodies, intermediate between the individual and the state, to officially represent the interests and concerns of different segments of society in social decision making (Schmitter, 1974, pp. 93–94). These corporate bodies may represent workers in general, owners in general, or particular segments of each group. For example, different segments of the workforce in an industry – for example, creative talent and support staff – may have separate associations, and different groups of owners – for example, small suppliers and large manufacturers – may have separate associations as well.[4]

What makes democratic corporatism "democratic" is that it articulates a strategy for deepening the democratic character of social decision making.[5] The idea is to strengthen secondary associations in the economy so that these associations can take on various rule making, rule applying, and compliance monitoring functions. An economy reformed along these lines is more democratic in the sense that more important aspects of economic life are taken out of the sphere of market competition and brought under the control of processes in which the relevant parties deliberate with each other and agree on appropriate standards and policies.[6]

It is common to think of corporatism as a governance structure that is tied to the industrial mode of production, a paradigm that is part of a bygone era in advanced Western economies. But corporatism is by no means tied to mass production. Consider that today's knowledge economies rest on a foundation of research that is carried out in universities. Higher education in countries such as the United States is governed by a structure with significant corporatist elements. In most American universities, students, faculty, and staff have their own associations, and representatives from each of these groups participate – along with administrators and trustees – in making decisions about policies that govern the institution. Beyond the boundaries of the university, there are encompassing national bodies that represent the perspective of students, faculty, and staff in decision-making processes that affect the higher education sector as a whole. For example, the American Association of University Professors (AAUP) represents the interests of faculty at the state and national level.

Corporatist structures can be found in other parts of advanced economies as well. Most major professional sports leagues in the United States – including professional basketball, professional football, and major league baseball – have players' associations that meet regularly with owners' associations to make rules and policies that structure competition between teams. Similar structures exist in the arts. In the movie industry, organizations such as the Screen Actors Guild (SAG) and the Motion Picture Editors Guild (MPEG) represent the interests of creative talent and shape the character of competition between studios. Even the codetermination system in Germany covers technologically advanced sectors of the economy, such as the production of designer chemicals that are quite far from the factory-based, mass production paradigm.

Another common view is that corporatism assumes or institutionalizes the social division between a capitalist class and a laboring class. This view stems, in part, from the fact that many corporatist structures in the world today evolved out of a conflict between owners and workers, where some accommodation of worker demands was necessary to maintain the social peace. Corporatist structures may have developed out of a conflict between these classes, but it would be a mistake to think that corporatism has no purpose or point apart from this conflict. Democratic corporatism in particular would have a point, even if society overcame this class division altogether. Consider the following hypothetical situation. Suppose that the medical field evolves to the point where most medical practices are owned not only by the doctors who work in them, but also by the nurses, assistants, technicians, and other people who work in them. If the entire medical field consisted of partnerships of this sort – worker-owned cooperatives – would there be any point to corporatist intermediation in this sector of the economy?

The answer is yes. Intermediation would involve explicit rule making to regulate competition between medical practices, but the representatives in these deliberations would not represent workers and owners; they would represent different segments of the overall class of worker-owners. For example, the process might incorporate representatives from a nurse's association, a doctor's association, an association of support staff, and so on. Without corporatist intermediation, widespread practices in the medical field would be the product of competition between medical practices. This would be true even if workers owned the practices. The point of intermediation in this sector would be to create an avenue for explicitly shaping the course of competition between these firms, and doing so in a way that reflects the values and interests of participants in production.

Democratic corporatism is a normative model of economic governance in that it does not simply describe the pattern of social coordination that we see in certain societies. Even European countries that have certain elements of democratic corporatism built into their institutional framework seem to lack an adequate degree of deliberation. Democratic corporatism is an ideal that we should strive for, an ideal that is partly realized in existing institutions, but is by no means identical with them.

There is much more that could be said to develop the idea of democratic corporatism, but the contrast between a liberal market POD and a democratic corporatist POD should be clear enough for my purposes at this point. The question is whether Rawls's theory offers us moral grounds for adopting one of these arrangements over the other.

What Is Stability? Why Does It Matter?

The central claim of this chapter is that Rawls's theory, as a whole, should be understood to support the pursuit of a democratic corporatist POD rather than a liberal market POD. My argument turns on the moral ideal of stability; so, starting in this section, I develop a more detailed account of this ideal. I focus on three questions: what kind of stability is relevant from the moral point of view? Why is this kind of stability morally relevant? And how does a social arrangement achieve this kind of stability?

According to Rawls, a just social arrangement is a configuration of society's basic institutions that conforms to the demands of his two principles of justice. Much like any other social arrangement, a just arrangement will have a complex relationship with the body politic. Social institutions will, on the one hand, shape the political movements that develop over time by shaping the fundamental motivations of citizens. For example, institutions will shape the motivations of citizens by shaping their education and early childhood experiences. On the other hand, social institutions will themselves be shaped by these political movements. For example, the laws will be shaped by the legislative changes enacted by successful electoral campaigns. This reciprocal relationship forms the background for stability.

A just social arrangement is stable in the morally relevant sense when it creates conditions such that any threat to the just character of society's basic institutions will engage the moral sensibilities of the people and lead them to take action and restore the just character of the institutional framework (Rawls, 1999, pp. 399–401). For example, suppose that changes in birth rates and internal migration patterns lead to a situation in which one region of the country has many times the population of the other regions. But suppose that this region still has the same level of resources devoted to the education of its people. Without any intervention, it is likely that the conditions of fair equality of opportunity would no longer hold: a talented and motivated child born into the overpopulated region would have worse life prospects than a similarly talented and motivated child born into some other region. If we are living in a just social arrangement that is stable in the morally relevant sense, the unfairness of the educational system would engage the moral concerns of the people, and political forces would emerge in society to change educational funding policy and restore the conditions of fair equality of opportunity.

Let us call the type of stability that is relevant from the moral point of view *stability for the right reasons*. A social arrangement is stable for the right reasons when it generates a shared sense of justice in citizens and this sense of justice is strong enough to move them to do what is necessary to maintain the just character of their basic institutions over time.

Stability in general is often seen as merely a practical consideration. The intuitive idea is that justice is the end and that we should take the best means to achieving this end. A stable arrangement is the best means to achieving the end because a stable arrangement would take fewer resources to maintain and would be more likely to persist over time. Any just arrangement that is unstable is objectionable because it involves a waste of social resources and presents a more serious risk of disintegrating over time.

Although this is a natural way to think about stability, it is misleading because stability is not just a practical consideration; it is a substantive requirement of morality. To see why, consider that morality often requires that we adopt certain forms of self-management. For example, people have an interest in bodily integrity, and this interest gives rise to a moral prohibition against certain forms of assault. But the interest in bodily integrity also gives rise to a moral requirement that we should take appropriate steps to ensure that we respect the prohibition. Among other things, morality requires that we avoid situations in which we might be tempted, against our better judgment, to assault others, and it requires that we cultivate in ourselves good habits of restraint and anger management. In this way, morality requires not only that we act in certain ways, but also that we take steps to make sure that we will act in these ways.

Much the same thing holds in the case of political morality. For example, individuals have an interest in free expression, and this interest gives rise to a moral requirement that citizens should provide each other with a legal right to express themselves. But there is a danger that we may not provide each other with these legal rights. When faced with social unrest and political disagreement, a democratic majority among us may be tempted to silence dissent by compromising the legal right of free expression. Here the interests that individuals have in free expression justify not only the moral requirement that we should recognize a legal right of free expression, but also a moral requirement that we should take appropriate measures to ensure that we will not unjustly limit these legal rights in difficult circumstances. There are many measures that we might take along these lines, and one of these is to cultivate an appropriate sense of justice in ourselves, a sense of justice that will move us to do the right thing when we are tempted improperly to constrain basic rights.

The idea of self-management offers a basic account of the moral significance of stability for the right reasons. Political morality requires not only that we frame our institutions in a certain way, but also that we take adequate measures to ensure that we will maintain this framework. When our institutions are stable for the right reasons, we meet this second demand by cultivating an appropriate sense of justice in ourselves. The problem, however, is that the explanation as it stands is lacking in one important respect. The idea of self-management can explain why measures to ensure stability are in general morally significant, but it does not explain what is distinctively important about a form of stability rooted in a shared sense of justice.

To sharpen the point, suppose that we could arrange our political system so that it worked more like a market. Under ideal conditions, a market will lead self-interested actors to a Pareto optimal outcome, even though none of them cares about generating such an outcome. Suppose that we could arrange our political system along similar lines. Whenever our basic institutions deviate from the principles of justice, the system would give individuals an incentive to enter the political forum to correct the injustice. No one would actually *care* about social justice; individuals would be led by their own self-interest to act in ways that maintain the just character of their basic institutions. What would be morally objectionable about an arrangement that is stable, but not stable in virtue of a shared sense of justice (Rawls, 1993, pp. 143–144; 2001, p. 185)?

In his later work, Rawls is explicit that, even if it were possible for an arrangement to be stable in virtue of a system of incentives, political morality requires that the social order should be stable in virtue of a shared sense of justice (Rawls, 2001, pp. 185–186).[7] We might put the argument in the following way. Political morality requires that, through our basic institutions, we should respect members of society – both ourselves and others – as "rational" and "reasonable." On the one hand, we must respect members of society as having the capacity to formulate their own ideas about the good life. But on the other hand, we must also respect members of society as having the capacity to regulate their pursuit of their own good in light of a conception of fair cooperation. If we arrange our basic institutions so that they maintain their just character simply by giving people an incentive to act in the right ways, we would respect ourselves as rational persons, but we would not respect ourselves as reasonable persons. Through our basic institutions, we would express the judgment that we are not capable of regulating our pursuit of the good in light of a conception of cooperation on fair terms. Moreover, we would express the judgment that we are not capable of participating fully in the political relationship, a relationship in which each of us offers and accepts fair terms from the others. By establishing a system of institutions that operate as a kind of Platonic guardian of social justice, we treat ourselves as if we lacked the moral powers to take our place in society as full citizens.[8]

What makes stability for the right reasons distinctively important, then, is that political morality requires not only that we should ensure that our institutions will be just, but also that we should treat ourselves (and each other) as reasonable persons in the process. If we used a system of economic incentives to induce the right behavior in ourselves, we would express a judgment that we were not capable of being full participants in the political community. Respect for our own potential as moral agents requires that we cultivate an appropriate sense of justice in ourselves and then address social injustices by calling attention to these injustices and relying on each other (within reason) to do what is required to maintain a just social order.

Recall that I asked three questions about stability. The first two questions have been answered – that is, what kind of stability is morally significant, and why? The third question is: how does a social arrangement achieve stability for the right reasons? I take it that a social arrangement does so mainly by cultivating an appropriate sense of justice in citizens. If a just social arrangement tends to generate a strong sense of justice in citizens, and this sense of justice is widespread among the various groups in society, then (other things being equal) it is more likely that political forces will emerge in society to sustain the just character of its basic institutions whenever this is threatened. But if the sense of justice is weak and limited to only a few social groups, then it is less likely that the right kind of political forces will emerge in the face of a threat. Much will depend, then, on how just institutions cultivate a sense of justice in individuals, and I turn now to Rawls's account of this process.

The Sense of Justice

Rawls conceives of the sense of justice as a particular kind of attachment to the principles of justice. People with a sense of justice want to comply with the rules of a social order that conforms to these principles. They also want "to work for . . . the setting up of just institutions," and to work "for the reform of existing ones when justice requires it"

(Rawls, 1999, p. 415). But the sense of justice also involves a distinctive pattern of reactions to the failure to live up to the requirements of these principles. People with a sense of justice are not merely disappointed when their social order does not conform to the principles: they feel guilty when their institutions fail to conform; they feel indignant for the people who are unfairly treated; and, when the circumstances are appropriate, they will apologize and seek forgiveness from the victims of social injustice. The story of moral development in *A Theory of Justice* explains how people in a society that is publicly regulated by the two principles of justice will form this distinctive type of attachment to the principles.

Reciprocity is the central engine of normative attachment on Rawls's account. When others show that they care about us, we naturally come to care about them in return. In caring about others, we care not only about their welfare, but also about living up to their expectations. Moreover, we experience distinctively moral sentiments, such as guilt and remorse, when we fail to live up to these expectations (Rawls, 1999, pp. 425–429). For example, when our parents love us as children, we naturally come to care about them in return, and once we form this attachment it is also natural for us to feel guilt and remorse if we fall short of their expectations. In a just society, individuals experience evident care and concern from the other members of society, and this care and concern eventually leads them to form an attachment to the underlying principles that unify the association.

The attachment develops in three stages. The first stage is the morality of authority. When individuals are born into a just society, their parents love and care for them, and they come to love and care for their parents in return (Rawls, 1999, pp. 405–406). This attachment manifests itself (among other things) in a desire to follow the rules that their parents set out in the household. Many of these rules incorporate the requirements of social justice (e.g., no stealing) but children cannot appreciate the connection between the rules and the principles of justice themselves. At this stage, the outlook of individuals in a just society is a "morality of authority" in the sense that their feelings toward the rules of a just social order arise out of their attachment to certain authority figures, namely their parents.

The second stage in the process is the morality of association. Individuals in a just society eventually take part in a wide range of associations, including churches, clubs, orchestras, firms, political parties, unions, and so on. Individuals who join these associations form bonds with other members, and these bonds lead to an attachment to the ideals that define expectations in the group (Rawls, 1999, p. 412). For example, an individual in a just society may join a labor union. When other members stand with him on the picket line, he experiences this as a contribution to his good, and he comes to care about his fellow union members in return. This social bond will lead him to want to live up to the union's shared conception of what makes for a good union brother, and to feel guilt and remorse if he fails to do so.

Associational ideals will often incorporate the requirements of social justice (e.g., a good union brother is not a thief), but people at stage two do not typically see the connection between these requirements and the principles of justice themselves (Rawls, 1999, p. 409). Their outlook is a "morality of association" in the sense that their feelings toward the rules of a just social order arise out of their attachment to the members of certain associations and groups.

The morality of association is often assumed to be an early stage of development, but Rawls clearly does not think that it is confined to childhood or adolescence. As he says, "this type of moral view extends to the ideals adopted in later life, and so to one's various adult statuses and occupations, one's family position, and even to one's place as a member of society" (Rawls, 1999, p. 409). What is distinctive about the morality of association, even in its most complex forms, is that our motivation to do what is right stems from an attachment to particular communities of individuals. For example, a politically active person who reaches this stage of development in a just society will treat the requirements of social justice as normative because other politically active people in his community care about these principles (Rawls, 1999, p. 414). His disposition to do what the principles of justice require, and his disposition to feel guilt and remorse when he fails to do so, are causally rooted in his attachment to friends, colleagues, and associates.[9] The morality of association represents a kind of morality of social belonging, something that is common in the emotional life of adults as well as children.

The final stage in the process is the morality of principles. I will discuss this stage further in the next section, but the basic idea is the following. When individuals in a just society enter public life, they take up positions in which they have to balance the competing claims of different individuals and groups. This puts them in a position to see how the social order answers to the principles of justice and how it contributes to the good of everyone in society. When people see how the institutional order has contributed to their own well-being and the well-being of those that they care about, they come to form an attachment to the organizing principles of the institutional order. At previous stages, their desire to comply, and their corresponding feelings of guilt and remorse, stemmed from an attachment to their parents or to the individuals in particular social groups. But now these dispositions are independent of these attachments. Individuals at this stage want to comply with the principles of justice, and they feel guilt and remorse when they fail to do so, and they would have all of these dispositions even if other members of society were indifferent to the requirements of justice. Their outlook is a "morality of principles" in the sense that they have an unmediated attachment to the principles of justice themselves.

Participation in Public Life

A key feature of the process of moral development, for my purposes, is the transition between the early stages of the morality of association and the morality of principles.

People at the second stage of moral development have a moral sensibility that does not extend beyond their associational ties.[10] They participate in a wide range of associations, care about the other people in these associations, and are normatively attached to the ideals connected with their roles in these associations. But their moral outlook does not extend beyond these horizons. People at stage two, particularly those who do not participate in public life, will not have a normative attachment to the principles of justice themselves (Rawls, 1999, p. 414). What they care about fundamentally at this stage is conforming to socially defined notions of being a good father or mother, a good neighbor, a good coworker, and so on. If requirements of social justice are incorporated into these ideals, then people at stage two will treat them as normative.

But if requirements of justice are not incorporated into these ideals, then they will not treat them as normative.

The fact that people have a moral sensibility that extends only as far as their associational ties matters from the standpoint of stability because it limits the social response to injustice. Imagine that a social injustice emerges in society and that citizens have only advanced to an early stage of the morality of association. Since their outlooks extend only as far as their associational affiliations, the only citizens who would be morally concerned about an emerging injustice would be those who have some sort of associational connection to it, namely (a) citizens who have a personal relationship with the victims or (b) citizens whose associational ideals require them to respond.

Imagine, for example, that changing migration patterns lead to overloaded school districts in one part of the country. Children in this region now have a less than equal opportunity to succeed. If everyone is at the second stage of moral development, the injustice would move the parents, teachers, and friends of the young people affected because they have a relationship with the victims. It would also move school administrators, political officials, and activists whose role ideals require them to respond to injustices of this kind. But insofar as the sense of justice in society is rooted in associational ties, the injustice would not necessarily move anyone else. After all, most people would not have a specific relationship with the young people affected and they would not belong to associations whose role ideals require a response. It follows that a political movement to rectify the injustice may be quite small and insufficient to generate the appropriate changes in society's basic institutions.

At the third stage of moral development, however, people's moral sensibilities are no longer rooted in their associational lives. They care about all aspects of social justice, not just those aspects that have a place in their associational ideals. They care about failures of social justice, even when they have no associational connection to the victims. And their concern is fully independent in the sense that they would continue to care about social justice, even if the people around them ceased to care. This development is important from the standpoint of stability because a just society is more stable when its members have this kind of attachment to the principles of justice.

Imagine that the same injustice that I described above emerges in society, but now citizens have all advanced to the morality of principles. Since everyone is attached to the principles of justice, they all care about the fact that society is falling short of the requirements of the two principles. Anyone who was confronted with the fact that certain people have less than equal opportunity in society would feel guilt and indignation, and they would want to do something to rectify the situation. Of course, those who have a personal connection with the victims – parents, teachers, and friends – would be moved more strongly to act, as would administrators, political officials, and activists, whose associational ideals require them to act (Rawls, 1999, p. 416). But the mere fact of social injustice would move everyone in society, even those without any associational connection to the injustice. It follows that a political movement to rectify the injustice will be stronger and more widespread because it will appeal to a moral sentiment that is shared by everyone.

What leads people to make the transition between the morality of association and the morality of principle? The factor that Rawls cites is participation in the political life of the community (Rawls, 1999, pp. 414–415). In a just society, some subset of the population (perhaps quite small) will take part in public life by serving in a legislative capacity, serving as a judge or jury member, or simply by taking an active interest in public affairs. These individuals take part in the process of making and interpreting the laws in society, and this requires them to step back from the concerns that occupy them in their day-to-day activities to consider issues that affect many disparate individuals, associations and groups:

> In a well-ordered society ... citizens who take an interest in political affairs, and those holding legislative and judicial and similar offices, are constantly required to apply and interpret [the principles of justice]. They often have to take up the point of view of others, not simply with the aim of working out what they will want and probably do, but for the purposes of striking a reasonable balance between competing claims and for adjusting the various subordinate ideals of the morality of associations. (Rawls, 1999, p. 414)

As citizens adjust and extend the legal framework in society, they are forced to develop their understanding of the two principles of justice and to apply this understanding to various legislative and judicial problems. Over the course of time, these activities bring citizens to see (a) how the social order as a whole answers to the principles of justice and (b) how the social order affects everyone's interests.

Rawls believes that we have a natural disposition to become attached to the organizing principles of a social arrangement when we see how this arrangement has contributed to our good and the good of the people that we care about. He describes this institutional form of reciprocity in his third psychological law of moral development:

> This law states that once the attitudes of love and trust, and of friendly feelings and mutual confidence, have been generated in accordance with the two preceding psychological laws, then the recognition that we and those for whom we care are the beneficiaries of an established and enduring just institution tends to engender in us the corresponding sense of justice. We develop a desire to apply and to act upon the principles of justice once we realize how social arrangements answering to them have promoted our good and that of those with whom we are affiliated. (Rawls, 1999, p. 415)

The central idea is that when we feel how the social order has cared for us and the people that we care about, we respond instinctively by internalizing its organizing ideals. Over the course of the first two stages of development, we come to care about family, friends, neighbors, and coworkers. When we take part in public life, we see how the social order answers to the principles of justice, and how the order has affected our interests. For example, we see how protections for the rule of law have protected our families, friends, and associates from violence and arbitrary persecution. Similarly, we see how protections for the liberty of conscience have protected the various religious, cultural, and scientific associations that we care about. Seeing how the social order has cared for us, and the people that we care about, we form an attachment to the ideals of the social order. We want to maintain institutions that live up to these ideals, and to further the degree to which our institutions live up to them. We also feel guilt and remorse when we and our fellow citizens fail to live up to these requirements. Moreover, these dispositions are no longer sensitive to the opinions, motivations, and expectations of those around us.

Three Distinctive Features of Rawls's View

At this point, I want to step back and put Rawls's account of moral development into some historical context. Let's say that a member of society becomes a "citizen" when he develops a sense of justice that regulates his pursuit of his own private self-interest. Rawls belongs to a long line of political thinkers concerned with how members of society become citizens. Like Rousseau, he thinks of citizenship as something that begins in childhood and evolves to higher stages. Insofar as he gives participation an important role to play in the process, he belongs to a more specific tradition that emphasizes participation, a tradition that includes Rousseau, Hegel, Tocqueville, and Mill.

One distinctive feature of Rawls's view is that he does not take thought and reflection to be the primary mechanism that brings individuals to become fully formed citizens. Although he formulates a complex philosophical argument in favor of the two principles of justice, he does not believe that the members of a just society internalize these principles simply because they come to appreciate the philosophical justification for them. What makes individuals into citizens is rather a nondiscursive feature of human nature, namely reciprocity – our natural tendency to care about those who manifestly care about us. In essence, Rawls believes that we can become attached to moral ideas, not only because we think that they express moral truths, but also because we have a particular historical connection to them. His third psychological law implies that people who grow up under utilitarian institutions will form an allegiance to utilitarian principles (as long as they have benefited in the right ways from these institutions); people who grow up under religious institutions will form an allegiance to the corresponding religious principles (as long as they have benefited in the right ways); and so on.[11] What drives the process is not thought and reflection, but our natural response to caring concern.

Another distinctive feature of Rawls's view is that citizenship is not rooted in a sympathetic identification with other members of society. It is common to think of citizenship in terms of broadening the perspective of individuals so that they care not only about their own good, but also about the common good of the community. In one sense, Rawls rejects this idea because he does not think of citizens as being moved by a sympathetic identification with the good of all members of society, or even with the good of the least advantaged group. Sympathy of this kind is a relatively weak form of motivation and it is difficult to imagine how citizens in general could sympathize with more than a tiny circle of associates (Rawls, 1999, pp. 155, 437–438). What motivates citizens, on Rawls's view, is not sympathy, but a commitment to liberal democratic ideals such as equal liberty and fair equality of opportunity. People internalize the ideals of their political culture, and it is a normative attachment to these ideals, rather than some identification with the common good, that leads them to maintain just institutions.

Finally – and most importantly for my purposes – Rawls's view is distinctive because of the way that it conceives of the function of participation. We might describe this function as *transparency*. The social order is, by assumption, actually regulated by the two principles of justice, and in virtue of this fact, it actually contributes to the good of each member. But the mere fact that the social order contributes to everyone's good does not mean that individuals will be able to see and appreciate this. When most people spend most of their waking hours at work or raising a family, there is no guarantee that anyone will be able to see and appreciate how they benefit from the social order. Participation in public life raises citizens up out of their daily lives so that they can see how the social order contributes to their good. Participation contributes to the development of a freestanding attachment to the principles of justice because it puts people in a position to see, feel, and appreciate the caring concern that is embodied in the social order. And the natural response to this experience is for people to reciprocate by forming an attachment to the organizing principles of the arrangement.

Democratic Corporatism and Participation

We now have an account of the moral ideal of stability. Political morality requires that our basic institutions should be both just and stable for the right reasons. To be stable for the right reasons, our institutions must generate a sense of justice that moves us to do what is necessary to maintain the just character of the social order. And participation is key because participation puts us in a position to appreciate what the social order has done for us, which in turn will lead us to form a free-standing normative attachment to its organizing ideals.

Let us return now to the comparison between the liberal market POD and the democratic corporatist POD. Recall that these two arrangements share the basic features of a just POD, but differ in the way that they coordinate the economy. The liberal market POD relies mainly on markets to coordinate the economy, while the democratic corporatist POD also makes significant use of corporatist deliberation and rule making. Once we understand the nature of stability, and in particular the transition from the morality of association to the morality of principles, we can see that the liberal market POD suffers from an important weakness. The problem is that participation is limited under this arrangement, perhaps quite limited, so it is not clear that the movement from the early stages of the morality of association to the morality of principle will be widespread.[12]

We can distinguish two more specific problems. One problem is that only a small fraction of society is likely to spend any significant amount of time taking part in the political life of the community. The number of legislators and judges in a modern society is relatively small, and even if we include other significant positions in the government bureaucracy (e.g., leading officials in agencies, such as the Department of Justice and the Federal Trade Commission), the total number of dedicated political offices is still quite small. Perhaps the most important political office in society is the office of citizen, which all competent adults occupy. Rawls's account of moral development seems to rely on participation in electoral politics to draw the largest number of people into the morality of principles. But he himself recognizes that "in a well-governed state only a small fraction of persons may devote much of their time to politics" (Rawls, 1999, p. 200). A large body of evidence about political participation in the United States, both in electoral politics and in other forms of political activity, seems to support this view (Wolfinger and Rosenstone, 1980; Verba and Nie, 1987; Rosenstone and Hansen, 2003).

A second problem is that participation is episodic. Even among the politically active segment of the population, the fraction that participates in the political process may be made up of different people in each election cycle. So if 60% of the population participated in each of the last three presidential elections, the percentage of people that participated in all three may only be 30% (Rosenstone and Hansen, 2003, pp. 53–56). Taking the argument one step further, even among those who participate consistently, election after election, there is reason to doubt that this form of participation could fundamentally alter their motivations. If people step out of their daily concerns just long enough to follow an election every four years, it is hard to see how this episodic involvement in public affairs could generate a fundamental change in their character.

A democratic corporatist POD addresses the participation problem by greatly expanding the sphere of political activity. In a democratic corporatist regime, workers, managers, and owners in an industry would participate in rule-making activities that structure economic competition between firms. In developing these rules, participants would have to formulate a conception of their *legitimate interests*, that is, interests that they could legitimately ask others to recognize within a social order regulated by the two principles of justice. This would require them to develop an understanding of these principles and to use this understanding in shaping their positions. Higher-level officials in representative associations would obviously have to engage in this kind of reasoning, but rank-and-file members would have to do so as well when they elect these officials. In deliberating with each other about the merits of different ways of structuring the rules of competition, people in an industry come to see how various aspects of the social order answer to the principles of justice and how they and their associates benefit from these arrangements.

An example will help to illustrate. The National Basketball Association (NBA) is the premier professional basketball league in the United States. It is governed by a corporatist structure in which franchise owners and players each have organizations that represent their interests and participate in making decisions about rules that structure the competition between teams. Interactions between the National Basketball Players Association (NBPA) and the owners (represented by the league itself) generally take the form of bargaining, where each side aims to advance its own interests. But there are many instances in which the two sides must deliberate about rule changes, where these deliberations involve wider social and political ideals.

A case in point is the eligibility of high school players for the NBA draft (Rosner, 1998).[13] This has been a long-standing issue for the league. The 2005 collective bargaining agreement (CBA) restricted eligibility to players who are at least 19 years old and one year removed from high school. The league argued, in part, that the new, tighter restrictions were necessary to keep scouts and agents out of high school gyms. This would prevent young people from being seduced by promises of fame and fortune in basketball, reinforcing the mission of high school education and protecting the long-term interests of young people. Many players, however, argued that the rule was unfair. In effect, an 18-year-old citizen (most often black) could be drafted into the army to die for his country, but he could not be drafted by a professional basketball team. In the past, players have also argued (and the league agreed) that young players who are often in economically depressed circumstances should be able to enter the draft when they face extreme financial pressures.

The debate surrounding high school eligibility illustrates how corporatist rule making can bring players and owners to formulate some of the central ideals of the social order, such as fairness, equality of opportunity, and racial neutrality, and to formulate some view about how institutions such as high schools, colleges, and the NBA fit into a scheme that aims to realize these ideals. It is not hard to see how these deliberations could also bring players and owners to understand how their well-being and the well-being of the league is connected with broader features of the social order, such as a public education system that teaches kids about the game from a young age and redistributive mechanisms that ensure that there is an audience that can afford to pay for tickets.

The expansion in the sphere of political activity under democratic corporatism addresses both elements of the participatory deficit in a liberal market POD. First, it addresses the small fraction problem. Only a small fraction of people in a mass democracy is likely to devote much of their time to electoral politics, but most adults in a modern society are involved in the moneyed economy. Democratic corporatism incorporates a form of political decision making into the structure of work life, and in doing so, it weaves an engagement with public affairs into a large sphere of social life that would otherwise be devoid of this kind of engagement. Second, it addresses the episodic participation problem. Even those who participate in electoral politics in a liberal market POD are likely to participate only from time to time. Work, on the other hand, occupies most people for most of their waking hours. By incorporating a form of political decision making into the structure of work, the democratic corporatist POD would foster a steadier engagement with the public life of the community.

Besides expanding the scope of political activity in society, a democratic corporatist POD also achieves a certain degree of clarity. Rawls argues that a social order will give rise to a stronger sense of justice when individuals can see clearly how it expresses a concern for their good (Rawls, 1999, pp. 438–439). For example, in a social order regulated by the principle of utility, it may require a certain mastery of economics and statistics for individuals to see how they gain from various laws and policies. But anyone living under a social order regulated by the two principles can see clearly that the arrangement will not sacrifice his fundamental freedoms for the sake of minor economic gains. Democratic corporatism achieves further clarity by creating a forum in which citizens can see how the social order contributes to their good. As part of their work lives, citizens will formulate a conception of the principles of justice, and they will come to see how specific individuals and specific firms benefit from a social order built on these principles. This brings them to see in an especially clear and concrete way how they benefit from the order.

Another significant feature of democratic corporatism is that it highlights the way that a just social order contributes to the good of individuals in their work lives. Other things being equal, a social order will generate a stronger response in us when it contributes to an aspect of our lives that is more important to us. Given the prominent place that work occupies in the concerns of people in the modern world, the fact that democratic corporatism clarifies the impact of just institutions in this sphere of life is important: the recognition of a contribution in this sphere is likely to have a more powerful effect on our commitment to the organizing principles of society.

I want to add one final consideration in support of the democratic corporatist POD. The argument in this section has certain affinities with the well-known arguments of John Stuart Mill (1994, book IV) and Carole Pateman (1970). Mill and Pateman argue that participation in collective decision making at work can help to educate citizens, transform their motivations, and lead them to take a more active role in politics. Self-confidence figures prominently in this line of reasoning. Pateman, for example, argues that participating in collective decision making at work encourages people to think that they can make a difference in the world and this in turn leads them to take a more active role in politics at all levels (Pateman, 1970, pp. 45–53). The emphasis on self-confidence distinguishes the Mill–Pateman argument from the Rawlsian argument, which focuses not on citizens' self-confidence, but on their concern for social justice. Nonetheless the Mill–Pateman argument lends further support to the case for a democratic corporatist POD. If increased participation in collective decision making at work improves a person's overall sense of efficacy, then we have a further reason to think that a democratic corporatist POD will be more stable for the right reasons: citizens under this arrangement will believe more strongly that they can make a difference and therefore they will be more likely to act on their sense of justice when they see some fundamental unfairness in their basic institutions.

Objections

Rawls's theory as a whole should be understood as providing a moral argument in favor of a democratic corporatist POD over a liberal market POD. Although both arrangements could meet the demands of the two principles of justice, the democratic corporatist arrangement answers better to the moral ideal of stability. The democratic corporatist POD greatly expands the sphere of engagement with public affairs by weaving a form of engagement into the work world. According to Rawls's own account of moral development, this wider sphere of engagement will lead to a more principled and widespread commitment to social justice, a commitment that will move more people to respond more forcefully as social injustices arise over time.

I want to address three objections to my argument. One objection says that we could address the participatory deficits of the liberal market POD in other ways besides altering our economic institutions. For example, instead of expanding the scope of political activity through corporatist deliberation in the economy, we could do so by encouraging civic engagement in town hall meetings, local school councils, community-based policing efforts, and so on.[14] With adequate measures outside of the economic sphere, a liberal market POD could be just as attractive from the standpoint of stability as a democratic corporatist POD.

The problem with this objection is that it does not come to terms with the unique position that the economic sphere occupies in modern social life. Most people spend most of their waking hours at work. They organize much of their lives around their professional aspirations, and they form many of their most important relationships in and through the workplace. Given the degree to which people are invested in their work, it is hard to see how society could address the participatory deficits in the liberal market POD without making substantial changes in the economic sphere. People simply do not spend enough time and energy in town hall meetings and school councils for participation in these arenas to substantially reshape their motivations.

A second objection says that we could achieve most of what the democratic corporatist POD achieves under a "mixed" POD that does not constrain our economic liberty. In a well-known article, Richard Krouse and Michael McPherson (1986) argue for a POD that allows individuals to form economic associations that are either worker controlled or privately owned. If there are positive externalities to worker-controlled cooperatives, Krouse and McPherson argue that society could use subsidies, tax breaks, and other measures to increase the size of the worker-controlled sector until it would produce the relevant benefits at the right levels. For example, if worker-controlled cooperatives encourage the formation of an appropriate sense of justice, society could subsidize the worker-controlled sector of the economy until it was large enough to generate a widespread and principled commitment to social justice. The attraction of the mixed POD is that it would not prohibit the formation of privately owned businesses and therefore would not constrain the liberty of individuals to form economic associations according to their preferences.

Many have argued that worker-controlled enterprises are important from the standpoint of stability, but the Rawlsian argument that I have formulated in this paper does not focus on worker control.[15] The focus of the argument has been on expanding the public sphere. To foster a stronger and more widespread commitment to social justice, people must engage in public life, see how their activities fit into a social order regulated by the principles of justice, and see how they benefit from these institutions. The democratic corporatist POD expands the public sphere by creating rule-making forums in which workers and owners deliberate with each other about how to regulate their industries. But it is not clear that the mixed POD does anything comparable. Even if almost all production in society took place in worker-controlled cooperatives, these cooperatives would presumably operate as private competitors in the marketplace. Those involved in cooperatives would think strategically with each other about how to beat the competition, but there is no reason to think that they would engage in deliberations that would bring them to conceive of their social order and the ways in which they benefit from it. So there is no reason to think that the mixed POD would generate the same benefits as a democratic corporatist POD.

It is also worth noting that a democratic corporatist POD has no obvious disadvantages when it comes to "economic liberty" in Krouse and McPherson sense. Most corporatist arrangements in the world legally prohibit the formation of large enterprises that do not take part in corporatist decision-making processes, but we could certainly imagine a different kind of arrangement. Society could allow people to form enterprises that take part in corporatist self-regulation or do not take part, and it could use subsidies, tax breaks, and so forth to expand the sphere of corporatist deliberation. It may turn out, of course, that this is very expensive, in which case it may be easier to simply require businesses of a certain size to participate in corporatist self-regulation. But the important point is that a democratic corporatist POD is in exactly the same position with respect to "economic liberty" as a mixed POD.

Finally, some may wonder whether we have an empirical basis for thinking that citizens will have a stronger sense of justice under a democratic corporatist POD. Any discussion of possible institutional arrangements always involves controversial claims about how human beings will develop and act under different circumstances. But there are two sources of empirical support for the stability argument. First, there is a large body of evidence that shows that reciprocity is a fundamental aspect of human nature, one that has played an important role in the evolution of the species, and one that continues to play a role in shaping society, even in the economic sphere (Gintis, Bowles,

Boyd and Fehr, 2005). This lends support to Rawls's general views about how human beings form attachments.

Second, we have a significant body of empirical evidence regarding existing arrangements that are similar to the democratic corporatist POD in important respects. The literature on corporatism has tended to focus on the economic performance of corporatist arrangements (Hall and Soskice, 2001),[16] their historical origins (Katzenstein, 1985; Streeck and Yamamura, 2001), and their prospects for survival in an age of globalization (Kitschelt, Lange, Marks, and Stephens, 1999; Streeck and Thelen, 2005; Gourevitch and Shinn, 2005). But perhaps the best study of the social consequences of corporatism is Arend Lijphart's *Patterns of Democracy* (1999), which takes corporatism as one element of a broader pattern of governance that we see in European social democracies – what he calls "consensus democracy." Controlling for various factors, consensus democracy is correlated with greater economic equality, higher voter turnout, more spending on social welfare (as a percentage of GDP), lower rates of incarceration, and greater spending on foreign aid (as a percentage of GNP) (Lijphart, 1999, chapter 16; Wilensky, 2002). One reasonable explanation for these correlations is that people who grow up in these societies develop a stronger and more widespread commitment to principles of social fairness and mutual support that are implicit in the political culture.

Conclusion

Rawls envisions a just society as one in which citizens are moved by a liberal democratic spirit, a spirit defined by a commitment to the two principles of justice. Social institutions in a just society are themselves a product of this sensibility, as it moves citizens and legislators to remake their social order in the face of changing circumstances. But the liberal democratic spirit does not come out of nowhere – it must be cultivated and encouraged. On Rawls's view, society nurtures the sense of justice by putting people in a position where they can appreciate how the social order embodies a caring concern for their interests and the interests of the people that they care about.

The problem with a liberal market POD is that it submerges people in economic competition for most of their lives. Instead of putting people in a position to appreciate the caring concern embodied in the social order, it puts people in circumstances where they experience the social order mainly as a frustrating constraint on the pursuit of their own private ends. A democratic corporatist POD, by contrast, lifts people up to give them a different perspective. By participating with others in regulating the parts of the economy in which they are most involved, citizens come to appreciate how the social order contributes to their good and the good of those that they care about. This fosters a more powerful and widespread attachment to the principles of justice, and, in this way, democratic corporatism answers better to the moral ideal of stability.

Notes

1. For helpful comments on previous drafts of this paper and for many discussions about its main themes, I would like to thank Samuel Freeman, Thad Williamson, Martin O'Neill,

Nien-hê Hsieh, Tim Scanlon, Joshua Cohen, and Carol Gould. I read Stuart White's illuminating contribution to this volume too late to incorporate it into my discussion, but I share his concerns and agree with many features of his argument.

2. Rawls also sometimes says that more substantive considerations may figure into the choice between these arrangements. See Rawls (2001, pp. 178 – 179).
3. I take it that the process that leads to an agreement is a "deliberation" when: (a) each party wants to adopt an arrangement that promotes his own interests but also gives fair consideration to the interests of others, and (b) each party attempts to convince the others to adopt a certain arrangement by presenting arguments that show that the arrangement advances everyone's interests in a fair way. For the distinction between deliberation and bargaining, see Cohen (1997), Habermas (1996), and Gutmann and Thompson (1996).
4. Democratic corporatism departs from many mainstream models in that it is not exclusively state-centered. Schmitter (1982), for example, thinks of corporatism as consisting primarily in a form of interest representation at the level of state legislatures and state agencies. Union representation on corporate boards would not obviously count as a form of corporatism on his view. Many modern theorists do not share the state-centered view of corporatism. See, for instance, Cawson (1986), Pekkarinen, Pohjola, and Rowthorn (1992), and Wilensky (2002).
5. The idea that we can deepen the democratic character of society by strengthening and empowering secondary associations is one that democratic corporatism shares with associationalist theories, such as those developed by Joshua Cohen and Joel Rogers (1993, 1995) and Paul Hirst (1994) (among others). I elaborate on the democratic character of democratic corporatism in Hussain (2009).
6. Democratic corporatism also departs from many mainstream models of corporatism in that it says that representative bodies must deliberate with each other to reach agreements. Many classical accounts of corporatism share this deliberative perspective. Hegel, for example, thinks of the legislative process as one in which representatives from the various corporations in society (in the lower house) represent each corporation's distinctive perspective on the common good in legislative deliberations. Agreements emerge not through a process of bargaining, but a reasoned discussion about the common good. See Hegel (1991, sections 309–315); see also G.D.H. Cole (1920).
7. By contrast, in *A Theory of Justice* (1999), Rawls seems to hold the view that it is simply not possible, as a practical matter, for a social arrangement to be stable unless people are moved by a corresponding sense of justice. See Rawls (1999, pp. 401, 431–432).
8. This raises a question about Rawls's attitude toward the market. The ideal of respecting citizens as reasonable individuals rules out the possibility of arranging society so that people are led to maintain just institutions through a system of incentives alone. But a just POD would rely on markets to provide individuals with incentives to act in ways that improve everyone's life prospects (especially those of the least advantaged). Why is relying on incentives to encourage citizens to engage in the right forms of economic activity not disrespectful to them, when relying on incentives to encourage them to engage in the right forms of political activity is? In either case, it seems that we bypass their moral sensibilities and merely address their rational self-interest. The worry that I raise here parallels the well-known critique of Rawls developed by G.A. Cohen (2008). See Rawls (1999, p. 415).
9. A person at stage two does not comply with the principles of justice merely strategically, as a means to securing social approval. A person at stage two has a genuine disposition to treat the principles as intrinsically reason giving, but this disposition is causally dependent on the attitudes and expectations of others. So if the people around him stopped expecting others to conform to the requirements of the principles of justice, he would no longer be disposed to treat them as intrinsically reason giving.

10. A moral sensibility that is circumscribed by associational ties has important features in common with the condition that Alexis de Tocqueville (1969) calls "individualism." See also Stuart White's contribution to this volume (Chapter 6).
11. Here I follow Edward McClennen's interpretation of the third principle of moral development (McClennen, 1989).
12. I take it that Rawls himself would not think this is a problem. Rawls's implicit view seems to be that most people in a just society will not reach the morality of principle. Only the political class – legislators, judges, engaged citizens – will reach this stage, and this is enough to maintain the stability of a just regime. I disagree with Rawls on this point. My argument in the section above on participation in public life suggests why a widespread morality of principle would be better from the standpoint of stability. See also Stuart White's contribution to this volume.
13. See Rosner (1998). Thanks to Scott Rosner for a helpful discussion about this case.
14. The classic study of democracy in town councils is Mansbridge (1983). For a discussion of local school councils and community-based policing, see Fung (2004).
15. For stability-based arguments for worker control, see Clark and Gintis (1978) and Wolff (1977).
16. Some of the claims made in the enormous literature on the economic performance of corporatist, neocorporatist, and coordinated economic regimes are broadly relevant to social justice, insofar as corporatist arrangements tend toward greater equality in the distribution of income and do a better job of developing skills.

References

Cawson, A. (1986) *Corporatism and Political Theory*, Blackwell, Oxford.
Charkham, J. (2005) *Keeping Better Company: Corporate Governance Ten Years On*, 2nd edn, Oxford University Press, Oxford.
Clark, B. and Gintis, H. (1978) Rawlsian justice and economic systems. *Philosophy & Public Affairs*, 7, 302–325.
Cohen, G.A. (2008) *Rescuing Justice and Equality*, Harvard University Press, Cambridge, MA.
Cohen, J. (1997) Deliberation and democratic legitimacy, in *Deliberative Democracy* (eds J. Bohman and W. Rehg), MIT Press, Cambridge, MA.
Cohen, J. and Rogers, J. (1993) Associations and democracy. *Social Philosophy and Policy*, 10, 282–312.
Cohen, J. and Rogers, J. (1995) *Associations and Democracy*, Verso, London.
Cole, G.D.H. (1920) *Guild Socialism*, Frederick A. Stokes, New York.
Fung, A. (2004) *Empowered Participation: Reinventing Urban Democracy*, Princeton University Press, Princeton.
Gintis, H., Bowles, S., Boyd, R., and Fehr, E. (eds) (2005) *Moral Sentiments and Material Interests: The Foundations of Cooperation in Economic Life*, MIT Press, Cambridge, MA.
Gourevitch, P.A. and Shinn, J. (2005) *Political Power and Corporate Control: The New Global Politics of Corporate Governance*, Princeton University Press, Princeton.
Gutmann, A. and Thompson, D. (1996) *Democracy and Disagreement*, Harvard University Press, Cambridge, MA.
Habermas, J. (1996) *Between Facts and Norms*, MIT Press, Cambridge, MA.
Hall, P.A. and Soskice, D. (eds) (2001) *Varieties of Capitalism: The Institutional Foundations of Comparative Advantage*, Oxford University Press, New York.
Hegel, G. (1991) *Elements of the Philosophy of Right* (ed. A. Wood), Cambridge University Press, Cambridge.

Hirst, P. (1994) *Associative Democracy*, University of Massachusetts Press, Amherst.
Hussain, W. (2009) The most stable just regime. *Journal of Social Philosophy*, 40, 412–433.
Katzenstein, P.J. (1985) *Small States in World Markets*, Cornell University Press, Ithaca, NY.
Kitschelt, H., Lange, P., Marks, G., and Stephens, J.D. (eds) (1999) *Continuity and Change in Contemporary Capitalism*, Cambridge University Press, Cambridge.
Krouse, R. and McPherson, M. (1986) A "mixed"-property regime: Equality and liberty in a market economy. *Ethics*, 97, 119–138.
Lijphart, A. (1999) *Patterns of Democracy*, Yale University Press, New Haven.
Mansbridge, J. (1983) *Beyond Adversary Democracy*, University of Chicago Press, Chicago.
McClennen, E. (1989) Justice and the problem of stability. *Philosophy & Public Affairs*, 18 (1), 3–30.
Mill, J.S. (1994) *Principles of Political Economy*, Oxford University Press, Oxford.
Pateman, C. (1970) *Participation and Democratic Theory*, Cambridge University Press, Cambridge.
Pekkarinen, J., Pohjola, M., and Rowthorn, B. (eds) (1992) *Social Corporatism: A Superior Economic System?* Oxford University Press, Oxford.
Rawls, J. (1993) *Political Liberalism*, Columbia University Press, New York.
Rawls, J. (1999) *A Theory of Justice*, rev. edn, Harvard University Press, Cambridge, MA.
Rawls, J. (2001) *Justice as Fairness: A Restatement* (ed. E. Kelly) Harvard University Press, Cambridge, MA.
Rosenstone, S.J. and Hansen, J.M. (2003) *Mobilization, Participation, and Democracy in America*, Longman, New York.
Rosner, S. (1998) Must Kobe come out and play? *Seton Hall Journal of Sport Law*, 8 (2), 539–574.
Schmitter, P. (1974) Still the century of corporatism? *The Review of Politics*, 36 (1), 85–131.
Schmitter, P. (1982) Reflections on where the theory of neo-corporatism has gone and where the praxis of neo-corporatism may be going, in *Patterns of Corporatist Policy-Making* (eds G. Lehmbruch and P. Schmitter), Sage, London.
Streeck, W. and Thelen, K. (eds) (2005) *Beyond Continuity: Institutional Change in Advanced Political Economies*, Oxford: Oxford University Press.
Streeck, W. and Yamamura, Kozo (eds) (2001) *The Origins of Non-Liberal Capitalism*, Cornell University Press, Ithaca, NY.
de Tocqueville, A. (1969) *Democracy in America* (ed J. P. Mayer), Harper & Row, New York.
Verba, S. and Nie, N.H. (1987) *Participation in America; Political Democracy and Social Equality*, University of Chicago Press, Chicago.
Vitols, S. (2001) Varieties of corporate governance: Comparing Germany and the UK, in *Varieties of Capitalism* (ed P. A. Hall and D. Soskice), Oxford University Press, Oxford, pp. 337–360.
Wiedemann, H. (1980) Codetermination by workers in German enterprise. *The American Journal of Comparative Law*, 28, 79–82.
Wilensky, H. (2002) *Rich Democracies*, University of California Press, Berkeley.
Wolff, R.P. (1977) *Understanding Rawls*, Princeton University Press, Princeton.
Wolfinger, R. and Rosenstone, S. (1980) *Who Votes?* Yale University Press, New Haven.

10

Property-Owning Democracy or Economic Democracy?

David Schweickart

Thirty-two years ago, in one of my first publications, I argued that Rawls, given the value commitments expressed in *A Theory of Justice*, should be a socialist (Schweickart, 1979). I argued that the model of democratic, worker-self-managed market socialism developed in my dissertation (not yet published) was more compatible with Rawlsian justice than the welfare state capitalism that I, along with everyone else I knew who had read the book, *assumed* was being defended in *A Theory of Justice*.

When my article, "Should Rawls Be a Socialist?" came out, I sent an offprint to Rawls (whom I had never met) with a one-sentence accompaniment, "Am I right?"

I received a short reply. Rawls pointed out to me that he had claimed that a "property-owning democracy" was compatible with his principles. He had not said that capitalism was so compatible. He had not delved deeply into the capitalism–socialism question in his book. Perhaps, he said, he should have done so.

It had not occurred to me until that moment that a "property-owning democracy" might be something other than capitalism, but that puzzling thought didn't linger in my head for long. I continued to assume that Rawls was a good social democrat, an advocate of Keynesian-liberal capitalism; indeed I cast Rawls as a representative Keynesian-liberal in two of my books, *Capitalism or Worker-Control?* (1980) and *Against Capitalism* (1993).

It was not until reading Perry Anderson's remarkable article several years ago (2005), "Arms and Rights: Rawls, Habermas and Bobbio in the Age of War," that I began to reconsider. Commenting on *Justice as Fairness: A Restatement*, Anderson asks, "What about Rawls's view of existing societies?"

> Rawls's answer is startling. After observing that favorable material circumstances are not enough to ensure a constitutional regime, which requires a political will to maintain it, he suddenly – in utter contrast to anything he had ever written before – remarks, "Germany between 1870 and 1945 is an example of a country where reasonably favorable conditions existed – economic, technical and no lack of resources, an educated citizenry and

more – but where a political will for a democratic regime was lacking. One might say the same of the United States today, if one decides our constitutional regime is democratic in form only".

Anderson is stunned:

The strained conditional – as if the nature of the American political system was a matter of decision – barely hides the bitterness of the judgment. This is the society Rawls once intimated was nearly just, and whose institutions he could describe as "the pride of a democratic people." In one terse footnote, the entire bland universe of an overlapping consensus capsizes. (Anderson, 2005, pp. 37–38)

Did Rawls's own views about the justice of welfare state capitalism shift over the years and become more critical, or did he later make explicit what he had felt from the beginning? I'm not sure. But it is clear now that the later Rawls did *not* think that welfare state capitalism could satisfy his principles of justice. In *Justice as Fairness: A Restatement* he is explicit:

Welfare state capitalism rejects the fair value of political liberty, and while it has some concern for equality of opportunity, the policies necessary to achieve that are not followed. It permits very large inequalities in the ownership of real property (productive assets and natural resources) so that the control of the economy and much of political life rests in few hands. And although the name "welfare-state capitalism" suggests welfare provisions may be quite generous and guarantee a decent social minimum covering the basic needs, a principle of reciprocity to regulate economic and social inequalities is not recognized. (Rawls, 2001, pp. 137–138)

According to Rawls, neither laissez-faire capitalism, nor welfare state capitalism, nor "state socialism with a command economy supervised by a one-party state" will satisfy his principles of justice. However, a suitably structured "property-owning democracy" or "liberal socialist regime" might. As for the latter two options, "justice as fairness does not decide between these regimes" (Rawls, 2001, p. 139).

Should it? Should my original questions still be answered in the affirmative? In this chapter I will revisit my original seven-count indictment of capitalism to see if it holds up against a Rawlsian "property-owning democracy," an economic system that still features widespread private ownership of means of production, but which is, as Rawls later clarified, quite distinct from "welfare state capitalism." I will compare a specific economic model that fits Rawls's description of a property-owning democracy with a specific model of a liberal socialist regime, namely my own version of Economic Democracy.

The Indictment

In "Should Rawls Be a Socialist?" I offer a seven-count indictment of capitalism. I then compare what I took to be Rawls's liberal "welfare-state capitalism" with a model of socialism I then called "worker-controlled socialism," which I now call "Economic Democracy." I argue that a liberal welfare state capitalism suffers the defects highlighted my indictment far more than worker-controlled socialism; hence, given the normative commitments expressed in *A Theory of Justice*, Rawls should abandon his neutrality. My indictment of capitalism was (and remains) as follows:

- Capitalism promotes an unjust distribution of wealth.
- Capitalism is incapable of resolving the problem of unemployment.
- Through the sales effort, capitalism generates a system of irrational wants and needs.
- Capitalism dehumanizes workers at the workplace by arranging production without workers' consent, so as to inhibit the exercise of imagination, creativity, and control.
- Capitalist growth channels workers and resources into areas that have little relation to social needs or preferences. (The *kind* of growth is non-optimal.)
- Capitalism is oriented toward growth for the sake of growth, even when growth has undesirable social consequences. (The *rate* of growth is non-optimal.)
- Capitalism is an economic system that is inherently unstable, prone to recession and/or inflation in ways that Economic Democracy is not.

Background Institutions for Distributive Justice

In Section 43 of *A Theory of Justice*, Rawls lays out some "background institutions for distributive justice." These are intended to describe the supporting institutions of a "properly organized democratic state that allows private ownership of capital and natural resources." "These arrangements are familiar," he says, "but it may be useful to see how they fit the two principles of justice. Modifications for the case of a socialist regime will be considered briefly later" (Rawls, 1971, p. 275).

The reader will note that Rawls's description of the regulatory institutions he is proposing as being "familiar" suggests a defense of the welfare state. However, he does say a few pages later that "the aim of the branches of government is to establish a democratic regime in which land and capital are widely though not presumably equally held. Society is not so divided that one small sector controls the preponderance of productive resources" (Rawls, 1971, p. 280). He is clearly aware that such equality does not exist at present. In questioning the need for progressive taxation in his just society, he warns the reader against misunderstanding his argument. "It does not follow that, *given the injustice of existing institutions*, even steeply progressive income taxes are not justified when all things are considered" (Rawls, 1971, p. 279, emphasis added).

Rawls proposes four branches of government to insure that the economy satisfies his two principles of justice. The first of these is the Allocative Branch, designed to keep the economy competitive and to compensate for market externalities. This branch will enforce anti-trust laws, and it will use such taxes and subsidies as are required to bring market prices into line with social costs and benefits. The point here is to keep the economy efficient. Economists of all stripes (Milton Friedman included) agree that the government should inhibit the formation of monopolies and should intervene when market transactions have significant "neighborhood effects," namely costs (or benefits) to third parties not participating in the transactions. Both of these conditions undercut the efficiency of free market exchange.[1]

Rawls shows himself to be a Keynesian with his Stabilization Branch, whose mission it is "to bring about reasonably full employment in the sense that those who want work can find it" by maintaining strong effective demand (Rawls, 2001, p. 276). Here Rawls reflects the then-dominant view among economists that by employing an appropriate mix of monetary and fiscal policies, an economy can be "fine-tuned" so as to sail smoothly between the Scylla of unemployment and the Charybdis of inflation.

The Transfer Branch sets the social minimum. Rawls's difference principle requires that all inequalities work to the benefit of the least well-off segment of society. This principle is operationalized by having a branch of government specifically charged with seeing to it that the social minimum be set as high as it can be without killing the goose whose golden eggs fund this minimum. The point is to insure that "the total income of the least advantaged (wages plus transfer payments) is such as to maximize their long-range expectations (consistent with the constraints of equal liberty and fair equality of opportunity)" (Rawls, 2001, p. 277). Rawls suggests that this social minimum can be achieved "either by family allowances and special payments for sickness and employment, or more systematically by such devices as a graded income supplement (a so-called negative income tax)" (Rawls, 2001, p. 275).

Finally there is the Distributive Branch, which has two distinct charges: (1) to raise the revenues that justice requires and (2) to keep inequalities of wealth within bounds. To raise the revenues necessary for the public provision of various benefits (e.g., education and health care) and for the transfer payments that the difference principle requires (e.g., the negative income tax), Rawls proposes a flat-rate expenditure tax. One pays in proportion to how much one consumes. To deal with inequalities, we should "tax inheritance and income at a progressive rate (when necessary)," and adjust "the legal definition of property rights" so that fair equality of opportunity and the value of political liberty are not put into jeopardy, which they are "when inequalities of wealth exceed a certain limit" (Rawls, 2001, pp. 278, 279).

At first sight, these four "background institutions" would seem to give us a Keynesian-liberal welfare state. The government plays a major role in the economy. It employs anti-trust legislation to keep the economy competitive. It imposes the requisite taxes to insure that prices reflect true social and environmental costs. It employs monetary and fiscal policies to keep the economy near full employment. It combines free public services with sufficient transfer payments to eliminate poverty. And it doesn't hesitate to employ progressive income and inheritance taxes to keep inequalities of wealth in check. This certainly looks like what Robert Heilbroner has dubbed "a slightly imaginary Sweden" (Heilbroner, 1992, p. 46).

In 1971 the United States did not seem to be too terribly far from this ideal. Paul Krugman, a winner of the Nobel Memorial Prize in economics, looks back with some nostalgia:

> Postwar America was, above all, a middle-class society. The great boom in wages that began with World War II had lifted tens of millions of Americans – my parents among them – from urban slums and rural poverty to a life of home ownership and unprecedented comfort. The rich, on the other hand, had lost ground. They were few in number and, relative to the prosperous middle, not all that rich. The poor were more numerous than the rich, but they were still a relatively small minority. As a result, there was a striking sense of economic commonality: Most people in America lived recognizably similar and remarkably decent material lives. (Krugman, 2007, p. 3)[2]

Yet even in those "Golden Age" years, Rawls had reservations. In discussing progressive taxation, he was explicit about "the injustice of existing institutions." There is also that curious phrase, a paragraph later, which he does not explicate, "the legal definition of property rights," which is to play a role, along with progressive taxation, in "securing the institutions of equal liberty in a property-owning democracy and the fair value of the rights they establish" (Rawls, 2001, p. 279). (More on this "curious phrase" below.)

Whatever Rawls may have been thinking at the time, his "Restatement," makes clear (as noted above) that he does *not* want his theory to serve as a justification of welfare state capitalism. A just "property-owning democracy" must be structured differently:

> The background institutions of property-owning democracy work to disperse the ownership of wealth and capital, and thus prevent a small part of society from controlling the economy and indirectly, political life as well. By contrast, welfare-state capitalism permits a small class to have near monopoly of the means of production. Property-owning democracy avoids this, not by the redistribution of income to those with less at the end of each period, so to speak, but rather by ensuring the widespread ownership of productive assets and human capital ... at the beginning of each period. (Rawls, 2001, p. 139)

A Non-Capitalist Property-Owning Democracy

Rawls's property-owning democracy is not to be identified with welfare state capitalism. (In Sweden, property ownership remains highly concentrated, so even a "slightly imaginary Sweden" won't do.) It is certainly not to be identified with Friedmanite laissez-faire capitalism. What then might such an economy look like? Rawls doesn't tell us. His four branches of government are to operate – but on what underlying set of economic institutions?

One might imagine a just property-owning democracy to be a decentralized society of small businesses and small farmers, a vision associated with E.F. Schumacher's classic *Small Is Beautiful* (1973), published two years after *A Theory of Justice*, but it is hard to imagine our transitioning back to such a state. Alternatively, one might envisage an economy whose productive enterprises are, materially, much like our own, but one in which "the legal definition of property rights" has changed. Specifically, we might imagine an economy composed of a mix of small, medium, and large enterprises, but one in which the *ownership shares* of the large corporations that dominate the economy are more or less equally distributed, and institutional mechanisms exist to preserve this equal distribution. Let us consider this second form of property-owning democracy in the comparison that follows.

A model of such a system was developed in the mid-1990s by economist John Roemer (1994, 1996). Roemer does not call his system a "property-owning democracy." He identifies it as a form of socialism. However, he does not want to identify "socialism" with "public ownership of the means of production," as the socialist tradition deriving from Marx has done: "The link between public ownership and socialism is tenuous, and I think one does much better to drop the requirement that 'the people' own the means of production from the socialist constitution. Socialists should want those property rights that will bring about a society that best promotes equality of opportunity for everyone" (Roemer, 1994, p. 20). (Economic Democracy, as we shall see, does embrace public ownership of [most] means of production.) Roemer describes his model as follows:

> The profits of firms are distributed to individual shareholders. Initially, the government distributes a fixed number of coupons or vouchers to all adult citizens, who use them to purchase the stock of firms, denominated not in regular currency but in coupons. Owning a share of the firm entitles the citizen to a share of the firm's profits. More realistically, citizens may invest their coupons in shares of mutual funds, which purchase shares of firms. One cannot purchase shares or coupons with money. People, however, can trade shares in firms for shares of other firms, at coupon prices. Thus prices on the coupon stock market will oscillate as they do on a regular stock market.
>
> Because money cannot be used on the coupon stock market, the small class of wealthy citizens will not end up owning the majority of shares. ... Everyone's coupon portfolio would be returned to the public treasury at death, and allocations of coupons would continually be made to a new generation of adults. (Roemer, 1994, pp. 49–50)

In effect, ownership shares of all major corporations are redistributed equally among the adult populations. But these shares can be neither purchased with nor sold for money. They can only be traded for other shares. The value of a share will deviate over time from its initial value, depending on how well the company is doing; hence individual portfolios will, over time, shift in value. Those doing better will pay higher dividends than those doing worse, and so one's "property income" may be higher or lower than average in any given year. However, unless every company in which one has a stake goes bankrupt, one will always receive *some* such income.

Since individuals cannot use their income to purchase additional shares from those who might be tempted to sell theirs, property will remain widely dispersed, and property income relatively equal. Since one's stock portfolio is returned to the public treasury at one's death, and those shares redistributed, ownership concentration over time is effectively blocked.

It seems clear: this model would qualify as a Rawlsian "property-owning democracy." Small and medium-sized privately owned businesses continue to exist. Large enterprises are also "privately owned" by their shareholders, in that shareholders are legally entitled to their proportionate share of the firm's profits, and they may "sell" their shares to anyone who wishes to buy them. However, the legal definition of the property rights of shareholders has been modified, in that buying and selling of shares may be effected only by means of the coupon currency, and one may not bequeath one's shares to one's heirs.

The economy continues to function as a market economy, subject to oversight and regulation by the state. Let us stipulate that Rawls's four "background institutions" serve as the regulatory agencies. Let us call this model POD, against which to set a model of Economic Democracy, henceforth to be designated ED.

Economic Democracy

Like POD, ED will be a competitive market economy, comprised of an array of small, medium, and large enterprises. As with POD, smaller firms operate pretty much as they do now. It is only the large firms that are different. Large firms are not privately owned. There are no shareholders. Large firms, the "commanding heights" of the economy, are "owned" by society as a whole. As with POD, there has been a change in the legal definition of property rights.

Although owned by society as a whole, a socialized enterprise is legally controlled by those who work there, not by the state. This control is democratic: one person, one vote. Workers elect a workers' council, which performs the functions that the board of directors performs in a capitalist corporation, namely appointing and overseeing management, approving or vetoing large-scale changes in company policy, approving or vetoing major investment projects.

Workers in a democratic firm do not receive fixed salaries or wages. A worker's income is a specified share of the company's net profits.[3] These shares need not be equal. Share size may vary depending on seniority, skill level, or level of responsibility, according to whatever standards the firm chooses to adopt (so long as they comply with societal anti-discrimination laws). Since everyone's income is tied directly to the firm's profitability, everyone is motivated to work conscientiously, and see to it that coworkers do the same – a fact that doubtless plays an important role in accounting for the impressive efficiency of most democratic firms (Schweickart, 2011a).

Societal ownership of the enterprises is manifested in several ways. First of all, enterprises are not bought or sold. They are communities, not commodities. Secondly, workers are obliged to keep the value of their enterprise intact. That is to say, they must maintain a depreciation fund. They are not permitted to sell off equipment and pocket the proceeds, or let the capital stock entrusted to them deteriorate in value. (A firm may decide to contract, but in such a case, the proceeds of whatever sales are involved go to the state, not to workers.) Thirdly, the enterprise must pay a leasing fee to the state, proportional to the capital assets under its control. That is to say, it must pay a flat-rate capital assets tax.

Workplace democracy is one fundamental structure that distinguishes ED from capitalism. The other is what I call "social control of investment." Although private or cooperative savings and loan associations continue to exist, which pay interest to savers and finance consumer spending (particularly home mortgages), all *business* investment is mediated though a network of *public* banks. Funds for these banks, to be loaned out to businesses, do not come from private individuals; they come from the capital assets tax (which is regarded as a leasing fee by democratic enterprises and as a property tax by the smaller privately owned businesses).

These funds are collected by the central government, then allocated to regions, and to communities within regions, on a per capita basis. That is to say, if region A has X% of the nation's population, it gets, each and every year, X% of society's investment funds.[4] These funds are then allocated to public banks within regions and communities, to be made available to businesses, private or democratic, wanting to expand production, upgrade their technologies, or develop new products. Loan officers in these banks – public employees – rank loan applications according to (a) the projected profitability of the investment request, (b) its job creating potential, and (c) whatever additional considerations the community wishes to impose. (Differential interest rates may be employed to guide investments in a desired direction, but bottom-line profitability is always a major consideration. Loan officers who make too many bad loans – of public funds – are subject to dismissal.)

ED Versus POD

How do POD and ED compare, relative to my seven-count indictment of capitalism? Am I still right that, given his value commitments, Rawls should be a socialist, or might he be equally justified in embracing POD? Let us see. My treatment will be somewhat schematic. We will ignore the small and medium-sized businesses, which are present in both models, and treat the models as being composed exclusively of shareholding and democratic firms, respectively. We will assume that managers of shareholding firms act as managers of capitalist firms are assumed to act, that is, striving always to maximize shareholder value. (We will modify this assumption below, when we look more closely at managerial motivation.)

I will also assume that financial markets in POD operate as they do under capitalism. Banks in POD will be private, not public, institutions: that is, they are owned by coupon shareholders.[5] In short, the POD we will be examining is essentially a capitalist economy in which stock shares are more or less equally distributed. (Later we will reflect on the differences a nationalized banking system might make to our comparative analysis.)

For ease of exposition, I will rearrange the order of the indictment charges.

Inequality

Clearly POD will be a more egalitarian society than any form of capitalism. Will it be as egalitarian as ED? There are two primary sources of inequality in ED: within firms, and among firms. Democratic accountability would doubtless reduce intra-firm inequality dramatically from what occurs in capitalist firms today, since these inequalities must be justified to the workforce. It is worth remembering that in the United States – a country not known for its egalitarian ethos – the highest paid *elected* official, namely the President, earns a salary of only $400,000 per year, which is roughly eight times the median household income in the country. When Rawls was writing his *A Theory of Justice*, the CEOs of the 100 top companies averaged 40 times the average pay of a full-time worker in the American economy. Now, these CEOs average 400 times the average worker's income (Krugman, 2007, p. 142).

Since POD firms are in essence capitalist firms, one might think that CEO compensation in such firms would obviously be higher than would be the case in a democratic firm. Clearly, upper management will have considerable leeway in setting their own salaries. Widely diffuse stockholders, with access to little more data than upper management provides them, are not likely to monitor salaries effectively, and, in fact, have little motivation to do so, since extravagant salaries at the top have minimal impact on the total profits to be distributed in a large corporation.

However, available evidence suggests that corporate culture is decisive here. US compensation packages are vastly out of line with CEO compensations elsewhere. Brian Barry cites figures indicating the ratio of top CEO to average worker to be

500:1 in the United States, 25:1 in Britain, 11:1 in Germany, 10:1 in Japan (Barry, 2005, p. 217). If the society in question is "well ordered" in a Rawlsian sense, with most citizens affirming a public conception of justice that includes the difference principle, we would expect pay differentials to be even lower. In principle they should be as low in a POD firm as they would be in a democratic firm, for the difference principle, in essence, allows inequalities only to the degree that they are necessary as incentives to secure optimal management. Since having good managers is as pressing a concern to workers in a democratic firm as it is to shareholders in POD, the financial incentives should be comparable. In practice, ED workers are better placed to monitor their managers than are shareholders in POD, but in an egalitarian culture the discrepancies between the two systems would not likely be large, if they exist at all.

Since both ED and POD are competitive market economies, we can expect the inter-firm inequalities to be similar. Some companies will be more successful than others. This fact counts against ED and in favor of POD with respect to income inequality. In ED a worker's income is derived entirely from her firm's profits.[6] In POD a worker receives part of her income as remuneration for work, but another part as dividends from her (presumably diversified) stock portfolio. The ED worker has, as it were, all her eggs in one basket – and hence is more vulnerable when her company's fortunes dip – and benefits more substantially during good times.

How then do the systems compare overall? If we grant an egalitarian cultural shift, the nod must be given to POD – although both systems will be vastly more egalitarian than capitalist economies, even social democratic ones.[7] But in POD, property income itself is relatively equal, and will therefore offset some of the inter-firm inequality inherent in a competitive market economy, a condition favoring POD over ED.

Unemployment

The key argument for the superiority of ED over capitalism is straightforward: capitalism *requires* substantial unemployment to function smoothly, whereas ED does not. Firm owners have interests that conflict sharply with those of their employees. Under capitalism labor is a cost of production. Thus owners want to get as much labor as possible from their employees for as little cost as possible, whereas employees are incentivized to do as little work as possible for the highest wage. There exists a fundamental disciplinary problem at the heart of every capitalist enterprise: how to compel workers to work diligently. The basic solution: the threat of unemployment. But for this threat to be credible, there must be replacement workers readily available, and conditions of unemployment must be relatively stark. Both of these conditions are fulfilled when unemployment is substantial; both diminish as the economy approaches the Rawlsian goal of "relatively full employment." (Capitalists do not want the unemployment rate to get *too* high, since workers are also consumers, but they don't want it to get too low either.)[8]

The situation is very different for a democratic firm. Workers who are incompetent or not pulling their weight may be fired, but the company cannot increase its profits by keeping wages down – for labor is *not* a cost of production. Everyone's income is a share of the profit, but "profit" here is the difference between sales and *nonlabor* costs. It follows that full employment is fully compatible with ED, but not with a healthy capitalism. Hence, in ED the government can – and should – serve as an employer of last resort (ELR), guaranteeing a meaningful, living-wage job to everyone who wants to work.[9] This is not feasible in a capitalist economy.[10]

Would ELR be feasible in POD? Labor remains a cost of production in this system as it is under capitalism. Managers are still charged with maximizing profits, so as to maximize shareholder value, and are rewarded for doing so. However, the shareholders in this case are fellow citizens with portfolios comparable to the workers in the firm. To be sure, an employee of the firm will benefit more if wages are raised at the expense of profits than conversely (assuming her stock portfolio contains other than those of the company for which she works), and if she can do less work for her wage than she is currently doing, but the owner/worker clash of interests is not so intense as it is under capitalism. Workers gain *both* from higher wages *and* from rising share values. It may well be that the threat of unemployment as the disciplinary stick to keep workers in line is less salient. The arguments of the pro-ELR economists (see note 10) would appear to have more force with respect to POD than they do with respect to capitalism.

In sum, ED fairs better than POD with respect to unemployment in theory, but in practice the difference might not be great.

Dehumanized work

A similar argument can be made regarding the quality of work life. Capitalist firms are strongly incentivized to replace skilled workers by unskilled workers, since unskilled workers cost less and tend to be more docile.[11] A capitalist firm has no interest in making work as skill-intensive and rewarding as possible, *unless* doing so would raise worker productivity enough to more than offset whatever wage increases the more skilled workers might demand or the inefficiencies such changes might produce. This tendency to "deskill" labor conflicts sharply with Rawls's "Aristotelian principle": "other things being equal, human beings enjoy the exercise of their realized capacities (their innate and trained abilities), and their enjoyment increases the more this capacity is realized, or the greater its complexity" (1971, p. 425).

The incentive structure is different in a democratic firm. There is no reason to suppose that workers would always give top priority to maximizing income. If they can reorganize their work processes so as to make them more satisfying, more skill enhancing, more in accord with "the Aristotelian principle," they may well choose to sacrifice a bit of "efficiency," and hence income, to do so.[12]

In principle, managers of POD firms are expected to behave the same as those of capitalist firms, but this might not be the case in practice. In capitalist firms, there are usually a few major shareholders well positioned to oversee management. Moreover, typically, CEOs and other senior administrators are offered company stock and stock options, so as to incentive them to maximize shareholder value. Under POD there are neither "major shareholders," nor stock options for managers. Hence managerial interests are less closely bound to owner interests than they are under capitalism. To be sure, their salaries are tied to company performance, but performance criteria might well be more flexible, not focused so exclusively on shareholder value.[13] Given the egalitarian culture of POD, managers would probably be reluctant to engage in the more brutal forms of deskilling and downsizing commonplace in capitalist firms.

It is fair, then, to say that democratic firms are better positioned to resist downsizing and deskilling than are POD firms, but the differential advantage may not be large. It must also be said: democratic firms are better positioned than POD firms to allow for a reorganization of work that makes jobs more meaningful at the expense of "efficiency." Workers in POD firms would not likely be given this option. So, overall, modest advantage to ED.

What kind of growth?

The kind of society in which we (and our children) will live is determined in significant measure by the kinds of investments our business enterprises, existing and new, choose to make. One might think that debate over investment priorities would be a major part of the political process in a democratic society. This is not the case in most capitalist societies. "The market" decides, not "the people." That is to say, those with money to invest make the decisions as to where to invest and in what, based on profit expectations. To be sure, the market does not decide everything. Public investment in infrastructure and other public goods must pass through the democratic process. Governments can also offer various incentives – low-cost loans and tax breaks – to nudge investors in one direction or another. But the bulk of investment decisions remain in private hands. This would also be the case in POD.

The market plays a significant role in resource allocation for future projects in ED, as it does in POD. The major difference has to do with *when* market forces come into play. Market forces do not determine the initial allocation of investment funds in ED, as they do in POD. The initial allocation is made by the national legislature, which typically applies the per capita rule. Investment funds flow to where the people are. This flow contrasts sharply with investment flows under capitalism. Typically, certain regions of a capitalist economy become "hot" for investors, while others go cold. Certain regions boom, while others decay. That is to say, people flow to where the investment funds are flowing – not the other way around.

When funds reach the regions, political decisions must then be made regarding how much of the investment funds are to be set aside for public investment projects, and what priorities, in addition to project profitability, banks should follow in loaning out the rest. Only after these decisions have been made do market forces come into play.

Two significant consequences follow from this difference in investment fund allocation: communities are more stable in ED, since investments flow to where the people are, and citizens will have more input into key decisions that will affect their communal quality of life. Every year communities receive their share of the national investment fund, so local governments have important decisions to make: How much of the funds should we allocate to public projects, how much to our local banks? What sorts of investments should we encourage the market sector to undertake, what sorts should we discourage? (Citizens will want to know what projects other communities have attempted that have worked out well, and what sorts have not.) Since such decisions impact significantly on residents, one would expect vibrant debate and an enhancement of the political culture. Given Rawls's commitment to "the good of community," he should favor ED over POD on this count.[14]

Rate of growth, nonrational persuasion, instability

One might argue that the ED investment mechanism would give us a less dynamic, less growth-oriented society than we would have under POD, where investment capital is less constrained. This may well be true, but this fact – if it is a fact – is not ethically decisive, since for Rawls growth is not, in and of itself, a value.

> It is a mistake to believe that a just and good society must wait upon a high material standard of life. What men want is meaningful work in free association with others, these associations regulating their relations to one another within the framework of just basic institutions. To achieve this state of things great wealth is not necessary. In fact, beyond some point it is more likely to be a positive hindrance, a positive hindrance at best if not a temptation to indulgence and emptiness. (Rawls, 1971, p. 290)

These reflections occur during Rawls's discussion of the question of "justice between generations" (Rawls, 1971, sections 44 and 45; see also Rawls, 2001, pp. 160–161). His concern is to specify a "just savings principle." Rawls wishes to debunk the idea that "time preference," the notion that humans value more immediate consumption over more distant consumption, is a valid *ethical* principle.[15] He worries that the "will of the electorate," influenced by "time preference," may be misguided in their judgment as to how much should be saved, saving too little as a result. He goes so far as to assert that conscientious government officials might be justified in trying to circumvent this will (Rawls, 1971, p. 296).

But Rawls seems not to have noticed that under capitalism – or POD – there is no institutional mechanism for people to engage in democratic will formation regarding how much savings a society should undertake. The size of the investment fund, which is derived from these savings, and which is a key determinant of economic growth, is the unplanned outcome of the decisions of individual savers. These savers are not motivated in their decisions – nor can they be expected to be so motivated – by the well-being of future generations. People save now so as to be able to consume later – either things they cannot afford to consume now or things they will need to consume after their incomes cease.

The problem is more serious and more complicated than Rawls seems to have grasped. "Saving" under capitalism is not a matter of consuming less now so that there will be enough left over for future consumption. The point is not to consume less so that the pie will last longer. The point is to consume less so that *the pie will get bigger*. At least this is the point from the societal point of view. The social utility of savings is quite distinct from individual utility. The point of capitalist financial institutions is to encourage people to save – by offering them financial inducements to do so – so that these funds may be made available to investors, who will use these funds to *increase* production.

But as Keynes (and experience) has made crystal clear, these two functions, saving and investing, are not nearly so neatly intertwined as classical economists had thought (Keynes, 1936). The motives of savers are quite distinct from the motives of investors; hence there is no reason to suppose that the quantity of money savers save will be the same as the quantity of money investors want to invest. Indeed, the basic problem in a modern capitalist economy, according to Keynes, is too much savings, not too little.[16] Indeed, saving, in and of itself, might be regarded as an antisocial act, deserving not reward but punishment. (Instead of receiving interest on your savings, perhaps you should pay a penalty tax.) The key point is: a healthy capitalist economy depends on strong effective demand. People must be able *and willing* to buy the goods that are being produced. If people *don't* spend, then the economy gets into trouble. Workers begin to be laid off, effective demand drops further, and we get a recession – or worse. (The current economic meltdown is making this point clear to all but the most obtuse anti-Keynesians.)

This analysis has gone a bit too fast. For it is not only consumers who spend – and thus keep up effective demand. Investors also spend, investors in the "real" economy, that is, those who borrow in order to build new production facilities or expand existing facilities, to bring new products to market, to introduce new, more productive technologies. So long as these investors have need of as much money as is being saved, demand will remain strong.

Herein, of course, lies the rub. Investors are not compelled to invest. They will not invest unless there are profitable investment opportunities beckoning. Investors, no more than savers, make their decisions based on consideration of "justice for future generations." Investors will not invest unless they can be reasonably sure that consumers can be enticed to buy the new goods that will be produced. "Investor confidence," as Keynes emphasized, is the key to a healthy capitalism. If investors do not invest, the economy slumps, we all suffer.

We can now see the strategic importance of advertising and the myriad other institutions involved in "the sales effort."[17] But this sales effort, insofar as it involves, massively, techniques of nonrational persuasion (i.e., techniques that go beyond providing consumers with full and complete information so that they may make considered decisions), should be deeply troubling to Rawls, who defines the good life as one that follows a rational plan, "one of the plans that is consistent with the principles of rational choice when these are applied to the relevant features of his situation, and that plan among those meeting this condition which would be chosen by him with full deliberate rationality" (Rawls, 1971, p. 408).

The problem is more serious still. If ever-increasing consumption is irrational as a life plan (for most people), it is even more irrational for society at large, given the ever-more apparent threats to planetary well-being posed by our exhausting both our nonrenewable resources and the capacity of our planet to absorb the waste products of our consumption. Capitalism, to remain healthy, requires sustained investor confidence. Sustained investor confidence requires ever-increasing consumption. But as economist Kenneth Boulding has pointed out, "Only a madman or an economist would believe that exponential growth can go on forever in a finite world" (cited by Olson, 1973, p. 3).[18]

In short my argument is this: In a capitalist society the rate of growth is not subject to democratic control. Economic stability requires that this rate remain high. To remain high, a high volume of nonrational sales persuasion is required. But a high rate of growth is ultimately ecologically unsustainable. The same argument applies to POD, since its financial institutions are the same as those of capitalism. Coupon corporations are as motivated as capitalist corporations to expand sales, so they can be expected to employ the same sorts of nonrational sales techniques as their capitalist counterparts. Private savers supply the funds for investment in both systems. If sufficiently lucrative opportunities are not apparent, savings will outstrip investment, effective demand will fall, and the economy will slump. POD, no less than capitalism, needs to keep growing to remain healthy, which means that POD, no less than capitalism, is ecologically unsustainable.

ED, by contrast, does not need to grow to remain healthy. A democratic firm is not incentivized to grow as is a capitalist (or POD) firm. This difference has long been recognized in the theoretical literature (Ward, 1958; Schweickart, 2011a). A capitalist firm tends to maximize total profits, whereas a democratic firm tends to maximize profit-per-worker. That is to say, a capitalist firm can double its profits if it doubles its scale of operation, whereas a democratic firm that doubles its scale of operation doubles the number of workers employed there and so leaves per-worker income unchanged.

This structural difference has many implications. It explains in part why cooperative firms, even when equally or more efficient than capitalist firms, do not, over time, come to dominate the economy.[19] More relevant to our concerns here: enterprise competition in ED is significantly less intense than it is under capitalism (and would be expected to be in POD). Democratic firms are concerned not to lose market share, but they have no interest in driving their democratic competitors to the wall.[20] Firms will also be less motivated to incessantly stimulate demand for their products, since they have less to gain from doing so, and need not fear being driven out of business by aggressive competitors. So the problem of nonrational persuasion is less acute in ED – and more easily amenable to regulation, if such regulation should be deemed necessary. Advertising and the other elements of the sales effort do not have the structural function that they have in capitalism of keeping demand high.

Even more important than the behavioral differences between democratic and capitalist firms are the differences between ED and capitalism (and POD) due to the differences in their financial structures. Since ED does not rely on private savers for its investment fund, it need not worry that savings might exceed investor demand. The size of the investment fund is determined by the capital-assets tax rate. It is not the unplanned outcome of private decisions. Should more funds be available than enterprises want to borrow, the excess can be rebated to the taxpayers or spent on public projects. The next year the tax rate can be cut. ED is in no way hostage to "investor confidence."

It follows that ED need not grow to remain healthy. A steady-state ED is non-problematic. This does not mean that technological innovation will cease in ED. Firms in ED can gain in two ways by introducing a more productive technology. They can increase their market share by undercutting their competitors' prices, and thus gain more income for themselves. Or, they can use their productivity gains to increase not their incomes but their leisure. (This latter option is not available to workers in a capitalist firm.) If a new technology allows them to produce more with the same amount of labor, they can employ it instead to produce the same with less labor – which means they can shorten their hours of work, or take more days off or longer vacations. Indeed, we might, over time, reach that stage envisaged by Keynes when speculating about "The Economic Possibilities for Our Grandchildren" – a stage that cannot be reached under capitalism:

We shall use the new-found bounty of nature quite differently than the way the rich use it today, and will map out for ourselves a plan of life quite otherwise than theirs.... What work there still remains to be done will be as widely shared as possible – three hour shifts, or a fifteen-hour week.... There will also be great changes in our morals.... I see us free to return to some of the most sure and certain principles of religion and traditional virtue – that avarice is a vice, that the extraction of usury is a misdemeanor, and the love of money is detestable, that those walk most truly in the paths of virtue and sane wisdom who take least thought for the morrow ... We shall honor those who can teach us how to pluck the hour and the day virtuously and well, the delightful people who are capable of taking direct enjoyment in things. (Keynes, 1963, p. 369)

POD Modified

I have argued that, when we compare ED with POD, apart from the issue of income inequality, ED fares better than does POD when confronted with my seven-count indictment of capitalism. Unemployment will (probably) be lower in ED; meaningful work will be (somewhat) more plentiful; the citizenry will have more democratic control over the direction of their economic development; they will be less subject to the nonrational sales techniques developed by modern capitalism; they will have more control over the pace of economic growth, and can, in fact, bring that growth rate down to an ecologically sustainable level without provoking an economic crisis.

The perceptive reader will note, however, that almost all the advantages I have enumerated derive from the fact that the financial sector in POD is homologous to the financial sector in a capitalist society. That is to say, POD relies on private savings for its investments, and private banks to allocate these funds. A property-owning democracy could choose to do otherwise. A property-owning democracy *could* nationalize its banking system. It could institute a capital assets tax to fund it.[21] A property-owning democracy could also mandate that worker representatives be given some of the seats on a coupon-corporation's board of directors. If these steps were taken, giving us POD+, the arguments I have made for the superiority of ED would pretty much collapse. POD+ firms would still be more expansion-oriented than ED firms, but with finance publicly controlled, their access to investment funds could be curbed. Such firms might be more aggressive in their sales effort than their ED counterparts, but the government could take measures take to curb abuses, if deemed serious, without worrying that a fall-off in consumption would trigger an economic recession.

Of course, with the government controlling the allocation of investments, with worker representation of corporate boards, and with restrictions in place to keep ownership widely dispersed, one would be hard pressed to call POD+ nonsocialist.[22] Hence my original claim would stand vindicated. Rawls *should* be a socialist.

Would he – or anyone else – have good grounds for choosing ED over POD+? Might there be some other case made for the superiority of ED over POD+, or vice versa, than the arguments set out in my indictment? Consider John Roemer's comment regarding the relative merits of his model (the one given in *A Future for Socialism*, which is essentially POD+) and a model such as ED:

> I think the principal weakness of the managerial-firm proposals [such as POD+] is that firms would not be democratically run. Although income would be more equally distributed, the relationship of the worker to her firm may not change much. ... The principal advantage of this model is that it involves probably the smallest change from actually existing capitalism, and therefore it perhaps has the largest probability of running as efficiently as capitalism does. (Roemer, 1994, pp. 50–51)

Given the economic havoc capitalist financial markets have recently wreaked, the efficiency argument is a lot less persuasive today than it might have been in 1994. But the fact that POD+ involves the smallest change from actually existing capitalism suggests a different argument, one that might well appeal to Rawls: "When a practical decision is to be made between property-owning democracy and a liberal socialist regime, we look to a society's historical circumstances, to its traditions of political thought and practice, and much else. Justice as fairness does not decide between these regimes" (Rawls, 2001, p. 139).

It might be argued that since POD+ more closely resembles capitalism than ED, it would be easier, practically, to move from our present-day capitalism to POD+ than to ED. Rawls might find such an argument compelling. It has prima facie plausibility. But a more careful analysis actually points to the opposite conclusion. A more convincing case can be made that ED is a more realistic goal than POD+.

Consider how such a transition to POD+ might come about. Stock shares in all major corporations would have to be redistributed to the adult population of the country, each getting a portfolio of equal value. But how would the government come to possess these stocks in the first place? They would have to be expropriated from their current owners – with or without compensation. This, needless to say, would be fiercely resisted by those whose stock would be expropriated, unless compensation were quite high. But high compensation would be unattractive to the vast majority, whose taxes would have to pay the bill. Moreover, if the economy is doing well, a movement calling for so radical a redistribution would have little chance of attracting much support in the first place.

If the economy is not doing well, things might be different. Consider a massive financial meltdown – unthinkable a couple of years ago, but not so hard to imagine at present. Suppose the stock markets collapse to the extent that they did during the Great Depression. Suppose a government is swept into power, backed by an aroused citizenry sick of bailing out the rich, committed to radical change (as opposed to a government backed by Wall Street, charged with saving the system with as little cost to the financial sector as possible.)[23] In this case expropriation can take place easily, for most shares are virtually worthless. Indeed the government could agree to purchase shares at *above* market value. In a sense the government would not be "expropriating" anyone's property. The markets have already done the expropriating. The government is merely picking up the pieces. This "buyout" (instead of "bailout") would not be expensive, since the stocks will be purchased for a tiny fraction of their former value. The government can print the necessary money, an appropriate response, since an economy in depression needs financial stimulus.

Now consider. What should the government do next? If it is determined to institute POD+, it will have to redistribute these seemingly worthless stock shares to the population at large. It will have to value them appropriately so that, when the economy recovers, all citizens will have portfolios of roughly equal value – a daunting task technically, and one, moreover, that might not have much popular appeal.[24]

It would be far simpler, would it not, to turn the now government-owned nonfinancial corporations over to their employees, to be run democratically?[25] (We might want to insist that they keep existing management in place for a certain time period, while they elect a workers' council, which will then decide what personnel changes, if any, they wish to make.) The financial sector, also under government control, could be restructured into a network of public investment banks, whose revenues would come not from private savings, but from a capital assets tax.[26]

Not only would this transition procedure be simpler than that to POD, but, given the total discredit into which financial markets have fallen, democratizing work would surely have more popular appeal than a plan that involves entrusting one's fate once more to those mysterious markets. It is also more in accord with the democratic values to which we constantly pay tribute.

Given the spike in unemployment that will accompany the crisis, the government should also propose itself as an employer of last resort, so as to absorb the excess workforce until the economy revives again. Which it should. For as our new president can remind the nation, there is nothing to fear but fear itself. We have not experienced a natural disaster. Our resources and skill base remain intact. We have experienced this crisis because our deeply flawed economic institutions have broken down. But with some fairly minor changes – minor from the point of view of the average citizen – we can get our economy up and running again. And now we will have a much better system: vastly more democratic, egalitarian, transparent, rational, and stable – one, moreover, that is no longer on collision course with our planet's ecosystem.

Might a transition to a more democratic economy, ED or POD, occur through a more gradual, piecemeal process, rather than via a massive economic crisis? Perhaps. But the more gradualist scenarios would also seem to favor ED over POD. It is easy enough to imagine governmental programs that would facilitate (via partial subsidization) worker buyouts of existing firms (Dow, 2003, chapter 12). If these firms are generally successful, political pressure might build to move more and more firms from the private sector to the democratic sector.

We can also imagine instituting a capital assets tax. This might have political traction. Since corporations have become so adept at avoiding the corporate income tax, replace that tax by a capital-assets tax. It would be simple to calculate: What is your stock price on December 31? How many shares has your company issued? What percentage of your sales are within the nation? Multiply these numbers together, then multiply that total by the flat-rate tax. That's what you owe.

Given the turmoil fresh in everyone's mind occasioned by the recent financial crisis, a case could surely be made for setting up a public banking system to compete with private banks. The public system would have job creation as its principal mandate, making its loans to local businesses or entrepreneurs. (At present one state in the United States has such a bank, the Bank of North Dakota, set up in 1919. A number of other states are now considering such a move.)

These initiatives all move the economy in the direction of Economic Democracy.

What might a move toward POD look like? The government could buy shares in major corporations, then distribute them to the citizenry. Since the explicit goal of this program is wealth redistribution, these stock purchases would be financed by taxing the wealthy. But to accomplish genuine redistribution, even gradually, the tax would have to be substantial, since currently the upper 1% (in the United States) own roughly 40% of the wealth. As Brian Barry has pointed out, to *reduce* the wealth of the ultra-rich, the tax rate would have to be substantially *higher* than the income that wealth generates (Barry, 2005, p. 191). That is to say, the ultra-rich would pay more in taxes than their entire income each year – very much more if they are ultra-ultra rich.[27] Needless to say, any such tax would be bitterly opposed – and, since the redistribution is gradual, most individuals wouldn't see much benefit: those dividends from a small stock portfolio (whose stocks could not be sold for cash, but only traded for other stocks). Support for such a policy would be hard to muster.

Our conclusion: POD+ would be vastly preferable to what we now have, but ED would be, for both theoretical and practical reasons (especially the latter), the better choice. Rawls should not only be a socialist. He should be an Economic Democrat.

Notes

1. Neighborhood-effect interventions typically involve taxing goods whose production or consumption generate negative externalities (e.g., goods whose production or consumption generates significant pollution) at a rate sufficient to provide the revenues required to redress third-party harm, and subsidizing the production of those goods that have substantial third-party benefits.
2. Krugman notes (2007, p. 18) that if we define a "billionaire" as someone whose wealth is greater than the output of 20,000 average workers ($1 billion in the mid-1990s), there were 13 in 1968. There are 160 now.
3. It should be noted that *labor* is not counted as a cost of production in a democratic firm; profit is thus the difference between sales and *nonlabor* costs. If a firm cannot make sufficient profits to keep all incomes above a specified minimum, the firm must declare bankruptcy, control of its assets passing to the state.
4. The national legislature may overrule this prima facie entitlement to account for special circumstances. Indeed, the national legislature could adopt some other formula for investment allocation, perhaps more explicitly in line with the difference principle. For reasons of simplicity and prima facie fairness, the model advanced here will use a per capita distribution. (One formula to be avoided is the one that would return to each region the capital tax revenues generated in that region. This formula all but guarantees a widening gap between richer and poorer regions – as the tragedy of Yugoslavia makes clear.)
5. In *A Future for Socialism* Roemer's banks are public banks – as in ED – but in *Equal Shares* banks have shareholders just like nonfinancial corporations. They too operate in the "coupon sector," and hence operate to maximize profits (Roemer, 1996, p. 21). POD will follow the *Equal Shares* model. What we will later designate POD+ will be the *Future for Socialism* model. The *Equal Shares* model also differs from the earlier model in that it allows firms (a) to create new shares and to exchange the coupons they receive in selling these shares for investment funds, and also (b) to buy back shares in circulation by purchasing coupons to do so with cash. These exchanges take place at the Treasury Department, the only agency authorized to exchange coupons for money. Thus, as under

capitalism, firms have two ways of securing investment funding: borrowing or issuing stock shares. The firms in POD may be assumed to operate this way, although this feature does not figure in the analysis that follows.

6. In practice workers are usually paid a weekly or monthly "wage," so that income is predictable, with "bonuses" paid at the end of the year, based on the firm's profitability. A certain portion of the firm's annual profit is put into a reserve fund, to cover times when annual profits do not cover the "wages" already paid out. When a worker leaves the firm, she receives that portion of the reserve fund to which she has contributed.

7. Social democratic welfare state capitalism is much more egalitarian than US neoliberal capitalism, but with property ownership concentrated, property income still produces massive pre-tax inequalities, which are only partially offset by redistributive taxation. Hence ED is significantly more egalitarian than welfare state capitalism, as my original paper argued.

8. The institution in a modern capitalist economy that keeps unemployment from getting too low is the central bank. When unemployment drops, workers gain power vis-à-vis capitalists, and so press for higher wages and more benefits. Firms raise prices to compensate, workers respond by pushing for higher wages still, and thus the "scourge of inflation" is unleashed. The central bank responds by raising interest rates and/or contracting the money supply, which forces businesses to cut back production – and lay off workers. The class character of this policy is hinted at by Paul Krugman, who writes, "It is one of the dirty little secrets of economic analysis that even though inflation is universally regarded as a terrible scourge, most efforts to measure its costs come up with embarrassingly small numbers" (Krugman, 1992, p. 52). No one likes to see rising prices, of course, but since inflation favors debtors over creditors, it is the latter group – people with money to lend as opposed to those who borrow – who really hate inflation. And, as John Kenneth Galbraith was fond of pointing out, people with money to lend generally have more of it than those who borrow. For more on this issue, see my *After Capitalism*, 2nd edition (2011, pp. 104–106).

9. In *After Capitalism* the government as employer of last resort is posited as a basic institution of Economic Democracy.

10. Although few contemporary economists are candid about this when addressing the general public, most believe that trying to achieve full employment (under capitalism) is a bad idea, that trying to force the unemployment rate below its "natural rate" (rebaptized NAIRU – the "non-accelerating inflation rate of unemployment") is a recipe for disaster. That is to say, most agree with my claim that unemployment is essential for (capitalist) economic stability. Most, but not all. See, for example the contributors to Warner, Forstater, and Rosen (2000), and those associated with the Research Center for Full Employment and Price Stability (University of Missouri-Kansas City): cfeps.org; and the Centre of Full Employment and Equity (University of Newcastle): e1.newcastle.edu.au/coffee.

11. The tendency of capitalism to deskill labor was noted by Marx in *Capital*, vol. 1. He quotes from Andrew Ure's 1835 treatise, *The Philosophy of Manufacture*: "By the infirmity of human nature, it happens that the more skillful the workman, the more self-willed and intractable he is apt to become" (Marx, 1967, p. 367). This tendency later evolved into "scientific management," promoted passionately by Frederick Winslow Taylor, a process described in detail in Braverman (1974).

12. "Efficiency" is in scare quotes. If "efficiency" means maximizing human happiness, not simply monetary profit, the choice of more satisfying work enhances efficiency.

13. For several decades following World War II, corporate executives had far more autonomy vis-à-vis shareholders than they do now. This was perceived to be a serious principal/agent problem, to be solved by more careful monitoring, giving stock options to executives, and

so forth. Corporations under POD would likely resemble those corporations more than the more purely capitalist ones of the present period. See John Kenneth Galbraith's classic *The New Industrial State* (1967) for a description of those bygone days – when CEOs thought it unseemly to set their salaries too high. Galbraith is emphatic and persuasive that the "technostructure" of a corporation did *not* strive to maximize profits, but to strike a balance among competing priorities.

14. "It is natural to conjecture that the congruence of the right and the good depends in large part on whether a well-ordered society achieves the good of community." This good, Rawls argues, is rooted in the "social nature of mankind" (Rawls, 1971, pp. 520, 522).

15. "Time preference theory" is a theory developed by economists to model certain economic behavior, but also – at its inception – to counter an important ethical critique of capitalism. For a discussion of this (spurious) counterargument, see Schweickart (1993, pp. 29–36).

16. This claim may strike Americans these days as extremely odd, since we are constantly told – correctly – that our national savings rate is now less than zero. However, much of the current crisis can be traced to the *global* savings glut, which has kept interest rates low, thus fueling the asset appreciation (stock market and real estate bubbles) that is at the core of the crisis. For more on this, see Schweickart (2011).

17. Although precise figures are hard to come by, it seems safe to say that in the United States expenditures on "the sales effort" is at least equal to what is spent on national defense. Advertising expenditures alone equal nearly half of what is spent on defense, and advertising is but a portion of the sales effort, which also includes the proliferation of retail outlets, research and development of products or product modifications with an eye to marketing potential, and much more. That the sales effort and national defense should consume comparable resources is not, from the point of view of the system, irrational, since keeping up effective demand is at least as important to the health and well-being of our society as is protecting us from external aggression. Indeed, a decline in consumer demand is turning out to be far more of a real threat to our national security than are whatever "external enemies" our astonishingly large Defense Department (with the help of the Department of Homeland Security) is protecting us against.

18. Note: the growth necessary for a healthy capitalism is indeed exponential growth, not merely steady growth, for investor confidence wanes when the *rate* of growth slows down. For an elaboration of this argument, see Schweickart (2009).

19. Rawls, in *Justice as Fairness*, observes that John Stuart Mill predicted that worker-owned firms – which he believed most working people would prefer – would eventually win out in competition with capitalist firms, but "since this has not happened, nor does it show many signs of doing so, the question arises whether Mill is wrong about what people prefer, or whether worker-managed firms have not had a fair chance to establish themselves" (Rawls, 2001, p. 178). It is a mistake to infer from the fact that democratic firms have not become dominant that workers prefer capitalist arrangements.

20. Nonprofit firms under capitalism behave much like democratic firms in this regard. Universities, for example, compete for students, do not want to see their enrollments drop, do not want to lose "market share" – but do not try to destroy or absorb their competitors. Small colleges compete quite effectively with large universities. The big fish do *not* swallow the little fish.

21. As noted above, Roemer's model in *A Future for Socialism* features a public banking system.

22. Unless one insists, contra Roemer, on making public ownership of means of production a defining characteristic of socialism.

23. "Wall Street gave $14.9 million to Obama's election campaign, the most for any campaign in history, with Goldman Sachs alone chipping in $1 million" (Foster and Holleman, 2010,

p. 18). Foster and Holleman also provide a listing (p. 15) of 21 highly placed administration officials and their connection to the financial sector.

24. It is worth noting that when Roemer proposed what I am calling POD+, the Soviet Union was in the process of transition. A transition from an economy in which all enterprises are state-owned to POD+ would be far more feasible than a transition from capitalism. The former transition was much on Roemer's mind at the time. (Personal communication.)

25. The Obama administration could have done this with bankrupt General Motors, when it took controlling interest in the company. Of course such a potentially world-historical experiment was not given the slightest consideration by Obama's Wall Street crowd.

26. That part of the finance sector dealing with home mortgages and consumer loans – as opposed to business investment – can be "reprivatized," that is, set up as a network of democratically run, nongovernmental Savings and Loan Associations that take in private savings, and loan these out to individuals wanting to purchase homes or big-ticket consumer items.

27. The math here is startling. If a billionaire makes 5% on his holdings, he takes in $50 million a year. To insure that he has less than a billion the following year, he needs to be taxed more than $50 million. Indeed, to reduce his billion to a million over, say, 10 years, his wealth would have to decline nearly $100 million a year. Leaving him, say $1 million for consumption, he should pay $149 million in taxes that first year, to bring his wealth down to $900 million. That is to say, his income tax rate would be $149/50 = 298\%$. If Bill Gates made a 5% return on his estimated $50 billion fortune, he'd take in $250 million a year in income. To whittle away his fortune over 10 years, he'd have to pay $5.25 billion in taxes that first year – 21 times his income. And the rates would go *up* each successive year.

References

Anderson, P. (2005) Arms and rights: Rawls, Habermas and Bobbio in the age of war. *New Left Review*, 31, 5–42.
Barry, B. (2005) *Why Social Justice Matters*, Polity Press, Cambridge.
Braverman, H. (1974) *Labor and Monopoly Capital: The Degradation of Work in the Twentieth Century*, Monthly Review Press, New York.
Dow, G. (2003) *Governing the Firm: Workers' Control in Theory and Practice*, Cambridge University Press, Cambridge.
Foster, J.B. and Holleman, H. (2010) The financial power elite. *Monthly Review*, 62, 1–19.
Galbraith, J.K. (1967) *The New Industrial State*, Houghton Mifflin, Boston.
Heilbroner, R. (1992) Where is capitalism going? Interview with Robert Heilbroner. *Challenge: The Magazine of Economic Affairs*, 35, 45–51.
Keynes, J.M. (1936) *General Theory of Employment, Interest and Money*, Harcourt and World, New York.
Keynes, J.M. (1963) Economic possibilities for our grandchildren, in *Essays in Persuasion*. Norton, New York.
Krugman, P. (1992) *The Age of Diminished Expectations: U.S. Economic Policies in the 1990s*, MIT Press, Cambridge, MA.
Krugman, P. (2007) *The Conscience of a Liberal*, Norton, New York.
Marx, K. (1967) *Capital*, vol. 1, International Publishers, New York.
Olson, M. (1973) Introduction, in *The No-Growth Society* (eds M. Olson and H. Landsberg), Norton, New York.

Rawls, J. (1971) *A Theory of Justice*, Harvard University Press, Cambridge, MA.
Rawls, J. (2001) *Justice as Fairness: A Restatement*, Harvard University Press, Cambridge, MA.
Roemer, J. (1994) *A Future for Socialism*, Harvard University Press, Cambridge, MA.
Roemer, J. (1996) *Equal Shares: Making Market Socialism Work*, Verso, London.
Schumacher, E.F. (1973) *Small Is Beautiful: Economics as if People Mattered*, HarperCollins, New York.
Schweickart, D. (1979) Should Rawls be a socialist? A comparison of his ideal capitalism with worker-controlled socialism. *Social Theory and Practice*, 5, 1–27.
Schweickart, D. (1980) *Capitalism or Worker-Control? An Ethical and Economic Appraisal*, Praeger, New York.
Schweickart, D. (1993) *Against Capitalism*, Cambridge University Press, Cambridge.
Schweickart, D. (2009) Is "sustainable capitalism" an oxymoron? *Perspectives on Global Development and Technology*, 8, 557–578.
Schweickart, D. (2011a) *After Capitalism*, 2nd edition, Rowman & Littlefield, Lanham, MD.
Schweickart, D. (2011b) Reading *Legitimation Crisis* during the meltdown. *Social Philosophy Today*, 27, 5–28.
Ward, B. (1958) Market syndicalism. *American Economic Review*, 48, 566–589.
Warner, A., Forstater, M., and Rosen, S. (eds) (2000) *Commitment to Full Employment: The Economics and Social Policy of William S. Vickery*, M.E. Sharpe, Armonk, NY.

Part Three
Toward a Practical Politics of Property-Owning Democracy: Program and Politics

11
Realizing Property-Owning Democracy
A 20-Year Strategy to Create an Egalitarian Distribution of Assets in the United States

Thad Williamson

The aim of this chapter is to elucidate a set of specific proposals for bringing into existence the basic elements of a Rawlsian property-owning democracy over a 20-year period, using the United States as an example. As I show, a relatively modest redistribution of wealth in the United States could easily finance a universal system of substantial assets holding, a reform that would substantially improve the life prospects of the majority of Americans. Importantly, this can be achieved through taxation focused *only* on the most wealthy (top 1%), and would not require draconian levels of taxation even of that group. I then go beyond the general remarks about property-owning democracy offered by Rawls to consider in detail three key issues: how to begin breaking up huge accumulations of wealth, how to distribute access to real property (land and housing) and cash savings widely, and how to alter who owns productive capital (i.e., the means of production). In the final section, I raise some questions left unanswered by Rawls's scheme of property-owning democracy, with particular attention to the extent of economic planning property-owning democracy in practice will require.[1]

Rawls never develops, nor purports to develop, a full-fledged, systematic account of property-owning democracy. What he has done is indicate the general outlines of the sort of political economy that might be consistent with justice as fairness. In the broadest possible terms, a property-owning democracy will be a market economy in which holdings of capital are widely dispersed across the population. The view is that fair equality of opportunity and limited inequality can be better achieved through a more broad-based distribution of initial holdings rather than by relying on the mechanism of "after-the-fact" redistributive taxation (Rawls, 1971). Needless to say (and as Rawls is well aware), this sparse account leaves many specific questions about how property-owning democracy can be implemented in practice unanswered.

In the next section I thus present a somewhat more detailed interpretive reconstruction of the property-owning democracy idea that builds upon the sketch Rawls provides. My aim is to describe an institutional configuration that could guarantee a meaningful share of property to *all* citizens, not just those who happen to be chosen to benefit from (dispersed) inherited wealth. Simply put, a property-owning democracy (POD) should not be a society in which some have property and others do not, combined with a cap on maximum property holdings or inheritance; call this interpretation of the concept "minimalist property-owning democracy." Rather, a POD should be a society in which *all* citizens have tangible (i.e., alienable) property, and enough of it to materially affect their life prospects and possibilities for exercising personal liberty. Here I follow DiQuattro's interpretation of Rawls as favoring a social system not based on class distinctions between owners and non-owners of capital and property (DiQuattro, 1983). This interpretation is also motivated by what might be termed a republican concern with fostering independence from domination by private interests, which in turn requires that individuals have sufficient economic holdings so as not to be forced into relations of social domination in order to secure their material existence (Pettit, 1998, Dagger, 2006; see also Hsieh, Chapter 7 in this volume).

Redistributing Wealth, I: Taxing Large Estates and Incomes

The *sine qua non* of a Rawlsian property-owning democracy is the creation of a society in which wealth (including savings, real property, and productive capital) is not held by a small minority of citizens, but is widely distributed. Wealth in the United States is now extraordinarily concentrated at the very top. In 2007, the wealthiest 5% of Americans, measured by net household assets, held nearly 62% of all wealth in the United States, including 72% of financial (non-home) wealth.[2] The top 1% of wealth holders in the United States held 34.6% of all wealth, including 42.7% of financial wealth and 49.3% of directly held stock and mutual funds (Wolff, 2010, tables 2, 9). And, at the very top, the richest 0.5% of Americans hold over 25% of total net worth (Mishel, Bernstein, and Allegretto, 2006, table 5.7).[3] Conversely, the bottom 60% of the asset distribution held just 4.2% of all wealth (Wolff, 2010, table 2). Further, the collapse in home and stock values since 2007, while reducing net asset levels across the board, have actually exacerbated levels of wealth inequality: economist Edward Wolff estimates that the value of median net assets plunged 36% between 2007 and 2009, compared to just a 17% drop in the mean. Simply put, households whose main asset is their home were hit much harder than rich households with diversified assets. In addition, the proportion of households with zero or negative assets increased rapidly, from 18.6% to 24.1% in just two years. Wolff thus estimates that in 2009, the share of net assets held by the top 1% of wealth holders rose to 37% (Wolff, 2010, pp. 33–34).

Mean wealth holdings of the top 1% of American households in 2004 totaled roughly $14.8 million (2004 dollars) (Mishel *et al.*, 2006, table 5.9).[4] Mean net assets for all households were roughly $430,000, with the median household having $78,000 (Mishel *et al.*, 2006, table 5.4). If a one-time redistribution were effected with the goal of providing all households with $100,000 in net assets, and all of the money were redistributed from that top 1% of households, the top 1% would still have about 70% of their current holdings.[5] In short, a redistribution of about one-third of current wealth held by the richest Americans could provide a strong cushion of security for each and every American household. This would result in a dramatic improvement in welfare – in particular for the bottom 40% of households, who hold an average of $2,200 in net assets. (Many of these households are in fact net debtors.)

Publicizing that fact must be a central goal of advocates of property-owning democracy. It is important to understand both the existing scale of inequality and the fact that redistribution on a scale which falls well, well short of "confiscatory" taxation would suffice to dramatically alter the degree to which the lower half of the economic distribution enjoy a meaningful measure of economic security.[6] But numerous difficult questions remain about *how* exactly to effect such an alteration.

Three general strategies can be distinguished. One would be, as just suggested, to pursue a one-time, large-scale redistribution, with the intent of altering the distribution of assets as rapidly as possible. The second would be to institute a more moderate package of taxes on wealth and high incomes that would operate slowly to level out inequalities over time – the path apparently favored by Rawls (1971), and the path which corresponds to most contemporary proposals for a wealth tax. The third approach would focus less on redistributing *existing* wealth, and instead focus on making sure *new* wealth is produced and distributed in a far more equitable manner.

In practice, all three strategies may well be required if anything like a property-owning democracy is to be achieved within a reasonable time frame (say the next 25 years). Roughly speaking, the proposal to tax away one-third of assets held by the top 1% to fund a universal system of assets holdings would involve redistribution of about $5 trillion in current dollars.[7] The political difficulties of effecting a redistribution approaching that scale are, to say the least, severe. Even a government committed to the goal of rapidly redistributing assets that managed to come to power and maintain strong popular support would face challenging dilemmas. Generally speaking, the larger the proposed intervention in the form of a wealth tax, the higher the likelihood of both (a) potentially unpleasant economic consequences and (b) inviting a political backlash that makes the long-term project of building a property-owning democracy unsustainable.

One economic difficulty is that wealthy households will seek and find ways to move their financial assets abroad so as to evade taxation, following the current example of many of the super-rich as well as many multinational corporations. Concerns about wealth leaving the country and global competitiveness have played a key role in persuading EU countries such as Spain and Sweden to reduce or abandon wealth taxation schemes in recent years. In the absence of a truly global taxing authority, this is not a difficulty that can be avoided, though it will be most severe for relatively small economies where wealthy households have relatively low exit costs. Physical, non-movable property (i.e., housing) represents a very large share of wealth holdings for the average American, but a relatively small proportion of holdings for most super-rich households. Cash assets in savings accounts can be transferred around the world instantly, and if a large-scale redistributive "moment" were known to be forthcoming in a single country, an exodus of such capital would be certain to follow.

How then could a property-owning democracy regime possibly get at accumulated wealth and counteract the problem of tax-evading capital flight (assuming for the moment highly favorable political conditions)? This is a problem Rawls never had to consider, since a presupposition of his theory of justice was the existence of a "closed," self-contained society and economy (Rawls, 1971). One route to a solution would be to enact policies that gave substance to that initial assumption – such as controls on capital flows, including taxation of cash assets leaving the country. Similarly, Brian Barry proposes implementing stiff penalties for "tax exiles," including not only loss of citizenship but loss of a right to return except for compassionate leave (Barry, 2005; see also Ackerman and Alstott, 1999, who propose similar measures). Another route is to impose taxes on those assets which are immovable – in particular, land – so as to capture what Henry George (1884) termed the "unearned increment." A third approach would be to settle for wealth taxes that are sufficiently modest – Edward Wolff (1996) has proposed a 0.3% wealth tax on the top bracket, while Ackerman and Alstott (1999) propose a 2% tax – to be unlikely to generate a serious tax refugee problem.

None of those approaches are entirely satisfactory if the goal is to achieve a large-scale redistribution of wealth in a short period of time. This leads us back again to a focus not on taxing estates of the living but on taxing intergenerational transfers of wealth, both *inter vivos* and at death. As usefully recounted by Jens Beckert (2007), the United States in fact has a rich political tradition dating back to Jefferson and extending through the Roosevelts of favoring high taxation of inherited wealth, and favoring it for reasons Rawls would appreciate: to break up large estates. This tradition was given political substance by the introduction of estate taxes in the Progressive Era; and sharp increases in top rates during the New Deal; indeed, at the time Rawls published *A Theory of Justice* (1971), top rates on estate taxation were some 77%, compared to 45% in 2009 and 35% in 2011 and 2012 (Jacobson, Raub, and Johnson, 2007, figure D; Sullivan, 2010).[8] (There was no estate tax altogether in 2010. Rates are scheduled to revert to 55% in 2013, but it is widely expected that the law will be changed again prior to 2013.) Nonetheless, wealthy estates have numerous ways they can avoid serious taxation at death, and while the nominally high rates of taxation on inheritance in the third quarter of the twentieth century may have moderated wealth distribution, it surely did not lead to the wide distribution of assets a genuine property-owning democracy would entail. Fiscally, the potential impact of higher estate taxes is relatively modest. In 2008, estate and gift taxes brought in nearly $29 billion in federal revenue, equivalent to about 1.14% of total federal tax receipts; in the 1960s and early 1970s, estate and gift taxes regularly approached or exceeded 2.0% of federal receipts, peaking at 2.6% in 1972 (Congressional Budget Office [CBO], 2009; US Budget Historical Tables, 2011, tables 2.1 and 2.5). Most realistic proposals for increasing the estate tax, or replacing the current system with a proper inheritance tax, projects revenue increases from stiffer taxes of roughly $40–60 billion a year (Cavanagh, Collins, Goldberg, and Pizzigati, 2009; Collins, Goldberg, and Pizzigati, 2010; this estimate is based on the "Sensible Estate Tax" legislative proposal of Washington Congressman Jim McDermott; see also Wolff, 1996.) While that total is far short of what would be required to finance a universal savings program, implementing stiffer inheritance taxes now could have very significant effects over the next 20 years as the baby boom generation enters retirement and the final stage of the life cycle (CBO, 2009).

The discussion so far indicates that there is no single policy instrument available capable of raising adequate funds to finance a universal system of savings that would provide substantial property to each household. Further, the goal of dispersing the largest estates quickly may not be practicable, given the limitations on implementing a steep wealth tax on the living and the inherently gradual process by which steep inheritance taxes shape the distribution of wealth. It is entirely possible, however, to specify a package of reforms aimed at increasing the effective taxes paid by the most wealthy that would be capable of generating enough revenue over a 10–20-year period to gradually finance such a system. Consider again the rough estimate that capitalizing a universal system of savings accounts, in which each household possessed roughly $100,000, would cost roughly $5 trillion; we may cautiously increase that estimate to $6 trillion to account for increasing population growth in the United States over the next decade. Measured out over a 12-year period, capitalizing such a system would require a more manageable investment (or redistribution) of roughly $500 billion a year. On the one hand, this is an impressive sum of money – nearly equivalent to the size of the annual defense budget in the United States and roughly equivalent to the current total of domestic discretionary (non-entitlement) spending. On the other hand, it is substantially less than the costs of either the Wall Street bailout or the Obama stimulus packages of 2008 and 2009, and would total about 3.5% of annual GDP.[9] Moreover, in economic terms these transfers are not equivalent to the "costs" of say, military spending; that is, the money transferred does not disappear from the economy. All that changes is who controls how the money is used.

Analysts at the progressive American think tank the Institute for Policy Studies (IPS) in 2009 spelled out a menu of tax proposals aimed precisely at raising taxes on the wealthy, which they estimate could in fact raise roughly $450 billion in new revenue a year (Cavanagh *et al.*, 2009; see also Collins *et al.*, 2010). An important feature of this set of proposals is the strong emphasis placed on increasing taxation of not just the wealth but also the incomes of the rich and super-rich, for it is with respect to income taxes that the most regressive changes have taken place in the United States over the past half-century. IPS thus calls for immediately eliminating Bush-era tax cuts on income and capital gains (projected additional revenue: $43 billion); creating a new top tax bracket of 50% for incomes over $2 million ($60–70 billion); taxing capital gains and dividends at the same rate as income from labor ($80 billion); introducing a financial transaction tax of 0.25% ($100 billion); reforming the estate tax so that it is paid by just 1 of 200 decedents, but at higher effective rates ($40–60 billion); shutting down overseas tax havens used by the wealthy and corporations ($100 billion); and ending a variety of subsidies for exorbitant CEO salaries ($18 billion). Over a 10–12 year period, taxation of this kind should produce an accumulation of over $5 trillion which could be used to steadily capitalize, year on year, a series of universal asset funds.[10]

Implementing this full menu of increased taxation on the wealthy is obviously a tall order politically. Linking these increased revenues to a systematic effort to capitalize a universal system of significant asset holdings over time would be equally challenging. The IPS report, for instance, links its proposed revenue streams to funding for important domestic priorities such as health care, environmental investments, and infrastructure. Since we can safely assume that a political coalition favoring property-owning democracy would also favor increased public investment to meet urgent needs of that kind, it is certain that a full-blown agenda to pursue both universal asset funding *and* a progressive domestic agenda would require identification of yet further new revenue streams, and/or substantial cuts in other parts of the budget, with military spending and subsidies for corporations being the obvious candidates. A further complication is that there are excellent practical and political reasons for making the creation of new assets programs *universal* – that is, not means tested with reference to currently held assets. While such public assets might be liable to taxation for households above a certain wealth level, making these programs universal would increase their fiscal cost very markedly – the practical result being that the $100,000 asset target per household would be reached either more slowly or at a greater tax bite. Given these considerations, if a system of universal asset holdings is to be recognized as a top political priority even among constituencies we should expect to be sympathetic to property-owning democracy, we must have a clearer conception of what that will entail.

Redistributing Wealth, II: The Structure of Universal Assets

An initial, rough starting point for thinking about how assets might be distributed in a property-owning democracy is to stipulate that each household should have access to roughly $100,000 (current dollars) in net assets (though for obvious reasons at any given moment numerous households will fall below this threshold). Those assets should generally be diversified, both as a check against "losing all" and to promote the full range of independence and free standing associated with ownership of property. To lack "property" might variously mean that one has no savings, that one has no physical property, or that one has no stake in productive capital. To lack savings and real estate is to be at a disadvantaged, insecure position vis-à-vis employers and landlords. Likewise, since political influence closely follows control of productive capital, if ownership of such is highly concentrated, then a class society in clear violation of Rawlsian principles of justice is the overwhelmingly probable result. It is thus proposed that in an egalitarian property-owning democracy, households should ordinarily have substantial quantities of all three types of property.

For the purposes of this chapter, I will focus on the individual adult as the unit of analysis, and assume that the $100,000 asset target noted above applies to households with exactly two adults.[11] This means that each adult should have access to $50,000 in publicly provided assets. (Note that this figure is less than the "stakeholder society" proposal of Ackerman and Alstott, in part because it is intended to be made available to all working-age adults, not just those currently under age 18. Note also that the figure of $50,000 will be steadily adjusted upwards as time goes on, assuming a mechanism is in place for linking dedicated revenue streams from taxation on the rich to ongoing capitalization of these funds.) It is proposed (as a starting point for discussion) that these assets take five principal forms: $10,000 for housing acquisition; $20,000 in cash assets ($15,000 in an unrestricted fund, $5000 in a restricted emergency fund); and $20,000 in ownership of productive capital ($10,000 in unrestricted investment capital, and $10,000 consisting of nontradable stock "coupons").[12] In the case of the housing, cash, and unrestricted investment funds, the accounts would be established at birth, with funds held in interest-bearing accounts until such time as they are used.[13]

How might this system be financed and implemented? Let us assume that beginning in 2012, $452 billion in revenue (derived from higher taxes on the very rich) were devoted to bankrolling an assets system, and that this amount would increase over time at the same rate as real per capita GDP growth (assumed for the sake of this example to total 1.75% per annum, after inflation).[14] Let us assume a (cautiously estimated) inflation-adjusted annual return of 2%.[15] In 2009 there were roughly 188 million residents under age 44 in the United States, and 79 million residents between ages 45 and 64 (United States Census Bureau, 2010, table T6). For the sake of the example, we assume that each of these residents will be eligible for the assets account.[16] It is proposed here that assets accounts be established for all persons aged 64 or younger, and that the public capitalize each account at the rate of $2000 per annum per person for persons aged 44 and below, and at the rate of $1000 per annum for persons aged between 45 and 64. In the first year, this would cost $455 billion (nearly equivalent to the size of the tax increases proposed by Collins et al., 2010). Persons would begin getting asset deposits at the lower rate once they turn 45, on the view that we should prioritize funneling assets to persons when they are younger, when they might have a large impact on life choices. (In practice, a more gradual sliding scale that more slowly reduces assets received year to year after roughly age 40 might be preferable.) Under this proposal, persons born in the United States in 2012 would accumulate just over $50,000 (in constant 2012 dollars) in the various asset funds before turning 18. (See Appendix for a complete table of these figures.)[17]

These assets should be semi-universal: that is, they should be provided to all persons as a matter of right without respect to income, but beginning at age 45 should become taxable on a steeply progressive scale according to the individual's net accumulated assets (private and public). Currently about 10% of households have net assets above $1 million (Mishel et al., 2006; Wolff, 2010), a reasonable threshold for making publicly received assets taxable.

Persons aged 65 and above are generally excluded from receiving new asset deposits. Over the long term, this will not constitute an injustice, as individuals born after the scheme's implementation can over the course of their lives expect to receive (assuming annual 1.75% increases in the sum of public deposits funded) over $185,000 in assets (constant 2012 dollars) from the public under this scheme, and upon retirement are assumed to have access to an adequate social security program as well as continued access to their unspent publicly provided assets.[18] In the short term, no injustice is involved with respect to those seniors being taxed to help fund this system, since the burden would fall exclusively on those already very rich. To be sure, mitigating the impact of accumulated inequalities on quality of life at the end of the life cycle is an extremely serious social justice issue any egalitarian society must address. But a universal asset program, whose intent is to equalize out life chances and political power over the course of the life cycle, is not the proper mechanism for addressing that issue; improving dramatically the quality of health care and elder care through public investments, and increasing social security payments for the low-income elderly via higher taxes on the retired rich, would be the more appropriate steps. Nonetheless, it might be politically advisable to link universal asset proposals with supplementary proposals to provide additional money (perhaps from taxes recycled on assets provided to the already affluent) to boost the income of nonrich retirees as part of a policy package intended to implement a property-owning democracy scheme.

To prevent misunderstanding, it is crucial to specify what this proposal does and does not cover. Contrary to Ackerman and Alstott's "stakeholder" proposal (1999), this version of universal assets is not envisioned as either a mechanism for assuring universal access to (debt-free) education, or as compensation for those citizens who cannot access publicly provided scholarships. (Of course, some assets will be used for educational purposes, and, as noted below, citizens can use future claims on assets as collateral for educational loans.) It is also to be distinguished from publicly funded child savings accounts, individual retirement accounts, and the use of tax mechanisms to create employee-owned firms (all of which may be useful complementary policies). It is also distinct from proposals to provide a universal income stream drawn from dedicated revenue sources (such as revenues or royalties derived from publicly owned assets), though this also may be a desirable policy when feasible. Most importantly, it is not intended to substitute for systems of universal social insurance. Rather, it is intended to provide citizens access to a *stable* and substantial bundle of assets that provides not just short-run but long-term security, fosters citizen independence and the capacity of citizens to pursue life plans of their own choosing, and promotes a more egalitarian political culture.

Note also that while this chapter does not discuss in any detail the macroeconomic impact of the proposed system of universal assets, two points are worth making. First, a well-functioning property-owning democracy shares with traditional social democratic politics the aim of a full-employment economy, in which government acts as an employer of last resort. Hence the following discussion pays little attention to questions of unemployment, and the sums of money discussed here are not intended to shepherd households through long stretches of unemployment. This is not to say that the question of how to achieve and sustain a full employment economy is straightforward, only that it is a problem that the asset program is not intended to address. Second, given that caveat, there is good reason to think that the redistribution proposed may in the long term have positive macroeconomic effects. The redistributions envisioned will offset the long-run trend toward growing inequality in the United States, a trend which numerous progressive and radical economists have identified as a key causal factor in both the 2008–2009 economic crisis and long-term trends toward stagnation under capitalism (Galbraith, 2008; Foster and Magdoff, 2009). Even so, it should be understood that the asset-widening initiative is not intended as a stimulus program to boost short- or medium-term consumption, and that the moral case for asset widening does not rest on its presumed or anticipated macroeconomic impact.

Cash assets

The purpose of providing universal cash assets is twofold. The first is to give citizens the capacity to undertake investments and risks they ordinarily might not be able to take. These include investments in moving, travel, business ventures, property acquisition, specialized education, or pursuing a career which often involves low income and high risk (as in the arts). The second is to provide a cushion, over and above other forms of social insurance, in the case of prolonged economic distress or the incursion of unexpected expenses not ordinarily covered by social insurance. Because universal cash assets are not intended as a substitute for generous provision of unemployment insurance and universal medical care or insurance (in particular), it is envisioned that most of the cash assets ($15,000) should be unrestricted, beginning in stages at age 18. Access to accumulated interest on the $5000 emergency fund should also be unrestricted (i.e., citizens may choose to spend the "endowment income" off this account each year). Access to the emergency fund itself might require filing of a statement of need, a meeting with a publicly provided financial counselor, and signing of a statement indicating understanding that the emergency funds cannot be replenished once used (except through gradual additions deposited into all accounts; see below). At a suitable age (perhaps age 35), individuals would acquire the right to deplete the emergency fund unconditionally. The government might also establish an emergency income insurance scheme so that individuals could use some or all of their $5000 emergency fund to buy an insurance policy, with the aim of obtaining a somewhat more generous emergency funding stream should the need arise, at the risk of losing the investment should emergencies never arise.

As to the unrestricted funds (totaling roughly $15,000 by age 18), one-third (roughly $5000) should be made accessible at age 18, one-half of the remainder (roughly $8500, counting new funds received plus interest) at age 23, and the remainder at age 28; citizens might petition for earlier access to the complete funding stream in cases where an especially compelling opportunity presents itself.[19] Generally speaking, caution in the use of these funds should be recommended to young adults; the government might set up a system of sub-accounts, for instance, in which individuals choose to place restrictions on their future use of the money, up to a certain age.

It might be cogently objected that the amount of money involved here is simply too small to make a major impact on individuals' lives. Considered in static terms, this objection has some force. If we consider the proposal dynamically and take into account both the ability of individuals to accumulate interest in the funds and the likelihood that citizens in a stable property-owning democracy will want to continue to increase (as practicable) the amount of assets individuals have access to beyond the $100,000 per household target, then the quantities of money involved become much more substantial. Consider the case of a child born in 2012, who turns 18 in the year 2030 at a time when (by assumption) the system of cash accounts provided here is fully in place. Assume that taxation on the rich continues to fund asset accumulation beyond 2030, starting at approximately $2700 (40% of which is deposited in cash accounts) and increasing 1.75% annually; and that these funds earn interest at the rate of 2% a year.[20] In scenario A, if the young adult accesses the money as quickly as possible, she will get (roughly) $5000 in 2030; an additional $8500 in 2035; an additional $16,000 in 2040; and still have $5000 left over in the "emergency fund." Assuming $5000 left in the reserve fund, this amounts to a cash stake of roughly $29,500. In scenario B, if the young adult waits until age 28 to access the unrestricted fund, she would acquire at that time a stake of roughly $31,500, again with $5000 remaining in the reserve fund. In scenario C, if the adult waits until age 35 to access the funds, the accumulated cash stake would be roughly $46,500, plus $5000 in the emergency reserve. Especially for persons who now have zero or negative net assets, these are quite substantial figures; and they do not count assets citizens would also hold in housing and productive capital (described below).

The key to this set of scenarios is not just the magic of compound interest but the presumed willingness of a public committed to property-owning democracy to continue to fund an ever-expanding system of universal assets. The utility of prioritizing asset growth vis-à-vis expanding social forms of wealth or other priorities is likely to be a hotly debated question. At a certain point, indeed, the public may choose priorities other than income growth, and a slower-growing economy would leave less funding available to expand assets. I would suggest, however, that the scale of an individual asset program must get very large indeed before a point of diminishing returns is reached; that is, individuals will continue to see very real benefit from an increase in the assets they are entitled to from $50,000 per capita to $100,000 and likely well beyond. Note also that the presumption of continually expanding the size of the assets pool partly offsets one of the obvious inequalities inherent in this system: the fact that those least endowed initially will have the greatest reason to spend the money while young, thus sacrificing the benefits of accumulated interest. Under the scenario sketched here, an adult (born in 2012) who spent all of their unrestricted funds at age 30 would by age 36 have access to over $12,000 in replenished cash and housing assets (see next section), with potential for accessing dramatically more funds by allowing them to accumulate for a still longer period of time, earning interest all the while. This of course would not amount to perfect equality, but would represent a massive equalization of asset holding, economic security, and practical freedom compared to the status quo.[21]

One important proviso needs to be added here. These cash stakes – like the housing and productive capital assets described below – should be considered inalienable. That is, it must be simply illegal to sell off one's future income stream. Like social security payments, the right to receive a citizen's stake can neither be bought nor sold. However, it should be legal for persons to offer their future *cash* assets (but not housing or productive capital assets) as collateral on a loan. To prevent exploitative loan arrangements, government might establish low-interest loans agencies for specified purposes – especially college education – to citizens who intend to use the future asset streams as collateral. Some reasonable limitations on this sort of loan arrangement would be desirable (for instance, limiting the maximum amount of collateral promised in a loan agreement to 10 years of asset payments) so as to prevent young persons from being swindled out of their stakes. It is also to possible to imagine small business and vehicle loans made on similar principles. Out-and-out "advances" on future cash streams from the government cannot be permitted, and private transactions involving "payday"-type loans should be tightly regulated; but reasonable loan arrangements that allow citizens to leverage their public assets in ways that dramatically expand the life choices available to them should be both permitted and facilitated.

Housing-based assets

With respect to housing, a reasonable policy goal would be to end nonvoluntary renting. This implies a norm in which households have significant holdings tied up in where they live. From the standpoint of egalitarian justice, this policy aim is not uncontroversial, so six important provisos need to be stated at the outset. First, in societies like the United States, home ownership has acted as a crucial pivot distinguishing the middle class from the poor, and many critics have rightly charged that public subsidies and policy generally has unfairly favored homeowners vis-à-vis renters (Dreier, Mollenkopf, and Swanstrom, 2001). The object of a property-owning democracy should precisely be to remove home ownership as an instrument of class distinction, by making it accessible to all, not a province from which one-third of the population is excluded. Second, there are good reasons to think that economic vitality, especially in urban areas, is enhanced by the availability of an impermanent (that is, rental) housing sector allowing persons (especially the young) to move in and out with minimal long-term commitments. A "voluntary" rental sector should and must continue to exist side by side with expanded home ownership; indeed, there is a strong case to be made for making rental payments at least partially tax deductible to offset the advantages now accruing to homeowners from the mortgage interest deduction. (Alternatively, the homeowner deduction itself might be abolished – with the taxes thus netted used to bolster the asset distribution program.) Third, "home ownership" need not always or even normatively take the form of single-family, detached housing. Use of community land trusts, cohousing arrangements, and limited equity cooperatives – collective forms of property ownership – may often be appropriate instruments for spreading ownership. Fourth, efforts to promote genuine control of real property via expanded ownership must be sharply distinguished from efforts to expand the *rate* of home ownership without undertaking a genuine transfer of assets – via subprime mortgages or other mechanisms intended to direct more lending to the poor. Indeed, a central aim of this proposal is to liberate poor households from becoming natural targets for predatory lenders. Fifth, this proposal is not dependent on the flawed assumptions that housing values will continually rise over time and that housing acquisition does not constitute a risk. Sixth, as Brian Barry has pointed out, providing funds to finance housing acquisition will be of little use unless the supply of housing is increased (Barry, 2005). This might be accomplished either through public construction of new affordable housing, appropriate incentives to housing developers, or (most novel) establishing a right for renters (after a set time period) to acquire property from landlords, should they choose.

The practical proposal for ending nonvoluntary renting is that government make available to each adult a one-time grant of $10,000 for making a down payment on a permanent residence, and access to matching funds on a 1 for 1 basis up to a further $5000 per person. Under this scheme, a single adult with no savings could claim $10,000 for a down payment; the same adult who commits $5000 in personal funds (perhaps from their unrestricted cash savings) could make a down payment of $20,000, of which $15,000 would be provided by the housing funds. A couple could likewise claim $15,000 each, for a total of $30,000 in public support.[22] (More complicated arrangements involving multiple families or households with more than two adults would also be permissible.) Adults would be allowed to claim this matching support one time, although those not claiming the matching funds on an initial purchase would later be allowed to claim those funds on either a new purchase or to acquire further equity in an existing home once such funds became available. Persons making use of the housing fund would be required to contribute a fixed percentage of the grant to a government-run mortgage insurance fund which would guarantee mortgage payments up to a fixed period for each household. In the event of chronic nonpayment of mortgages that exhausts such insurance, owners would be obliged to either draw down from other available cash assets or to sell their accumulated equity and leave the residence.

Twenty percent of annual funds distributed for housing ($80 a year and rising for adults age 18–44) would be used to capitalize the housing down-payment matching fund.[23] Following the cash assets model, the remainder of funds ($320 per capita for adults aged 18–44, $160 for adults aged 45–64) would be held in individual interest-bearing accounts, with additional funds added from the public coffers each year. In the typical case of a couple both born in 2012, each partner would at age 28 have roughly $15,100 in their housing funds, and hence could together make a down payment of about $30,200; if each committed a further $5000 from their unrestricted assets, with matching funds they could make a down payment of $50,200. Post-purchase, the buying household could instruct that further public funding of their housing account (roughly $1040 at age 28 for a two-adult household and rising each year to age 44 before falling by one-half at age 45) be devoted to paying down the principal of the loan, or alternatively, held (accumulating interest) as a reserve mortgage payment fund.

Prudence and recent experience suggest that individuals and couples using publicly provided funds to acquire housing should be obliged to follow basic guidelines regarding the cost of the property so acquired; buyers might be required to put 15–20% of the total value of the house down, on an (upwardly) sliding scale depending on demonstrated income level. As indicated above, expanding the supply of relatively modest homes and condominiums would be a needed accompaniment to this policy. Finally, it should be acknowledged that home ownership is not and need not be for everyone. At a suitable point (say age 28 or 30), adults who have not accessed their housing fund may request that this fund be merged with their unrestricted cash funds, and that they be issued a rebate for funds previously contributed to the down-payment matching fund. These adults would give up the right to access federal matching funds on a future housing purchase, but otherwise would not be penalized.[24]

Stock holdings

Finally, a critical component of property-owning democracy must be broadening the ownership of productive capital (i.e., the means of production). If property-owning democracy is to be considered a social ideal distinct from traditional capitalism, it cannot involve a small group of persons controlling the bulk of productive capital, as is presently the case. Three alternative possibilities present themselves: control of capital may rest with the workers of particular enterprises; it may rest with public institutions; or it may be held by smallholders, as individuals. The phrase "property-owning democracy" seems to privilege the smallholder answer, but in practice there is good reason to think POD must involve all three alternative forms of ownership. The plan for widespread stock ownership sketched here combines public ownership of corporations with both (a) individual rights to returns from capital and (b) giving individuals the chance to become small investors (in the traditional sense) in private enterprises. I leave aside here the question of how to encourage and nourish specifically worker-owned enterprises. Although there is very good reason to think a POD should encourage and assist worker ownership, by definition it cannot be a universal social policy; that is, not everyone can or will be a worker-owner. But everyone can (under the following proposal) come to have a meaningful share of the society's productive capital.

It is proposed that all citizens at age 18 acquire access to a universal capital fund, consisting of two components each initially capitalized at $10,000 per person. As with the other funds, it is assumed that as time goes on the size of these funds will increase due to ongoing public capitalization (starting at the level of $400 per annum per each component fund). The first fund would be usable for traditional, high-risk investing, the only requirement being that the funds used are invested in a productive business enterprise of some kind (not speculative activity). This could entail investment in a business owned by the individual herself, in a family business, in a partnership with other citizens, in a traditional publicly traded corporation, or in a traditional mutual fund.[25] Citizens could also use this money to join together with other workers in an enterprise to buy it out and become worker-owners. As with the other accounts, individuals could choose to save the $10,000 indefinitely and accrue interest in order to be able to make a larger investment later on. The purpose of this component fund, then, is to help underwrite entrepreneurial activity and relatively high-risk investment behavior. It is to be expected that many citizens making use of the funds in this way will lose their initial investments, although under the envisioned system of progressive recapitalization of all funds, they eventually would be able to accumulate sufficient savings to have another go.

The second fund would be quite different in purpose. Its aim would be essentially conservative: to guarantee each citizen a nonlosable stake in productive capital, and at least a modest income stream from corporate dividends. This fund would be modeled roughly on John Roemer's version of market socialism: citizens would be issued nontradable coupons good for buying shares in a series of publicly owned mutual funds (Roemer, 1994). These mutual funds in turn would buy shares of publicly traded corporations, and return annual dividends to coupon holders. Citizens would be able to shift their coupons from one public trust fund to another, but would not be able to redeem the coupons for cash; this fund would not function as a vehicle for speculating on stock prices. Citizens who wished could also transfer funds from the entrepreneurial fund (but not private assets) to the coupon fund. Assuming annual capitalization additions (starting at $800 year for both funds combined and increasing 1.75% annually), a person born in 2012 who put all their investment assets into the coupon fund would at age 35 possess roughly $53,700 worth of such coupons. If the coupons earned an annual dividend of 2%, this would amount to an additional $1075 of annual income.

Probably most citizens would not be so conservative, given the limited possibilities for large payoffs from the coupon fund. Indeed, the principal aim of the coupon fund is not to generate returns for the stockholders. Rather, the primary aim is to effect the gradual socialization of capital.[26] Roemer (1994) has shown in detail how changed ownership patterns – from ownership by a small minority to ownership by a broad public – can alter the calculus of corporations with respect to the generation of public bads and public goods. (Polluting rivers is more rational when the gains from doing so are concentrated and the costs diffuse than when both gains and costs from such an action are diffuse.) As time goes on and the publicly funded mutual funds hold more and more capital, their effective influence over the corporations they own will increase. If the funds were allowed to pursue broader goals than short-term dividend maximization, then managers of the funds could deliberately direct investment toward particular social goals – such as the creation of new environmental technologies or making new investments in the Mississippi Delta – and attract investment from coupon holders on the basis of those goals. Put another way, the mutual funds would become a vehicle by which each individual in the society could have a small impact on the allocation of capital investment. What gets invested in and where would no longer be the province of a very small group of capital owners. As noted below, this mechanism is indirect and cannot be seen as a substitute for direct economic planning by the state in cases in which that is appropriate or necessary. But existing experience with public pension and labor-controlled funds indicates that such funds both (a) have significant clout and (b) are capable of proactively advancing particular social goals through their investment decisions (Fung, 2001; Williamson, Imbroscio, and Alperovitz, 2002; Wright, 2010).

Individual Assets versus Common Wealth

As noted above, any plausible political coalition that adopts the aim of creating a property-owning democracy will have broader aims than the creation of a system of universal assets holdings. From the standpoint of advancing substantive equality of opportunity and securing the social basis of self-respect for all citizens, strong claims can be made that in the United States in particular, advancing common, public forms of wealth and assets should be at least as important a goal as expanding individual assets. The vast majority of egalitarians would, for instance, prioritize provision of universal health insurance over expansion of individual savings accounts, and strong cases can be made for also prioritizing expansion of badly under-supplied public goods such as access to childcare and efficient public transportation over individual asset building. Likewise, a strong case can be made for prioritizing improvements in the quality of public education and holding down tuitions at public colleges and universities over creating education-specific accounts to help individuals pay for college.

Advocates for property-owning democracy may respond in three kinds of ways when faced with the need for apparent trade-offs between pursuing a large-scale assets-based strategy and development and expansion of social wealth. First, they may accept the need for a compromise between the establishment of universal assets on a substantial scale and other social justice priorities. If we think of the $450 billion a year in new taxes on the most wealthy identified by the Institute for Policy Studies as representing a potential reserve fund for the financing of new social justice initiatives, a case can be made for reducing the proportion of funds annually devoted to capitalizing individual assets, so as to meet other needs. If the amount were reduced to $250 billion a year, for instance, it would then take some 27 as opposed to 18 years to fully capitalize the asset funds at the rate of roughly $100,000 per two-adult household.

Alternatively, it might be argued that it should be possible to finance both new forms of social wealth *and* individual assets. Strictly speaking, this is true, if we assume that it is politically plausible to implement not only the full suite of new taxes on the wealth suggested by IPS, but add to those yet further increases on the very rich (the 50% top income bracket suggested by IPS remains low by historic standards, for instance) as well as prudent cuts in other parts of the federal budget (again, most likely defense and corporate subsidies). From a rigorous egalitarian point of view, there is strong justification for pushing for as much redistributive taxation and expansion of both collective and social forms of assets as is politically feasible. At the moment, the IPS tax agenda alone already pushes beyond the boundaries of what is feasible. But what is politically feasible may change over time, especially if advocates for property-owning democracy succeed in any degree in making POD seem an attractive ideal worth paying for.

Finally, the fiscal limitations (even under the relatively optimistic framework we have been exploring) on new initiatives points to the importance for advocates of property-owning democracy of relying not only on redistribution of existing wealth, but the creation of new forms of public and social wealth. Both publicly owned enterprises and publically controlled resources are capable of generating new revenue streams (oil in Alaska, which provides a substantial dividend to all residents, being a leading if ecologically problematic example). Auctioning systems for scarce ecology-related goods – such as the right to emit carbon, and perhaps eventually, fossil fuels themselves – could generate additional public revenue. Likewise, government should act far more aggressively to claim for the public some of the fruits of government-sponsored high-tech research.

Equally important, a property-owning democracy should be concerned with encouraging new forms of enterprise that, from the beginning, more widely disperse productive capital and wealth. Encouragement of employee-owned firms is a particularly promising route to that end. Expanding tax benefits and technical assistance available to employee-owned firms, as well as providing workers a right of first refusal to acquire abandoned productive facilities, could help boost the formation of such firms. Perhaps more important would be the establishment of a publicly controlled bank dedicated to making loans to such firms; as numerous economists have shown, lack of access to capital is a primary reason why employee ownership is not already more widespread (Dow, 2003). Some of the public funds (holding assets on behalf of children before they reach age 18) might be devoted to the purpose of funding and nurturing democratic firms. Initiatives to establish employee-owned firms and other forms of community wealth should be seen as integral to a full-blown property-owning democracy, although under the proposal considered here they would not be the primary mechanism for guaranteeing to all citizens a substantial asset base.

Property-Owning Democracy as an Incomplete Ideal

This chapter has tried to establish two clear points. First, rich countries can afford, with a relatively modest long-term commitment (transfers equivalent to roughly 3.5% of GDP in the US), to incrementally establish a quite substantial, indeed generous, system of universal assets, provided to all citizens as a matter of right. Second, plausible mechanisms can be identified for ensuring that such assets are widely distributed in a *stable* fashion, namely one that will not quickly revert to a situation where a significant proportion of the population have no net assets.

That said, the sketch of property-owning democracy provided here is necessarily incomplete. For one thing, more work needs to be done to establish what the financial architecture of fully realized property-owning democracy might look like, and in particular what sort of financial institutions would be needed to steward the large funds of publicly provided assets involved in the proposal. For another, while the proposals discussed here should moderate wealth inequalities over time quite significantly, significant inequities would remain. This is a program for diluting huge fortunes and dramatically lifting the position of the most asset poor, not for dispersing large fortunes in any literal sense. Perhaps more significantly, much more careful and creative thinking needs to be directed to the question of how to organize finance within a property-owning democracy. The enormous increase in the size and importance of the financial sector since the 1970s within global capitalism, the extraordinary volume (and too often, irrationality) of speculative activity, and the risks (and actual damage) generated by these developments represents a major set of challenges that the Rawls of 1971 need not have considered. Long gone are the days in which discrete community-oriented financial institutions made relatively safe, targeted loans to underwrite local building and development, and in which banking and stock transaction activity were sharply separated. A thorough overhaul of the *structure* of financial institutions so as to limit the concentrated economic (and hence political) power of large institutions such as Goldman Sachs, reduce the risk of systemic economic damage generated by speculative activity, and ensure that the financial system fulfills the primary task of providing liquidity to meet real local needs is certainly a prerequisite for *any* serious program to forge a more stable and fairer economy. But it is particularly urgent for advocates of property-owning democracy for two kinds of reasons: first, the Rawlsian worry about the political effects of large concentrations of capital and the leverage this gives the biggest players over economic policy, a worry that is fully justified by events of recent years (Taibbi, 2010; Suskind, 2011); and second, simply because a property-owning democracy envisions giving all citizens quite substantial investment funds of their own, and it is essential that systems be devised to secure and protect these funds so that they may fulfill their purposes over the long term. The creation of new funds to manage citizens' public asset holding also presents many opportunities for investment in democratically governed firms, targeting investment toward high-poverty areas, and other positive possibilities. Much more work needs to be done on this set of issues.

Finally, we have left aside entirely the question of economic planning. Rawls's writings often demonstrate a preference for market-based allocations of resources. In my judgment, Rawls was correct to suggest that it might be possible to design a political-economic regime that generated a significantly more egalitarian distribution of income, assets, and life opportunities without recourse to economic planning, understood here as the comprehensive steering of capital investment by public bodies in order to attain particular social ends.

But while distributive justice may not necessarily require democratic planning, there may be other important social reasons for implementing at least partial democratic control over many types of capital investment (see Schweickart's discussion of this issue in Chapter 10 in this volume). In particular, redressing the ecological crisis and meeting the challenge of building an economy that minimizes the use of carbon over the next generation almost certainly will require governments to take a very active role in key sectors of the economy such as energy and transportation. Especially in light of the technical and economic challenges posed by climate change, there is good reason to believe liberal egalitarians must not shy away from embracing some forms of planning when necessary to achieve socially essential goals.[27]

Appendix: Accumulation of Capital Assets Over a 35-Year Period

This table shows year-by-year accumulation of *total* assets over a 28-year period for a child born after the start of the proposed scheme. As is shown, total accumulated assets would exceed $50,000 by age 18, and be nearly $100,000 by age 29, and over $140,000 by age 36 (if unspent to that point). To calculate the proportion of accumulated funds which would be in either (or contributed to) the cash assets or stock assets funds (*in toto*) at a given point in time, multiply any number by 0.4. To do the same for the individual portion of the housing assets fund, multiply any number by 0.16 (20% of housing assets funds go into a down-payment assistance fund). **All amounts are in constant (real) dollars.** 2012: At birth: $2000 asset fund established, earning 2% annually. Fund total at end of year: $2040. Annual contributions increase from $2000 at rate of 1.75% a year.

Year (age at birthday)	Starting funds	Annual contribution	Funds at end of year ([Starting funds + Annual contribution] × 1.02)
2013 (1)	2040	2035.0	4156.5
2014 (2)	4156.5	2070.6	6351.6
2015 (3)	6351.6	2106.8	8627.6
2016 (4)	8627.6	2143.7	10986.7
2017 (5)	10986.7	2181.2	13431.3
2018 (6)	13431.3	2219.4	15963.7
2019 (7)	15963.7	2258.2	18586.3
2020 (8)	18586.3	2297.8	21301.8
2021 (9)	21301.8	2338.0	24112.6
2022 (10)	24112.6	2378.9	27021.4
2023 (11)	27021.4	2420.5	30030.7
2024 (12)	30030.7	2462.9	33143.5
2025 (13)	33143.5	2506.0	36362.5
2026 (14)	36362.5	2549.8	39690.5
2027 (15)	39690.5	2594.5	43130.7
2028 (16)	43130.7	2639.9	46686.0
2029 (17)	46686.0	2686.1	50359.6
2030 (18)	50359.5	2733.1	54154.5
2031 (19)	54154.5	2780.9	58074.1
2032 (20)	58074.1	2829.6	62121.8

2033	(21)	62121.8	2879.1	66300.9
2034	(22)	66300.9	2929.5	70615.0
2035	(23)	70615.0	2980.7	75067.6
2036	(24)	75067.6	3032.9	79662.5
2037	(25)	79662.5	3086.0	84403.5
2038	(26)	84403.5	3140.0	89294.4
2039	(27)	89294.4	3194.9	94339.1
2040	(28)	94339.1	3250.8	99541.7
2041	(29)	99541.7	3307.7	104906.4
2042	(30)	104906.4	3365.6	110437.4
2043	(31)	110437.4	3424.5	116139.1
2044	(32)	116139.1	3484.4	122016.0
2045	(33)	122016.0	3545.4	128072.6
2046	(34)	128072.6	3607.4	134313.6
2047	(35)	134313.6	3670.6	140743.9

Notes

1. My thanks to Gar Alperovitz, Joe Guinan, Martin O'Neill, Alejandro Reuss, and John Schmitt for helpful detailed comments about this chapter.
2. I use the terms "net assets," "net worth," and "wealth" interchangeably in this chapter.
3. Figure for top 0.5% based on 2004 data (analogous data for 2007 is not yet published); because the share of the top 1% increased between 2004 and 2007, and there is no reason to think that distribution of wealth amongst the top 1% became less concentrated, the statement also holds for 2007. Source data for tables presented in Mishel *et al.* (2006) is a study by Edward Wolff of the 2004 Survey of Consumer Finances.
4. In the following estimates, I use the 2004 wealth numbers. The 2007 data (showing higher wealth levels across the board) offer a distorted picture of the actual quantity of wealth currently held by US households, since much of that wealth – an estimated 17% – was wiped out by 2009 due to the collapse of the housing bubble and the financial crisis (see Wolff, 2010). For the record, however, in 2007 the top 1% of wealth holders were estimated to have an average of $18.5 million in assets, a 26% increase from 2004; however, assets held by the bottom 40% of households (just $2,200) were unchanged over that same time period (Wolff, 2010).
5. Author's calculation based on data published in Mishel *et al.* (2006, table 5.7), based on 2004 dollars. Here is an abbreviated account of the math: In 2004, the wealthiest 1% of households held 8.5 times as much wealth as the bottom 60% of households, taken together. The top 1% had an average of nearly $14.8 million in assets. The top two quintiles (top 40%) had an average of well over $100,000. The middle quintile of households had an average $81,800 in assets, and the bottom two quintiles had an average of $2,200 in assets. To lift the middle quintile households from $81,800 to $100,000 in assets, and the bottom two quintiles from $2,200 to $100,000 in assets would require redistribution from the top 1% of just under $4.3 million in assets per household – still leaving those households with average assets of $10.5 million!
6. Why $100,000? The exact figure is not particularly important, but the number is selected for illustrative purposes for two primary reasons. First, it is substantial enough not only to catch attention but to raise the asset position of the majority of households, improving not

only their welfare but potentially expanding the range of life options available to the majority. It is important for political and substantive reasons to distinguish a serious universal assets program from welfare-motivated programs aimed at helping a poor minority. Second, the scale of redistribution required to achieve universal holdings of $100,000 per household, while certainly a stretch given the current political climate, is not altogether implausible, especially if carried out over a period of years. It might well be objected that the scheme proposed below is in fact too modest from the point of view of Rawls's theory of justice, since it still (as shown) leaves most of the wealth of the very rich intact. Certainly I do not contend that the proposed scheme is sufficient to realize the difference principle in any literal or even approximate sense. But it is a step in the right direction sufficiently large to be worthy of attention from even the most rigorous egalitarian, and the benefits it promises to confer on the majority of the population would be tangible and nearly immediately felt. Further, if successful, the scheme could build political support for yet further redistribution of assets in the more distant future. In addition, the scheme described below allows for incremental increases in the per household wealth level over time beyond the $100,000 mark.

7. Again, this estimate is based on 2004 asset levels as well as the 2005-2009 US Census estimate that there are 112.6 million households in the USA.
8. Tax burden on the wealthiest households has fallen across the board in the past 50 years. For instance, a recent historical study found that "the top 0.01 percent of earners paid over 70 percent of their income in federal taxes in 1960, while they paid only about 35 percent of their income in 2005." (Piketty and Saez 2007, p. 22; see also Colins, Goldberg and Pizzigati, 2010.) Piketty and Saez show that declining tax rates have to an extraordinary degree been limited to the top 0.5%, especially the top 0.1%, of households. Marginal tax rates for the population as a whole actually increased over the same time period.
9. Given previous debate about the merits of asset-based versus basic income approaches (Ackerman, Alstott, and Van Parijs, 2006), it may be worth noting that this same $500 billion could alternatively fund a universal income supplement of roughly $1600 per person (i.e., all 308 million US residents). This chapter presupposes that basic income alone does not achieve the core goal of property-owning democracy, namely having a society in which all members have meaningful assets and shares of capital. I also concur with Ackerman and Alstott's view that asset-based approaches are more likely to have a large impact on the sense of possibility enjoyed by individuals about how their life might go. Further, in my judgment, basic income proposals will also be more difficult to argue for politically in countries like the United States, because they can be more easily characterized as a "handout" than asset-based approaches. Nonetheless, there is no reason that a property-owning democracy could not also have a basic income component, perhaps tied to commonly owned resources, as in the example of the Alaska Permanent Fund (oil revenues) proposed by Alperovitz (2004). Indeed, the proposal below provides for a modest basic income consistent of dividends generated by nontradable shares of mutual funds. In addition, as will become apparent, the cash and housing assets transfer programs outlined here could in practice function as an income supplement for citizens as they get older; as seen below, restrictions on access to cash assets and housing assets gradually disappear as citizens get older. These restrictions represent a major difference between my proposal and that of Ackerman and Alstott, who reject any such restrictions on anti-paternalist grounds. My proposal in contrast places greater priority on ensuring that the wide distribution of property, especially productive capital, remains stable over time. For a useful rejoinder to anti-paternalist arguments against any restrictions on the use of "stakes" or state-provided funds, see White (2006). I take my proposal to be roughly consistent with White's

recommendation of a "hybrid" approach that combines features of both "capital grants" and basic income proposals.

10. Here I assume that the revenue raised by these taxes will rise over time due to economic growth sufficient to fully fund the program described below.

11. It is critical to make clear that all the dollar amounts in the proposal are inflation-adjusted ("real") dollars. Because the proposal involves long-term, ongoing transfers of funds, the nominal values would in practice be significantly different (presumably higher) than the figures noted here.

12. See Roemer (1994) for exposition of the idea of a coupon socialism.

13. These proportions are a modest revision of the proposal in Williamson (2009); here I have reduced the proportion of assets in housing and in stock, while doubling the proportion in cash assets so as to increase the flexibility individuals and households would enjoy. It is to be stressed that the exact composition of asset portfolios is not particularly significant; what is important is that the portfolios be diversified and that they meet the goal of providing all citizens with both a financial cushion and a share of productive capital, while protecting them from involuntary renting.

14. The 1.75% real per capita GDP annual growth figure is conservative, relative to growth rates achieved in the United States in the second half of the twentieth century, particularly the period between 1950 and 1973 when per capita growth rate was 2.45% (Maddison, 2001, p. 186, table A-1d). In light of recent economic problems, a cautious figure seems advisable for these projections. If actual growth achieved is higher than 1.75% per capita annually, funds deposited in capital accounts would grow quickly (assuming legislation was in place to link annual contributions to the per capita growth). Conversely, a slower-growing economy would produce a slower rate of accumulation in the accounts.

15. This projected 2% annual rate of inflation-adjusted return corresponds to the real long-term interest rates actually offered by the US Treasury in 2009 and 2010 (available at www.treasury.gov/resource-center/data-chart-center/interest-rates/Pages/TextView.aspx?data=reallongtermrate). I assume that as most of these assets will be time deposits, financial institutions will be able to offer interest rates higher than on conventional interest-bearing savings accounts. Further, some of these deposits may be invested in equities offering potentially higher rates of return if economic conditions are healthy. Generally speaking I wish to avoid making assumptions of rates of return that depart dramatically from real per capita growth in the economy as a whole. If in favorable circumstances it proves possible to achieve higher rates of return, that would allow a more rapid accumulation of individual assets.

16. I leave aside here the difficult question of how institution of a universal assets system might affect immigration policy, and whether stakes might be provided to noncitizens. The figures provided in the text are based on providing asset stakes to all residents, but in practice it is probably advisable to establish a legal residence or citizenship requirement for adults to access these funds so as not to (further) incentivize large-scale illegal immigration. Because children cannot access their funds until age 18, I see no reason to penalize children of illegal immigrants born in the United States who are constitutionally considered citizens from access to a full stake (doing so does not provide a short-run incentive for families to move illegally to the United States).

17. A major question, not taken up here, is what sort of financial institutions these deposits should be placed in. There are three major possibilities: creating new public financial institutions to handle these funds; using existing private banks; or using a network of locally and regionally scaled banks focused on community lending within a specific area. The spirit of property-owning democracy suggests that some combination of the first and

18. I do not treat here the complex question of whether citizens are expected to repay some or all assets received to the public at death. Note, however, that in contrast to Ackerman and Alstott (1999), funding for the proposed scheme is not dependent in any way on assets recycled back to the public at death. As a general approach, I would recommend treating all publicly provided assets held by citizens at death as equivalent to privately held assets and hence taxed at the appropriate rate on that basis. In addition, families should be able to acquire publicly provided life insurance to compensate families for the value of future asset payments not received by a family member due to premature death.
19. Once the emergency fund is fully capitalized at $5000, subsequent annual pay-ins as well as interest earned would accrue to the unrestricted fund, increasing payoffs citizens would be eligible for at ages 23 and 28. In cases where a citizen has tapped into the emergency fund, 25% of subsequent pay-ins would go to the emergency fund until it is recapitalized.
20. This assumes a starting-level annual payout in 2012 of $2000 with annual increases of 1.75% (as above). In the scenario described here, the level of new asset capitalization per capita in 2030 would be $2733, rising to $3251 by 2040. See Appendix.
21. Two unaddressed issues of practical importance are the transition problem and the issue of eliminating crippling private debts owed by millions of households. The scenarios discussed above involve the case of children whose accounts are capitalized year by year from birth and who gain access to their funds at age 18. But what of persons who are already adults at the time the scheme begins? A worry is that asset-poor households may spend year-by-year assets received on consumption as soon as they become available and hence fail over time to build up an asset base. One possible remedy is to offer incentives to households that save their year-by-year asset base, or use them for favored purposes (such as tuition or job training). Additionally, special encouragement and incentives might be given to net debtor households to retire their private debts (apart from long-term mortgages) as soon as possible after the implementation of the scheme. In general it should be noted that the creation of a publicly funded stream of assets capitalized year by year would offer many possibilities for creatively linking the financial streams to other desirable public policy aims. For instance, workers might use part of their cash assets to front the money for high-skill, "high-road" job training (Wright and Rogers, 2010, chapter 9) that is expensive for firms to undertake on their own, with the public providing insurance on assets used in this manner in case of job loss (so that workers do not take the risk of paying for job training that does not lead to a job).
22. It should be noted here that George W. Bush's administration funded a modest, means-tested program, the American Dream Downpayment Initiative, aimed at providing up to $10,000 (or up to 6% of the value of the home) in down-payment and closing costs assistance for qualified first-time buyers. For further details, see www.hud.gov/offices/cpd/affordablehousing/programs/home/addi/
23. Potentially this fund would need to provide grants to all adults in the nearly 40 million households currently renting, plus each advancing cohort of "new" adults seeking to acquire a first home. This method would immediately capitalize the down-payment matching fund at $18.2 billion a year, sufficient to provide matching funds of $5000 to 3.64 million people (1,820,000 two-adult households) a year. (Total housing sales in the United States of new and existing homes over the past decade have ranged from under 5 to over 7 million annually [Harvard Joint Center for Housing Studies, 2010, table A-2]). It is possible that short-term demand from first-time homebuyers for use of the matching funds

may exceed initial capacity, in which case the fund should be permitted to borrow against future contributions to meet demand; alternatively, the size of the public contribution to the matching fund might be increased. In the long term, as involuntary renting is minimized and the size of overall public contributions increases, it should become possible to reduce the 20% annual rate of contribution to the fund, or alternatively increase the size of the matching fund maximum assistance.

24. One further issue needs to be addressed, at least in brief: How do we prevent the housing assets program from becoming a subsidy for moving house as opposed to initial housing acquisition at the start of the program? Over the course of the life cycle, the program does not subsidize moving because the down-payment matching fund may only be accessed once in an individual's life, for initial housing acquisition. But what of people who already own homes when the program begins – should they also have access to the matching fund to acquire a new house? Since the purpose of the program is to end nonvoluntary renting, not to subsidize the dream houses of those who already own homes, my recommendation is no. Existing owners can use the funds in their account to pay down mortgages, however, or merge their accounts with their general cash accounts. A disadvantage of this answer is that it means that existing homeowners would help subsidize the housing acquisition of renters through their contributions ($80 a year, $40 for persons aged 45–64) to the down-payment matching fund. But this subsidy is quite small and its overall impact is progressive, and ought not be a major worry.

25. Mutual funds receiving publicly funded investment funds should be barred from investing in financial assets (a form of speculation).

26. There is no reason in principle why this scheme might not be combined with a "share levy" method of corporate taxation enabling workers (via unions or other associations) to gradually acquire ownership in the firms in which they work, as initially proposed by Rudolph Meidner. The basic idea is to require corporations to annually issue new stock controlled by worker associations equivalent to the corporate tax rate. See Wright (2010, pp. 230–234), for a recent discussion of share-levy plans; these plans do not require any public expenditure to get off the ground and amount to another form of a wealth tax (by gradually diluting the value of privately held stock). If combined with Roemer-type plans, the result would be corporations that over time become hybrids – partially worker-owned, partially publicly owned, with some remaining private investors.

27. One important general argument for planning is in order to remove the "structural constraints" on public policy produced by private dominance of productive capital, an argument made by Cohen (1989) and shared by Schweickart (see this volume) and other socialists. The argument here is that realizing political democracy and hence the fair value of political liberties requires that private owners of capital not be able to determine the shape of public policy by threatening to withhold or relocate investment.

References

Ackerman, B. and Alstott, A. (1999) *The Stakeholder Society*, Yale University Press, New Haven.
Ackerman, B., Alstott, A., and Van Parijs, P. (2006) *Redesigning Distribution*, Verso, New York.
Alperovitz, G. (2004) *America Beyond Capitalism*, John Wiley & Sons Inc., Hoboken, NJ.
Barry, B. (2005) *Why Social Justice Matters*, Polity Press, Cambridge.
Beckert, J. (2007) *Inherited Wealth*, Princeton University Press, Princeton.

Cavanagh, J., Collins, C., Goldberg, A., and Pizzigati, S. (2009) *Reversing the Great Tax Shift: Seven Steps to Finance Our Economic Recovery Fairly.* Institute for Policy Studies, Washington, DC.

Cohen, J. (1989) The economic basis of deliberative democracy. *Social Philosophy and Policy*, 6, 25–50.

Collins, C., Goldberg, A., and Pizzigati, S. (2010) *Shifting Responsibility: How Fifty Years of Tax Cuts Benefited the Wealthy.* Wealth for the Common Good. Available at wealthforcommongood.org/wp-content/uploads/2010/04/ShiftingResponsibility.pdf (accessed September 19, 2011).

Congressional Budget Office (CBO) (2009) *Federal Estate and Gift Taxes.* Economic and budget issue brief. Available at: http://www.cbo.gov/ftpdocs/108xx/doc10841/12-18-Estate_GiftTax_Brief.pdf (accessed September 23, 2011).

Dagger, R. (2006) Neo-republicanism and the civic economy. *Politics, Philosophy and Economics*, 5, 151–161.

DiQuattro, A. (1983) Rawls and left criticism. *Political Theory*, 11, 53–78.

Dow, G. (2003) *Governing the Firm: Workers' Control in Theory and Practice*, Cambridge University Press, Cambridge.

Dreier, P., Mollenkopf, J., and Swanstrom, T. (2001) *Place Matters: Metropolitics for the 21st Century*, University Press of Kansas, Lawrence.

Foster, J.B. and Magdoff, F. (2009) *The Great Financial Crisis: Causes and Consequences*, Monthly Review Press, New York.

Fung, A. (ed.) (2001) *Working Capital: The Power of Labor's Pensions*, Cornell University Press, Ithaca.

Galbraith, J. (2008) *Predator State: How Conservatives Abandoned the Free Market and Why Liberals Should Too*, The Free Press, New York.

George, H. (1884) *Progress and Poverty*, William Reeves, London.

Harvard Joint Center for Housing Studies (2010) *The State of the Nation's Housing 2010.* Available at www.jchs.harvard.edu/son/index.htm (accessed September 19, 2011).

Jacobson, D., Raub, B., and Johnson, B. (2007) *The Estate Tax: Ninety Years and Counting.* Washington, DC: Internal Revenue Service. Available at www.irs.gov/pub/irs-soi/ninetyestate.pdf (accessed September 19, 2011).

Maddison, A. (2001) *The World Economy: A Millennial Perspective. Vol. 2: Historical Statistics*, OECD, Paris.

Mishel, L., Bernstein, J., and Allegretto, S. (eds) (2006) *The State of Working America*, Economic Policy Institute, Washington, DC.

Petit, P. (1998) *Republicanism: A Theory of Freedom and Government*, Oxford University Press, Oxford.

Piketty, T. and Saez, E. (2007) How progressive is the U.S. tax system? A historical and international perspective. *Journal of Economic Perspectives*, 21, 3–24.

Rawls, J. (1971) *A Theory of Justice*, Harvard University Press, Cambridge, MA.

Roemer, J. (1994) *A Future for Socialism*, Harvard University Press, Cambridge, MA.

Sullivan, P. (2010) Estate Tax Will Return Next Year, But Few Will Pay It. *The New York Times* (Dec. 18), B1.

Suskind, R. (2011) *Confidence Men: Wall Street, Washington, and the Education of a President*, Harper, New York.

Taibbi, M. (2010) *Griftopia: Bubble Machines, Vampire Squids and the Long Con That Is Breaking America*, Random House, New York.

United States Budget Historical Tables (2011) Government Printing Office, Washington, DC. Available at www.gpoaccess.gov/usbudget/fy11/hist.html (accessed September 19, 2011).

United States Census Bureau (2010) *2009 Population Estimates*. Available via American Fact Finder at www.census.gov (accessed September 19, 2011).

White, S. (2006) The citizen's stake and paternalism, in *Redesigning Distribution* (eds B. Ackerman, A. Alstott, and P. van Parijs), Verso Books, New York.

Williamson, T., Imbroscio, D., and Alperovitz, G. (2002) *Making a Place for Community: Local Democracy in a Global Era*, Routledge, New York.

Williamson, T. (2009) Who owns what? An egalitarian interpretation of John Rawls's idea of a property-owning democracy. *Journal of Social Philosophy*, 40, 434–453.

Wolff, E. (1996) Time for a Wealth Tax? *Boston Review*, 21 (1), 3–6.

Wolff, E. (2010) *Recent Trends in Household Wealth in the United States: Rising Debt and the Middle-Class Squeeze – an Update to 2007*. Levy Economics Institute (Bard College) Working Paper No. 589. Available at www.levyinstitute.org/pubs/wp_589.pdf (accessed September 19, 2011).

Wright, E.O. (2010) *Envisioning Real Utopias*, Verso, New York.

Wright, E.O. and Rogers, J. (2010) *American Society: How It Really Works*, Norton, New York.

12

The Empirical and Policy Linkage between Primary Goods, Human Capital, and Financial Capital
What Every Political Theorist Needs to Know

Sonia Sodha

Rawls's account of property-owning democracy depicts a society in which productive assets are widely distributed. In the previous chapter, Thad Williamson sketched a proposal for long-term redistribution of financial assets in the United States, leaving aside questions about human capital and the equal development of human capabilities. But human capital development clearly must be a central concern of any just society. This chapter thus takes up three tasks. First, I provide a brief overview of Rawls's account of primary social goods and how it has helped inform subsequent development of the "capabilities" approach to justice associated with Martha Nussbaum and Amartya Sen. Second, I draw on social science evidence illustrating what we know about the links between skill development ("human capital"), financial assets, and the acquisition or development of what Rawls terms "primary goods" (or in Sen's terms, "capabilities"). Third, I describe and assess existing policy approaches in the UK to equalizing wide disparities in such capabilities, including education, health, and economic inequalities, and consider what policy reforms might be needed to ensure a fairer distribution of "primary goods" or capabilities.[1]

This chapter argues that there is an important role for financial redistribution – including, to some extent, asset-based policies – in any society. This comes from the need to ensure a decent social minimum for those who are unable to provide for themselves, and is in light of evidence that growing up and living in poverty is associated with a lack of many other important capabilities – for example, skills and good health. However, financial redistribution alone is not enough: there is no evidence that redistributing income or assets, by itself, will transform people's life chances. This is because the effects of living in poverty on someone's life outcomes are mediated through a range of important behavioral factors.

Primary Goods, Self-Respect, and Capabilities

Rawls calls "primary goods" those goods people need in order to pursue their conception of the good life. He defines these (Rawls, 2001, p. 58) as:

- the basic rights and liberties needed for people to develop and exercise their moral powers;
- the freedom to pursue opportunities consistent with their view of the good life;
- power and authority;
- income and wealth;
- the "social bases of self-respect."

Rawls argues that these primary goods are the resources needed by individuals in order to pursue their conception of the good life. Here, then, crops up the basic tenet of liberalism: everyone has the right to develop the autonomy and ability to pursue their own conception of the good life – what Rawls calls the "fundamental human interest." This right entails a right to certain liberties, such as the freedom of association, but also fair access to the primary goods or resources they need to pursue their conception of the good life.

The set of resources people are entitled to in order to pursue their conception of the good life is heavily contested by liberals – from right-wing libertarians, who would argue that people are entitled to only the minimal amount of liberties and financial resources, and that the rest is up to them; to liberals on the left, who would argue that we need to move toward much greater equality of opportunity in order to give people a fair chance to live a meaningful life.

There has been a rich debate in political philosophy about what people need in order to pursue their conception of the good life. A significant contribution has been made by Amartya Sen and Martha Nussbaum, who have argued that we need to move from focusing on the outcomes people actually achieve to the set of outcomes they can choose to achieve given the "capabilities" they have at their disposal. These resources span both economic resources and human capabilities – like good mental and physical health, skills, and knowledge. As we discuss below, the debate about what people need has rightly become an empirical debate, but there is also a normative issue about whether people are entitled to what they need.

In embedding his definition of primary goods within his theory, Rawls is aligning himself with thicker forms of liberalism which take the view that true freedom and autonomy require certain resources (such as human and financial capital), and can only be achieved if there is significant redistribution of these resources. However, it is also the case that his definition of primary goods remains fairly vague throughout his work, and is not necessarily informed by looking at the empirical evidence on what is most important in achieving a meaningful and autonomous life.

This is partly because some primary goods, such as power, authority, and the social bases of self-respect, may be felt to be intuitively important, but there is in fact little evidence of the extent to which they are important in affecting outcomes because they are difficult to operationalize and measure. However, it is also partly because it is impossible to evaluate the empirical evidence about what is needed to achieve a meaningful and autonomous life without coming to some conception of what a meaningful and autonomous life looks like. To a pure liberal, this is anathema: the state should be neutral between competing conceptions of the good life. But in practice this is impossible. Even setting up the original position is itself not a neutral step because it makes assumptions about what is and is not morally relevant to the original position.

In more practical public policy debates it is very common to look at indicators such as what income level people achieve, the extent of social mobility in a population, and a wider set of benefits such as life expectancy and good mental and physical health. An added complication is that some of these outcomes are themselves primary goods – for instance, being born into a richer family and enjoying good physical and mental health in childhood makes it more likely that people have access to financial resources later on. And some of the "primary goods" (such as good physical and mental health) that people might need to achieve their version of the good life (such as a higher income) might also be desirable ends in themselves.

Here I take the view that the objections to looking at these kinds of outcomes are mostly theoretical. While it is of course possible to pose a supposition that not everyone will want to earn more, or be socially mobile, or enjoy good health in adulthood, there is a sufficient social consensus around these outcomes to merit looking at the empirical evidence on the determinants of better life outcomes. Once this premise has been accepted, the debate about which resources are important to achieving these outcomes should become an empirical debate, not a normative one (Margo, 2007).

Primary Goods: The Empirical Evidence

The last two or three decades have witnessed the development of a rich evidence base on how certain resources and capabilities – such as human capital like skills and good mental and physical health, and financial capital like income and wealth – are related to good outcomes. Here I focus on two sets of capabilities in particular: skills and financial capital. There are, of course, other very important resources people need to live a fulfilled life, such as good health, decent housing, and happy and fulfilling relationships with family, friends, and colleagues.

Skills

The term "skill" refers to a learned ability or proficiency; and the skills needed to live an autonomous and fulfilled life span a diverse range of skill sets. I consider three broad categories of skill here: "core" skills such as literacy, oracy, and numeracy; "learning to learn" skills such as critical thinking and independent enquiry; and social and emotional competencies such as agency, motivation, and communication.

Historically, much of the focus in public policy has been on core skills like literacy, oracy, and numeracy. Without being able to read and write, to undertake basic arithmetic, and to communicate, people have no hope of being able to live fully autonomous lives in today's society. And this is reflected in the empirical evidence:

children who fail to develop good literacy and numeracy skills are much more likely to be permanently excluded from school, more likely to truant, more likely to be out of education, training, or employment aged 16 to 19, and ultimately go on to suffer a wide range of poorer outcomes (Every Child a Chance Trust, 2009a, 2009b). One estimate suggests that between six and nine out of every ten young offenders in the UK have poor language skills (Bercow, 2008). Not being able to communicate, to read and write, and to count, are hugely disabling.

Yet each year in England, eight in one hundred 11-year-olds leave primary school with literacy and numeracy levels lower than those of the average 7-year-old (Sodha and Margo, 2010). Many of those children will simply never catch up, and their lives will be blighted by their lack of these skills. Of course, these skills alone are not enough. There are a further two broad categories of skills people need to develop in order to live an autonomous life. The first set of skills are what are sometimes referred to as "learning to learn" or "metacognitive" skills: skills like independent inquiry, creative thinking, being able to work as part of a team, and being able to reflect on your own learning. These are skills that enable people to learn and to expand their own knowledge base. They are crucial for the modern labor market.

Metacognitive skills are more difficult to measure independently than skills like literacy and numeracy and have not been captured by longitudinal datasets in the same way as reading and writing ability, which would allow us to point to their independent effect. However, it is undoubtedly the case that these metacognitive skills are important in explaining why people with higher levels of qualification go on to enjoy better life outcomes. For example, in the UK, attaining the General Certificate of Secondary Education (GCSE) adds around 10% to wages over the life course compared to someone with no qualifications; GCE Advanced Levels (A-Levels) a further 15% for women and 20% for men; and a bachelor's degree a further 25% for women and 15% for men (Walker and Zhu, 2001).

The third important set of skills, or competencies, are social and emotional competencies. There is not a universal way of referring to this skill set: it has been variously dubbed social and emotional competencies (Weare and Gray, 2003), emotional intelligence (Goleman, 1995), emotional literacy, and soft skills, to name a few. However, this skill set contains several familiar skills and competencies (Weare, 2008):

- Self-understanding: having a positive and accurate sense of oneself, acknowledging one's strengths as well as recognizing responsibility toward others, and being realistic about one's limitations.
- Understanding and managing feelings: for example, knowing how to soothe oneself when troubled or angry, cheer oneself up when sad, and tolerate some degree of frustration.
- Motivation: showing optimism, persistence, and resilience in the face of difficulties; planning and setting goals.
- Social skills of communication, getting along with others, solving social problems, and standing up for oneself.
- Empathy: being able to see the world from other people's point of view, understand and enjoy differences, and pay attention and listen to others.

Again, the idea that these competencies are important is intuitive, but until recently there has been limited evidence. In the last decade, however, research has demonstrated that these are just as important as some of the more conventional skills like literacy and numeracy (Margo and Dixon, 2006). Analysis of longitudinal data that tracked people born in the UK in 1970 (the British cohort study) and captured data on some social and emotional competencies suggests they are just as important as the core academic skills in impacting on children's later life chances (Blanden, Gregg, and Macmillan, 2006). For example, a higher "application" score at age 10 was associated with 8.9% higher earnings at age 30 (controlling for a wide range of other factors), compared to 8.2% higher earnings for a higher mathematics score.[2] A higher "locus of control" score at age 10 was associated with 6% higher earnings at age 30.[3] There is also evidence that these competencies were particularly important for children from disadvantaged backgrounds for this cohort (Blanden et al., 2006).

Of course, there is a lot of overlap between these different skill sets – they are all interrelated and they impact on each other. But the idea that it is only traditional academic skills that matter is long outdated.

However, there are gaping social inequalities in the extent to which children and young adults develop these skills. For example, data show that only one in five young people from the poorest fifth of households got five A*–C General Certificate of Secondary Education (GCSE) scores including English and mathematics in 2006, compared to almost three-quarters of young people from the richest fifth of households – a gap of over 50 percentage points (Sodha and Margo, 2010). Socioeconomic background is more strongly associated with attainment in the UK than in many other European countries (Sodha and Guglielmi, 2009). We explore the reason for these social inequalities below.

Financial capital

Access to financial capital seems to matter greatly for life outcomes: children born into families with higher levels of household income tend to enjoy better life outcomes, controlling for other factors including skills. Again, this chimes with the simple intuition that people who do not have access to financial capital do not enjoy the same independence and freedoms – and ultimately the same ability to pursue the ends they wish – as those in more fortunate financial circumstances.

However, there is an important warning to make about the direction of causality between lack of financial resources and worse outcomes. The data showing an association between poor access to financial capital and poorer life outcomes do not establish causality, and it is likely that being poor impacts on life outcomes both directly (for example, the stress of getting by on an inadequate income may directly impact on someone's physical and mental health) and indirectly. For example, much of the 10-year gap in life expectancy for men from working-class and professional backgrounds is explained by the fact that they are less likely to go and see their doctor – leading to lower cancer detection rates – and are more likely to smoke. In the case of education outcomes, poorer children are more likely to have a poor-quality home learning environment, a fact which has an important impact on how they do at school. In the case of these indirect effects, it is unlikely that redistributing financial resources will change the behavioral mechanisms through which economic deprivation affects life outcomes.

Both political philosophers and economists make a distinction between income – the flow of an individual's or household's financial capital – and assets (or wealth or property) – the stock of an individual's or household's financial capital. This is an important distinction, both in thinking about what matters most for life outcomes (is it the flow or stock of capital, or both?) and in judging how the state can best impact that flow or stock of financial capital (through traditional welfare state policies that target redistribution of income, or through asset-based policies?).

Much of the research on outcomes looks at income level rather than asset stock, because it is much easier for researchers to capture in large surveys. However, it is equally important to look at asset ownership alongside income. Wealth in many ways offers a better snapshot of the resources people have access to at a certain point in time. For example, someone may have a low income in one month but have access to considerable assets to offset the short-term strain (Sodha and Reed, 2007).

Some have gone further, and have argued that asset or property ownership brings positive benefits over and above being an income store (Ackerman and Alstott, 1999). They argue that assets provide extra security – a financial cushion for when things go wrong, and an ability to cope with the risk of unexpected or large, one-off costs such as a car breaking down or a child starting school. This extra security is thought to enable individuals to take productive risks such as starting their own business or undertaking training. Analysis of the British National Child Development Study suggests that people aged 23 who had received at least £5000 of inheritance by the time of the survey in 1981 (in 1981 prices) were twice as likely to be self-employed in that year, controlling for other factors (Blanchflower and Oswald, 1998).

More controversially, some philosophers have argued that asset ownership affects an individual's sense of personal agency (the extent to which they can change future outcomes through their own actions) and time horizons, making them more likely to plan for the future. There is not much hard evidence on this, though, partly because there is a real difficulty in establishing the causal mechanism. Does greater personal agency and longer time horizons result in greater asset ownership (as some of the evidence in the section above suggests) rather than vice versa? Or, indeed, does the effect work both ways?

If arguments that there is something special about an asset or stock of financial capital that brings added benefits other than the income it represents are correct, we would expect that assets have an independent impact on positive outcomes over and above the impact that financial resource has through a measure of income. The evidence for this is weaker than the evidence about the importance of skills, or the importance of financial capital more generally, though this is partly because there has been less work done on the long-term impacts of asset ownership. However, one study has found that, among respondents in the British National Child Development Study, owning a financial asset of between £300 and £600 (at 2001 prices) was positively associated with a greater chance of employment and improved mental health outcomes at age 33, controlling for other factors (Bynner, 2001). However, this work did not control for the social and emotional competencies discussed above, so there is an important question about the causality that underpins this finding: is it that assets cause these positive outcomes, or is it that people who are more likely to own assets because of some underpinning factor like better motivation or entrepreneurship are also more likely to experience positive outcomes later on? The lack of evidence on this would suggest caution about policy makers putting too much stress on such arguments. The evidence on skills, outlined in the section above, is much stronger and less ambiguous.

Inequalities in access to financial resources are well documented. Income inequality in the UK is high and has not changed a great deal since 1992: in 2006/2007, the richest fifth of households received 42% of the share of total disposable income (National Statistics, 2009). Underpinning the increase in income inequality are increases in wage inequality: wage inequality increased dramatically in the United Kingdom between the late 1970s and the mid-1990s (National Equality Panel, 2010).

Wealth inequality is even more pronounced: it is approximately twice as high as post-tax income inequality (HMRC, 2006). The richest 1% of the population owned 21% of total wealth in the UK in 2003, while at the same time, the bottom 50% of the wealth distribution owned just 7% between them, and almost a quarter of the population owned assets worth less than £5000 (HMRC, 2006).

What is the Role of the State in Redistributing Primary Goods?

Skills

As noted above, socioeconomic background exerts a stronger pull on educational attainment in the UK than in several other developed economies, such as Finland and Canada.

When we look at where the state has traditionally been involved in trying to reduce inequality of skills – the education system – it quickly transpires that the quality of schooling has a limited impact on the extent to which people develop the skills that are so crucial to living an autonomous life. One estimate suggests that only about 14% of variance in achievement at school is down to school-level factors (Hirsch, 2007).

This is because the nature of a child's home environment has by far the most profound and lasting impact on the level of skills they develop – across all three broad skill sets outlined above. A mother's highest qualification level and the quality of a child's home learning environment is the strongest predictor of academic outcomes at ages 10 and 11 (Sylva *et al.*, 2008). One large-scale US-based study showed how children from families on welfare hear on average only 600 words per hour, compared to the 2100 words per hour children from professional families hear. This, unsurprisingly, has a lasting impact on communication and literacy skills (Hart and Risley, 1995). And parent–child relationships characterized by warmth and love, stability and authority best promote social, emotional, and behavioral development (Margo *et al.*, 2006). Levels of parental aspiration are also significantly correlated with better educational outcomes, and although they are more important for children from poor backgrounds, levels of aspiration tend to be lower amongst poor parents (Sodha and Margo, 2010).

In fact, by the time children start school at five, children from the richest income quartile who score in the lowest quartile of cognitive ability tests at 22 months have caught up with children from the poorest quartile who score in the top quartile of the tests – and they soon overtake them (Feinstein, 2003). Original Demos research using the Millennium Cohort Survey has shown that 1 in 10 five-year-olds start school without the behavioral skills they need to benefit from classroom learning – but that this rate is more than four times as high for children from the poorest fifth of families as the richest fifth (18.4% compared to 4.4%) (Sodha and Margo, 2010). The impact of family background cannot be underestimated.

Although the impact of schooling is less pronounced than the impact of parenting, 14% variance is by no means insignificant and good schools can help to counteract the negative impacts of a child's social background. Quantitative evidence suggests that the most important school-level factor on outcomes is quality of teaching (Margo, Sodha, Benton, and Withers, 2008). It is difficult to be as exact about how other features of the school impact on outcomes because they are less easily measured, but there is certainly evidence that teaching styles and school culture have an impact on attainment, social and emotional development, and pupil behavior (Sodha and Guglielmi, 2009). In particular, studies in the United States have found links between the "emotional quality" of the classroom (as measured by the warmth of adult–child interactions and adult skills in responding to children's needs) and progress in literacy and numeracy (Pianta et al., 2007).

What works in reducing inequality of skills? It is much easier for social researchers to point to why inequalities arise in the first place rather than what works in tackling them: it is easier to identify what makes a good parent or school than to identify what works in supporting poor schools, or in changing the attitudes or behaviors of parents who may have very negative experiences of education themselves and/or lack some of the key skills like literacy or numeracy.

This has certainly been reflected in the Blair and Brown governments' lack of success in tackling educational and health inequalities, which have remained large despite an explicit commitment to tackle them from the Labour government, and the creation of an early years services infrastructure for 0–5-year-olds and their families that included the introduction of Sure Start children's centers and an entitlement to free early years education (Sodha and Margo, 2010). Why this lack of progress?

To some extent, it is a reflection of the strength of the social forces at work – and some of the behavioral factors underpinning them – rather than a failure of policy (Sodha and Bradley, 2010). The way in which poverty manifests itself in poor outcomes is complex, as noted above. But while tackling socioeconomic inequalities has been an explicit objective of public service reform over the last decade, this objective has had to compete with others such as improving average standards and meeting threshold targets, which arguably have been given higher priority. It could also be argued that public service reform has not focused enough on these complex behavioral transmission mechanisms that link disadvantage to poor life outcomes.

Sodha and Bradley (2010) argue that there are five key features any public service agenda that seeks to reduce inequalities in education and health outcomes needs to have, as follows.

First, there has to be much stronger accountability for closing the socioeconomic gap in health, education, and employment outcomes across public services. While there has been a government commitment to tackling inequalities, these have not been reflected in accountability regimes. This means, for example, that schools are incentivized to focus on supporting children just below a simple "threshold" target (for example, those children just below the threshold of getting five A*–C GCSEs) rather than children – disproportionately from poorer backgrounds – who may be some way off.

Second, we need a better evidence base about the effectiveness of particular interventions in supporting children from poor backgrounds to better develop their skills. There have been promising developments in recent years, for example the piloting of the Family Nurse Partnership program in the UK. This is a program that works intensively with at-risk mothers in the prenatal stage and for two years after a child's birth to improve parent–child relations. It has been shown to have significant impact on child developmental outcomes. Another example is Reading Recovery, an intensive program of one-to-one tuition for 6-year-olds who are significantly behind their peers in reading ability, which has been tried and tested in the UK and has proven to be extremely successful (Sodha and Margo, 2010).

Third, and related to this, we need a better understanding of what the role of government is in promoting evidence-based interventions that work in local services, particularly in an era of decentralized services. While highly evidence-based programs like Family Nurse Partnership and Reading Recovery exist, they are not always taken up by local education and health providers. Sodha and Margo (2010) argue for a strong role for central government in building up the national training infrastructures required to deliver these programs, and in incentivizing local services such as schools, local authorities, primary care trusts, and children's centers to provide them from their autonomous budgets.

Fourth, there needs to be more early intervention across education, children and youth services, and health care – in other words, more intervention as soon as risk factors for a higher-level need develop. Early, evidence-based intervention has been shown to lead to more effective outcomes and costs for the state. Although there has been a strong policy focus on early intervention – for example in education in children's services – recent Demos research has shown how it is not widespread in local services up and down the country because of various structural barriers (Sodha and Margo, 2010). For example, local budgets (such as in education, health, and youth justice) tend to be siloed. So while it may make good sense from the perspective of a child's outcomes and the overall budget spent on a child for a health service to spend some money on a service upfront, the savings might accrue to a different part of the state (for example, the youth justice system) and so the budget might not be available in the health service. Early intervention also requires upfront investment to save money over a longer time frame, perhaps even longer than a decade.

Fifth, there should be more "intelligent" needs-based targeting (as opposed to income- or area-based targeting) in interventions aimed at improving education and health outcomes (Sodha and Margo, 2010). In too many services, targeting is far too blunt although there are incredibly powerful – yet light touch – evidence-based screening tools that can be used to identify individuals in need of extra support and direct them toward evidence-based interventions. For example, the Strengths and Difficulties is a screening tool for children's behavioral development. It takes the form of a simple five-minute questionnaire to parents, and it predicts clinical mental health problems with 81–91% accuracy. Parallels can be drawn with medical services, in which diagnostic assessment is used much more effectively. We require a better system of "triage" in services for children and families, and in public health. Better outreach with low-income households, which are often the hardest to reach, also has to be a key feature of an intervention strategy.

Financial capital

Very few politicians and policy makers (at least in the UK) would disagree with the objective of reducing inequality in the development of skills and human capital in young people – although there may be fundamental disagreements about the best way to do it. However, redistribution of financial capital is much more contentious. Even if we start from the view that redistribution is instrumental (to ensure everyone has enough primary goods) rather than an end in itself, there will be a huge amount of disagreement about what level of redistribution that entails. This is perhaps partly because tackling inequality of income and assets is more explicitly zero sum than reducing inequality of skills.

What level of financial resource do people need in order to be able to live an autonomous and fulfilled life? Of course, there is no easy answer to this question. There have been attempts to define what level of resource is needed to achieve a socially acceptable minimum standard of living, however. The best known example of this in the UK is the Joseph Rowntree Foundation's Minimum Income Standard (Sodha and Bradley, 2010). The Minimum Income Standard (MIS) is defined as the level of financial resources required to achieve a socially acceptable standard of living that enables people to participate in society. It is derived from budget standards that are developed by members of the public asked to reach consensus on the items needed to achieve this standard of living for different types of household, with input from professional experts. Originally produced in 2008, it has now been updated for 2010. A single adult with no children needed a weekly net income of £174 to achieve the MIS in 2010; a couple with two children, £403.

For most households, the MIS falls between the official income poverty threshold in the UK (60% of median income) and the median income. There are thus many people whose net income falls below the MIS: to put this in context, there were 13.4 million adults, and 3.9 million children, living in relative income poverty (after housing costs) in the UK in 2008/2009. A single person on income support gets less than half the income they need to reach this standard. And a single person needs to earn at least £14,400 a year before tax to achieve the MIS; but the minimum wage in 2010/2011 is only £11,560 for someone working a 37.5-hour week. Indeed, there are more adults and children living in poverty in working households than in workless households in Britain: 60% of poor adults live in working households, as do 61% of poor children (Lawton, 2009).

There are a number of dimensions that need to be considered in a debate about financial redistribution by the state. The first is the important question of what the role of redistribution is in getting people up to a minimum standard of living. Working full time at the minimum wage is not a guarantee of achieving a minimum income standard, or even, for many households, a guaranteed route out of poverty. Redistribution can be used to boost low wages, and this was certainly the approach of the last Labour government in Britain, which used in-work benefits to boost the incomes of households with people in low-paid jobs. However, it can be argued that this situation is far from ideal: for the sake of an individual's dignity and autonomy, workers have the right to a wage that enables them to achieve an acceptable standard of living. This raises a fundamental set of questions relating to the economy, including the shape of the labor market with respect to wages, skills, and productivity. As reflected by increasing inequality in wages, and a growing concentration of jobs in low-skill and high-skill sectors (with a shrinking share of mid-skill jobs), the British economy has become reliant on low-skill, low-paid service jobs. The result of this is an increasingly polarized labor market, with growing numbers of people trapped in low-paid work that does not offer a route out of poverty, let alone progression to highly skilled jobs. So although the state has a role in financial redistribution, it has an equally important role in trying to create the kind of economy which produces a more equal earnings distribution in the first place. The debates about how the state can do this are very current in the wake of the global financial crisis and consequent economic downturn. How to achieve this kind of economy is not yet well understood, and there will always be people unable to work in the labor market due to disability or caring responsibilities, so there will always be some role for financial redistribution.

A second key issue in relation to financial redistribution is what kind of conditionality should be attached to it. What should be expected of citizens in exchange for a guarantee that they will have sufficient financial resources to live autonomously? The UK, like other Anglo-Saxon democracies, has moved further down the path of conditionality in the last three decades. So now, a condition of receiving benefits from the state is that those who are deemed able to work are actively looking for work, and, in some cases, accept available jobs. Whilst there are imperfections in how this system works, there is widespread consensus in the political domain about conditionality. Rawls himself moved toward conditionality in his later work (see, for example, Rawls's discussion of the "Malibu surfers" in *Justice as Fairness*, 2001, p. 179).

A third issue is the extent to which redistribution should be means tested. It would be possible to have a redistribution system that paid everyone an income or asset grant regardless of their level of need. In practice, however, most redistributive systems rely heavily on means testing. Means testing brings disadvantages: the more accurate it is, the more intrusive it tends to be. It can also be stigmatizing and can create disincentives to move into work or to build up assets. In an ideal world, there might be a conditional citizen's income paid to all those fulfilling basic obligations (for example, working or caring, for those who are able), funded through higher taxation, but the political difficulties of introducing the levels of taxation that would be needed to fund this would be immense.

A fourth issue is how an individual's need is assessed. Traditionally welfare state capitalism has been concerned with income levels rather than asset stocks, using income as a proxy for people's wealth.[4] It has often been argued that for the state to means test using wealth rather than income would be overly intrusive, expensive, and also act as a disincentive for people to save and build up their own assets. These arguments are practically very persuasive.

The fifth key issue is what *form* redistribution should take: is encouraging a build-up of financial capital over the life course best done through income- or asset-based welfare policies? In other words, if holding an asset is seen as a positive, there is a distinction to be made between different ways of getting an asset: a person saving from their income stream, and being able to access an asset in another way (for example through inheritance or an asset grant).

One argument is that redistribution should be wholly income based and it should be left to people to decide whether or not to save up assets, regardless of whether or not they have positive impacts. Some people do not have enough resources to save in the first place, and a decent income-based redistribution would get around this. But people also do not save because their time horizons are too short – for example, even with government incentives to save, many people do not save enough to ensure a decent standard of living in retirement.

There are many different kinds of asset-based policies that have been proposed in the UK, but there are some fundamental differences between them. The proposed policies can be thought of as falling into three main categories:

1. Policies that encourage people to save when it would make sense for them to do so and they are not already doing so. These policies are based on the assumption that people's time horizons are too short. Examples of this include tax relief for pensions contributions, and the Saving Gateway in the UK, a matched saving scheme for people in low-income households (Sodha and Lister, 2006). They are based on quite anti-liberal and paternalistic assumptions about people's behavior but are designed to minimize the impact of "irresponsible" lack of saving on the rest of the population.
2. Policies that give people an asset grant on top of a system based on income-based redistribution – because of the extra benefits assets are thought to confer on top of being a store of income. Some proposals have been for very large grants when people embark on adulthood (see, for example, Ackerman and Alstott, 1999).
3. Policies that capitalize future streams of income – for example, policies that propose the capitalization of future benefit streams such as housing benefit (Wind-Cowie, 2009). These are based on the opposite kind of arguments to policies in the first category – the assumption is that people are better placed to decide how they spread their spending than government, that capitalizing future benefits streams gives people access to opportunities they would not otherwise have, and that if people "squander" their asset, they forfeit their right to the continuous income stream they would have received should they not have chosen to capitalize their future benefits.

Asset-based policies in the UK fall mainly into the first category. For example, tax relief on pensions contributions, the Child Trust Fund, and the Saving Gateway are all policies primarily designed to increase saving behavior.

The Child Trust Fund (CTF) was introduced by the Labour government. Every child born from September 2002 onward received a Child Trust Fund account with a £250 endowment at birth, with a further £250 top-up at age 7, with parents encouraged to save into the account and children from low-income families getting double the government deposit. The account is locked until the child reaches the age of 18. This policy was abolished by the new Conservative–Liberal Democrat government in 2010. The Saving Gateway was a matched saving scheme for people on low incomes piloted by the Labour government. People on low incomes saving into the account received a proportion of the amount they saved from the government to top up their savings – up to a limit over two years. The Labour government intended to roll this out nationally, offering low-income savers 50p for every pound saved over two years, to a maximum of £600. Plans to roll this out were scrapped by the new government, however. Although the CTF has elements of stakeholding in it, in practice these arguments have had a weaker pull on how the policy has been implemented than arguments about saving behavior (Finlayson, 2008).

In practice, what we have in the UK with respect to redistribution goes some way to providing a minimum safety net, but is a long way off a theoretical ideal in which everyone – including those who are not able to work – has conditional access to the financial resources they need to achieve a socially acceptable minimum standard of living. The state has a role in financial redistribution, primarily through income-based redistribution, but also through the first category of asset-based redistribution in which people are encouraged to save and build up assets for the medium and long term. But financial redistribution by itself is not adequate: people have a right to be able to earn enough to secure a decent standard of living through their job. This presents a much more complex challenge to the state, and to society more widely, that rests on us moving toward an economy in which there is less wage and skills inequality in Britain. In the past few decades in Britain, the wage share of GDP has decreased compared to profit share – and within that wage share, there has been growing wage inequality (National Equality Panel, 2010).

A major remaining question is how redistribution should be funded. Just as income is one of the main indicators the state uses to assess need, it is also used as the primary way of assessing individuals' means to contribute. (We leave aside the issue of business taxation here.) There is a significant imbalance between the taxation of income earned through labor, and the taxation of wealth – or the income stream that wealth provides through investment returns.

Wealth in the UK is mainly taxed through two taxes: inheritance tax (IHT) and capital gains tax (CGT). Inheritance tax is a tax on estates, levied when owners die. The first £325,000 of an estate can be passed on tax free, and wealth above this threshold is subject to a 40% tax. There are exemptions, including transfers to spouses, charities and small gifts, and reliefs for agricultural property, and family and private business. People can also make gifts tax free so long as they live for seven years after they are made. Inheritance tax is a tax paid by around 6% of estates (Brown, 2006).

Capital gains tax is a tax on gains to people's wealth over a period of time – in other words, a tax on unearned income. It is a transactions tax: people pay the tax at the point of sale of assets that have appreciated in value. People pay a tax rate of 18%, and each person has a CGT tax-free allowance (£10,1000 in 2009/2010). However, there are significant exemptions. People's homes are completely exempted, meaning that any increases in the value of their homes go untaxed during their lifetime, a tax bonus of around £14.5bn in 2007/2008 (HM Treasury, 2009, table A3.1). Second, the amount of gain that is taxable on other assets decreases over time to just 60% after 10 years for nonbusiness assets, and 25% after two years for business assets. This represents a tax bonus of £6.8bn a year in 2007/2008 (HM Treasury, 2009, table A3.1).

There are significant problems with both these taxes. IHT is very easy for the wealthy to avoid because they can afford to pay for expensive tax-avoidance advice. It is true the government has in recent years made an effort to close some loopholes, such as those on trusts, but the biggest loophole is impossible to close without fundamental reform: people can always avoid the tax if they are wealthy enough to gift their wealth while they are living, so long as they live for seven years after the gift. The moderately affluent tend to pay the tax disproportionately because their wealth tends to be locked up in their homes and is harder to gift: one estimate is that inheritance tax receipts are only 16% of what they would be were IHT not so easy to avoid (Wadsworth, 2006).

As a result these taxes capture only a very small fraction of the total increase in wealth in the UK each year. For example, the UK property market alone increased in value by over £400 billion in 2006 (Halifax, 2006), but IHT and stamp duty taxes in that same year raised only £14 billion (HM Treasury, 2006) – capturing about 4% of the increase in value.

It is unfair and inconsistent that windfall gains in housing value, which simply represent a transfer of wealth from non-owners to owners, and derive in the main from restraints on house building and area-based infrastructure investment, go untaxed altogether until death, whereas earned income is subject to tax on an annual basis. IHT is an imperfect way of taxing windfall gains – and because it is more distanced from the principle of taxing gains to wealth than, say, CGT, it is more difficult to make the case for it on this basis.

There is a good case, therefore, for reforming the system of wealth. The first way of doing this would be by bringing housing wealth more fully into the tax system, for example through an annual tax on land value, levied by owners, set at a percentage of land value (say 0.5% to 1%). This kind of tax would have a number of advantages. First, it would capture some of the huge gains in land value that are just a transfer of wealth from non-owners to owners without some of the distortionary impacts that making people's homes eligible for CGT would have on buying and selling decisions (McLean, 2006). Second, it would be difficult to avoid as land cannot be easily moved or hidden. Third, it could have important macroeconomic benefits by helping to stabilize property prices in high-demand areas, and increasing investment in low-demand ones (Muelbauer, 2006).

A second potential reform would be changing the system of taxing intergenerational transmissions of wealth so the affluent cannot avoid tax by gifting their wealth seven years before they die. One option would be a tax on gifts rather than inheritance. If the starting point is that transmission of financial wealth between adult generations should be taxed to some degree, this should apply to all transmission of financial wealth between adult generations, not just those at deaths. Such a tax could either take the form of a tax on the gifts that donors make, or a tax on the recipients of gifts, as was proposed by the Fabian Tax Commission, above an annual limit (Patrick and Jacobs, 2003). This would see an increase in the number of bequests and gifts that would become taxable – and if introduced in conjunction with a land tax could see a significant reduction in the rate applied: it could be much lower than the 40% IHT rate applied at the moment.

While both of these are quite radical options for reform and would require much practical work on how they would be implemented, they have the potential to tackle some of the unfairness in the current system of wealth taxation.

Conclusion

This chapter has set out the extent to which wide inequalities exist in two key "primary goods" – financial and human capital – and looked at the role of the state in addressing these inequalities. In terms of financial distribution, the priority needs to be ensuring that citizens who fulfill their obligations to society (by working or caring, if they are able) have access to the financial resources needed to achieve a socially acceptable minimum standard of living. This should partly be through income-based, and to some extent, asset-based, redistribution. But redistribution can only achieve so much, and ensuring that people are able to earn a decent wage that enables them to achieve a decent standard of living is just as important in a fair society. In terms of tackling inequality in skills, the state must focus on supporting children from disadvantaged backgrounds in accessing the same kinds of opportunities as their more affluent peers, through education, health, and family services.

Asset redistribution has an important role to play in enhancing equality of opportunity, although the likely impact of such redistribution on deep-seated inequalities in life chances is limited, especially given current political constraints on the scale of redistribution. Even if political circumstances become more favorable in the future, any serious program for redressing existing inequalities of opportunity must pay due attention to the multiple and overlapping reasons – financial and nonfinancial – why socioeconomic status tends to be transmitted across generations. This is equally true whether such an effort is conceptualized as building on the accomplishments of existing welfare states, or as part of a more radical effort to construct a genuine property-owning democracy.

Notes

1. I would like to thank Simon Hampson and Stuart White for their very helpful comments on earlier drafts of this chapter.
2. "Application" is a measure of young people's dedication and concentration (Blanden et al., 2006).
3. "Locus of control" refers to the extent to which people see events as being within their control – people with an internal locus of control see them as being within their control, people with an external locus of control as outside of it (Rutter, 1954). It is therefore linked to the idea of personal agency.
4. It should be noted that there are simple asset tests for several benefits in the UK – these usually operate as a threshold. There are also, of course, benefits that take into account needs like disability and the number of children in a family.

References

Ackerman, B. and Alstott, A. (1999) *The Stakeholder Society*, Yale University Press, New Haven.

Bercow, J. (2008) How speech, language and communication are linked to social disadvantage, in *Getting in Early: Primary Schools and Early Intervention* (ed. J. Gross), Smith Institute and Centre for Social Justice, London.

Blanchflower, D. and Oswald, A. (1998) What makes an entrepreneur? *Journal of Labour Economics*, 16, 26–30.

Blanden, J., Gregg, P., and Macmillan, L. (2006) *Accounting for Intergenerational Income Persistence: Non-cognitive skills*, Centre for the Economics of Education, London School of Economics, London.

Brown, G. (2006) *Budget Statement*, HM Treasury, London.

Bynner, J. (2001) Effects of assets on life chances, in *The Asset Effect* (eds J. Bynner and W. Paxton), Institute for Public Policy Research, London.

Every Child a Chance Trust (2009a) *The Long Term Costs of Literacy Difficulties*, 2nd edn, Every Child a Chance Trust, London.

Every Child a Chance Trust (2009b) *The Long Term Costs of Numeracy Difficulties*, Every Child a Chance Trust, London.

Feinstein, L. (2003) Inequality in the early cognitive development of British children in the 1970 cohort. *Economica*, 70, 73–98.

Finlayson, A. (2008) Characterising New Labour: The case of the child trust fund. *Public Administration*, 86 (1).

Goleman, D. (1995) *Emotional Intelligence*, Bantam Books, New York.

Halifax (2006) UK Private Housing Stock Worth £3.8 Trillion. Press release January 15, 2007.

Hart, B. and Risley, T. (1995) *Meaningful Differences in Everyday Parenting and Intellectual Development in Young American Children*, Brookes, Baltimore, MD.

Hirsch, D. (2007) *Experiences of Poverty and Educational Disadvantage*, Joseph Rowntree Foundation, York.

HMRC (2006) Table 13.5: Distribution Among the Adult Population of Marketable Wealth (Series C). Available at http://www.hmrc.gov.uk/stats/personal_wealth/table13-5-2001-03.pdf

HM Treasury (2006) *Budget 2006: A Strong and Strengthening Future*, HM Treasury, London.

HM Treasury (2009) *Building Britain's Future: Budget 2009*, HM Treasury, London.

Lawton, K. (2009) *Nice Work If You Can Get It: Achieving a Sustainable Solution to Low Pay and In-Work Poverty*, Institute for Public Policy Research, London.

Margo, J. (ed.) (2007) *Beyond Liberty*, Institute for Public Policy Research, London.

Margo, J. and Dixon M., with Pearce, N. and Reed, H. (2006) *Freedom's Orphans: Raising Youth in a Changing World*, Institute for Public Policy Research, London.

Margo, J., Sodha, S., Benton, M., and Withers, K. (2008) *Those Who Can?* Institute for Public Policy Research, London.

McLean, I. (2006) The politics of land tax – then and now, in *Time for Land Value Tax* (eds D. Maxwell and A. Vigor), Institute for Public Policy Research, London.

Muelbauer, J. (2006) Property taxation and the economy, in *Time for Land Value Tax* (eds D. Maxwell and A. Vigor), Institute for Public Policy Research, London.

National Equality Panel (2010) *An Anatomy of Inequality in the UK: Report of the National Equality Panel*, National Equality Panel, London.

National Statistics (2009) *Income Inequality: Little Change Since the 1980s*.

Patrick, R. and Jacobs, M. (2003) *Wealth's Fair Measure: The Reform of Inheritance Tax*, The Fabian Society, London.

R. Pianta *et al.* (2007) Classroom effects on children's achievement trajectories in elementary school. *American Educational Research Journal*, published March 5, 2008 as Online First.

Rawls, J. (2001) *Justice as Fairness: A Restatement* (ed. E. Kelly), Harvard University Press, Cambridge, MA.

Rutter, J. (1954) *Social Learning and Clinical Psychology*, Prentice Hall, New York.

Sodha, S. and Lister, R. (2006) *The Saving Gateway: From Principles to Practice*, Institute for Public Policy Research, London.
Sodha, S. and Reed, J. (2007) Mind the wealth gap? The politics of resource inequality, in *Politics for a New Generation* (eds N. Pearce and J. Margo), Palgrave Macmillan, Basingstoke, and Institute for Public Policy Research, London.
Sodha, S. and Margo, J. (2010) *Ex Curricula*, Demos, London.
Sodha, S. and Bradley, W. (2010) *3D Poverty*, Demos, London.
Sylva, K. et al. (2008) *Final Report From the Primary Phase: Pre-school, School and Family Influences on Children's Development During Key Stage 2*, Department for Children, Schools and Families, London.
Wadsworth, M. (2006) *Tax, Benefits, Pensions: Keep it Simple Part 2*, Bow Group, London.
Walker, I. and Zhu, Y. (2001) *The Returns to Education: Evidence from the Labour Force Surveys*, DfES Research Report 313, The Stationery Office, London.
Weare, K. (2008) Developing social and emotional skills in school to help combat disadvantage, in *Getting in Early: Primary Schools and Early Intervention* (ed. J. Gross), Smith Institute and Centre for Social Justice, London.
Weare, K. and Gray, G. (2003) *What Works in Developing Children's Social and Emotional Competence and Wellbeing?* Department for Education and Skills, London.
Wind-Cowie, M. (2009) *Recapitalising the Poor*, Demos, London.

13

The Pluralist Commonwealth and Property-Owning Democracy

Gar Alperovitz

Increasing recognition that John Rawls's principles of justice – or any other attractive conception of egalitarianism – cannot be satisfied even by an ideal form of "welfare state capitalism" presents important new intellectual challenges. One of the most urgent tasks facing progressive intellectuals and scholars is the development of carefully considered systemic alternatives that help move the intellectual debate forward beyond the traditional political-economic paradigms, and, in particular, beyond the sterility of the traditional contrast between corporate capitalist and state socialist models. Essential to this process is an analysis of the emerging political-economic context, on the one hand, and on the other, the identification of structural building blocks of a democratic political-economic system design that can nurture values of democracy, equality, liberty, and ecological sustainability. This essay takes up that task in the context of twenty-first-century American politics.

An implicit assumption in most established quarters is that there will inevitably be a return to some form of economic and political "normalcy," that systemic issues are not serious – and that once the recession is behind us we will get back to a reasonably normal growth path. However, a number of increasingly intractable problems – the profound and growing fiscal crisis, deep levels of stagnating income (hence radically new Keynesian problems), intense global trade competition, an inability to adequately regulate domestic and international financial institutions, to name only a few of the large-order challenges we face – suggest there are reasons to believe that ongoing and perhaps deepening political and economic difficulties will continue. If so, the economic and financial crises of 2008 and 2009 may well define the opening moments of a longer period of economic difficulty and social decay. This trajectory points in the direction of an unusually structured systemic crisis, not simply an economic or political crisis – and, in turn, to quietly increasing discussion of serious long-term systemic change possibilities.

The underlying problem is that, broadly speaking, the political system is simply no longer able to solve many critical problems that are driving the crisis – not able to solve

Property-Owning Democracy: Rawls and Beyond, First Edition. Edited by Martin O'Neill and Thad Williamson.
© 2012 Blackwell Publishing Ltd. Published 2012 by Blackwell Publishing Ltd.

them, that is, in more than a fragmentary way. Although it is unquestionably possible to achieve certain gains, in many areas the gains are fragmentary *compared with the problems and long-declining social, economic, and environmental trends.* Commonly the kinds of policies that are politically feasible recall the much-hailed 2007 legislative achievement that improved the minimum wage in the United States. This produced an increase from $5.15 an hour to $7.25 an hour over three years – something very useful and positive. But viewed in longer-term perspective it also offered a pitiful illustration of underlying weakness: the inflation-adjusted minimum wage was more than $2 higher (nearly $10 an hour in 2009 dollars) in 1968. The newly achieved level was lower in real (inflation-adjusted) terms than it was when John F. Kennedy was President more than four decades earlier, in 1961 (Economic Policy Institute, 2009).

In this illustration, as in numerous other areas, the underlying capacities of traditional social democratic politics are simply insufficiently powerful to provide an adequate trend-altering response to emerging challenges. In most advanced nations, the power of such politics is intimately related to the power of organized labor. Yet most American progressives are loath to face up to the fact that the American labor movement has long been in the process not only of decline, but of radical decline. It has fallen from a peak membership of 35% of the labor force in the mid-1950s to just 6.9% in the private sector today, 11.9% overall (Bureau of Labor Statistics, 2011). This reality, along with America's unusual racial and ethnic divisions, is a key reason why (after allowing for certain historically path-dependent – and very late! – partial exceptions like health care) most progressive social democratic proposals based on European precedents are unlikely to be achieved in more than modest form in the United States.

Although I would welcome whatever can be done, the traditional hope of steadily and progressively reforming capitalism following the best liberal welfare state and corporatist precedents is not likely to be realized. Even allowing for Obama administration achievements, in fact, what we are beginning to experience in many areas is a process of slow decay, one in which reform achieves sporadic gains, but the long-term trends of stagnant or growing inequality, economic dislocation, failing democratic accountability, deepening poverty, ecological degradation, and greater invasions of liberty (as well as growing imprisonment, especially of minorities) continue to slowly and quietly challenge belief in the capacities and moral integrity of the overall system and its governing elites. Although we may experience momentary periods of important renewal, accordingly, the emerging era appears likely to be one in which truly fundamental values – equality, liberty, meaningful democracy, ecological sustainability – will be increasingly thwarted by real-world trends. If so, and given the emerging constraints on traditional politics, both serious liberal reform and genuine conservatism are likely to falter. We may, in fact, be entering upon a sustained period in which the classic elements of a legitimation crisis – a time involving profound challenges to the moral and practical integrity of the state – begin quietly coming to the fore.

What might this mean for alternative political-economic approaches? Consider three analytical ways of thinking about serious progressive change in different longer-term political-economic contexts:

1 The first begins with conventional progressive assumptions about the emerging historical context and what it implies: namely, the context will essentially allow for a

slow but steady reforming extension of the past. (Or possibly a "pendulum swing" or "countervailing power" notion of upward and onward reform.) Both imply attempting better regulation, improved social expenditures (financed by progressive taxation), and various related "reforms," but no major change in capitalism as a system.

2   A second historically conventional way of thinking about the nature of the emerging context follows something like the traditional Marxist analysis: namely, there are reasons to believe the system will collapse – which suggests the possibility of "revolution," or, alternatively, a crisis sufficiently powerful to generate a "New Deal"-scale response. (In the collapse scenario, I suspect, however, that what might actually happen is that the system would move dramatically to the right rather than the left.)

3   A third analytic judgment is that the system neither achieves serious "reform" nor collapses into revolution. This possibility I think is the most likely. It suggests a long and sustained period of fragmentary reform which (give or take an occasional exception) does not solve major problems – accompanied by long-term social, economic, and in many areas environmental decay, and attended (in the first instance and phase of development) by disillusionment, questioning and experimentation.

In an ongoing, long-term context of "stalemate and decay," over time, and in due course beyond the first disillusionment, the long, slow, and "evolutionary reconstruction" of institutions and ideas, both local and national, may (or may not) be possible. If it is possible, the process would likely take several decades, would be messy and difficult, and would appear as fragmentary and incomplete for some time before a new synthesis was achieved. Plausible partial analogies are "prehistory" eras – like the long, quiet, building decades prior to the populist and progressive eras, or the several-decade period that led up to the American revolution itself. In my judgment, we are well into a context of "stalemate and decay" that is already forcing – I use the word carefully – *forcing* – a new questioning, a new level of experimentation and development (especially locally), and a new exploration of "big picture" systemic ideas both about policy and about models – as well as the specific modalities of change appropriate to the nature of the specific historical context we are entering. The modality of most interest to me in this context involves what I think is usefully termed the "evolutionary reconstruction" of institutions at the base of the society – leading later perhaps to extensions of principles so developed to national applications.

A central intellectual problem that must be confronted is whether it is feasible even in theory to develop an institutional architecture that allows for true democratic control of any advanced political economy. The two main traditional progressive strategies for controlling corporate behavior – anti-trust and various forms of regulation – are both now increasingly understood to be deeply compromised: the attempt to use the former in more than marginal ways is almost a forgotten relic of history. And repeated studies of "regulatory capture" have shown that various forms of regulation are commonly narrowed, and often redirected, by the powerful corporate interests they seek to control. In socialist systems, many studies also demonstrate that in practice powerful institutional economic actors commonly dominate planning and other policy mechanisms.[1]

What long-term structural arrangements might even in principle be capable of achieving and sustaining an advanced democratic political economy? The traditional socialist argument is that democratic control ultimately will require some form of social ownership of significant industry. In a society like our own in which the top 1% owns just under 50% of all investment capital and the top 5% owns roughly 70% of such capital, that answer, I believe, is correct (Alperovitz and Daly, 2008, p. 5). However, it is hardly sufficient even in broad, long-term theoretical terms. A first critical question is: "What form?" A second and third are: "What else would be required?" And: "Are there any real-world experiences which suggest the practicality and feasibility of a new approach?"

Recent studies suggest that what is actually happening "on the ground" in a number of key areas involves the build-up of a mosaic of entirely different institutions that suggest the possible direction of new answers – and, further, a process which at this stage of development is both peaceful and evolutionary. In the United States alone, literally thousands of real-world efforts that illuminate how alternative wealth-holding principles can work in practice have developed in communities throughout the nation over the last several decades. The range of social or "common" ownership models suggest a "pluralist" vision that may ultimately nurture greater diversity, decentralization, and democratic control of crucial economic institutions and processes.

At the heart of the various models is the principle that ownership of the nation's wealth must ultimately be shifted, institutionally, to benefit the vast majority. Although I favor the term "pluralist commonwealth" to describe what a political economy anchored in democratic ownership of wealth-holding institutions would look like, there is an important and obvious overlap between this conception and Rawls's ideas about property-owning democracy. Like a property-owning democracy, the "pluralist commonwealth" insists on both the centrality of the question of who owns capital, and the desirability of building a system in which such control is no longer dominated by tiny elites.

The "pluralist commonwealth" offers a diverse institutional model. In some areas, traditional public ownership will clearly be appropriate. In Medicare and Medicaid, we already have a nationalized partial health insurance system, and this is ultimately likely to be expanded, as in connection with the so-called "public option." European experience provides numerous other practical (and, new studies demonstrate, demonstrably efficient) public ownership precedents to draw upon, and such experience underscores the obvious fact that private US corporate control is not the only practical economic option (Alperovitz and Dubb, 2007). The United States has already nationalized auto firms, insurance companies (A.I.G.), and housing finance agencies (Fannie Mae and Freddy Mac). Although this has been done in crisis contexts, a line has clearly been crossed, and future possibilities are likely to build beyond current practice. If (as is likely) future financial crises force the question, it is possible that major investment banks may be nationalized: if they are too big to fail, and if effective regulation is simply not feasible politically, the alternative is "breaking them up" – but this, history shows, is simply a formula for the "big fish to eat the little fish," bringing us back to very large structures that simply cannot be controlled politically.

For at least some large industries, the most appropriate structure of ownership is likely to be something close to that suggested by James Meade some time ago. In the first instance this involves establishing some form of national "Public Trust" or other agency that would own major controlling interests (ultimately perhaps nearly all stock) in very large corporations (Alperovitz, 2006, pp. 23–27, 70–80). Within a new public investment framework, different groups of investment managers would compete with each other in managing chunks of the public portfolio (as investment managers commonly do today in both private and public pension fund investing). Larger ecological and other noneconomic criteria for investment would be set by government trustees, in a manner analogous to the kinds of criteria that are imposed today in California by the California Public Employees' Retirement System (CalPERS). Such strategies, though modest and flawed in their current limited range of demands, have demonstrated a growing capacity to bring together economic efficiency and larger political goals. They also maintain a substantial degree of market competition. Critical from the perspective of longer-term democratic control is the possibility they suggest for a system of public accountability and transparency – and the accrual of major portions of profits to the public (Alperovitz, 2006, pp. 233–234).

For many industries there is no way around something like the Public Trust form of social ownership as a first approximation. However, such a mechanism alone – a partial analogue for large industry to some "market socialist" models – would hardly be adequate to achieve democratic accountability. Here (as in the case of direct public ownership models) the power of large enterprises – and of the market – would likely continue to substantially dominate even a fully realized system of social ownership of this kind.

Countering this power requires the *systematic* development of local democratic experience, along with its precondition: community economic stability. Any serious "pluralist commonwealth" model must give great emphasis to the strategic arguments of earlier theorists like de Tocqueville and John Stuart Mill, and of modern theorists like Jane Mansbridge, Stephen Elkin, and Benjamin Barber, who hold that over the long haul only if a strong and participatory version of democratic experience is nurtured at the local level can there ever be a strong, participatory capacity for democratic control in the nation at large.

Note carefully: The emphasis on local community democratic experience is different from (though certainly related to and compatible with) participatory control of enterprises, large and small. Although many theorists interested in cooperatives and worker participation and control rightly urge the importance of such efforts, a major gap in much systemic discussion is a general lack of interest in the conditions required to achieve democratic *governance* in local experience – which is to say the conditions of meaningful local, everyday municipal democracy.

Both because of their importance in ownership terms, but also to achieve the economic stability required ultimately for local democratic governance, any serious model must aim also to steadily develop new local ownership institutions, especially worker-owned and other community-benefiting firms. Most important are enterprises that are practical, anchored locally (i.e., rarely pull up stakes and leave by virtue of their ownership), and which either alter inequality directly or use profits for public or quasi-public purposes (or both). Employee-owned firms, cooperatives, neighborhood-owned corporations, and a wide range of municipal and social enterprises, along with municipal and state-investing agencies, are among the key locally based institutions of the "pluralist commonwealth."

Worker-Owned Firms

That individuals work harder, better, and with greater enthusiasm when they have a direct interest in the outcome is self-evident. The obvious question is: why aren't large numbers of businesses organized on this principle? The answer is: roughly 11,400 are. Indeed, 13.7 million Americans now work in firms that are partly or wholly owned by the employees, six million more than are members of unions in the private sector (Bureau of Labor Statistics, 2011; National Center for Employee Ownership, 2011).

Appleton (Co.) in Appleton, Wisconsin (a world leader in specialty paper production) became employee owned when the company was put up for sale by Arjo Wiggins Appleton, the multinational corporation which owned it – and the 3300 employees decided they had just as much right to buy it as anyone else (Dresang, 2001; Appleton Ideas, 2006). Reflexite, an optics company based in New Avon, Connecticut, became employee owned in 1985 after 3M made a strong bid for the company and the founding owners, loyal to their workers and the town, chose to sell to the employees instead (Case, 1992). W.L. Gore – the maker of Gore-Tex apparel – has been owned, since 1974, by (currently 9500) worker-owners in 30 countries around the world (W.L. Gore and Associates, 2011).

Although there are 300–500 traditional worker co-ops, most worker-owned businesses are organized through "employee stock ownership plans" (ESOPs). Technically an ESOP involves a "trust" which receives and holds stock in a given corporation on behalf of its employees. What is positive about this mechanism is that it offers major tax benefits for the creation of large numbers of worker-owned firms – especially when an original owner retires and decides to sell to the employees. What is negative is that although there are exceptions, in the main the ESOP form is not at this stage organized democratically.

Several considerations suggest, however, that greater democratic control of ESOPs is likely to develop. First, many ESOP companies – more than 25%, according to one report (Wirtz, 2007) – are already majority owned by workers. Of these, the National Center for Employee Ownership estimates 40% already pass voting rights through to plan participants. Second, as workers accumulate stock their ownership stake tends to increase. Annual ESOP Association member surveys indicate that in 1982 only 20% of ESOP Association member companies were majority ESOP-owned companies; by 2000, that figure was 68% (Democracy Collaborative, 2005, p. 59).

It is conceivable that as more and more ESOPs become majority owned, workers will simply ignore the fact that some have little power. On the other hand, the more likely probability – as an editorial in *Business Week* observed in 1991 – is that ultimately workers "who own a significant share of their companies will want a voice in corporate governance." In Ohio a survey completed in the mid-1990s found that employee ownership was becoming more democratic over time, with three times as many closely held companies passing through full voting rights to ESOP participants as had occurred in a previous (1985–1986) survey. Beyond this, new efforts by various local groups and the United Steelworkers and others to develop cooperatives along the lines of the Mondragón effort in the Basque country of Spain aim to expand worker ownership in a much more direct and democratic form (Dunkin, 1991; Logue and Yates, 2001; USW News, 2009).

Municipal Enterprises

An extraordinary range of local municipal efforts embodying pluralist commonwealth-related principles also exist. One of the most important areas of activity is land development. As early as 1970 the city of Boston embarked on a joint venture with the Rouse Company to develop the Faneuil Hall Marketplace (a downtown retail complex). Boston kept the property under municipal ownership. One study estimates that in the project's first decade the city took in 40% more revenue than it would have collected through conventional property tax (Frieden and Sagalyn, 1989, p. 169). Entrepreneurial "participating lease" arrangements for the use of public property are now common. Alhambra, California, for instance, earns approximately $1 million a year in rent revenues from a six-acre holding it leases to commercial tenants (Williamson, Imbroscio, and Alperovitz, 2002, pp. 157–159).

A fast-growing arena of new activity involves Internet and related services. In Glasgow, Kentucky the municipally owned utility offers residents electricity, cable, telephone services, and high-speed Internet access – all at costs lower than those of private competitors. The city also has access to an "intranet" which links local government, businesses, libraries, schools, and neighbors (Glasgow Electric Plant Board, 2007). Tacoma, Washington's broadband network "Click!" also offers individuals and private companies Internet and cable service, as does Cedar Falls, Iowa (Click! Network, 2007; Cedar Falls Utilities, 2008). More than 700 public power utilities have equipped their communities with such networks (American Public Power Association, 2008).

Municipalities have also been active venture capital investors, retaining publicly owned stock in businesses that hold promise for the city's economy. A survey conducted in 1996 found that more than a third of responding city governments reported venture capital efforts of one kind or another (Clarke and Gaile, 1998, pp. 72, 79–86). During the 1990s the publicly owned New York Power Authority and two private companies formed a joint investment pool of $60 million, which yielded $175 million at the end of the first five years of operation (Brodoff Communications, 2000). Many smaller cities have created local venture funds that make investments in the $500,000 to $2 million range (Bowman, 1987, p. 4; Clarke and Gaile, 1998, p. 84).

Other areas of innovation include health services and environmental management. Denver Health is a municipal enterprise which has transformed itself from an insolvent city agency ($39 million in debt in 1992) to a competitive, quasi-public health care system ($54 million cash reserves in 1997) delivering over $2.1 billion in care for the uninsured over the last 10 years (Moore, 1997; Denver Health, 2008). Denver Health operates a satellite system of eight primary care centers and 12 school-based clinics and employs some 4000 Denver area residents (Nuzum, McCarthy, Gauthier, and Beck, 2007; Denver Health, 2008). Hundreds of municipalities also generate revenues through landfill gas recovery operations which turn the greenhouse gas methane (a by-product of waste storage) into energy. Riverview, Michigan, one of the largest such recovery operations, illustrates the trend. Riverview's sale of gas for power production helps produce enough electricity to continuously power over 5000 homes. Royalties covered initial costs of the effort in the first two years of operation and now add to the city's cash flows (DTE Energy, 2011; City of Riverview, 2011; EPA, 2011).

Building Community: Neighborhoods and Nonprofits

The neighborhood-based community development corporation (CDC) combines the community-serving mission of a nonprofit organization with the wealth-building and ownership capacities of an economic enterprise. The CDC is a hybrid self-help entity that operates at both the community-building level and the economic level, and exhibits micro-level applications of pluralist commonwealth principles.

One leading example is New Community Corporation (NCC) in Newark, New Jersey – a CDC which employs 2300 neighborhood residents and generates roughly $200 million in economic activity each year. Profits help support day-care and after-school programs, a nursing home, and four medical day-care centers for seniors. NCC also runs a Youth Automotive Training Center; young people who complete its courses are guaranteed jobs offering $20,000-plus starting salaries (Rusch, 2001, p. 5; Guinan, 2003).

Since the 1960s, 4600 neighborhood-based CDCs have come into being in American communities. Most are not nearly as large and sophisticated as the leaders, but all employ wealth-related principles to serve "small publics" in geographically defined areas. The assets they commonly develop center above all on housing, but many also own retail firms and, in several cases, larger businesses (National Congress for Community Economic Development, 2006, p. 15; Sirianni and Friedland, 2001, p. 59).

Other nonprofit organizations have picked up on the underlying principles of development (Massarsky and Beinhacker, 2002; Emerson, 2003). A leading example is Pioneer Human Services (PHS), in Seattle, Washington. Initially established with donations and grants, PHS is now almost entirely self-supporting. PHS provides drug- and alcohol-free housing, employment, job training, counseling, and education to recovering alcoholics and drug addicts. Its annual operating budget of nearly $60 million is 99% supported by fees for services or sales of products. PHS's various social enterprises employ nearly 1000 people and include a light metal fabricator employing theoretically unemployable people, which manufactures parts for Boeing and other customers; a food buying service which distributes food to other nonprofit organizations; and two restaurants (Pioneer Human Services, 2005; Dubb, 2006).

State and National Innovators

A number of larger efforts based on pluralist commonwealth principles have also emerged in recent years, especially at the state level. Particularly interesting are a group of sophisticated developments that point in the direction of practical – even dramatic – applications of the most radical and far-reaching strategies.

Historically, several states have had considerable experience with significant scale efforts. For instance, the state-owned Bank of North Dakota – founded in 1919 – currently manages $3.5 billion in assets and earned $57 million in profits in 2008 (Bank of North Dakota, 2009). The Wisconsin State Life Insurance Fund has assets of over $75 million and has coverage in force totaling over $200 million (Wisconsin Legislative

Audit Bureau, 2002; Williamson *et al.*, 2002, p. 154). More recent developments include venture capital initiatives in more than half the states, which involve direct public investment and ownership in companies by state agencies (Heard and Sibert, 2000, pp. 48–49). A typical example is Maryland's Enterprise Investment Fund, which provides promising high-tech start-ups with up to $500,000 in capital in exchange for the state receiving equity shares and a guarantee from the firm that it will continue to operate in Maryland for at least five years.

At the federal level, public ownership of stock in specific corporations is also a long-established (if little discussed!) tradition. In the post 9/11 airline bailout, for instance, the Bush administration demanded a 10-year option to purchase a third of America West's stock at $3 per share in exchange for federal loan guarantees (Kesmodel, 2002; Wong, 2003). Similarly, in 1980, as part of a $1.5 billion loan guarantee for the Chrysler Corporation, the government received 14.4 million warrants, representing 10–15% of Chrysler stock.[2] Again, in 1984, the government through the FDIC (Federal Deposit Insurance Corporation) took a controlling ownership position (over 80%) in connection with the $8 billion bailout of Continental Illinois Bank. Other precedents can be traced back to World War II (Reich and Donahue, 1985). The recent government investments and takeovers follow in a long line of developmental history.

Perhaps of greatest significance – and suggestive of future possibilities – are federal, state, and municipal public employee retirement system boards. These institutions now control roughly $2 trillion in total assets (Barrett and Green, 2007). At the national level the Federal Reserve Board manages a pension fund of this kind, and more than two million federal employees are involved in a similar public pension program which owns and manages over $200 billion (Financial Markets Center, 2000; US Census Bureau, 2003, table 521; Thrift Savings Plan, 2008). Critically, many public pension funds have begun to explore new ways to use their ownership position for public purposes. For instance, as of 2006, in California CalPERS had pension fund placements totaling $8.3 billion in the state's economy (Lifsher, 2007). CalPERS also emphasizes information disclosure and the independence of boards of directors – and it enforces transparency, environmental performance and other standards in many of its international investments (California Public Employees Retirement System, 2008; Nesbitt, 2001).

The state of Alabama also actively pursues pluralist commonwealth-related strategies. Retirement Systems of Alabama (RSA) – which manages the state employee and teachers' pension system – has invested in numerous local Alabama industries, in some cases also helping create worker-owned firms (Williamson *et al.*, 2002, p. 182). An even more suggestive effort is the Alaska Permanent Fund, which invests a significant portion of revenues derived from oil development on behalf of citizens of the state. In 2008, a high payout year, each individual state resident, as a matter of right, received dividends of just over $2000 – more than $10,000 for a couple with three children (Alaska Permanent Fund Corporation, 2008, 2011).

CalPERS, RSA, and related efforts offer precedents for using public ownership strategies to achieve greater public oversight of corporate practices, and to help achieve state and community economic goals. The Alaska Permanent Fund takes us one step further: It is an on-the-ground operating system that demonstrates the feasibility of the kinds of far-reaching public trust proposals which might ultimately be advanced at the national level. Although each approach differs in specifics – and are at this stage incomplete – all are based on the principle that capital can and should be accumulated and managed in socially accountable ways.

It is also important to note that many of these emerging ownership-altering forms of wealth have demonstrated a capacity to develop much broader political support than most realize. Though they have progressive redistributive and community-building impact, *at the local level* they are rarely divisive. Because of their practical problem-solving capabilities they are often supported by independents and even moderate Republicans – a fact that also suggests political possibilities for splitting traditional conservative political groupings. Many "community wealth" initiatives also resonate with new, ecologically serious approaches to "the commons," and to the larger principles of sustainability.

There is also ample room in the pluralist commonwealth model for small and medium-sized businesses, for new-era "sustainable businesses," and for a diverse and eclectic mix of economic institutions that now often find their larger economic and value priorities thwarted by the operation of our current corporate-dominated form of capitalism. None of the existing models, of course, are adequate at this stage of development. The question is whether over time they might provide evolving precedents for – and a basis upon which to build – more fully realized efforts.

Integrated Advances and Further Possibilities[3]

The New Deal famously drew upon – and then extended the principles inherent in – efforts that had previously been developed in the state "laboratories of democracy." Recent developments in Cleveland, Ohio, one of the nation's hardest-hit rust-belt industrial cities, suggest how evolutionary possibilities can develop in ways that draw upon but also transcend the kinds of local institutional experiences that are now becoming commonplace. A model of community-owned enterprises targeted at sectors that are inherently heavily financed by the public has begun to develop powerful momentum. This momentum, in turn, suggests principles both for local development and for longer-range structural changes in American capitalism.

At the heart of the strategy is a new form of integrated cooperative economic organization. The Cleveland "Evergreen Cooperative Initiative" comprises an evolving series of worker-owned companies that are both financed by – and feed funds back into – the Evergreen Cooperative Development Fund. The goal is not simply one cooperative, but an integrated network of worker-owned businesses that are financed by a revolving fund designed both to continuously expand the network and to keep jobs anchored in the community.

Evergreen also draws heavily on the experience of the above-noted Mondragón Cooperative Corporation in the Basque Country of Spain, the world's most successful large-scale worker cooperative network model (now employing 85,000 workers in more than 120 industrial, service, and financial cooperatively owned businesses).

What makes the model of potentially far-reaching relevance is its relationship to sectors of expanding public procurement and investment. The strategy aims to capture ever-greater shares of spending in health, energy, and other key sectors in a way that both changes ownership patterns and helps stabilize the local community economy.

The approach is also thoroughly "green," but the goal is not simply green jobs; it is "green ownership."

The flagship of the effort, the Evergreen Cooperative Laundry (ECL), has targeted health care, which is currently approaching 18% of the GDP, as an obvious sector of expanding public investment. Launched in October 2009, the $5.7 million laundry already has landed contracts to wash 3.5 million pounds of laundry annually, roughly one-third of the laundry's ultimate business goal. After a six-month initial "probationary" period employees can begin to buy into the company through payroll deductions of 50 cents an hour over three years (for a total of $3000). If the company meets its sales projections, employee-owners are likely to have built up a $65,000–85,000 equity stake in the business over eight to nine years – a substantial amount of money in an area where most people live on about $18,000 a year.

ECL has the smallest carbon footprint of any industrial-scale laundry in northeast Ohio, and, in all probability, the entire state. Just how "green" are its operations is illustrated by a simple fact: most industrial-scale laundries use three gallons of water per pound of laundry (the measure common in industrial-scale systems); ECL uses just eight-tenths of a gallon to do the same job.

An employee-owned, community-based energy company – Ohio Cooperative Solar – has also begun large-scale installations of solar panels on the roofs of the city's largest nonprofit health, education, and municipal buildings; OCS also has weatherized more than 200 homes. Another business in development (construction began in October 2011) is Green City Growers, designed to build and operate a year-round hydroponic food production greenhouse in the midst of urban Cleveland. The 3.25-acre facility will be capable of producing more than 3 million heads of fresh lettuce and 300,000 pounds of (highly profitable) basil and other herbs a year. Other community- or worker-owned enterprises in the R&D stage include firms oriented to weatherization, recycling, equipment maintenance, and records retention. Organizers project an initial complex of 10 companies that will generate roughly 500 jobs over the next five years.

The overall strategy is not only to go "green" but to intentionally design and position all the co-ops as the greenest firms within their sectors. This is important in itself but even more important is the fact that the new green companies are aiming for a competitive advantage in getting the business of hospitals and other "anchor institutions" that are trying to shrink their carbon footprint.

Strikingly, the effort has substantial backing not only from progressives but from a number of important members of the local business community as well. Co-ops in general, and those in which people work hard for what they get in particular, cut across ideological lines – especially at the local level where practicality, not rhetoric, is what counts in distressed communities. There is also a great deal of national "buzz" among activists and community development specialists about "the Cleveland model." Given the challenges facing many urban areas, there is little doubt that variations on the model are likely to be developed in other cities. Moreover, within universities and other so-called "anchor institutions" that are tied to specific locales there has been a quietly developing trajectory of supporting expertise on how to use procurement budgets to help local communities. For instance, the University of Pennsylvania, a leader in the field, has developed techniques that reward university administrators in part on how well they do in meeting their local purchase targets (Dubb and Howard, 2007, pp. 63–64).

What makes the Cleveland effort of potentially much greater significance, however, is that its basic design suggests principles for a larger, "pluralist" economic approach that could also be applied in hard-hit industries and working-class communities around the nation. The model, again, takes us both beyond traditional capitalism and traditional models of socialism. The key linkage is between national sectors of expanding public activity and procurement with a new local economic entity that both broadens ownership and is deeply anchored in the local community economy. In the case of health care, the linkage is also to a sector in which some implicit or explicit form of "national planning" – the movement toward universal health care – will all but certainly increase public influence and concern with how funds are used.

Beyond this, consider what might happen if the stock the government and union owned in 2009 in General Motors had been used to reorganize the company along full or joint worker ownership lines – and the new General Motors' product line were linked to a serious plan to develop the nation's mass transit and rail system. Since mass transit is a sector that is all but certain to expand, there is every reason to plan its taxpayer-financed growth and integrate it with new community-stabilizing ownership strategies.

The possibilities, in fact, are extraordinary. There are currently some 164,000 public transit vehicles in operation in the United States, a number that will inevitably increase as rail and bus rapid transit service increases. In 2007, public authorities nationwide acquired roughly 600 rail and subway cars along with roughly 15,000 buses and smaller "paratransit" vehicles. Total current capital outlays on vehicles alone amount to $3.8 billion; total annual investment outlays (vehicles plus stations and other infrastructure) are $14.5 billion (American Public Transportation Association, 2009a, p. 16).

The American Public Transportation Association (APTA) estimates that a $48 billion investment in transit capital projects would generate 1.3 million new green jobs within two years. There are also strong reasons to expedite the retirement of aging buses and replace them with more efficient energy-saving vehicles with better amenities such as bike racks and GPS systems – and this could add to further public procurement requirements (American Public Transportation Association, 2009b).

The Obama administration has also endorsed a strategy for making high-speed rail a reality in the United States. In an April 2009 statement announcing the strategic plan, the President observed: "A major new high-speed rail line will generate many thousands of construction jobs over several years, as well as permanent jobs for rail employees and increased economic activity in the destinations these trains serve" (US Department of Transportation, 2009). The 2009 stimulus package included an $8 billion "down payment" for investments in high-speed rail. Amtrak has identified 10 corridors ripe for new or upgraded high-speed rail service, and the states are also involved. In November 2008, voters in California approved a $10 billion bond to build a high-speed rail system running from San Francisco to Los Angeles (Gertner, 2009). There are also opportunities for bipartisan support: House Republican whip Eric Cantor, who led the opposition to Obama's stimulus plan, has teamed with liberal Democrat Bobby Scott to lobby for an extension of high-speed service to Amtrak's Washington to Richmond, Virginia route (Cantor and Scott, 2009).

Even more dramatic possibilities are suggested by experts concerned with the impact of likely future oil shortages. Canadian scholars Richard Gilbert and Anthony Perl, projecting dramatic future increases in the cost of all petroleum-based transportation, have proposed building 25,000 km (15,000 miles) of track devoted to high-speed rail between now and 2025. Along with additional, incremental upgrades of existing rail lines to facilitate increased and faster service, they estimate total investment costs at $2 trillion – roughly $140 billion each year for 15 years (Gilbert and Perl, 2008, pp. 248–288).

All of this clearly defines an inevitably expanding economic sector – and one that also will inevitably be heavily dominated by public funds and public planning. The striking fact, however, is that there are currently no US-owned companies producing the kind of equipment needed for high-speed rail. Nor are American-owned companies producing subway cars (although some foreign-owned firms assemble subway cars in the United States.) In the absence of a deliberate effort to create a national capacity to produce high-speed rail equipment, the United States in general, and California and other regions in particular, will likely end up awarding contracts for production to the French firm Alstom, the acknowledged world leader in production of very high-speed trains, or other firms from abroad. The newly established American firm US Railcar, formed in 2009, is hoping to tap into that market and reestablish a domestic train-building capacity, using a next-generation "diesel self-propelled railcar" designed by the now-defunct firm Colorado Railcar as a prototype (US Railcar, 2009).

The notion of using America's coming increase in orders for high-speed rail equipment and other mass transit vehicles to help achieve important economic goals has already been grasped by some public officials. In July 2009, Wisconsin awarded the Spanish firm Talgo a $47 million contract negotiated by Governor Jim Doyle to build two 14-car trains for the Milwaukee to Chicago route. The trains will be built in Wisconsin, possibly at the recently closed General Motors factory in Janesville; 80 jobs are expected to be created immediately, with prospects for further expansion in the future (Sandler, 2009). Retirement Systems of Alabama, a public pension fund with a long history of proactive investments in the Alabama economy, has gone further: in 2009 RSA made an additional loan of $275 million (on top of an earlier loan of $350 million) to railway car producer National Alabama to complete construction of a production facility in the state. Interestingly, RSA has also begun to confront the ownership issue, and is acquiring a 20% stake in the firm (Bronner, 2009).

The longer-term logic and implications of all this becomes even more obvious when it is realized that by 2050 another 130 million people are projected to be living in the United States; by 2100 the "high" Census Bureau estimate is over one billion (US Census Bureau, 2003). Providing infrastructure and transportation for this expanding population will generate a long additional list of required equipment and materials that a restructured group of vehicle production companies could help produce – and, at the same time, help create new forms of ownership that also help anchor the economies of the local communities involved.

As reflection upon the transportation issue in general (and the fate of General Motors in particular) suggests, the pluralist commonwealth principles implicit in the Cleveland and other efforts point to the possibility of a new and important strategic approach. It is one in which economic activity related to sectors that are inherently heavily financed by the public is used both to help create and give stability to enterprises that are more broadly owned, and to target jobs to local communities in distress. The "model" does not, of course, rely only on public funds; as in Cleveland it also serves a private market, hence faces the "discipline" of the market. (There is no reason General Motors should stop producing automobiles – and hopefully it will produce energy-efficient ones.)

We are, of course, a long, long way from developing a sophisticated near-term national policy approach like that suggested for transportation – to say nothing of the fully developed principles of a genuine systemic alternative. On the other hand, as we have noted, historically the development of models and experiments at the local and state level have often provided the principles upon which subsequent national policy drew when the moment of real decision arrived. It is none too early for serious progressives to begin to think both about the Clevelands of the world and about the possible implications they may have for one day moving the nation in a very practical way toward a new pluralist systemic vision.

Challenging the Ideology of Unconstrained Wealth Inequality

Ultimately there cannot be effective democracy – hence, control of major economic actors – unless inequality is altered in fundamental ways. The top 1% currently receives more income each year than the bottom 150 million Americans. The share of the top 1% has doubled from 9–10% to 19–22% of all income in recent years (Saez, Piketty, and Atkinson, 2009). Attempts to achieve significant trend-changing improvements in such realities via traditional tax-and-spend strategies have been largely blocked for many, many years; the main battle in recent years has involved attempts simply to reverse Bush-era tax reductions rather than to aggressively achieve positive progressive change. Challenging and changing the ownership of capital to benefit both workers and local, state, and national publics is important for distributional reasons as well as to negate the power associated with private corporate ownership.

The examples provided so far illustrate the fact that there are numerous plausible ways to institutionalize democratic principles of wealth and capital holding. But these various examples cannot evolve into the basis for an alternative political-economic system unless the rationale for larger features of the existing regime is also confronted. Challenging the inequality of wealth means directly challenging the *ideology* that justifies its concentrated ownership. The standard Rawlsian strategy for addressing inequality is to challenge the notion that individuals can in any strong sense *deserve* either the wealth they inherit or fruits garnered from their own talents and efforts; persons can have "legitimate expectations" about the rewards they will get once a political-economic institutional framework has been established, but the claims of "desert" in itself play no role in the formulation of that framework (Rawls, 1971).

Whatever the philosophic merits of that argument, it is clearly one which ordinary people find difficult to accept; most people think that "desert" is a relevant moral consideration in distributive justice. But in the modern technological era, accepting a role for desert need not lead to a validation of massive wealth inequalities. In fact, a proper understanding of the ways in which wealth has been and continues to be created leads us to precisely the opposite conclusion – that because society as a whole is primarily responsible for our accumulated wealth and knowledge, a narrow slice of humanity (roughly the top 1% of industrialized nations) has no right to capture the lion's share of such wealth. In recent work, Lew Daly and I have sketched out principles for an alternative conception of distributive justice that accepts the moral claims of desert, but gives due weight to the fact that most of the wealth present in advanced societies is a *social* product, not the result of individual persons or firms (Alperovitz and Daly, 2008).

The starting point is the observation that our national output in any given year or period has far more to do with our inherited productive capacity – the fruit of long-run technological change and cumulative knowledge – than with current contributions in the marketplace. Nobel laureate economist George Akerlof puts the key point succinctly: "Our marginal products are not ours alone." The value we attribute to today's labor and capital, he explains, is "due almost entirely to the cumulative process of learning that has taken us from stone-age poverty to twenty-first century affluence." And thus, "our current standard of living" is something we "owe" to the past (Akerlof, 2000).[4]

Robert Solow's pioneering work on economic growth helps us understand the importance of cumulative learning and other forms of social value. In 1957, Solow published a brief but powerful article that applied a new growth model he had developed to measure the relative importance of various factors of production (labor, capital, and so on) as sources of economic growth. What Solow found was that most productivity growth was due to a "shift" in the production function, a change in output beyond what could be explained by changes in the supply of conventional inputs such as labor and capital. The remainder, now commonly called the "Solow residual," essentially represents an increase in the efficiency – not an increase in the amount – of the combined conventional inputs (Solow, 1957).

Specifically, Solow found that nearly seven-eighths of productivity gains in the first half of the twentieth century, about 88%, could not be accounted for by measuring conventional inputs of labor and capital (Solow, 1957). Strikingly, only one-eighth of the gains could be attributed to increases in the supply of capital, capital accumulation being conventionally thought to "play a large part in explaining growth, not just a small supporting role," as Moses Abramovitz later wrote in interpreting the new growth discoveries (Abramowitz, 1993, p. 218). The large share of growth unaccounted for by conventional measures could only be attributed to "technical change in the broadest sense," Solow concluded (Solow, 1987).

Economic journalist David Warsh summarizes the case in his book *Knowledge and the Wealth of Nations* as follows: "Here was the answer to the question of why the economy kept climbing the mountain of diminishing returns." It had little to do with labor or capital accumulation, he confirms. Instead, "'[t]echnical progress,' the growth of knowledge as measured by the [Solow] Residual, was creating the new wealth" (Warsh, 2006, p. 147). If the magnitudes suggested by Solow's work are roughly accurate over time – as subsequent research (i.e., Bluestone and Harrison, 1996) has suggested – this presents extraordinary problems for conventional moral arguments about the inherent deservingness of all market rewards, large and small. The individual's contributions at any point in time are extremely modest compared to the contributions of society. And, accordingly, if deservingness is the test, the individual's reward should be equally modest.

If the public share of national income is to rise enough to meet the social challenges we now face, we need to develop and promote a better understanding of the types and magnitudes of social value that drive economic growth. Lacking a better empirical understanding of the economic impact of common assets – most importantly our expanding inheritance of scientific and other forms of productive knowledge and know-how – public debate will continue to be controlled by moral arguments pitting strong assumptions of individual "deservingness" in the private economy against equally strong assumptions of "undeservingness" in the development of public policy.

Yet, if we are serious in holding that contribution matters, then – as the Solow study and many others demonstrate – society "deserves" much more than many believe, and all members of society should share in the common fruits. This basic idea – that the wealth generated by common assets should be generally shared – has been advocated by many thinkers and leaders well within the liberal tradition, including Thomas Paine, John Stuart Mill, L.T. Hobhouse, David Lloyd George, and Franklin D. Roosevelt; and, more recently, Robert Dahl and Herbert Simon. Simon, in particular, a winner of the Nobel Memorial Prize in economics, began to redeploy this concept in a forceful attack against the growing inequalities of recent decades. As he stated shortly before his death in a speech to the American Political Science Association, in 2000:

> If we are very generous with ourselves, I suppose that we might claim that we "earned" as much as one fifth of [our income]. The rest is the patrimony associated with being a member of an enormously productive social system, which has accumulated a vast store of physical capital, and an even larger store of intellectual capital – including knowledge, skills, and organizational know-how held by all of us. (Simon, 2000, p. 756)

In understanding that much of the value created today derives from a common "patrimony" of cumulative infrastructure and knowledge, we are able to redefine the moral debate, not by rejecting the principle of deservingness but by applying the principle more rigorously, exposing and challenging the private capture of societal wealth and crediting society for its contributions in an equally traditional sense.

One of the most penetrating advocates of these ideas, Leonard Trelawny Hobhouse, understood the moral task in a way that resonates strongly today. As he wrote in his influential 1911 book *Liberalism*, "The true function of taxation is to secure to society the element in wealth that is of social origin, or, more broadly, all that does not owe its origin to the efforts of living individuals." Hobhouse was very careful to distinguish his argument from more radical collectivist positions. It is only by crediting social value, he argued, that genuine individualism could be preserved. An "individualism which ignores the social factor in wealth" is no individualism at all, but rather a type of "private socialism" that "deprive[s] the community of its just share in the fruits of industry and so result[s] in a one-sided and inequitable distribution of wealth" (Hobhouse, 1994, p. 91).

Private socialism occurs when the wealth generated by common assets is not generally shared but captured by a small minority and when, at the same time, the public absorbs the losses when the wealthy fail. From the growth of inequality to the current Wall Street bailouts, this is precisely what we have today. It is time to dismantle this morality of private socialism – first, by crediting society for the value it creates, and second, by recapturing that value for common purposes.

Conclusion

Given the dead ends now facing most traditional progressive strategies, a central question is whether Americans can achieve a practical and common-sense understanding of the principle that some form of social, public or quasi-public ownership of capital is both necessary and possible. In the absence of this understanding, we cannot expect to move beyond the difficulties now facing traditional social democratic politics in many countries, and progressive efforts in the United States. A new understanding is required if we are to develop coherent new systemic designs, and if we are to alter long-decaying social and economic trends.

But if changing the ownership of capital is important, then precisely *how* is this idea to be demonstrated and conveyed to large numbers of Americans in everyday life? The best answer to that question entails the further development of real-world forms that embody new ownership principles. In the near term, the various practical efforts may be as important for what they teach about possibilities as what they accomplish in altering major trends. In this sense they are both precedents and instruments of education that help teach the practicality and common-sense nature of new principles. Not only are such efforts already politically viable; over time, there are reasons to believe they could help generate principles upon which major (viable) large-order responses to some of the major national problems we face can be based.

History shows that those who assume that nothing fundamental can ever change have repeatedly been proven wrong. It is appropriate – even urgent – that we clarify the principles and content of what might ultimately become the basis of a serious pluralist democratic vision – and that we do so in ways that both build upon and extend and refine what can be learned from emerging democratic experience as that experience accumulates in the era of stalemate, difficulty, and decay.

Notes

1. President Woodrow Wilson (1913, p. 202) wrote that "If the government is to tell big business men how to run their business, then don't you see that big business men have to get closer to the government even than they are now? Don't you see that they must capture the government, in order not to be restrained too much by it? Must capture the government? They have already captured it." Galbraith (2008) provides a recent in-depth analysis of the phenomenon.
2. The Chrysler bailout legislation also required Chrysler to create an ESOP. See Logue and Yates (2001, p. 85).
3. The Democracy Collaborative at the University of Maryland, of which the author is a founding principal, has played a direct role in these developments and much of this

information is taken from our direct on-the-ground experience. For published information on the Evergreen model, see also Howard, Dubb, and Alperovitz (2009), Yates (2009), Alperovitz, Howard, and Williamson (2010).
4. Akerloff response in Baumol (2000).

References

Abramovitz, M. (1993) The search for the sources of growth: Areas of ignorance, old and new. *Journal of Economic History*, 53 (2).

Akerlof, G. (2000) "Comment" on William J. Baumol, "Rapid economic growth, equitable income distribution, and the optimal rate of innovation spillovers," in *Economic Events, Ideas, and Policies: The 1960s and After* (eds G.L. Perry and J. Tobin), Brookings Institution, Washington, DC.

Alaska Permanent Fund Corporation (2008) *Permanent Fund Dividend Program*. Available at: www.apfc.org/home/Content/dividend/dividend.cfm (accessed September 20, 2011).

Alaska Permanent Fund Corporation (2011) *Annual Dividend Payouts*. Available at: www.apfc.org/home/Content/dividend/dividendamounts.cfm4 (accessed May 16, 2011).

Alperovitz, G. (2006) *America Beyond Capitalism: Reclaiming Our Wealth, Our Liberty and Our Democracy*, John Wiley & Sons, Inc., Hoboken, NJ.

Alperovitz, G. and Daly, L. (2008) *Unjust Desert: How The Rich Are Taking Our Common Heritage*, The New Press, New York.

Alperovitz, G. and Dubb, S. (2007) *Public Enterprise – A Historical Evaluation and an Assessment of Its Role in a Pluralist Commonwealth Economy*, National Center for Economic and Security Alternatives (NCESA), Working Paper, May 25.

Alperovitz, G., Howard, T., and Williamson, T. (2010) The Cleveland Model. *The Nation*, 290 (8) (March 1, 2011) 21–24.

American Public Power Association (APPA) (2008) *Quick Summaries of Major Issues*, APPA, Washington, DC. Available at: http://appanet.org/pressroom/index.cfm?ItemNumber=17992&navItemNumber=21052 (accessed September 20, 2011).

American Public Transportation Association (APTA) (2009a) *2009 Public Transportation Fact Book*, APTA, Washington, DC. Available at: http://www.apta.com/gap/policyresearch/Documents/APTA_2009_Fact_Book.pdf (accessed September 20, 2011).

American Public Transportation Association (APTA) (2009b) *Legislative Alert*, APTA, Washington, DC. January 7. Available at: http://www.apta.com/gap/legupdatealert/2009/Documents/2009january07.pdf (accessed September 20, 2011).

Appleton Ideas (2006) *About Appleton*. Available at: www.appletonideas.com/Appleton/jsps/ourcompany.do?langId=-1&catalogId=239327&storeId=139327 (accessed September 20, 2011).

Bank of North Dakota (2009) Bank of North Dakota Celebrates 90 Years. Available at: http://www.banknd.com/email/pressrelease/bndpressrelease07282009_2.htm (accessed September 21, 2011).

Barrett, K. and Greene, R. (2007) The $3 trillion challenge. *Governing* (Oct.). http://www.governing.com/articles/0710pension.htm (accessed September 21, 2011).

Baumol, W. (2000) Rapid economic growth, equitable income distribution, and the optimal range of innovation spillovers, in *Economic Events, Ideas, and Policies: The 1960s and After* (eds G. Perry and J. Tobin), Brookings Institution, Washington, DC, pp. 3–42.

Bluestone, B. and Harrison, B. (1996) *Growing Prosperity*, Houghton Mifflin, New York.

Bowman, A. (1987) *Tools and Targets: The Mechanics of City Economic Development*. National League of Cities, Washington, DC.

Brodoff Communications (2000) Giuliani Administration to Reinvest in Successful High-Tech Venture Capital Fund, Brodoff, New York (July 18). Available at: http://www.brodoff.com/pressreleases_08.htm (accessed September 21, 2011).

Bronner, D. (2009) Expanded Commitment to The Shoals. *Advisor* (Mar. 9). Available at: http://www.rsa-al.gov/About%20RSA/Pubs%20and%20forms/RSA%20Pubs/Advisor/2009/Mar09Advisor.pdf (accessed September 21, 2011).

Bureau of Labor Statistics (BLS) (2011) Union Members in 2010. Available at: http://www.bls.gov/news.release/pdf/union2.pdf (accessed November 1, 2011).

California Public Employees Retirement System (2008) Facts at a Glance: Corporate Governance (June 2008). Available at: https://www.calpers.ca.gov/eip-docs/about/facts/corpgov.pdf (accessed September 21, 2011).

Cantor, E. and Scott, B.(2009) Letter to Secretary LaHood, US Department of Transportation: April 23. Available at: http://www.bobbyscott.house.gov/index.php?option=com_content&task=view&id=387&Itemid=62#letter (accessed November 1, 2011).

Case, J. (1992) E.O.Y. 1992: Collective effort. *Inc.*, 14 (1), 32.

Cedar Falls Utilities (2008) About the Communications Utility. Available at: http://www.cfu.net/about/community-benefits.aspx (accessed September 23, 2011).

City of Riverview (2011) Land Preserve welcome page. Available at: http://cityofriverview.com/LP.html (accessed September 23, 2011).

Clarke, S. and Gaile, G. (1998) *The Work of Cities*, University of Minnesota Press, Minneapolis.

Click! Network (2007) About Us. http://www.click-network.com/AboutUs/tabid/88/Default.aspx (accessed September 21, 2011).

Democracy Collaborative (2005) *Building Wealth: The New Asset-Based Approach to Solving Social and Economic Problems*, The Aspen Institute, Washington DC.

Denver Health (2008) About Denver Health. Available at: http://www.denverhealth.org/portal/AboutDenverHealth/DenverHealthOverview/tabid/267/Default.aspx (accessed September 21, 2011).

Dresang, J. (2001) It's a Gamble on Paper. *Milwaukee Journal Sentinel* (Nov. 11) 1D.

DTE Energy, DTE Biomass Energy (2011) Riverview Gas Producers, LLC (Riverview, MI). Available at: http://www.dtebe.com/aboutus/successStories/riverview.html (accessed September 23, 2011).

Dubb, S. (2006) Interview of Mike Burns, CEO, Pioneer Human Services, March 9, Democracy Collaborative, College Park, MD.

Dubb, S. and Howard, T. (2007) *Linking Colleges to Communities: Engaging the University for Community Development*, The Democracy Collaborative at the University of Maryland, College Park, MD.

Dunkin, A. (1991) The Real Strengths of Employee Ownership. *Business Week* (July 15), p. 156. Available at: http://www.businessweek.com/archives/1991/b322283.arc.htm (accessed September 21, 2011).

Economic Policy Institute (EPI) (2009) *Minimum Wage Issue Guide*. May. Available at: http://www.epi.org/publications/entry/tables_figures_data/ (accessed September 21, 2011).

Emerson, J. (2003) Total foundation asset management: Exploring elements of engagement within philanthropic practice. Stanford Graduate School of Business Research Paper No. 1803 (February). Available at: https://gsbapps.stanford.edu/researchpapers/library/RP1803.pdf (accessed September 21, 2011).

EPA (2011) LMOP partner profile: Riverview Land Preserve. Available at: http://www.epa.gov/lmop/partners/profiles/riverviewlandpreserve.html (accessed September 23, 2011).

Financial Markets Center (2000) Uncivil service: Pension rebellion stirs the Fed. *FOMC Alert*, 4 (5), 1–9.

Frieden, A. and Sagalyn, L. (1989) *Downtown, Inc.*, MIT Press, Boston.

Galbraith, J. (2008) *Predator State: How Conservatives Abandoned the Free Market and Why Liberals Should Too*, The Free Press, New York.
Gertner, J. (2009) Getting Up To Speed. *New York Times* (June 14). Available at: http://www.nytimes.com/2009/06/14/magazine/14Train-t.html?pagewanted=print (accessed September 21, 2011).
Gilbert, R. and Perl, A. (2008) *Transport Revolutions: Moving People and Freight Without Oil*, Earthscan, London.
Glasgow Electric Plant Board (2007) FAQ. http://www.glasgowepb.net/faq.html (accessed September 21, 2011).
Guinan, J. (2003) Interview of Mary Abernathy of New Community Corporation, August 26. National Center for Economic & Security Alternatives, Washington DC.
Heard, R. and Sibert, J. (2000) *Growing New Businesses with Seed and Venture Capital: State Experiences and Options*, National Governors Association, Washington, DC.
Hobhouse, L.T. (1994) *Liberalism and Other Writings*, Cambridge University Press, Cambridge.
Howard, T., Dubb, S. and Alperovitz, G. (2009) Help Wanted: Green Businesses Seek Worker-Owners. Walk to Work. Good Benefits. *Yes! Magazine* (Summer issue), pp. 44–45.
Kesmodel, D. (2002) United Holds Loan Talks With Feds. *Rocky Mountain News* (April 13), p. C1.
Lifsher, M. (2007) Study Touts CalPERS' Benefit to Economy. *Los Angeles Times* (Sept. 19). Available at: http://articles.latimes.com/2007/09/19/business/fi-calpers19 (accessed September 21, 2011).
Logue, J. and Yates, J. (2001) *The Real World of Employee Ownership*, ILR Press, Ithaca, NY.
Massarsky, C. and Beinhacker, S. (2002) Enterprising nonprofits: Revenue generation in the nonprofit sector. Yale School of Management – The Goldman Sachs Foundation Partnership on Nonprofit Ventures. Available at: http://www.ventures.yale.edu/docs/Enterprising_-Nonprofits.pdf (accessed May 12, 2008).
Moore, J.D. (1997) Denver role model. *Modern Healthcare*, 27 (15), 68.
National Center for Employee Ownership (2011) A Statistical Profile of Employee Ownership. Available at: www.nceo.org/main/article.php/id/2/ (accessed September 21, 2011).
National Congress for Community Economic Development (2006) *Reaching New Heights: Trends and Achievements of Community-Based Development Organizations*, NCCED, Washington, DC.
Nesbitt, S. (2001) The "CalPERS Effect" on Targeted Company Share Prices. *Directorship*, 27 (5), 1–3.
Nuzum, R., McCarthy, D., Gauthier, A. and Beck, C. (2007) *Denver Health: A High-Performance Public Health System*, The Commonwealth Fund, New York.
Pioneer Human Services (2005) *2004 Annual Report*, Seattle: WA: Pioneer Human Services.
Rawls, J. (1971) *A Theory of Justice*, Harvard University Press, Cambridge, MA.
Reich, R. and Donahue, J. (1985) *New Deals: The Chrysler Revival and the American System*, Times Books, New York.
Rusch, K. (2001) *The Emerging New Society*, The Democracy Collaborative, College Park, MD.
Saez, Emmanuel, T. Piketty, and T. Atkinson (2009) "Top Incomes in the Long Run of History" NBER Working Paper No. 15408, October.
Sandler, L. (2009) Super Steel Could Build Trains without Jeopardizing Contracts. *Journal Sentinel* (Aug. 7).
Simon, H. (2000) Public administration in today's organizations and market. *PS: Political Science and Politics*, 33 (4).
Sirianni, C. and Friedland, L. (2001) *Civic Innovation in America*, University of California Press, Berkeley.

Solow, R. (1957) Technical change and the aggregate production function. *Review of Economics and Statistics* 39 (3).

Solow, R. (1987) Nobel Prize lecture. Available at: http://nobelprize.org/nobel_prizes/economics/laureates/1987/solow-lecture.html (accessed September 21, 2011).

Thrift Savings Plan (2008) *Thrift Savings Plan Highlights*, January–February. Available at: http://www.tsp.gov/forms/highlights/high08a.pdf (accessed September 21, 2011).

US Census Bureau (2003) 2002 Statistical Abstract of the United States, US Bureau of the Census, Washington, DC.

US Department of Transportation (2009) President Obama, Vice President Biden, Secretary LaHood call for US high-speed passenger trains. Available at: http://www.dot.gov/affairs/dot5109.htm (accessed September 24, 2011).

US Railcar (2009) *High-Speed Rail in the United States: Opportunities and Challenges*, US Railcar LLC, Columbus, OH.

USW News (2009) Steelworkers Form Collaboration with Mondragon, the World's Largest Worker-Owned Cooperative. Available at: http://www.usw.org/media_center/releases_advisories?id=0234 (accessed September 21, 2011).

Warsh, D. (2006) *Knowledge and the Wealth of Nations: A Story of Economic Discovery*, Norton, New York.

Williamson, T., Imbroscio, D. and Alperovitz, G. (2002) *Making a Place for Community: Local Democracy in a Global Era*, Routledge, New York.

Wilson, W. (1913) *The New Freedom: A Call For the Emancipation of the Generous Energies of a People*, Doubleday, Page and Company, New York.

Wirtz, R. (2007) Employee Ownership: Economic Miracle or ESOPs Fable? *The Region* (June), Federal Reserve Bank of Minneapolis, Minneapolis.

Wisconsin Legislative Audit Bureau (2002) An Audit of the State Life Insurance Fund. Report 02-18 (November). Available at: http://www.legis.state.wi.us/lab/PastReportsByDate.htm (accessed September 21, 2011).

W.L. Gore and Associates (2011) About Gore. Available at: http://www.gore.com/en_xx/aboutus/index.html (accessed September 21, 2011).

Wong, W. (2003) US Airways Makes Cuts And Leave Bankruptcy. *New York Times* (Apr. 1), p. C3.

Yates, J. (2009) The Evergreen Cooperative initiative: Can "anchor institutions" help revitalize declining neighborhoods by buying from local cooperatives? 23rd Annual Ohio Employee Ownership Conference. Ohio Employee Ownership Center, Kent State University, pp. 44–47.

14

Is Property-Owning Democracy a Politically Viable Aspiration?

Thad Williamson

At the start of this volume, Simone Chambers (Chapter 1) provided a rich discussion of the ambiguous politics of John Rawls. Chambers shows how Rawls's preferred set of economic arrangements implied a systemic critique of modern capitalism and its incompatibility with socially just institutions and policies. Succeeding chapters in Part One explored the idea of "property-owning democracy" (POD) from a variety of angles, including its historic roots, its philosophical justification, and the connections between Rawlsian property-owning democracy and republicanism. Parts Two and Three have taken up the political economy of property-owning democracy, with the aim of specifying in some detail what it might look like and what sorts of policies and institutional developments might help bring it into being, as well as the aim of critically assessing what a property-owning democracy might and might not accomplish. In this closing chapter, we turn full circle by once again returning to the question of *politics* in a more explicit way. In this chapter I pose the question of whether it is possible to imagine a politics of property-owning democracy that did not compromise the essentially radical nature of the idea yet also might, over the medium and long term, prove politically viable in a nation like the United States with its many distinct strands of conservative and neoliberal political opinion and its formidable power structure (i.e., corporate and financial economic and political power, as well as the political influence of the rich, the super-rich, and their ideological compatriots.) The answer to that question may, of course, well prove to be "no." This chapter aims to make the case for a more positive (albeit uncertain) answer to that question.

The thrust of my argument is this: property-owning democracy is a quite distinct ideal from welfare state liberalism, just as late-nineteenth-century American populism was a quite distinct ideal from middle-class progressivism (Goodwyn, 1976). Consequently, it is a mistake, or at least premature, to draw strong conclusions from the weakness of American liberalism over the past generation about the future prospects of a form of populist or radical politics that is both (a) explicitly redistributionist and (b) argues not for redistribution from the middle and upper-middle classes to the poor

---

Property-Owning Democracy: Rawls and Beyond, First Edition. Edited by Martin O'Neill and Thad Williamson.
© 2012 Blackwell Publishing Ltd. Published 2012 by Blackwell Publishing Ltd.

via taxation, but for redistribution of access to and control over wealth and capital from the *very* rich to almost everyone else. Further, it is also a mistake to presume that developing a substantive politics of property-owning democracy requires, in the first instance, an unlikely revival of trade unions or other building blocks of traditional social democratic politics, or an unlikely embrace by democratic publics of full-bore Rawlsian egalitarian principles. Acceptance of the basic (negative) idea that our economic and political life ought not be dominated by a narrow self-serving elite, and the basic (positive) idea that extremely wealthy countries ought to provide sufficient resources to each citizen to allow them to construct and carry out a meaningful life plan, without being excessively burdened or motivated by economic necessity, is sufficient to get the idea of property-owning democracy off the ground. What proportion of Americans (or citizens in other advanced nations) might be receptive to arguments for these ideas in practical form cannot be known in advance of a serious effort to forward them.[1]

Why a Politics of Property-Owning Democracy Is Needed

We begin by making a brief detour into contemporary political realities, with the aim of showing *why* a politics of property-owning democracy is so sorely needed. The election of Barack Obama as President in 2008 triggered a wave of optimism in the United States (and elsewhere) about the possibility of serious political change in the USA and a reversal of a 30-year drift toward greater income and wealth inequality and increased corporate power. These long-term trends have taken the United States very, very far away from the idea of a society characterized by equal political liberties, substantive equality of opportunity, and moderate, ethically justifiable inequalities. Not only did Obama run and win on what (relative to American politics) was a plainly progressive agenda, he took office in the midst of the worst economic crisis seen in America since the 1930s.

Soon after being elected, however, Obama enlisted big-name economic advisors with experience from the Clinton presidency – especially former Treasury Secretary Lawrence Summers and his protégé Timothy Geithner – to lead his own economic team. Both men had deep ties to Wall Street as well as a long record of supporting neoliberal, free-market policies of the kind that helped spawn the economic crisis. In office as Obama's Treasury Secretary, Geithner crafted a "bailout" plan for financial institutions that offered massive, publicly guaranteed incentives to the private financial sector to buy up bad loans accumulated by banks, eschewing the more straightforward and less risky option of simply nationalizing the banks, firing management, and cleaning away the bad assets (Kuttner, 2010; Suskind, 2011).

Equally significant, Obama appointed a task force composed primarily of financial experts to tackle the crisis in the automobile industry and force General Motors (GM) and Chrysler to either declare bankruptcy or come up with an acceptable business plan, in exchange for government loans. The resulting bankruptcy and subsequent restructuring of General Motors, which saw the federal government take a majority stake in the company, took as its premise the reduction of industrial jobs and the scaling back of production; indeed, part of the revised strategy for the "new" GM involved the closing of 14 (of 47) plants in the United States, increasing the proportion of cars built for the

US market in low-wage countries such as Mexico, and extracting severe concessions from labor, most notably a two-tier wage structure in which new workers are hired at much lower wages than existing workers. The priority has been to restore GM to profitability as quickly as possible so as to make the firm attractive to a new private buyer (Rattner, 2010). Alternative approaches that prioritized preserving jobs and communities over the companies' financial profits, or that connected the idle productive facilities of GM to the need to build mass transit equipment and other "green" products were rejected, if they were contemplated at all by decision makers. (The account of Rattner, 2010, suggests they were not.) The result is that a "progressive" President, strongly supported by organized labor, in effect used public money to help a failed, incompetently managed company shut down more production and eliminate more jobs in order to restore corporate viability. GM issued an initial public offering in shares in November 2010, and the federal government was expected to sell its remaining stake by the end of 2011.

Taken on its own terms, analysts such as Robert Kuttner view the GM takeover as a good example of the sort of approach government should have taken with the large financial institutions – for instance, using the power of government to force out bad management. Indeed, optimistic appraisals of both the GM and even the TARP (Troubled Asset Relief Program) interventions might point to it as an example of the capacity of government to take public stakes in private institutions with beneficial consequences (the American economy did stabilize, and cars sold by GM increased from 2009 to 2010). But from a perspective critical of the concentration of economic power in the United States, and critical of the traditional capitalist mode of production, these interventions represent a major missed opportunity.

Indeed, Obama's approach to the economic crisis – conceptualizing the problem as how to preserve traditional capitalist arrangements – is the almost-inevitable consequence of the lack of a well-articulated, coherent alternative vision of the post-crisis political economy in which markets play a subordinate and not a leading role. Simply put, progressive political forces have lacked a compelling account of how the political economy should be organized so as to best realize liberal, democratic, and egalitarian values. Most mainstream progressive politicians in the United States take the structure of the current political economy for granted, and speak in terms of ways to enhance opportunity and ease social pain within the current system. In short, mainstream liberal and progressive politicians practice (at best) a politics of what Rawls would term welfare state capitalism. To be fair, they do so in a political climate which is often hostile to even minimal norms of redistribution or any effort to question the distribution of society's wealth and resources. But the recent financial and economic crisis demonstrates both the limitations of liberalism and why having a much better developed vision of the alternative to which the society should aspire is a political necessity if those limitations are to be overcome.

For example, a progressive governing regime that had committed itself to the goal of forging a property-owning democracy could have approached the automobile industry bailout with a quite different set of priorities. From the standpoint of property-owning democracy, there is no inherent moral value in having a large automobile producer generate profits that flow to a (relatively) small group of private investors. There is, however, a moral value to preserving jobs and communities. Moreover, there is a moral value in broadening ownership of productive assets and in employees having democratic control over the companies for which they work. Both sorts of considerations point strongly in the direction of using public funding either to buy the companies outright on behalf of the public for the long term, or to reestablish the companies as employee-owned enterprises. Additional steps likely would have been required to make such re-formed companies viable over the long term (such as assistance in converting plants from car production to mass transit vehicles). The important point is that a governing party motivated by the ideal of property-owning democracy would have seen the failures of the auto industry as an opportunity to restructure ownership in a more democratic fashion, not an occasion to do whatever is required to restore traditional capitalist ownership patterns (Williamson, Dubb, and Alperovitz, 2010).

This excursus into contemporary politics is intended to illustrate one crucial point: there is tremendous political significance in whether or not progressive governing parties are guided by a substantive conception of the kind of society and kind of political economy they intend to build. Where such a conception is lacking, the default assumption that a capitalist political economy is desirable and inevitable will remain unchallenged and play a key role driving crucial policy decisions. As many authors have noted, since the collapse of "actually existing socialism" left parties throughout the West have generally failed to offer a plausible and attractive social ideal that represents a genuine alternative to (as opposed to mild improvement within) capitalism and capitalist social relations. The difficulty is more severe in the United States in that the Democratic Party – the party purporting to represent workers – has *never* offered or embraced such an alternative, instead advocating for at best a more extensive welfare state. Indeed, during the 1980s and 1990s the "centrists" dominating party leadership – including most especially Bill Clinton – embraced the neoliberal agenda, especially on issues of trade, financial deregulation, and "welfare reform."

Property-Owning Democracy and Public Opinion

It is in this context that Rawls's vague but suggestive discussion of property-owning democracy is of particular *political* interest. In my view, if Rawls's original intent in *A Theory of Justice* was to articulate and argue for a set of philosophical principles capable of becoming the consensus view undergirding political debate in a country such as the United States, his project has clearly failed (see Chambers, Chapter 1). Even among relatively egalitarian thinkers, there is no consensus on the philosophical content of social justice, and in the wider political arena, it is clear that public opinion in America strongly opposes key features of Rawls's thought, including especially his rejection of pre-institutional moral desert and his commitment to the difference principle.

But as Joshua Cohen (2003) and many others have observed, the aspiration to build a consensus on well-defined principles of social justice within the context of a democratic society was always a flawed enterprise, based on an inappropriate application of norms within academic philosophy (the assumption that in principle better arguments can be identified and come to be widely accepted) to the practical world of politics. The more relevant question is whether it is possible to establish a conception of both broad principles of justice *and* measures to implement those principles capable of winning and maintaining majoritarian support in actually existing democratic societies. This means shifting the terms of debate from philosophical to political terrain, and from ideal to nonideal theory. Posing the question this way abandons any aspiration to consensus, and admits from the outset that many persons and organizations will oppose both the institutional proposals and their normative rationales.

This does not mean that ideal theory is a useless enterprise – I concur with Ingrid Robeyns's assessment (2008) that ideal theory can play a modest but vital role in indicating the broad direction in which society should move. It also does not mean that progressive political actors should refine their proposals to accord with the current views on distributive justice of the "median voter" in actually existing capitalist societies. It does mean, however, that proposals should take seriously public opinion on these matters, in just this sense: far-reaching institutional proposals must be built on moral principles that *could* plausibly be understood and embraced by a stable political majority.

What implications does that requirement have in the context of the United States (and the other "advanced" industrialized countries)? I would suggest that there is in fact widespread public support for two legs of Rawls's three-legged distributive justice stool: the principle of substantive equal opportunity, and the principle of equal political liberty. The fact that life chances are so strongly shaped by the quality of education one receives and the sort of neighborhood one happens to live in strikes many Americans as fundamentally unfair (Ryan, 2010). Thoughtful conservatives are sensitive to this criticism, which is why they often contest empirical claims about the intergenerational transmission of class status, and why many claim that voucher programs and other market-based approaches to public education are the best way to improving struggling urban schools. There is no question that a great many citizens are misinformed about the degree to which class position is influenced by initial starting points, and that many affluent persons in particular lack an accurate understanding of the reality of poverty, both as a sociological fact and as a lived human experience. But I would contend that even in the United States, a stable majority of citizens would endorse the core Rawlsian principle that one's initial socioeconomic position should not have a major influence upon long-term life chances.[2] Almost no one in American public life defends explicitly the view that we *ought* to have a social system characterized by sharp class distinctions in power and resources, and that one's class position *ought* to be primarily a function of who your parents are or were.

Similarly, almost no one in American public life explicitly endorses the view that large corporations *ought* to have more political influence than ordinary citizens, or that the views of persons with greater income and wealth should have more sway over political outcomes than the views of the less well endowed. To be sure, many conservatives argue that huge inequalities in political influence are an inevitable consequence of "free speech," and that ability to use as many resources of one's own to influence politics is a fundamental freedom for both individuals *and* corporations that trumps any concern about maintaining political equality. In *Citizens United v. Federal Election Commission*, the current conservative majority on the Supreme Court endorsed the (widely unpopular) view that corporate political speech must receive the same protection as individual political speech. This is an example where a society-wide consensus on a substantive principle of justice is not likely to be reached. But it is also an example in which the contradiction between public opinion (generally wary of corporate political power) and actual institutional practices creates the potential for future reform efforts.

Indeed, it is a significant fact that large proportions of Americans believe government is currently influenced much too heavily by the rich and well connected and by corporations.[3] These data suggest that a stable political majority could in fact be forged that endorsed the Rawlsian idea that we should aspire to build a society in which neither the rich nor powerful corporations are able routinely to secure policy and administrative outcomes favorable to their interests. To be sure, arguably that majority has not yet been mobilized – for instance, while there was much public resentment in the United States toward bank executives who claimed bonuses after their institutions were bailed out by the federal government, that resentment did not translate into a coherent political force capable of altering the terms and priorities of the various federal bailouts of 2008 and 2009. But arguments from the basis of a concern for equal political liberty have a large potential audience in the United States.

It is much less plausible, however, to suppose that a stable political majority could endorse the difference principle itself. Most Americans believe that moral desert (in what Rawls would term the pre-institutional sense) should be a relevant consideration in determining how resources are distributed to individuals. Politically efficacious arguments for reducing inequality of *outcome* must recognize that fact. Allowing desert back into the picture does not mean sanctioning unlimited inequality of outcome, however; on the contrary, powerful arguments for reducing existing inequalities on the basis (in part) of a concept of desert are available. At the top end of the spectrum, Gar Alperovitz and Lew Daly have persuasively argued that the marginal contribution made to individual capitalists, entrepreneurs, and inventors in our knowledge economy is slight compared to the much larger contribution of humanity's collected accumulation of knowledge (Alperovitz and Daly, 2008). At the other end of the scale, David Miller (1999) and others note the widespread popular belief that persons of modest means who work ought to be afforded a decent living and not live in constant fear of losing one's livelihood, health care, housing, and so on; the implicit claim is that workers *deserve* a raise – that is, more than the market currently awards them. Benjamin Page and Lawrence Jacobs thus report that the median respondent in a 2007 survey of 608 Americans favored wage increases of 10–25% for sales clerks, skilled and unskilled factory workers, small shop owners, and even doctors, but lower salaries for heart surgeons and corporate CEOs (Page and Jacobs, 2009, p. 42).

There is also good reason to believe that a stable majority could endorse the idea of providing a minimal social baseline on the basis of need, as well as social insurance to compensate for harms caused by events out of one's control (such as job loss and accidents). Page and Jacobs find that 67% of Americans support government-provided jobs for the unemployed, 73% favor government-backed universal health coverage, 68% believe government "must see that no one is without food, clothing, or shelter," 76% support a minimum wage high enough to lift a family out of poverty, and 87% support government spending "whatever is necessary to ensure that all children have really good public schools they can go to" (Page and Jacobs, 2009, pp. 58–72, 91–92). Page and Jacobs also find that majorities of Republicans share these views (but for a discussion of how conservative political views impact attitudes toward distributive justice, see Bartels, 2009). Importantly, from the standpoint of property-owning democracy, majorities of Americans also support the views that "Our government should redistribute wealth by heavy taxes on the rich" (favored by 56%) and that estates larger than $100 million ought to be taxed at a rate of at least 25% (favored by 60%).

These findings suggest that public opinion as such is not the principal obstacle to a politics aimed explicitly at reducing severe inequalities. Taken together, it is plausible to believe a stable political majority in the United States could endorse the principles of substantive equality of opportunity, substantive political equality, and modifying market-generated inequalities to reflect considerations of perceived desert (in particular people getting less than what they are held to deserve) and human need. Those principles are sufficient to undergird a strong argument that the top 1% ought not control nearly so large a proportion of society's wealth as at the present, and that we should move in the direction of something like property-owning democracy. Further agreement on the proposition that society's inequalities ought to be organized so as to benefit the least well off is *not* required to make the judgment that the inequalities characteristic of contemporary capitalism violate *widely shared values*, and that we should seek a systemic alternative. To be sure, this conclusion will not be obvious to many Americans: advocates for property-owning democracy must argue for both the idea and its necessity. The point here is that they may do so by arguing from shared values that are by no means alien to American political culture. Indeed, the most pressing political task is precisely to describe a coherent, systemic alternative that has a fighting chance of gaining the endorsement of a stable political majority within the foreseeable future.

Property-Owning Democracy Versus the Welfare State, Revisited

Close readers of this volume will note a tension between my argument here – that property-owning democracy may be a viable political project in a country like the United States *even if* we assume most Americans will reject the difference principle as an appropriate vantage point to evaluate our institutions for the foreseeable future – and the argument of Martin O'Neill in Chapter 4, where O'Neill contends that the difference principle offers the most decisive reason for favoring property-owning democracy over "welfare state capitalism." If one accepts O'Neill's argument, the question may arise: why should we be concerned with property-owning democracy if its underlying normative basis is a principle of justice that most citizens reject, or at least find strange and unfamiliar?

In my view, the answer to that question depends on what society one is talking about, the strength of the welfare state and its underlying social base in a particular country, as well as the ideological, cultural, and historical context being considered. In nations with highly developed welfare states, strong labor unions, strong norms about distributive justice, and relatively effective mechanisms for insulating money from politics, then it may make little sense for progressive political forces to focus effort on creating a property-owning democracy simply for the sake of equal political liberty and equal opportunity, taken alone. The United States at present is certainly not such a country. Simply put, its patchy welfare state does too little to alleviate poverty and bolster economic security (Hacker, 2008); millions of working families even if employed face lifetimes of low security and low power at work, as well as low wages (Greenhouse, 2008; Wright and Rogers, 2010); and politics from the local to national levels are typically dominated by powerful economic interests. Indeed, the complacent pluralism of mainstream American political science has given way to increasingly alarmed assessments from leading scholars about the inability of American politics to contain sharply rising income and wealth inequalities since the 1970s (Jacobs and Skocpol, 2007; Bartels, 2009). More often, in fact, public policy in recent years has acted to exacerbate inequality (Hacker and Pierson, 2010). Even the steps taken by the Obama administration to extend health care coverage utterly failed to challenge the existing political economy of health insurance in the United States: Obama's political strategy was to buy off those private interests likely to be most wary of a health care bill (i.e., the pharmaceutical industry), at a heavy cost to the public interest (Taibbi, 2010; Suskind, 2011; but for a more positive assessment see Jacobs and Skocpol, 2010).

In this context, the politically relevant question is not whether a well-designed property-owning democracy might do a better job than a strong welfare state in realizing the difference principle (though I concur with O'Neill's judgment that it would). Rather, the politically relevant question is whether a politics of property-owning democracy might emerge that would be a more powerful vehicle for realizing equal opportunity and political equality than existing forms of liberal, reformist politics. (Indeed, nothing in O'Neill's argument, which is concerned with the *possibility* of realizing these principles under more familiar forms of capitalism, speaks against this political conclusion that a politics of property-owning democracy would in practice be more conducive to these goals.) In the context of the United States, I concur with Gar Alperovitz's judgment (2004; see also Chapter 13) that traditional social democratic-type politics faces too many obstacles – the large-scale and federalist structure of the country (allowing internal capital mobility), the nation's racial history, weak and declining organized labor, the sheer political muscle of financial and corporate interests – to achieve its stated goals, even when such goals are modest. Philosophical debate over the morality of the difference principle is, except in a very indirect way, essentially irrelevant to the practical politics of the United States at this moment in history. The practical question in the USA is whether and how a politics capable of realizing values that are widely shared in the political culture but persistently violated in practice might emerge in response to long-term negative trends and the evident weakness of conventional liberal and progressive remedies. This way of characterizing the problem may not, of course, apply to all advanced capitalist countries, especially those with strong welfare states and where organized labor remains quite strong.

The Viability of Property-Owning Democracy

One dimension upon which an alternative must be plausible is its normative basis. An alternative must be explainable and defensible with reference to normative values that are widely (not necessarily universally) shared. If the argumentation above is correct, then property-owning democracy meets this criterion, insofar as it appeals primarily to the values of substantive equality of opportunity and of equal political liberty. Strong arguments for widely dispersing property and breaking up large inheritances can be anchored in the view that society should not consist of intergenerationally transmitted social classes and that the most economically privileged members of the society should not control the political system.

But this alone does not show that property-owning democracy is a politically viable project. Attention must be paid to three other dimensions of viability: whether the proposal is in fact internally coherent and plausibly functional; whether the proposal accords with the "culture and history" of a given country's self-understanding; and finally, whether the proposal is capable of attracting constituencies who will fight in the political arena on its behalf. This chapter will set aside the (critical) question about the internal coherence of property-owning democracy, and instead focus on these last two questions.

Rawls himself called attention to questions of culture and history as potentially decisive in judging whether property-owning democracy is better suited than democratic market socialism to fulfill the principles of justice in a given situation. The strong implication is that in countries like the United States with a weak tradition of socialist politics and strong cultural fascination with entrepreneurship, property-owning democracy may be appealing in ways that any form of "socialism" cannot be.

There is some justification for this inference. To argue for property-owning democracy does not require that one challenge the institution of property, the ideal of the market, or the virtues of entrepreneurship. Nor does it require one to make an argument on behalf of the necessity of democratic social planning. Instead, the argument can be framed colloquially in terms of ideas like "private property is such a good idea, that everyone should have some," "everyone should have a chance to make something of themselves," and "everyone should have the independence that property affords." Indeed, support for broadening ownership of property has often been voiced by conservatives in the United States, including Ronald Reagan (1987), who praised employee ownership of enterprise as the next phase in the development of capitalism and "the path that befits a free people." In this sense, property-owning democracy seems a good fit for a nation of what Page and Jacobs (2009) call "conservative egalitarians."

It is far too simple to leave the question at this, however. First, it is important not to understate the degree to which the property-owning democracy idea challenges entrenched cultural norms in the United States. Consider the surprising rehabilitation of the word "socialism" in the American political lexicon since the fall of 2008, when Republican activists began describing Barack Obama's very modest proposals for increasing taxes slightly on the wealthiest households as "socialist." While these attacks failed to sway moderate voters, they did force Obama to state that he was not a socialist and pledge his support for capitalism. On the one hand, this episode seems to confirm the view that "socialism" remains a toxic label in American politics and that "property-owning democracy" is a better rhetorical vehicle for arguing for redistribution. On the other hand, the episode also makes clear that the right wing in the United States will vociferously attack *any* substantive proposal for redistribution of wealth or income – especially proposals of the scale needed to give property-owning democracy substance.

The key point is that advocates of property-owning democracy in the United States would be quite wrong to think that using that term will spare them from being labeled as socialists and otherwise red-baited by conservative activists. One unanswered question, then, is whether such attacks would succeed in dissuading moderates or even some liberals from taking property-owning democracy seriously. Would the prospect of such attacks by vociferous conservatives cause liberal politicians to retreat from embracing property-owning democracy? If moderates and liberals can be scared off by charges of being "socialist" from embracing quite substantial redistribution of assets, then prospects for property-owning democracy attaining support from a politically stable majority are bleak indeed. At a minimum, both the general public and progressive political leaders will have to develop a far more nuanced understanding of the differences between command (Soviet-style) socialism, market socialism, property-owning democracy, welfare state capitalism, and laissez-faire capitalism than is characteristic of most public debates.[4]

To successfully develop that understanding will require that property-owning democracy be clearly defined and given institutional and policy substance. In its essence, property-owning democracy consists of two distinctive planks: systematically redistributing wealth away from the top 1% (or top 0.1%) of households, and establishing mechanisms by which each household in the United States could come to control meaningful assets. Property-owning democracy (on Rawls's conception) also must involve expanded provision of certain public goods (especially universal health care) via familiar welfare state mechanisms, but it is the emphasis on altering who holds wealth that makes property-owning democracy distinctive. Another way to assess the question of the long-term political viability of property-owning democracy, then, is to ask whether we could imagine the public supporting (a) concrete proposals to expand wealth ownership and (b) serious proposals to redistribute wealth away from the very top.

Elsewhere I have argued that a property-owning democracy should aim to provide all households with (a) stable ownership of real property (i.e., housing), (b) a reserve of cash assets, and (c) a meaningful share of productive assets (Williamson, 2009; see also Chapter 11 in this volume). I have further suggested that if the worst-off households in the United States had on average roughly $100,000 in net assets nested in some combination of these three kinds of wealth, it would represent an enormous improvement in welfare of these households and also be an enormous step toward realizing the values of equality of opportunity and equal political liberty.

Already there are significant policy precedents for "asset development" in all three of these areas (see Sherraden, 2005; Sodha, Chapter 12 in this volume). Similarly, policies to nurture community development corporations, employee-owned firms, cooperatives and other forms of place-based enterprise are widespread and in most cases uncontroversial, especially in distressed communities (Williamson, Imbroscio and Alperovitz, 2002; Alperovitz, Chapter 13 in this volume). Incremental policy steps in the direction of providing citizens greater assets *are* politically attainable in the United States at present, so long as they are relatively small in scale and do not involve challenging politically powerful constituencies. The political difficulty for advocates of property-owning democracy is not with the idea that it is desirable for ownership to be more widespread or the idea that government should pursue "asset-based" social policies or provide support to community-rooted, democratically organized firms. Rather, the greatest obstacles lie in (a) bringing such policies to sufficient scale to have a large impact on the distribution of assets and (b) undertaking redistribution of narrowly held assets so as to make such a larger-scale asset-building initiative possible.

The Core Issue: The Morality of Large-Scale Taxation of the Very Rich

Indeed, the most severe difficulty facing serious property-owning democracy proposals is likely to revolve around the morality of dramatically increasing taxation of wealth and inheritances of the rich and super-rich. Since the 1990s, conservative activists have waged a surprisingly effective campaign against the estate tax, claiming it amounts to a "double tax" or a "death tax." They also crafted a narrative claiming that family farmers and small business owners were being forced to sell by the tax, even though in reality the tax affects only a tiny minority of households. At bottom, the most important conservative argument against the estate tax is the moral claim that individuals have the right to pass on accumulated wealth to whoever they wish, and that restrictions on this right amount to an unjustified curtailment of liberty.

As political scientists Michael Graetz and Ian Shapiro (2005) pointed out, responses to this argument from most congressional Democrats focused on pragmatics rather than principle: Democratic leaders claimed that the federal coffers could not afford a tax reduction on the richest Americans. But this response falls short because it does not meet the moral issue at stake. Advocates for property-owning democracy must advance their own moral argument for the morality of redistributing accumulated wealth in order to build a consensus on behalf of not just existing taxes on accumulated wealth but dramatically increasing such taxes over time. In addition, they should craft proposals for increased taxation in ways that isolate and target the most extreme concentrations of wealth amongst the top 0.1% of households.

Four kinds of moral argument can be made on behalf of wealth distribution of this kind – two of which challenge the claim that individuals have an untrammeled right to control and dispose of property, one which appeals to quasi-utilitarian principles, and one which appeals to the kind of society that substantial redistribution for the sake of a property-owning democracy would produce.

The first argument straightforwardly holds that property rights are socially constructed, and that individual claims to wealth and income come only in the context of a set of social rules which have been established to regulate property (Murphy and Nagel, 2002). This is a quintessentially Rawlsian argument, and one that would be endorsed by almost all nonlibertarian political philosophers. But it runs counter to the understanding of many American conservatives (and libertarians), who adhere to a natural rights understanding of property in which individuals have strong claims to whatever property they happen to hold upon which the state cannot intrude. Here again is a point where universal consensus on a crucial principle of justice is impossible, at least in the American context. Further, it is not entirely clear that the Rawlsian understanding of property – which challenges the common view that citizens have a moral right to their pre-tax income and wealth – can in fact secure support of a stable majority in the United States. Ideological battle on this point is likely to be fierce, should property-owning democracy in fact gain political headway in coming years.

A second sort of argument more specifically challenges the prerogatives of extremely wealthy households by arguing that modern fortunes made by persons such as Bill Gates owe more to our inherited accumulation of knowledge than to individual achievement. The claim here is not simply (as Rawls would agree) that society provides the institutional framework in which fortunes can be generated, and hence society should have a claim on those fortunes; it is that wealth creation relies on the steady accumulation of knowledge and technical advances, to which the entire society contributes. The innovations Bill Gates helped spawn and the money he subsequently made lie less to his own brilliance and effort than to the steady accumulation of knowledge about computers over the course of the twentieth century (much of it directly funded by the US government). Contrary to the impression left by heroic portrayals of Gates and similar figures, there are strong reasons to believe that the personal computer explosion and the networking revolution would have taken place even without the existence of Gates and Microsoft; the specific history and timing may have been different, but the long-run outcome would have been the same. This argument, articulated in detail by Gar Alperovitz and Lew Daly, is of potential interest to advocates of property-owning democracy because rather than arguing that the question of "desert" is simply immaterial to who should get what, it challenges desert-based explanations for the accumulation of enormous fortunes on their own terms. If we truly believe that individuals should only be rewarded according to their contributions, then it is quite clear that society should have a very substantial claim on the private fortunes generated by, for instance, the computing revolution, in view of society's essential contribution to that revolution (Alperovitz and Daly, 2008).

The remaining moral arguments on behalf of breaking up large estates are consequentialist in nature. The claim that redistributing wealth away from those now living extraordinarily exorbitant lifestyles so as to underwrite the distribution of a meaningful share of assets to the millions of households with few if any net assets would generate a huge net increase in aggregate welfare is highly plausible – and hence can be defended on not only egalitarian but utility-maximizing grounds.

Equally important, advocates of dispersal of wealth can and should provide an attractive, persuasive account of the kind of society that large-scale wealth distribution would make possible. This means calling attention not just to the shares of wealth that poor and middle-income households would possess under a full-blown property-owning democracy, but to the moral consequences of such a shift: namely, a society in which economic security and the freedom to make truly independent choices about how one will live one's life would be near-universal, not the domain of a small minority. Closely related, advocates for wealth distribution will want (and often need) to invoke a conception of community, in three senses: first, by insisting that we share a common fate with fellow citizens, and hence that we should structure our institutions on a principle of social inclusion and overturning invidious class distinctions; second, by clearly pitting the establishment of universal mechanisms for ensuring access to property and wealth in opposition to the narrow control of property by a small segment of the society; and third, by making a claim about the meaning of the nation's cultural ideals, and asserting that *we* are the kind of nation that takes fairness and liberty seriously enough to be sure everyone has a piece of the pie and a legitimate opportunity. The establishment of a system of universal assets holdings in the United States on anything like the scale envisioned in Chapter 11 would itself have profound long-term effects on what it means to be an "American," as it would on any other nation that adopted such a program.[5]

As historian Ben Jackson shows, historically successful appeals by radical and egalitarian politicians in the USA and the UK have often employed such rhetorical strategies, by contrasting the good of the community with the narrow interests of the few, and claiming that egalitarian proposals "expressed the traditions, values, and interests of their communities; that among other things, redistribution expressed the fairness and solidarity of the national character" (Jackson, 2009, p. 239). To paraphrase Franklin D. Roosevelt's appeals on behalf of the New Deal, a practical politics of property-owning democracy must claim that its adoption would lead to a "happier, safer, more American America" (quoted in Jackson, 2009, p. 240). The near-disappearance of such language from mainstream American political discourse (the failed presidential campaign of John Edwards was a partial exception) speaks in my judgment more to the capture of both political parties in the United States by corporate-oriented elites rather than to lack of public receptiveness to such a message. As Jackson reminds us, too, citing statistics (however astonishing), let alone formal philosophical argumentation, is rarely if ever in itself adequate as a political strategy; stories need to be told. In the case of property-owning democracy the stories to be told involve not just the traditional contrast between the exorbitant, wasteful lifestyles of the idle super-wealthy and the struggles and deprivation of the poor, but the contrast between the kinds of constraints ordinary working-, lower-middle, and middle-class citizens now face as they seek to make their way in the world and the opportunities that would be opened up by property-owning democracy. Advocates for property-owning democracy must craft stories about POD both as a vehicle for liberation from crushing financial pressures and as a mechanism for individuals to become more truly themselves. Advocates for POD must then in turn link those individual narratives to a collective story about "America becoming more American."

Are these arguments and appeals, either alone or taken together, capable of legitimating the idea of large-scale transfer of wealth from the top 0.5% or top 0.1% in order to finance universal assets holdings? To reiterate, the question is not whether these arguments will face fierce opposition – they will. The question is whether a stable political majority *could* eventually endorse these ideas. That question cannot be answered simply with references to Americans' current preferences and ideas about taxation, wealth, and capitalism. As suggested already, most Americans and elected officials lack the kind of nuanced understanding of different possible political-economic systems which Rawls outlines, and liberals and progressives in the United States have in recent decades only rarely made explicitly moral critiques of wealth inequality a central theme. If property-owning democracy and its associated proposals are to have viability, they must be strenuously argued for in the political arena.

This brings us to the fourth relevant consideration regarding POD's political plausibility – whether concrete political actors willing to struggle on its behalf can be identified. Advocates for property-owning democracy necessarily must engage in what we might term (borrowing a phrase from Gramsci) a "war of position." In such a war of position, ideas matter, but so too do interests. One key move in the "war of position" over the legitimacy of accumulated wealth is to focus redistributive proposals on the very top of American society. As noted in Chapter 11, redistribution of just 30% of the net wealth held now by the wealthiest 1% of households would suffice to capitalize all households in the United States with roughly $100,000 in assets. It might well be smart politics to focus even more tightly at the top 0.1%; after all, the top 1% consists of over three million people, many of whom are politically active and could be expected to defend their interests aggressively. Moreover, many Americans aspire to join the top 1%. But the lifestyles led by the top 0.1% of society are a world apart from the experience of the vast majority of Americans, even relatively affluent Americans (Frank, 2007). Publicizing the excesses of this group and contrasting it with the unrealized possibility of providing every American a very decent assets portfolio could be an effective political strategy.

From Moral Critique to Mobilization: Who Would Be For Property-Owning Democracy?

A moral critique of extreme concentrations of wealth and the absurd use of resources it generates is crucial, but will not in itself be sufficient to make property-owning democracy politically viable. Constituencies must be mobilized on its behalf. One complicating feature of property-owning democracy is that organized labor, the bedrock of social democratic politics in advanced industrialized countries, is unlikely to be the most enthusiastic supporter of property-owning democracy, at least initially. Strong arguments can be made that a full-blown property-owning democracy would enhance the bargaining power of labor dramatically (see Hsieh, Chapter 7 in this volume), but the distinctive features of POD do not directly impact workplace conditions and worker power. In practice, advocates for property-owning democracy should (as suggested by several contributors to this volume) embrace community wealth-building initiatives, including worker ownership of firms, that preserve jobs from corporate outsourcing, and should stress that establishing a system of savings accounts for all households could dramatically improve the well-being of low-wage service workers.

There is no reason why organized labor could not in time endorse the goals and tactics of property-owning democracy, but other constituencies likely must play the lead role. The cultural ideals to which POD appeals are individualistic and entrepreneurial, and stand in tension with labor's traditional emphasis on solidarity. In a provocative essay, Roberto Unger (2006) has suggested that the "left" should in fact move away from over-identification with the fading industrial working class, and instead develop a politics that speaks to the aspirations of the "petit bourgeoisie" – individuals struggling to build better lives for themselves with very limited resources, often through self-improvement (education) and entrepreneurial activities. The average young person of modest means in the United States today does not often aspire to be a well-paid, unionized industrial worker with good benefits, whose material well-being is entirely dependent on the well-being of the union (and the employer). Rather, the aspiration is to have sufficient human capital (skills and abilities) and resources to make one's own way in the world and to be independent of any particular job or economic context.

Property-owning democracy, properly advertised, should have particular appeal for persons fitting this description. A difficulty, however, is that this stratum is generally not well organized politically; indeed, the political sensibilities of the petit bourgeoisie may often lean in a libertarian direction. A key goal in organizing on behalf of property-owning democracy then must be to win the explicit support of organizations representing young persons in general (such as student associations) and young entrepreneurs in particular.

Another major category of potential supporters of property-owning democracy are racial minorities in the United States, especially Hispanics and African Americans. Together these groups comprise roughly 29% of the population, a figure that is projected to rise to 35% by 2030 and 42% by 2050 (US Census, 2009). As has been well documented, the median wealth of white households today ($143,600) is over 15 times higher than the median wealth of African Americans households ($9300) (Wolff, 2007, Table 10; based on 2007 figures). This tangible legacy of America's history of slavery and racial discrimination has received increasing attention from scholars and activists in recent years (Oliver and Shapiro, 2006; Conley, 2009). Redressing this situation has often been linked to the question of reparations for slavery. Whatever the moral merits of that case, the subject of large-scale slavery reparations remains a political nonstarter in the United States. However, a universalist program to distribute assets widely and to tax away a larger share of the holdings of the wealthiest Americans could achieve many of the same practical aims as a reparations policy. One can particularly imagine African American business people and entrepreneurs enthusiastically supporting a serious assets-based approach, in preference to expansion of the traditional welfare state.

Indeed, the prospect of building a society in which each person has sufficient assets to "make something of themselves" as well as tangible stake in property has potential appeal across social class lines. The politics of a property-owning democracy cannot be traditional working-class politics. Rather it must be a politics of the working class and the economically excluded in alliance with the middle class, in antagonism to a quite narrow group of wealth holders at the economic pinnacle of society. Without support of the bulk of the middle class, this politics cannot succeed (Elkin, 2006). As suggested above, appeals to the ideals of equal opportunity and of equal political liberty may carry considerable political weight with the American middle class, and it is fortuitous that institutional proposals for property-owning democracy do not need to be framed in terms of more controversial arguments about the scope of permissible inequality of results.

This is not to say that winning over the middle class toward property-owning democracy will be an easy proposition. Four kinds of obstacles can be identified. First is the tendency of many middle-class persons to identify with and valorize the very wealthy; the United States is generally not a society characterized by cultural hostility toward the super-rich. Increasing the level of resentment and antagonism toward the super-rich may well be a prerequisite of building popular support for serious taxation of wealth, but few politicians (least of all Barack Obama) are willing to cast their politics in terms of social antagonism; progressive politicians in the United States prefer the language of community and "we're all in it together." Communitarian rhetoric that draws no distinctions between the interests of the vast majority and those of the very wealthy will not be powerful enough to underwrite dramatic levels of redistribution. A politics of property-owning democracy with real traction cannot be a politics without enemies.

The second obstacle is ideological opposition to increased taxation, often rooted in the "everyday libertarian" view that individuals ought to be able to keep whatever they have accumulated because they have "earned it" (Murphy and Nagel, 2002).

A third, related obstacle is a general lack of sophistication, or perhaps just lack of information, about the general differences between socialism, different types of capitalism, and conceptions of property-owning democracy, and about the likely consequences of different sorts of tax policies. Opponents of a wealth tax will try to argue that the middle class will be hurt by higher taxes on the very rich. While a wealth tax should be carefully designed so as to minimize the plausibility of such distortions, any concrete proposal must be accompanied by relentless demonstration of how the middle class stands to benefit from substantial redistribution aimed at the top.

The fourth and final obstacle is in some ways the flip side of the first: a reluctance of some middle-class Americans to join into political coalition with working- and lower-class Americans, a reluctance that often is tied to ideological views about poverty and its causes that tend to blame individuals and individual behavior rather than policies and structure. Property-owning democracy may offer a more promising route to building the needed measure of cross-class solidarity compared to traditional welfare state capitalism, insofar as its aims are to provide citizens with a measure of independence and to reduce the need for citizens to be sustained by means-tested welfare payments. One of the oldest saws in conservative discourse about poverty in the United States (often repeated by George W. Bush) is that if you give a man a fish, you feed him for a day, but if you teach a man to fish, you feed him for a lifetime. Property-owning democracy can be framed as a vehicle for independence and self-reliance, a way to both teach a man or woman to fish and provide a rod with which to do so.

Conclusion: Going Public With Property-Owning Democracy

There is no way to judge whether these obstacles are insuperable in advance of a serious, sustained effort to engage the general public with the idea of property-owning democracy. The place to begin is by dramatizing several startling facts of which most Americans are unaware: the degree to which wealth is concentrated, and the fact that the United States could easily afford to establish a system affording to each citizen a quite substantial amount of property, at a cost roughly equivalent to the cost of recent wars, the annual military budget, or the sticker price of the 2008–2009 financial bailouts (see Williamson, Chapter 11). A program of popular education about the basic facts of inequality of wealth and opportunity in the United States needs to be combined with an effort to educate opinion makers and politicians on the fact that there are a variety of plausible alternatives to neoliberal forms of capitalism that are quite different in character than Soviet-style socialism.

A small number of intellectuals and activists in the United States have in fact been engaged in such activities for some time, but they have yet to impact the broader public consciousness in a lasting way. The adoption of some or all of a property-owning democracy platform by a prominent interest group or organization could have some impact; so too might the formation of grassroots study groups in the spirit of feminist "consciousness-raising." Popular education regarding the economy, how it works, and the contradiction between the enormous wealth holdings of the top fraction of society and the highly stressed economic existence experienced by most people is a precondition for generating a social movement on behalf of a concerted effort to broaden wealth ownership.[6]

At some point, however, prominent public figures (such as politicians) will need to begin talking about property-owning democracy in a serious way, both in soapbox style and in concrete political campaigns. Since 2008, numerous dogmas about the virtues of the free market have been abandoned, and ordinary people and opinion makers have begun to ask increasingly probing questions about capitalism. As the crisis continues, interest in long-run alternatives to capitalism is likely to increase. Now is thus an opportune time to make a serious effort to launch a discussion of plausible systemic alternatives.

At its heart, property-owning democracy is a fairly radical proposal based on fairly moderate normative principles. Once confronted with the practical reality that capitalism-as-usual no longer delivers functional or sustainable, let alone just, outcomes, democratic publics in the United States and elsewhere might eventually view property-owning democracy as an attractive alternative – if it is argued for persistently, persuasively, and creatively. This does not mean that property-owning democracy is the best possible alternative to capitalism, or that it alone can solve all of the fundamental problems capitalism generates. In particular, Rawls's conception of property-owning democracy has little to say directly about the fundamental question of how finance should be organized in a market society, and too little to say about environmental issues and how we might in practice shift to an economic system oriented around ecological sustainability rather than endless growth. A full-blown political-economic alternative must address those issues, and efforts to do so necessarily must go far beyond the guidance Rawls provides. Nonetheless, pursuing some version of property-owning democracy – that is, some systematic effort to broaden the distribution of wealth and assets in a serious way, within the context of a market society – is probably the most politically plausible route to seriously challenging and altering to capitalism over the next generation. The social changes and leveling of political power it promises to deliver could lay the groundwork for yet further movements in the direction of a just and democratic political economy in the more distant future.

Notes

1. As this volume went to press, the Occupy Wall Street (#OWS) movement was launched, with the aim of protesting against economic and political inequality in the USA (and elsewhere). The staying power and long-term trajectory of this movement is uncertain at this early point, but the adoption of the theme of contrasting the "99%" with the "1%," as well as the

favorable response of many people to the protest, are worth noting. At a minimum, the movement's emergence reinforces this chapter's primary argument: that a populist economic critique of the domination of the economy and of politics by a plutocratic minority has significant political potential in the United States.

2. In an analysis of 20 years of survey data (1984–2004), Bartels (2009, p. 131) reports that 88% of Americans "agree strongly" (60.5%) or "agree somewhat" (27.5%) that "Our society should do whatever is necessary to make sure that everyone has an equal opportunity to succeed." To be sure, it is not clear that middle-class Americans would take this principle as far as Rawls would like. Whereas Rawls would like to minimize the impact of socioeconomic position on long-term outcomes as much as feasible and consistent with the institution of the nuclear family, most middle-class and affluent Americans regard intergenerational transfers of funds for the purpose of paying for college, down payments on first homes, first motor vehicles and the like as not just morally permissible but laudable (i.e., the mark of a caring parent). But this does not necessarily imply that such persons would oppose or reject measures intended to increase the capacity of poorer, lower-asset Americans to confer opportunities and advantages on *their* children. Believing one has a moral obligation to one's children to use available assets to improve their life chances in the context of a society that is highly unequal and where the consequences of falling out of the middle class are severe is not inconsistent with also believing that it would be better and more just if the society were organized more fairly (greater equality of opportunity, less inequality of outcome). Nonetheless, this poses a tricky political problem for advocates of a property-owning democracy – how to articulate the case for equalizing the resources and opportunities provided to the next generation without alienating or excessively threatening middle-class families who are now able to pass on advantages out of their own resources (i.e., the middle-class family that scrimps and saves in order to be able to live in a locality with a "good" public school district); and how to distinguish between intergenerational transfers of wealth that are intended to provide the next generation with a good "start" and those transfers characteristic of the super-rich (i.e., transfers that allow the children of the rich to control enormous amounts of wealth and capital while living a highly opulent lifestyle in which work is optional.)

3. In 2000, for instance, a *Business Week* poll found that 74% of Americans believed that large companies have too much political power; only 40% said the same of labor groups, and 2% said small business had too much power (*Business Week*, September 11, 2000). Other polls over the past 10 years have consistently generated similar results.

4. Note, however, that if more nuanced understanding were widespread, Rawls apparently believed that property-owning democracy might fare better in the American context not only than market socialism but than welfare state capitalism: property-owning democracy better exemplifies the idea of independent, free-standing citizens than does a system with a class of people more or less permanently dependent on public support.

5. For a useful discussion of how egalitarian politicians in the past have framed egalitarian demands in terms of a language of national community see Jackson (2009). An interesting related question is whether a system of universal asset distribution ought to be linked to or paired with increased civic obligations (i.e., a program of universal national service, required voter registration). Here I simply observe that in some political cultures (including likely the United States) linking increased civic entitlements with increased civic obligations may increase the political and cultural appeal of property-owning democracy; such a dual program in effect creates thicker citizens whose lives are more obviously and explicitly connected to the larger (national) political community than is now the case in the United States.

6. Again, the international "Occupy" protests that began on Wall Street in Fall 2011 and quickly spread across the U.S., as well as to other countries, may prove to be an embryonic form of such a movement. At any rate, the protests have provided an unusual opportunity for public discussion and public education concerning the inequality of wealth and its possible remedies. It is worth noting here (in light of Simone Chamber's chapter in this volume) that while Rawls himself may have never made it to the barricades, at least some of his ideas did. In a visit to London in October 2011, I viewed a sign consisting of a single printed page posted on a wall nearby the "Occupy London" protests at St. Paul's Cathedral. The poster read as follows: "In constant pursuit of money to finance campaigns, the political system is simply unable to function. - John Rawls." The quote is from Rawls's final published essay, "The Idea of Public Reason Revisited," reprinted in the expanded 2006 edition of his Political Liberalism, pp. 449–450.

References

Alperovitz, G. (2004) *America Beyond Capitalism: Reclaiming Our Wealth, Our Liberty and Our Democracy*, John Wiley & Sons, Inc., Hoboken, NJ.

Alperovitz, G. and Daly, L. (2008) *Unjust Deserts: How the Rich Are Taking Our Common Inheritance and Why We Should Take It Back*, New Press, New York.

Bartels, L. (2009) *Unequal Democracy: The Political Economy of the New Gilded Age*, Princeton University Press, Princeton.

Cohen, J. (2003) For a democratic society, in *The Cambridge Companion to Rawls* (ed. S. Freeman), Cambridge University Press, Cambridge, pp. 86–138.

Conley, D. (2009) *Being Black, Living in the Red*, 2nd edn, University of California Press, Berkeley.

Elkin, S. (2006) *Reconstructing the Commercial Republic: Constitutional Theory After Madison*, University of Chicago Press, Chicago.

Frank, R. (2007) *Richistan: A Journey Through the American Wealth Boom and the Lives of the New Rich*, Random House, New York.

Goodwyn, L. (1976) *Democratic Promise: The Populist Movement in America*, Oxford University Press, Oxford.

Graetz, M. and Shapiro, I. (2005) *Death by a Thousand Cuts: The Fight Over Taxing Inherited Wealth*, Princeton University Press, Princeton.

Greenhouse, S. (2008) *The Big Squeeze: Tough Times for American Workers*, Knopf, New York.

Hacker, J. (2008) *The Great Risk Shift: The New Economic Insecurity and the Decline of the American Dream*, Oxford University Press, New York.

Jackson, B. (2009) The rhetoric of redistribution, in *In Search of Social Democracy* (eds J. Callaghan, N. Fishman, B. Jackson, and M. McIvor), Palgrave Macmillan, Basingstoke.

Jacobs, L. and Skocpol, T. (eds) (2007) *Inequality and American Politics: What We Know, What We Need to Learn*, Russell Sage Foundation, Thousand Oaks, CA.

Jacobs, L. and Skocpol, T. (2010) *Health Care Reform and American Democracy: What Everyone Needs to Know*, Oxford University Press, New York.

Kuttner, R. (2010) *A Presidency in Peril*, Chelsea Green, White River Junction, VT.

Miller, D. (1999) *Principles of Social Justice*, Harvard University Press, Cambridge, MA.

Murphy, L. and Nagel, T. (2002) *The Myth of Ownership: Taxes and Justice*, Oxford University Press, New York.

Oliver, M. and Shapiro, T. (2006) *Black Wealth/White Wealth: A New Perspective on Racial Inequality*, 2nd edn, Routledge, New York.

Page, B. and Jacobs, L. (2009) *Class War? What Americans Really Think About Economic Inequality*, University of Chicago Press, Chicago.

Pierson, P. and Hacker, J. (2010) *Winner-Take-All Politics: How Washington Made the Rich Richer – And Turned Its Back on the Middle Class*, Simon and Schuster, New York.

Rawls, J. (2006). *Political Liberalism*, expanded edition, Columbia University Press, New York.

Rattner, S. (2010) *Overhauled: An Insider's Account of the Obama Administration's Emergency Rescue of the Auto Industry*, Houghton Mifflin, New York.

Reagan, R. (1987) Project economic justice. Speech, August 3, 1987, Washington DC. Available at: http://www.cesj.org/homestead/strategies/regional-global/pej-reagan.html (accessed September 22, 2011).

Robeyns, I. (2008) Ideal theory in theory and practice. *Social Theory and Practice*, 34, 341–362.

Ryan, J. (2010) *Fives Miles Away, A World Apart: One City, Two Schools, and the Story of Educational Opportunity in Modern America*, Oxford University Press, New York.

Sherraden, M. (ed.) (2005) *Inclusion in the American Dream: Assets, Poverty and Public Policy*, Oxford University Press, Oxford.

Suskind, R. (2011) *Confidence Men: Wall Street, Washington, and the Education of a President*, HarperCollins, New York.

Taibbi, M. (2010) *Griftopia: Bubble Machines, Vampire Squids and the Long Con That Is Breaking America*, Random House, New York.

Unger, R. (2006) *What Should the Left Propose?* Verso, New York.

US Census (2009) *Population Projections, 2010–2050*, Table 4, available at http://www.census.gov/population/www/projections/2009comparisonfiles.html (accessed September 22, 2011).

Williamson, T. (2009) Who owns what? An egalitarian interpretation of John Rawls's idea of a property-owning democracy. *Journal of Social Philosophy*, 40, 434–453.

Williamson, T., Dubb, S., and Alperovitz, G. (2010) *Climate Change, Community Stability, and the Next 150 Million Americas*, Democracy Collaborative, Washington, DC.

Williamson, T., Imbroscio, D., and Alperovitz, G. (2002) *Making a Place for Community: Local Democracy in a Global Era*, Routledge, New York.

Wolff, E. (2010) *Recent Trends in Household Wealth in the United States: Rising Debt and the Middle-Class Squeeze – an Update to 2007*. Levy Economics Institute (Bard College) Working Paper No. 589. Available at: www.levyinstitute.org/pubs/wp_589.pdf (accessed September 23, 2011).

Wright, E.O. and Rogers, J. (2010) *American Society: How It Really Works*, Norton, New York.

Index

Note: Abbreviations used within the index are: ED = economic democracy; FEO = fair equality of opportunity; POD = property-owning democracy; WSC = welfare state capitalism

Abramovitz, M. 280
Ackerman, B. 36, 48, 67, 85, 134, 228, 230, 232, 243n
advertising 213, 214
agrarian societies 34–5, 36
Akerlof, G. 280
Alaska Permanent Fund 274–5
Alperovitz, G. 13, 94n, 243, 292, 294, 298
Alstott, A. 36, 48, 67, 85, 134, 228, 230, 232, 243n
Anderson, P. 201–2
arbitrariness, moral 23–6
arbitrary interference at work 154–6
arts, corporatist structures 183
association, morality of 187–90, 192
attachment, principles of justice 187–90, 191–2
Attlee, C. 43
authority, morality of 187
automobile industry 277, 278–9, 288–90
autonomy
　corporate executives 219–20n
　legitimating private property 56, 59, 60, 65–7, 69–70
　redistribution of resources for 250–1, 258–62, 263
　skill development for 251–3, 255–8, 263

Baker, J. 170
Baldwin, S. 39, 41
banking sector 6, 75–6
　in an economic democracy 207–8, 218–19n
　a long-term US wealth-redistribution strategy 239
　in a pluralist commonwealth 269, 273
　in a POD+ 215, 217
Barber, B. 270
Barry, B. 208–9, 218, 228, 235
basketball 193–4
Baumol effect 165
Beckert, J. 228
Belloc, H. 37–8
Bergmann, B. 169, 170, 175
Boulding, K. 213
Brettschneider, C. 9
Britain *see* UK
Buber, M. 142
Burtt, S. 123n
Bush, G.W. 245n, 274, 279, 302

California Public Employees' Retirement System (CalPERS) 270, 274
capabilities 249, 250
　see also primary goods; talents
capital assets tax 207, 214, 217
capital dispersal
　gender justice and care 172–4
　Rawls's criticism of WSC 79, 80–1, 83, 85–6, 87, 88–90
　see also productive capital; wealth distribution
capital flight, tax-evading 227–8
capital gains tax (CGT) 261, 262

capitalism
  background institutions for justice   203–5
  conceptual history of POD   35–48
  economic democracy distinguished from   207
  economic democracy–POD comparison   208–15
  economic democracy–POD+ comparison   215–16
  institutional analysis of justice   2–7
    democratic corporatism   180–97
    difference principle and   21–2, 78, 87–91, 93, 110, 111, 116
    Rawls's critique of WSC   3, 5–6, 75–93, 119, 133, 149
    see also property-owning democracy
  political viability of POD in the USA   302–3
  Schweickart's indictment   202–3, 208–15
  US economic crisis (2008)   288–90
care work, gender justice   163–76
cash assets, US wealth-redistribution strategy   230–1, 232–4, 241, 296
central banks   219n
Centre of Full Employment and Equity (CofFEE)   219n
Chambers, S.   7, 71n, 287, 290
charities, welfare rights   69–70
Chesterton, G.K.   37
Child Trust Fund (CTF)(UK)   260–1
children
  care of   164–5, 166, 167, 168, 169–72, 173–4
  financial capital   253, 254, 255–6, 260–1, 263
  skill development   251–3, 255–8, 263
Chrysler Corporation   274, 282n, 288
Churchill, W.   40
citizenship
  republican or liberal   129–43
    property-owning democracy   133–4
    stability of justice as fairness   129–30, 134–6, 138–9, 143
    Tocquevillian sociology   130, 136–41, 142–3
  republicanism of Rawls's liberalism   130–3
  roots of   191
Citizens United v. Federal Election Commission (US Supreme Court)   6, 291

civic humanism   131, 132
class
  democratic corporatist POD   183
  political viability of POD in the USA   287–8, 291, 300–2, 303–4n
Cleveland, cooperative economic organization   275, 276, 277, 278–9
codetermination system   182, 183
coercive exclusion from property   55, 56–64, 65, 70
Cohen, G.A.   9
  difference principle critique   101–2, 108, 109–11, 113–14, 116, 120–2
  insulation strategy   82
Cohen, J.   24, 84, 144n, 145n, 198n, 290
Cole, G.D.H.   41, 44, 198n
collective ownership
  conceptual history of POD   36, 40–1, 43–4, 46, 48
  legitimating private property   61
command economy socialism   2–3, 202
commercial republicanism, rise of   34–6
commodification of care welfare regime   169, 170, 171–2, 174–5
community development   273, 275–7
Community Development Corporations (CDCs)   273
competencies (skills)   251–3, 255–8, 263
competition see economic competition
conditionality, state benefits   259
consensus democracy   197
Conservative Party (UK)   33, 37–40, 41, 43, 46–7, 95n
consumption
  economic growth   212, 213
  a US wealth-redistribution strategy and   232
contractualist justification of private property   54, 55, 56–64, 66, 71
cooperatives   196, 214, 271, 275–7
co-partnership schemes   38–9, 42, 45
corporate political speech   5, 6, 291–2
corporate regulation   268
corporatism see democratic corporatism
corruption, political   81–4, 173
  see also fair value of political liberties
crime rates   70
Crosland, A.   42, 44
culture

political viability of POD and 295–6, 298–9, 300
politics of egalitarianism 23–7, 28–9

Dagger, R. 4, 100, 103–4, 111, 112, 124–5n
Dahl, R. 142, 281
Daly, L. 280, 292, 298
Daniels, N. 96–7n, 103
Davis, D.W. 29n
debts, private 245n
Declaration of Independence (US) 18
De Francisco, A. 129, 143n
democracy, consensus 197
democracy in POD 81
　democratic corporatist form 182
　Rawls's criticism of WSC 81–4, 93, 119
　see also democratic personality, the ills of
democratic citizenship, equality of see political equality
democratic corporatism 180–97
　forms of POD compared 181–3, 184, 192–5
　political participation 188–90, 191–7
　sense of justice 185–8, 196–7
　stability 180–1, 184–6, 189, 192, 195
democratic equality 103, 114
democratic personality, the ills of 129, 130, 136–40, 141–3
democratic socialism see liberal democratic socialism
democratic societies, social psychology of 129–30, 134–43
De Rerum Novarum (papal encyclical) 37
desert principle 25–6, 279–81, 290, 292, 298
diachronically combined welfare regime of care 169, 174–5
difference principle 19
　G.A. Cohen's critique 101–2, 108, 109–11, 113–14, 116, 120–2
　liberal republicanism 107–22
　political implications 18, 21–4, 26–9
　political viability of POD in the USA 290, 293–4
　Rawls's criticism of WSC 78, 87–91, 93
　workplace democracy 152
DiQuattro, A. 21, 96n, 124n, 226
disabled people 164–5, 168
distributism (distributivism) 37–8

Dodds, E. 41–2
domination
　liberal republicanism 102–9, 118, 121–2
　Rawls's criticism of WSC 87–91
Durkheim, E. 145n
duties, natural 131

ecological sustainability 213–14, 239, 240–1, 267, 270, 275–6, 303
economic competition
　background institutions for justice 204
　democratic corporatist POD 181, 182, 183, 193
　in an economic democracy 206–7
　economic democracy–POD comparison 209, 214
economic crises 5–6, 232, 266–7, 288–9
economic democracy (ED) 201–18
　background institutions for justice 203–5
　indictment of capitalism 202–3
　model of 206–8
　non-capitalist POD 205–6
　POD compared 208–15
　POD plus (POD+) compared 215–18
economic efficiency
　distributive justice institutions 203
　economic democracy–POD+ comparison 216
economic equality see social and economic (in)equality
economic growth
　as a cumulative process 280–1, 292, 298
　ED–POD comparison 211–15
　a US wealth-redistribution strategy and 232
economic planning 240–1
economic policy, conceptual history of POD 42–5
economic power, fair value of political liberties 81–4
economic production
　in a democratic corporatist POD 181–3, 193
　in an economic democracy 207
　economic democracy–POD comparison 212–13, 214
　Solow residual 280–1, 298
　work effects of widespread ownership of assets 149–59

Eden, A.   39–40, 41, 47, 95n
education
　aim of POD   79, 134
　democratic corporatist structures   182
　financial capital–outcome relation   253, 255–6
　political viability of POD in the USA   291, 302–3
　Rawls's criticism of WSC   79, 86–7, 91–2
　skill development   251–3, 255–8, 263
Edwards, J.   299
egalitarianism
　conceptual history of POD   33–6, 39, 40–1, 42–8
　gender justice and care   163–76
　liberal republicanism as base for   101–23
　political viability of POD in the USA   299
　politics of   17–29
　see also equality/inequality
elderly people
　care of   164–5, 166, 168, 169
　US wealth-redistribution strategy   231–2
elections
　funding of   118–19
　participation in   193
Elkin, S.   4, 140, 270, 301
emergency funds, wealth redistribution   233
emotional competencies   252–3
employee stock ownership plans (ESOPs)   271, 282n
employment see work and workers; workplace democracy
equality/inequality
　background institutions for justice   203, 204
　democratic   103, 114
　economic democracy–POD comparison   208–9
　ideology of unconstrained inequality   279–82
　legitimating private property   59, 66, 68
　liberalism–republicanism convergence   102–9
　life outcomes   253–5
　a long-term US wealth-redistribution strategy   225–41, 296
　pluralism and   19–21, 103
　political viability of POD in the USA   291, 292–4, 295–6, 297–303

principle of justice   19
　G.A. Cohen's critique   101–2, 108, 109–11, 113–14, 116, 120–2
　liberal republicanism   107–23
　political implications   18, 21–4, 26–9
　political viability of POD in the USA   291, 293–4
　Rawls's criticism of WSC   76, 78, 80–1, 82–91, 93, 119, 149
　see also difference principle; fair equality of opportunity (FEO) principle
public political culture   23–7, 28–9
skill development   253, 255–8, 263
spheres of defined   18–19
UK redistribution strategies   258–62
work   149, 156–7, 158–9
see also egalitarianism
Esping-Andersen, G.   91
estate taxation
　UK   261, 262
　USA   228, 229, 297, 298
eugenics 95–6n
exclusion, welfare rights as compensation for   53–71

fair equality of opportunity (FEO) principle   19
　aim of POD   80, 81, 134
　political viability of POD in the USA   291, 293
　Rawls's criticism of WSC   78, 80, 81, 84–7, 93
fair value of political liberties   77–8, 80, 81–4, 93
　liberal republicanism   108, 112, 115, 116–22, 123
　political viability of POD in the USA   291, 293
　workplace democracy   152
fairness, justice as see justice as fairness
family care welfare regime   169, 170–2, 174–5
Feldman, S.   30n
feminist criticisms of Rawls's theory   177n
financial capital, as primary good   253–6, 258–62, 263
　see also income; wealth distribution
financial crises   288–9
　global savings   220n

pluralist commonwealth and 266–7, 269
political viability of POD and 292
public banking systems 217
relevance of POD 6, 240
financial redistribution *see* wealth distribution
financial sector 6, 75–6
  bailout of 288, 292
  in an economic democracy 207–8
  economic democracy–POD+
    comparison 215–18
  organization in a POD 240, 303
  savings 212
  see also financial crises
Folbre, N. 165
fraternity, ideal of 157–8
free markets
  restraints 203
  welfare rights 69–70
free speech 291–2
Freeman, S. 72n, 78, 85–6, 90–1, 93, 97n, 152, 157, 159n
Friedman, M. 4, 203
functional capital 41
fundamental equality 18–19
  utilitarianism and 23

Gaitskell, H. 42, 45
Galbraith, J.K. 219n, 220n
Gates, B. 221n, 298
Gaus, G. 108
GCE Advanced Levels (A-Levels)(UK) 252
Geithner, T. 288
gender justice 163–76
General Certificate of Secondary Education (GCSE)(UK) 252–3, 257
General Motors 277, 278–9, 288–90
George, H. 228
Germany, codetermination system 182, 183
Gilbert, R. 278
good life, primary goods for pursuit of 250
government role
  background institutions for justice 203–5
  in an economic democracy 207–8, 211
  justifying private property 55, 56–65, 69–70
  in a POD+ 216–17
  primary good redistribution 255–62
  republicanism 104
Graetz, M. 297

Gramsci, A. "war of position" 300
Grimond, J. 42
guild socialism 41
Gutmann, A. 65

Harrington, J. 34
Haslanger, S. 166
Hayek, F.A. 2
health inequalities 256–8
health insurance 269, 294
Hegel, G.W.F. 145n, 191, 198n
Heilbroner, R. 204
Herzog, D. 123n
high-speed rail systems 277–8
higher education sector 182
Hirst, P. 198n
Hobhouse, L.T. 40–1, 281
Hobson, J.A. 41
Hochschild, J. 25, 26
Holmes, S. 58, 70
household debt 245n
household work 167–8, 170
housing-based assets, US redistribution strategy 230–1, 234–6, 241, 296
housing finance agencies (Fannie Mae and Freddie Mac)(US) 269
housing value, UK redistribution strategies 261, 262
Hsieh, N. 10, 49, 112, 226, 300
human capital 249, 251–3, 255–8, 263
  care work 171, 174
  Rawls's criticism of WSC 79, 80–1, 86–7, 91–2
Hussain, W. 11, 141
Hutton, G. 42

ideal political theory 1, 2, 20, 291
in-kind resources, right to 65–6, 67–8
incentivization to work
  in an economic democracy 207
  economic democracy–POD comparison 209–10
  moral inconsistency in 102, 109, 110, 113–14, 121
income
  background institutions for justice 203, 204
  conceptual history of POD 41, 45–6, 47, 48

income (*Continued*)
  in an economic democracy 207
  economic democracy–POD
    comparison 208–9
  gender justice and care 174, 176
  large-scale taxation of the very rich
    297–300
  legitimating private property 65, 66–8, 70
  life outcomes 254, 255
  long-term strategy for US wealth
    distribution 229
  meaningful work 154
  minimum 3, 134, 204, 258, 267
  moving toward POD 218
  political viability of POD in the USA 292, 295
  politics of egalitarianism 22, 25–6
  Rawls's criticism of WSC 88, 89–91, 149
  right to basic 66–8, 70, 156
  UK redistribution strategies 258–61
  workers as property owners 156
individualism 137–8, 139–40, 141–3, 281
inequality *see* equality/inequality
inflation 219n
inherited productive capacity 280–1, 292, 298
inherited wealth *see* intergenerational transmission of advantage
Institute of Economic Affairs (IEA, UK) 42
Institute for Policy Studies (IPS, USA) 229, 238–9
institutional analysis of justice 2–7
  democratic corporatism 180–97
  difference principle and 21–2, 28, 78, 87–91, 93
    G.A. Cohen's critique 110, 111, 116
  liberal republicanism 105–7, 115–16, 121–2
  pluralist commonwealth 269–82
  Rawls's criticism of WSC 3, 5–6, 75–93, 119, 133, 149, 201–2
  republicanism of Rawls's liberalism 131–2
  see also laissez-faire capitalism; liberal democratic socialism; property-owning democracy;   welfare state capitalism
insulation of political–economic spheres 82–3
intergenerational justice 212

intergenerational transmission of
    advantage 79, 81, 85
  background institutions for justice 204
  gender justice and care 173, 174–5
  long-term strategy for US wealth
    distribution 228
  political viability of POD in the USA
    297–300, 303–4n
  UK redistribution strategies 261–2
intermediation, democratic
    corporatism 182, 183
investment
  in an economic democracy 207–8
  economic democracy–POD
    comparison 211, 212–14, 215
  economic democracy–POD+
    comparison 215
  economic planning 240–1
  gender justice and care 176
  in a pluralist commonwealth 270, 271, 272, 274
  a US wealth-redistribution strategy
    230–31, 232–3, 236–8, 240

Jackson, B. 8–9, 55, 95n, 163, 299, 304n
Jacobs, L. 25, 292–3, 295
Jay, D. 42–5, 49n
Jefferson, T. 34, 228
jobs *see* work and workers
just institutions *see* institutional analysis of justice
just savings 212
justice, principles of 19–20
  background institutions for 203–5
  basic liberties 114–15
  democratic corporatist POD 193, 194, 197
  difference principle *see* difference principle
  G.A. Cohen's critique 101–2, 108, 109–11, 113–14, 116, 120–2
  liberal republicanism 102–11, 112, 113–23
  moral development 187–90, 191–2
  political participation 191–2
  political viability of POD in the USA 290, 291–2, 293–5
  public reason 27
  Rawls's criticism of WSC 9, 76, 77–91, 93, 119, 149

sense of justice 186–8
stability 184, 185, 189
workplace democracy 152
justice, sense of 185–8, 196–7
justice as fairness 1–7
 aims of POD 134
 in an economic democracy 207
 moral inconsistency 101–2, 109–11
 politics of egalitarianism 18, 19, 21
 principles of justice *see* justice, principles of
 public reason 20–1, 27
 republican citizenship 129–43
 stability 129–30, 134–6, 138–9, 143, 184
 widespread ownership of productive assets 133, 151, 152–9
Justice as Fairness (JF, Rawls) 2–3
 Anderson on 201–2
 background institutions for justice 203–5
 criticism of WSC 3, 75–9, 80–2, 85–90, 149, 202
 liberalism and republicanism 112, 132
 POD+ and 216
 primary goods 250
 worker-owned firms 220n
 workplace democracy 152

Kaldor, N. 42
Kennedy, J.F. 267
Keynes, J.M. 44–5, 212, 214–15
Keynesian economics 39, 43–5, 201, 204, 212–13, 214–15, 282
King, L. 145n
knowledge economies 182
 accumulation of knowledge 280–1, 292, 298
Krouse, R. 22, 113, 195–6
Krugman, P. 204, 208, 219n
Kymlicka, W. 25

labor *see* work and workers
labor unions *see* trade unions
Labour Party (UK) 5, 8, 91, 97n
 conceptual history of POD 42–5, 46
 primary goods redistribution 256, 258–9, 260–1
laissez-faire capitalism 2–3, 202
 welfare rights 55
Lane, R.E. 25
Larmore, C. 103, 107, 108, 123–4n

left egalitarian POD tradition 34–6, 40–1, 42–6, 48
legitimacy
 liberal principle of 56
 politics of egalitarianism 17–29
 of private ownership of property 53–71
Leo XIII (Pope) 37
Lewis, A. 42
liberal democratic socialism 2, 3–7, 76, 202
 conceptual history of POD 46, 47, 48
 economic democracy 201–18
 republican citizenship and 142
liberal market POD 181, 184, 192–5, 197
liberal republicanism 101–23
 G.A. Cohen's difference principle critique 101–2, 108, 109–11, 113–14, 116, 120–2
 liberal republican political economy 112–14
 liberalism–republicanism convergence 102–9
 political agency 102, 103, 105–7, 108–9, 114–20, 123
 see also republican citizenship
liberalism
 convergence with republicanism 102–9
 primary goods 250–1
Liberal Party (UK) 40–2, 44, 45, 46–7
libertarians, private property 53, 56–7, 58, 61, 64
liberty principle 19, 27
 the basic liberties 114–15
 liberal republicanism 107–8, 112, 114–23
 political viability of POD in the USA 291, 293
 Rawls's criticism of WSC 76, 77–8, 80, 81–4, 93, 119
 workplace democracy 152
life chances, in the USA 291
life outcomes, financial capital and 253–6
Lijphart, A. 197
Lippmann, W. 42
literacy skills 251–2, 256, 257
Lloyd George, D. 281
local ownership institutions 270, 271–3, 275–7
Locke, J. 9, 64, 72n, 123n

Macmillan, H.   39, 95n
Mandle, J.   97n
Mansbridge, J.   199n, 270
Marx, K.   89, 94n, 101–2, 108, 125n, 153, 205, 219n
Marxists and Marxism   1, 6, 108–9, 115, 120, 125n, 268
materialism   138–9, 141–3
McCloskey, H.   25, 30n
McPherson, M.   22, 113, 195–6
Meade, J.   3, 8, 22
    aims and features of POD   79–81, 92
    choice of work   156, 161n
    conceptual history of POD   33–4, 41–3, 44–6, 47, 48, 95n
meaningful work   153–4
means of production *see* production, means of
means testing   259
Meidner, R.   246n
men, care work   167, 169, 170, 171, 173–4, 176
metacognitive skills   252
middle class, political viability of POD   287–8, 301–2, 303–4n
Mill, J.S.   62, 140–1, 191, 194–5, 220n, 270, 281
Miller, D.   94n, 130–1, 141, 292
Minimum Income Standard (MIS)   258
Mondragón Cooperative Corporation (Basque Country/Spain)   271, 275
Mont Pelerin Society   42
moral arbitrariness   23–6
moral development   187–90, 191–2
moral inconsistency in Rawls's theory   102, 109–11
morality, stability and   184–6
Moriarty, J.   153
mortgages   235–6
Motion Picture Editors Guild (MPEG)   183
municipal enterprises   272
Murphy, L.   71n, 96n, 297

Nagel, T.   21, 23, 71n, 96n, 297
National Basketball Association (NBA)   193
National Basketball Players Association (NBPA)   193
National Centre for Employee Ownership (US)   271
natural duties   131

natural law, private property   58–9
natural rights, private property   297–8
natural talents *see* talents
needs
    assessment   259
    interventions based on   257–8
    resources to meet   65–6, 67–8, 250
neighborhood-based community development   273
neoliberal POD tradition   33, 42, 46–8
neo-republican political economy   102, 111, 112, 114
neutrality in the liberal state   132
New Community Corporation (NCC)(US)   273
New Deal (US)   65, 268, 275, 299
nonprofit organizations   273
Nozick, R.   53
numeracy skills   251–2, 256
Nussbaum, M.   168, 249, 250

Obama, B.   5, 220–1n   277, 288–9, 294, 295
Okin, S.   171, 177n
O'Neill, M.   9, 112, 123n, 126n, 142, 152, 160n, 172–3, 293–4
opportunity, equality of *see* fair equality of opportunity (FEO) principle

Page, B.   25, 292–3, 295
Paine, T.   35–6, 37, 47, 281
parent–child relationships   255–6, 257
    see also children, care of
Pateman, C.   67, 160n, 194–5
Patten, A.   123n, 131, 143n
Peacock, A.   42
Pence, G.   159n
Perl, A.   278
personal responsibility ethos   25, 28–9
Pettit, P.   103, 105–6, 121–2, 123–4n, 160n
pluralism
    civic humanism and   131
    (in)equality and   19–21, 103
pluralist commonwealth   266–82
    long-term structural possibilities   275–9
    municipal enterprises   272
    national-level innovation   274
    neighborhood-based community development   273

nonprofit organizations 273
   state-level innovation 273–5
   wealth inequality ideology 279–82
   worker-owned firms 271, 275–7
policy analysis of justice 2
political agency 102, 103, 105–7, 108–9, 114–20, 123
political corruption 81–4, 173
   see also fair value of political liberties
political culture 23–7, 28–9
political equality 18, 19
   liberalism–republicanism convergence 102–9
Political Liberalism (Rawls)
   basic liberties 114–15
   minimum income 3
   politics of egalitarianism 20
political liberties, fair value see fair value of political liberties
political morality, stability and 185–6, 192
political participation 130–3, 139–42, 143
   democratic corporatism 191–7
   moral development 189–90, 191–2
political party funding 118–19
political relevance of POD 5–7
political viability of POD 227, 228–9, 238–9, 287–303
politics of egalitarianism 17–29
power
   liberal republicanism 104
   property for vs. property for use 40–1
   Rawls's criticism of WSC 81–4, 87–91
primary goods (capabilities) 249, 250–1
   financial capital 253–6, 258–62, 263
   skills 251–3, 255–8, 263
   state role in redistributing 255–62
   see also talents
principles, morality of 188–90, 192
private socialism 281–2
production
   in a democratic corporatist POD 181–3, 193
   in an economic democracy 207
   economic democracy–POD comparison 212–13, 214
   Solow residual 280–1, 298
production, means of
   conceptual history of POD 36, 37–9, 48
   a non-capitalist POD 205–6, 237–8

Rawls's criticism of WSC 80–1, 83, 85–6, 87, 88–90, 93
productive capital 7
   in an economic democracy 207
   in a pluralist commonwealth 269–82
   a US strategy for redistribution of 236–8, 296
   work effects of widespread ownership of 133, 149–59
   see also production, means of
productive enfranchisement 150–9
property-owning democracy (POD)
   aims and features 76, 79–81, 134, 172–3
   background institutions 205
   democratic corporatist 180–97
   fuzzy borders with WSC 91–3
   institutional alternatives 2–7
   conceptual history of POD and 35–6, 47–8
   difference principle and 21–2, 78, 87–91, 93, 293–4
   economic democracy 201–18
   gender justice and care 163–76
   pluralist commonwealth 269–82
   political viability of POD in the USA and 293–4
   Rawls's criticism of WSC 3, 5–6, 75–93, 119, 149, 201–2
   work and 149–59, 207, 209–11, 214, 216, 217
   institutional implications 10–12
   gender justice and care 164, 171–6
   work–asset ownership relation 149–59
   liberal market–democratic corporatist contrast 181, 184, 192–5, 197
   modified (POD+) 215–18
   non-capitalist 205–6, 237–8
   see also property-owning democracy plus (POD+)
   in practice 12–13
   an incomplete ideal 239–41
   a long-term strategy for the USA 225–41
   a near-term strategy 249–63
   ownership-altering forms in the USA 266–82, 296–7
   political viability 227, 228–9, 238–9, 287–303
   theoretical foundations 8–10

property-owning democracy (*Continued*)
  conceptual history   33–48, 95n
  liberal republicanism   101–23
  politics of egalitarianism   17–29
  public justification of private property   7, 53–71
  Rawls's criticism of WSC   75–93, 119, 133
  republican citizenship   129–43
property-owning democracy plus (POD+)   215–18
property rights   53–71
psychology of democratic societies   129–30, 134–43
  see also moral development; reciprocity
public banking system   207–8, 217, 218–19n   239, 269, 273
public justification of private property   53–71
public life, participation in *see* political participation
public ownership
  conceptual history of POD   38, 41, 43, 47
  a non-capitalist POD   205–6, 237–8
  US wealth-redistribution strategy   237–8, 239
public political culture   23–7, 28–9
public reason   20–1, 27–9
public transport   277–9
public trust form of ownership   270, 274–5
Putnam, R.D.   140

racial minorities   301
radicals and radicalism
  conceptual history of POD   34–6, 42–6, 48
  politics of egalitarianism   17–18, 21–3, 29
rail networks   277
Reagan, R.   295
reciprocity
  legitimating private property   56, 59, 60–3, 65
  liberal republicanism   105–7
  moral development   190, 191–2
  Rawls's criticism of WSC   78, 149
  sense of justice   187, 196–7
  stability of justice as fairness   135–6, 138–9, 140–1
  see also difference principle
republican citizenship   129–43
  property-owning democracy   133–4

republicanism of Rawls's liberalism   130–3
  stability of justice as fairness   129–30, 134–6, 138–9, 143
  Tocquevillian sociology   130, 136–41, 142–3
republicanism
  commercial   34–6
  Rawls's liberalism and *see* liberal republicanism; republican citizenship
Research Center for Full Employment and Price Stability (CFEPS)   219n
resource rights   65–6, 67–8
Retirement Systems of Alabama (RSA)   274, 278
rights
  Paine's social   35–6
  private property–welfare parity   53–71
  to property   297–8
Robeyn, I.   10–11, 291
Roemer, J.E.   3, 205–6, 215–16, 218n, 220n, 237–8, 244n, 246n
Rogers, J.   145n, 198n, 245n, 294
Roosevelt, F.D.   228, 281, 299
Röpke, W.   42
Rousseau, J.-J.   34, 53, 55, 59–60, 63–4, 71
rules, corporatist structures   181, 182, 183, 186–7, 193–4

sales techniques   213–14
Sandel, M.   96n, 103, 130, 132
savings
  ED–POD comparison   212–13, 214
  UK redistribution strategies   259–61
  US wealth redistribution   229
Scanlon, T.M.   54, 56, 97n
Schmitter, P.   182
Schweickart, D.   7, 11–12, 94n, 246n
schooling, skill development   251–3, 255–8
  see also education
Schumacher, E.F.   205
Screen Actors Guild (SAG)   183
Seldon, A.   42
self-confidence   194–5
self-employment   151
self-management   185
self-respect   250
  liberal republicanism   103, 121
  Rawls's criticism of WSC   87–91, 149
  work and   149, 151, 153, 155, 258–9

Sen, A. 2, 249, 250
sense of justice 185–8, 196–7
The Servile State (Belloc) 37
Shapiro, I. 297
share ownership *see* stock and share ownership
Shenfield, A. 42
Silver, B.D. 29n
Simon, H. 281
Skelton, N. 8, 38–9, 95n
skills 251–3, 255–8, 263
Skinner, Q. 103, 130, 143n
slavery 301
Smith, A. 35, 161n
Smith, P. 113
social capital 140
social competencies 252–3
Social Democratic Party (SDP)(UK) 46
Social Democratic Party (SAP)(Sweden) 91
social and economic (in)equality 18, 19
  conceptual history of POD 33–48
  difference principle 21–4, 26–9, 78, 87–91
    liberal republicanism 101–2, 107–22
  early 21st-century US asset distribution 226–7
  economic democracy–POD comparison 208–9
  education about 302–3
  gender justice 163–76
  ideology of unconstrained inequality 279–82
  life outcomes 253–5
  a long-term US redistribution strategy 225–41, 296
  pluralism and 19–21
  public political culture 23–7, 28–9
  Rawls's criticism of WSC 81, 82–91, 119, 149
  skill development 253, 255–8, 263
  UK redistribution strategies 258–62
  viability of POD in the USA 292–4, 295–6, 297–303
  work 149, 156–7, 158–9
social order 186–8, 190, 191–2, 193–4
social psychology of democratic societies 129–30, 134–43
  see also moral development; reciprocity
social rights 35–6
socialism
  command economy 2–3, 202
  conceptual history of POD 36–48
  legitimating private property 55
  liberal democratic *see* liberal democratic socialism
  a non-capitalist POD 205–6, 237–8
  political viability of POD in the USA 295–6, 302
  private 281–2
  of Rawls 201
society
  basic structure of 110–11, 116–17
  economic growth and 280–1, 292, 298
socioeconomic system
  inequalities in *see* social and economic (in)equality
  POD as 80–1
sociology of democratic societies 129–43
Sodha, S. 12–13
Solow, R. 280–1
sports, corporatist structures 183, 193–4
stability 184–6
  democratic corporatism 180–1, 189, 192, 195
  justice as fairness 129–30, 134–6, 138–9, 143
The Stakeholder Society (Ackerman and Alstott) 48, 85, 230, 232
state (command economy) socialism 2–3, 202
state role
  background institutions for justice 203–5
  in an economic democracy 207–8, 211
  justifying private property 55, 56–65, 69–70
  in a POD+ 216–17
  primary good redistribution 255–62
  republicanism 104
state welfare *see* welfare state capitalism (WSC)
status
  harms to 87–9
  of work 156–8
Steenbergen, M.R. 30n
stigma, welfare recipients 67–8
stock and share ownership
  economic democracy–POD comparison 210
  economic democracy–POD+ comparison 216–17

stock and share ownership (*Continued*)
  employee stock ownership plans   271
  moving toward POD   218
  in a non-capitalist POD   205–6, 237–8
  a US wealth-redistribution strategy
    230–1, 236–8, 241
Stoker, G.   145n
Summers, L.   288
Sunstein, C.   58, 70
Supreme Court
  corporate political speech   291–2
  public reason   28
Sweden   11, 91, 205
  wealth taxation   227
  welfare state costs   175
synchronically combined welfare regime of
  care   169, 174–5

talents   102, 109, 121
  politics of egalitarianism   24–6
  see also primary goods
Tawney, R.H.   41
Taylor, C.   103, 159
tax-evading capital flight   227–8
tax transfers
  aim of POD   79, 81, 134
  background institutions for justice   203,
    204, 205
  conceptual history of POD   35, 36, 39, 41,
    42, 43–4, 45–6
  in an economic democracy   217
  gender justice and care   173, 174–5
  large-scale taxation of the very rich
    297–300
  a long-term US strategy for wealth
    distribution   225–30, 238–9
  moving toward POD   218
  political viability of POD in the USA   295,
    297–300, 301–2
  Rawls's criticism of WSC   79, 81, 85,
    88–90
  UK strategies   261–2
  welfare state capitalism   3
teaching styles   256
technological advances   280–1, 298
Thatcher, M.
  conceptual history of POD   33, 47
  council housing   95n
A Theory of Justice (Rawls)   1

background institutions for justice   203
capitalism–socialism question   201
feminist critiques   177n
institutions of justice   3, 4, 17
meaningful work   153
moral development   187–90, 191, 192
POD–WSC distinction   149
political viability in the USA   290
politics of egalitarianism   18, 19–20,
  24–5, 26
Thomas, A.   9
Thompson, D.   65
Tocqueville, Alexis de   130, 136–41, 142–3
trade unions
  conceptual history of POD   44, 45–6, 47
  decline in the USA   267
  democratic corporatist POD   182, 198n
  political viability of POD in the USA   300
trespass   60–1

UK
  care work   167
  conceptual history of POD   33, 37–48,
    95n
  council housing   95n
  income inequalities   255, 258
  political relevance of POD   5, 6
  primary goods   249
    financial capital   254, 255–6, 258–62
    skills   252, 253, 255–8
  wealth inequalities   255
  welfare state as egalitarian strategy   48
unemployment
  ED–POD comparison   209–10
  in a POD+   217
  a US wealth-redistribution strategy   232
  see also work and workers
Unger, R.M.   300
universal assets   230–8, 239–40, 241–2, 296
universities   182
Ure, A.   219n
USA
  background institutions for justice   204–5
  community development   273, 275–7
  democratic corporatist structures   182,
    183, 193–4
  democratic regime   202
  early 21st-century asset distribution
    226–7

federal-level ownership innovations   274
gender justice and care   165–6, 167, 171, 175
health insurance   269, 294
high-speed rail   277–8
ideology of wealth inequality   279–82
income inequalities   208–9, 229, 267
inverted totalitarianism   119
labor movement decline   267
meaningless consumerism   75
morality of taxing the very rich   297–300
municipal enterprises   272
nonprofit organizations   273
pluralist commonwealth   266–82
political participation   192
political relevance of POD   5–6
political viability of POD   287–303
public political culture   24–6
public transit systems   277–9
racial minorities   301
sales effort expenditure   220n
savings   220n
skills development   255, 256
slavery   301
social class   287–8, 291, 300–2, 303–4n
state-level ownership innovations   273–5
Tocqueville's democratic society   136–8, 139
wealth redistribution strategy   225–41, 296
welfare state as egalitarian strategy   48
welfare state weakness   293–4
worker-owned firms   271, 275–7
workfare   72n
utilitarianism   23
  legitimating private property   62, 69
  moral development   191

Van Parijs, P.   67, 73n, 75, 93, 111, 125n, 156, 160n,

Wall, S.   126n
Wall Street   216, 220–1n, 229, 282, 288
Walzer, M.   53, 96n, 108
Warsh, D.   280
wealth, ownership-altering forms of 269–82, 296–7
wealth distribution   5, 7
  aim of POD   79, 80, 134

background institutions for justice   204
conceptual history of POD   34–6, 37–8, 39, 40–4, 45, 47, 48
desert principle   279–81, 298
gender justice and care   173–5
ideology of unconstrained inequality   279–82
legitimating private property   60–4, 67, 68
life outcomes   254, 255
moving toward POD   218
political viability of POD in the USA   293, 295, 296, 297–300, 301–3
politics of egalitarianism   22, 23
Rawls's criticism of WSC   79, 80–4, 85, 87–91, 119
in Tocqueville's democratic society   136
UK strategies   259–60, 261–2
a US long-term strategy   225–41, 296
  individual–common wealth trade-offs   238–9
  POD as an incomplete ideal   239–41
  taxation   226–30, 238–9
  universal assets structure   230–8, 239–40, 241–2
Webb, Sidney and Beatrice   37
Welch, C.   145n
welfare rights   53–5, 61, 63–71
welfare state, republican citizenship   142
welfare state capitalism (WSC)   2–3
  background institutions for justice   203–5
  conceptual history of POD   35–6, 37, 39–40, 42, 43, 45–6, 47–8
  difference principle and   22, 78, 87–91, 93, 293–4
  fuzzy borders with POD   91–3
  gender justice and care   163–76
  integration of POD with elements of   47–8
  legitimating private property   55, 68
  needs assessment   259
  political viability of POD in the USA and   293–4
  Rawls's criticism of   3, 5–6, 75–93, 119, 133, 149, 201–2
  Schweickart's indictment   202–3
  work   149–59
welfarism   53–4
White, S.   9–10, 41–2, 112, 199n
Williamson, T.   7, 12–13, 30n, 172–3, 175, 249, 272, 274

Wilson, W. 282n
Wolff, E. 226, 228
Wolin, S. 119
women
  Family Nurse Partnership Program 257
  gender justice and care work 167–8, 169, 170, 171, 173–4, 176
work and workers 149–59
  arbitrary interference at work 154–6
  background institutions for justice 203–4
  conceptual history of POD 37, 38–9, 41, 42, 44, 45–6, 47
  dehumanization 210–11, 258–9
  democratic corporatist POD 182, 183, 194–6, 198n
  economic democracy 207
  economic democracy–POD comparison 209–11, 214
  gender justice and care 163–76
  incentivization 102, 109, 110, 113–14, 121, 207, 209–10
  meaningful work 153–4
  needs of those unable to work 66, 68
  in a pluralist commonwealth 271
  in a POD+ 216, 217
  political viability of POD in the USA 292, 295, 300–1
  right to work 64–5, 66, 67–8
  status of work 156–8
  UK income inequalities 258–61
  US economic crisis (2008) 288–90
  US income inequalities 208–9, 229, 267
  a US wealth-redistribution strategy 232, 237, 239
  workers as property owners 156–8
worker-owned firms 183, 220n, 236–7, 239, 270, 271, 275–7, 295
workplace democracy 152, 154–6
  democratic corporatist POD 182, 194–6, 198n
  in an economic democracy 207
  gender justice 173–4
  in a POD+ 217
  a US wealth-redistribution strategy 239
  US worker-owned firms 271
Wright, E.O. 7, 28

Young, I.M. 158–9

Zaller, J. 25, 30n